Best wishes

The Life and Secrets

of

Almina Carnarvon

The Life and Secrets of Almina Carnarvon

A Candid Biography of The 5th Countess of Carnarvon
Of Tutankhamun Fame

By

William Cross, FSA Scot

Updated Version, With Expanded Footnotes

ISBN 10 1-905914-08-3
ISBN 13 978-1-905914-08-1

Published by
William P. Cross
58 Sutton Road
Newport
Gwent
NP19 7JF
United Kingdom

For Tony Leadbetter

My Lady's Dear Boy

" you cannot bottle up news, particularly news which in interest and
importance is the legitimate possession of the whole world"
Valentine Williams.

Introduction

One day in May of 1969, an ambulance raced to number 19, Hampton Road, Bristol, an unremarkable terraced house, where a housekeeper had found her 93-year-old mistress choking on a piece of gristle from a homemade chicken stew. The unconscious woman was rushed to Frenchay Hospital, but all efforts to revive her failed, and she died soon after.

The deceased was no mere statistic of nonagenarian mortality, and no ordinary citizen of Bristol. She was Almina, Countess of Carnarvon, widow of the 5th Earl of Carnarvon, the aristocrat-adventurer who, with sidekick Howard Carter, discovered and emptied the tomb of Tutankhamun [1] in Egypt's Valley of the Kings, and whose untimely death is believed by many to be evidence of a curse of the pharaohs.

But the 5th Countess of Carnarvon was much more than the legendry Earl's wife. Almina was a well-known figure in her own right in London society: one of the last great eccentric aristocrats of the 19th and 20th centuries; a pioneer in nursing; and quite possibly a descendent of one of the richest, most powerful families in European history, and the mother of a son whose true bloodline may show that the family *still* have an additional ancestor to declare.

What follows is the as yet untold story of a daughter, a wife, a mother, a lady, a Countess, and a long and colourful life.

Chapter 1
1876–1893
Daughter Almina

A mysterious beginning

The year 1876 is notable for many things. Queen Victoria was crowned Empress of India by her Prime Minister, Benjamin Disraeli. Alexander Graham Bell was granted a patent for an invention he called the telephone. Melvil Dewey invented his classification system. The United States celebrated its centenary. And Almina Victoria Marie Alexandra Wombwell, destined to be the 5th Countess of Carnarvon, was born.

In the late spring of that year, a heavily pregnant, well-to-do Frenchwoman stepped out of number 20, Bruton Street, London and made herself comfortable in a hansom cab bound for Victoria railway station. Marie Wombwell, aged 30, was leaving behind her Mayfair abode – on a street that great statesmen had called home and which would one day become H.M. Queen Elizabeth II's birthplace [2] – to return to her native Paris, where she would welcome her second child into the world.

But Marie never made it to the London to Dover train or the subsequent crossing to Calais; indeed she didn't even make it to Victoria. Gripped by early labour in the back of the lowly hansom cab, she was diverted to an address in Bayswater where, on 14 April, she gave birth to a daughter: Almina.

Almina's birthplace, at first glance, appears an obscure location to deliver a baby. Number 18, Bayswater Terrace, Bayswater was a hotel, described as "an establishment for families and gentlemen"[3] – certainly a less fashionable address than Mayfair or Paris. Yet this place was an ideal retreat: a sanctuary that offered protection for *all* the parties concerned from the watchful eyes and chattering tongues of London society commentators.

For Marie was estranged from her husband of eight years, Frederick Charles Wombwell, and it wasn't quite clear *who* exactly had fathered her daughter...

Marie Wombwell née Boyer

Almina's mother, Marie Felicie Boyer (*c*.1846–1913) came from continental stock which straddled French and quasi-Spanish –South American heritage. She was the daughter of Alexandre Antoine Boyer, a financier, and Marie Victoria de los Dolores de Gogorza, of Paris. The Boyers were old French aristocrats, indeed, through their association Almina would grow up to speak fluent French with no hint of an accent, using the 'pre-guillotine pronunciation'[4]. Marie's father, Alexandre Boyer, was an astute Parisian businessman involved in banking and property letting, but he also merits being counted as an inspired French-South-American colonist. Marie's mother, Marie Victoria de los Dolores de Gogorza, provided an infusion of respectable Spanish-South American blood : she was born in Maracaibo, Venezuela. [5]

It had not been an easy pregnancy for Almina's mother, with emotional traumas and readjustments, since her father, Alexandre Boyer, had died in Paris, on 11 November 1875 [6] , and her mother was remarried within a year of this tragedy. [7]

Almina's mother, Marie was best known as being a Frenchwoman, but she *also* once claimed that *her* birthplace was Venezuela, in South America.[8] The likelihood is that she was born in France. Nonetheless, there is evidence of settlement by the Boyers in Maracaibo, the second City of Venezuela, from the 1840s.[9] Records of the Boyer family's financial wheeling and dealing exist here until at least the end of the 19th century. [10]

Fred Wombwell

The man named as Almina's father, Frederick ('Fred') Charles Wombwell (1845–1889), came from a strong lineage. He was a descendant of Robert de Wombwell who lived at the time of King Stephen. He was the youngest of the four sons of Sir George Wombwell, the 3rd Baronet of Wombwell (1792–1855). Fred's mother Georgina (née Hunter; 1807–1875) was the daughter of Thomas Orby Hunter MP of Crowland Abbey, Lincolnshire.

For Fred, Newburgh Priory in North Yorkshire was home. To this day the Wombwells have their family seat there, at Easingwold near Coxwold. The site was once an Augustinian priory, granted by King Henry VIII to Antony Belasyse, from whom the Wombwells descended – in fact, one of Fred's kin was the daughter and heiress of the last Lord Fauconberg. The priory is famed for its collection of Cromwellian relics; Mary Cromwell (a daughter of Oliver, the great Protector) was the wife of the second Lord Fauconberg.[11]

After a public school education, Fred lived off allowances from family trust funds. This brought him a handsome income of 500 pounds a year. In his early twenties he featured regularly in the *Sporting Intelligence* section of newspapers, but from 1863 – and after coming of age at 21 – his press coverage reveals a weaker, flawed character. He divided his time between the racing circuit (he owned several horses) and engaging in a lavish social life. Thus, whilst the Carnarvon guidebooks mistakenly refer to Fred as a "Captain"[12], Almina's birth certificate is closer to the mark when it describes Fred's occupation as a "Gentleman."

Fred was often in the company of his older brother Captain Henry (Harry) Herbert Wombwell (1840–1926), and the two enjoyed a reputation as promising gentleman-riders of the English county and French turf during the 1860s and 1870s. The brothers were great friends of the hapless Henry Rawdon-Hastings, 4th Marquis of Hastings (1842–1868), and they rode the Hastings' horses and socialised extensively with the Marquis – travelling often to Scotland (to the Marquis' seat at Loudon Castle, Ayrshire) and cruising across Europe's waterways aboard the Hastings' fine yachts.

In London Fred kept rooms at Limmer's Hotel, Bond Street, a rough establishment frequented by the dregs of the sporting world.[13] Fred's brothers Harry and Ulick (1834–1886; another soldier, with the rank of Colonel) were like-minded frequenters of Limmer's. But the youngest Wombwell brother Fred. was also forced, at times, to live with his widowed mother, Lady Georgina, at John Street, Berkeley Square, London[14], for too often Fred's frivolous nature with money left him stoney-broke.

The youngest Wombwell brother should have been comfortable: at the age of 21 he had inherited the sum of 20,000 pounds. But in the year that followed he had run up large debts and made promissory notes against his inheritance. Debt stalked him at every turn, and he acquired a reputation as a rakish young man who did not pay his way, and provoking creditors' wrath. Worse still, his close friend Henry, the Marquis of Hastings, was embroiled in a scandal, having stolen a friend's fiancée. The friend was Henry Chaplin[15], later a senior British Cabinet minister. Hastings frittered away the family fortune and enraged a mob of creditors (which would lead to his ultimate ruin and death a few years later at the tender age of 26).[16] To escape being swept into the Hastings affair and the inevitability of confrontation with moneylenders including probable arrest, Fred, in panic, fled to France.

The union of Fred and Marie

It seems likely that Almina's mother, Marie Boyer, first met Fred when he took refuge in Paris. There, he was described as a regular *"citoyen de Londres"*[17] who joined the throngs on the Parisian scene, seeking gentlemanly pleasures, gambling and riding at such sporting events as the Grand Prix. Subsequent meetings with Marie Boyer may have been in England. The Boyers often visited London for the English social season and the horse racing.[18] Marie was in England during 1864 and 1865 for the wedding of her two sisters, who were both matched to English aristocrats: Eleanor Marie Boyer (d.1897) married Walter Buckler Lethbridge (1845–1907), the sixth and youngest son of Sir John Hesketh Lethbridge[19] and Victoria Francisca Boyer (1841–1899) married Lord Henry Howard (1837–1898), the heir to the Earl of Effingham.[20]

On 12 January 1868 it was Marie's turn to be the blushing bride at St Mary's Church, Marylebone. Fred was 23 years old, Marie was 21. The bride was described as being radiant and calm. Her dress was of "grey silk, and she wore a white bonnet trimmed with orange flowers"[21].

The wedding was a quiet affair; the guests comprised only a few relations and friends. On Marie's side was her sister Victoria, Lady Howard. On Fred's side cronies from the turf sat alongside friends from the Royal Horse Guards where his brother Harry, the best man, was a serving officer.[22] Also present was Fred's much respected elder brother, Sir George Orby Wombwell (1832–1913) – the 4th Baronet, hero of the Charge of the Light Brigade's famous dash of 1854 and, according to *Vanity Fair* magazine, "the best-dressed man in London"[23] – and with him his attractive but aristocratically snooty wife Lady Julia, a descendant of the past British Prime Minister Sir Robert Peel.[24] After the ceremony a sumptuous wedding breakfast was laid on at Harry's house in Berkeley Square. Then the very happy couple took a long and leisurely honeymoon on the Continent, where they both had many friends and family offshoots.

Cracks appear

Following the wedding, Marie and Fred were often in residence in Paris. [25] Their first child, a boy, Frederick Adolphus Wombwell (1869–1912) [26], was born in the French capital on the eve of the city's disruption during the Franco–Prussian War and the ensuing bloody Paris Siege. To his considerable credit, Fred took part in these dangerous wartime proceedings alongside other Englishmen. He is recorded as bringing much needed medical supplies on horseback from Versailles, in perhaps his finest ever ride. [27]

Between 1870 and 1872, Fred and Marie lived at 3 Bryanston Street, London[28] . They stepped-out in the very best of circles – for example, they're listed as guests at a ball held by the Prince and Princess of Wales at Windsor Castle on 4 July 1870, and Fred was an enthusiastic member of the Zoological Society of London. Yet away from the facade of gentility and decorum, tensions in the relationship existed.

The turf, not Marie, was Fred's true love. After his marriage he gave up his ownership of his racehorses, and was merely a gentleman rider. He had small glory – eight wins in one season, earning him the rank of 11th place with dozens of riders competing. But he was frequently injured in falls and in one accident lost all his teeth.

Off the race track, Fred was frequently in trouble with the law for conduct that his cronies in taverns would no doubt class high jinks, but that shamed and angered his wife and family. He was charged with non-payment of a series of accounts run up with a Bond Street jeweller named Ryder when he was still under age. [29] A verdict was given against him for 40 pounds and 15 shillings, and with it an indelible piece of English case law, *Ryder versus Wombwell,* "on a gentleman's necessaries and the use of the defence of infancy."[30] In another court case, in 1872, Fred's financial situation was laid bare when his complaint that his valet, John Macdonald, had stolen from him was dismissed by the jury because it felt the man had some justification: as "during the period the prisoner was in Mr Wombwell's service that gentleman was labouring under some pecuniary pressure and in consequence the prisoner's wages and disbursements were not regularly met".[31] In the space of a few days further disaster struck the Wombwell household, when Fred was declared bankrupt. [32] More public humiliation followed with unpleasant newspaper headlines when, in 1875 Fred was arrested for trespassing and poaching game on land owned by his in-laws, the Effinghams. He continued to break the law even whilst awaiting sentence. By 1876, at the time Marie was fleeing to France to have her baby, Fred had a further writ hanging over him in a case in the King's Bench division of the High Court. [33]

These acts were the last straw for Fred's brother Sir George, the Wombwell Baronet. The youngest Wombwell's antics were setting tongues wagging ferociously amongst his brother's law-abiding connections. And Marie was equally disappointed: it seemed marriage had not reformed Fred, her husband was ruined financially, and little more than a gentleman poacher.

At some point in time, Marie and Fred became estranged and separated. [34] But it would be unfair to hold Fred entirely accountable for the breakdown of his marriage. Marie, too, played her part. She had set her sights on being of influence in London Society, and Fred could not fulfil her ambitions for grandeur. So she was drawn to another man who perhaps could: Baron Alfred de Rothschild.

Enter Baron Alfred de Rothschild

Alfred Charles de Rothschild (1842–1918) was a wealthy, eccentric banker, a partner, with his brothers Nathan Mayer (1840–1915) and Leopold Nathan (1845–1917), in the Jewish banking house N.M. Rothschild and Sons. The bank was named after their grandfather, Nathan Mayer Rothschild (1777–1836), who came from Germany to England in 1798. The Rothschilds made inroads in Manchester and London, eventually establishing a banking business at New Court, St Swithin's Lane, London. Their many European family members formed other branches, quickly extending a financial grip on the world stage, funding governments as well as businesses and private citizens in wars and in new-fangled buildings, engineering projects and national infrastructures. The Rothschilds were rewarded with British titles and their wealth brought them into contact with politicians, royalty and titled foreigners. They became influential, and remained so for several decades of the 19th and 20th centuries.

Alfred is described as being "a little man"[35] with a dark complexion, sporting carefully curled and oiled whiskers. A dapper figure, he was famed for wearing a scarlet carnation of a particular tint, one for the morning and one for the evening, all the year round. Although a successful businessman (he was the first Jew to be a director of the Bank of England, but was forced to resign from the post after breaching confidentiality[36]), he's described as "a fop, a hypochondriac, and something of a poseur".[37] One contemporary described him bitterly as having "a good heart, but a mean and miserable little mind"[38]: Rothschild was hugely generous to others in need[39] and in support of good causes, but he could also be blunt and irritable.[40]

Alfred was renowned for his colourful hospitality, entertaining all manner of guests, royalty included – indeed, he often entertained the heir to the throne, Albert (Bertie) (later King Edward VII), at supper. His lavish Buckinghamshire home, in the manner of a French chateau, called Halton House, was the setting for particularly memorable entertaining.[41] Here, Alfred was ringmaster in his own private circus/zoo, conductor (complete with diamond-encrusted baton) of his own orchestra and chief of a private fire brigade. He dressed in costumes to match all his warped, expensive, camp and sometimes-madcap frivolities and pastimes.[42] There was no doubt that chez Rothschild guests enjoyed a unique brand of hospitality:

> "A footman, followed by a powdered footman with a trolley, would enter and enquire politely "Tea, coffee or a peach off the wall, sir?"
> "Tea, please."
> "China tea, Indian tea, or Ceylon tea, sir?"
> "China, if you please."
> "Lemon, milk, or cream, sir?"
> "Milk please."
> "Jersey, Hereford, or Shorthorn, sir?"[43]

It was to this vibrant, lively world – and the riches that afforded it – that Marie Wombwell was drawn. She probably came to know Alfred through her father, Alexandre Boyer. Alfred and Alexandre moved in the same circles in the banking world, and Alfred (who spoke French) spent time in both Paris and London, combining his role as a financier with his love of observing culture and purchasing art.[44]

Alfred and Marie some how found their common ground: they shared a passion for music, especially for the opera. Soon (it is said) they were often to be seen together on the theatre scene in London and Paris.

Marie saw Alfred's friendship as a way of social climbing. There's little doubt that the two enjoyed a very close relationship, including it is inferred, during Marie's marriage to Fred, actually living together. [45]

Thus: when Marie fell pregnant in 1875, it naturally raised the question: who was the father of her child?

The question of paternity

The Carnarvons have been eager to accept Alfred as Almina's father. The Rothschild is, of course, a more acceptable ancestor than the disgraced Fred Wombwell. Thus Fred Wombwell is largely omitted from the Carnarvon history. [46] Instead, Marie Boyer is proclaimed the "mistress" of Baron Alfred de Rothschild. According to intimates, Almina was convinced that she was Alfred's natural daughter (although in the 1925 court case of *Dennistoun v Dennistoun*, (see Chapter 8) in which she became embroiled after her second marriage to Lieutenant Colonel Ian Onslow Dennistoun (1879–1938), she maintained that Alfred was *only* her "guardian"). But Almina's only son, Henry George Alfred Marius Victor Francis Herbert (1898–1987), 6th Earl of Carnarvon, celebrates his mother's illegitimacy in his memoirs, *No Regrets,* published in 1976.[47] *He* proclaims that Alfred de Rothschild was Almina's true biological father.

Yet the claim that Marie conceived a baby with Alfred – or indeed, was his lover at all – is not an entirely convincing proposition, for several reasons.

First and foremost, Alfred never acknowledged Almina as his daughter. His last will and testament (from 1918) would have been the ideal vehicle for confessing: all his brothers were dead and he was about to die. But there was no declaration: he referred to Almina only as the "Countess of Carnarvon". [48] He did, however, make Almina the principal beneficiary of his will, transferring a significant part of Rothschild wealth out of his immediate family without offering his direct heirs (who faced large death duties) any explanation. [49] He met all the costs of obtaining Almina's title for her and left her £50,000 from his £1.5 million estate as well as his London home at 1 Seamore Place, Mayfair with its fabulous contents, valued at almost £500,000.[50] Yet this may just as well be the action of a loving benefactor, rather than a father.

Then there is the question of timing. When Marie became pregnant in the weeks during the autumn of 1875, there is no evidence to show the exact whereabouts of either Fred or Alfred. Indeed, neither party may have been Marie's lover at the time. Yet at this time Alfred was far from free to indulge in an affair. According to the Paris newspaper *Figaro* as late as December 1875 (only four months before Almina's birth) Alfred was about to marry "the widow of a diplomatist".[51] Further details on this match appeared in the English press: "Preparations are being made on a costly and extensive scale for the marriage of Mr Alfred de Rothschild with an English lady, the widow of a former member of the British Embassy in Paris."[52]

Whilst this evidence of the banker's betrothal does not sweep away the paternity claim over Almina, it undermines the insistence by those who make the claim that Alfred possessed a monogamous adoration of Marie. Alfred's proposed marriage must introduce reasonable doubt that his love child was due to come into the world a few months later.

Furthermore, it is naive to assume that Alfred's close friendship was something special. He did not bestow fancy and expensive gifts exclusively on Marie Wombwell or in fact devote the lion's share of his time to her; he lived the life of a frivolous bachelor and was closely associated with several other women, especially amongst the era's actresses and musical *artistes*. Yet he was likely disinclined to take any of these women as a lover, because the foppish Alfred was almost certainly a homosexual.

From this perspective, any claim of Alfred's paternity is challenged in the 1988 landmark study of the Rothschild dynasty: *Rothschild: A Story of Wealth and Power.*[53] Author Derek Wilson directs our attention to events 100 years *before* the 6th Earl's memoirs. In 1895, the year Almina married Lord Carnarvon, Alfred made an immense gift of a marriage settlement upon the couple of upwards of £300,000.[54] He also paid off Carnarvon's personal and gambling debts amounting to a further £150,000. Some have suggested that Alfred's generosity proves that he and Almina were blood-related. But Wilson has a different explanation. It was in 1895 that the sex trials of playwright Oscar Wilde took place, highlighting Wilde's homosexual acts that extended to a circle of gay men and boys whose liaisons crossed social classes. At this time, others with the same instincts as Wilde sought to cover-up their secret lives. Wilson infers that Alfred de Rothschild was one of those who feared exposure, and that he may have contrived a ready-made family to prevent or save himself from detection and downfall.

Derek Wilson has reinforced his opinion recently. He told the author:

> It is generally known in the [Rothschild] family (or at least amongst those who have any interest in past scandals) that Alfred was homosexual and that would certainly have been something the Rothschilds would have paid handsomely to keep quiet.[55]

Some have found evidence of Almina's parentage in her very name.[56] They argue that Almina's Christian name is derived from a fusion of 'Al' (from Alfred) and 'Mina' (from Alfred's pet name for Marie). Because the name is so unusual, it is argued that it must signify that she is the love child of Marie Boyer and Alfred de Rothschild. But the name is *not* unique; and in any case names are not evidence of substance. Those determining Almina's names also decided that she should have the monarch's name, Victoria, and the name of the wife of the Prince of Wales, Alexandra. [57]

A further unsatisfactory element is the time taken to register Almina's birth. Shortly after Almina's birth Marie whisked her new daughter off to France. Because she had no intention of returning to England, she neglected to register the child's birth as required by English law. It was only four years later, on 24 November 1880, that an English birth certificate officially recorded Almina's birth in Britain.

The certificate is certainly imbued with an air of authority. The informant, who declared he had delivered Almina, was William Priestley, MD, of 17 Hereford Street, Mayfair. He was no back street quack or just someone who had happened to be passing the scene: he was Sir William Overend Priestley, MD, LLD, MP (1829–1900), an eminent obstetric physician and gynaecologist. With his credentials a request of the authorities for retrospective registration was unchallengeable.[58]

Certainly, Almina's records are not without fault – her death certificate, for instance, records her place of birth as France.[59] (It was

Lord Porchester, Almina's grandson Henry, the 7th Earl of Carnarvon and renowned horse racing manager to the present Queen, who registered her death, and he cannot be faulted for his mistake: Porchester's much-loved "granny" enjoyed exhibiting an air of *grandiosité* about her French roots. But as she indicated in the 1911 Census return, Almina was indeed born in London.) But those who argue that the name Alfred de Rothschild should appear in place of Fred Wombwell on Almina's birth certificate must question the timing of the registration and the relative ease with which Marie could have declared Alfred's paternity if, indeed, he was the father. For by 1880, when the late registration took place, the dust had settled on memories. If Marie and Alfred were unreservedly devoted to each other then why, given the gap between Almina's birth and the issue of a birth certificate, not be honest about Almina's parentage? Alternatively, a French birth certificate, albeit contrition, might also have been considered an apt solution to record Alfred's (or another's) paternity.

The Rothschild family have also undermined the paternity claims. According to Derek Wilson (who interviewed several of them for *Rothschild: A Story of Wealth and Power*) some of those alive in the 1980s had serious doubts about Almina's claims. Wilson is merciless in attacking Almina, describing her as "a grasping, extravagant, vicious, wilful, unprincipled woman".[60] Wilson's principal source of information was Dr Miriam Rothschild (1908–2006), the much-respected scientist whose father, Charles, was Alfred's nephew. According to Wilson, Miriam "undoubtedly knew much about the secret life of Alfred, the Edwardian roué".[61] Miriam went no further in public than to state that Porchey, the 6th Earl (whom she knew very well), only *claimed* to be Alfred's grandson.[62] But this may well have been a case of following the party line; the author has seen evidence in a letter from Miriam to suggest that, in private, she withheld this doubt, favouring Almina's daughter Lady Evelyn, on account of her physical resemblance to other Rothschild women.[63] However, equally, in the eyes of another beholder, Lady Evelyn (it was said) takes after her maternal grandmother, Marie Boyer.[64]

Clearly, more evidence is required to obtain a definitive answer to the question of who exactly Almina's father was. A good place to start was once thought to be the Alfred de Rothschild Scrapbook, which Almina inherited from Alfred and which on her death was placed in Highclere Archives, the Carnarvon family's repository of its past triumphs and disasters.[65] With a recent Herbert sourced biography of Almina offering *no evidence whatsoever* on the subject, this route is now discounted. [66] Of course, a DNA test would be conclusive: there are several surviving Rothschild bloodlines to compare with alleged Carnarvon specimens.

Yet ultimately, whatever the truth of Marie's relationship with Alfred, those in high-class Society circles were convinced that Marie was Alfred's mistress and Almina " the presumed fruit of a blatant union" [67]. Thus Marie was snubbed by the Wombwells *and* the Rothschilds, who saw the pairing as scandalous, especially as Marie was still married to Fred Wombwell, and a mismatch on economic, moral and religious grounds. Behind her back Marie was maliciously dubbed *Mrs Wombchild* or sometimes *Mrs Rothwell.* [68]

There's little doubt that Marie wanted to get rid of her embarrassment of a husband and work her way up the echelons of London Society to the very top. Becoming Mrs Alfred de Rothschild would have achieved this. Yet she never instigated divorce proceedings against Fred, and even after her husband's death Marie remained Mrs Wombwell. It seems that whatever Alfred and Marie were to each other, they weren't soul mates.

Almina's childhood

An intimate of Almina maintains that soon after her birth and being taken to France, her mother raised her in Paris. There, "Alfred visited often and looked after her education by employing the services of a private tutor who made her study hard". [69] She spent "much of her childhood hidden away" [70] in Parisian hotels until her teenage years, when she moved to London. In her later life she affectionately recalled the magic and bustle of gay Paris. She loved returning to the city and travelling down to the coastal resorts on the French Riviera.

In England in 1882, during a visit from France, she was a child bridesmaid, in the company of her mother and Fred (making a rare reappearance) when her cousin Julia Wombwell, (one of Sir George and Lady Julia's daughters) married Lord Cremorne, later the 2nd Earl of Dartrey. Following that, the first occasion that Almina merits mention in her own right is on the marriage of Cecilia Wombwell (another of Sir George and Lady Julia's daughters) to William Graham Menzies in 1890. The 13-year-old Almina sent a diamond spray as a present. The same wedding list has separate gifts from Mrs F Wombwell and Alfred de Rothschild.

Exit Fred Wombwell

Fate intervened to end Fred Wombwell's parental rights. Upon the death of his brother Colonel Adolphus Ulick Wombwell in 1885, Fred and his brother Harry inherited an annuity of 2,000 pounds. This gave Fred's starved finances a much-needed boost. But his health was shattered: he was latterly unable to ride at all. He lingered towards death with his sporting friends around him, and died from an abdominal condition at 12 Brunswick Terrace, Hove, Sussex[71] on 7 July 1889, in his 44th year. Fred's obituary in the *Nottinghamshire Guardian* of Saturday 13 July 1889 records:

We regret to announce the death at Brighton on Sunday, after a lingering illness, of Mr Frederick Charles Wombwell, youngest brother of the present baronet. Mr Wombwell, who was born on July 12 1845, leaves a son and daughter. He will be very much missed in sporting circles and on the Thames for he was an ardent boating man.

Prior to his demise, Fred had spent part of his time living at Box, Hampton, Middlesex, cohabiting with a spinster named Caroline Sophie Jones. In his last will and testament, Caroline is named one of his trustees, and he made modest provision for her two sons. But Fred did not forget his first family. In painfully affectionate terms, he left family pictures to his wife Marie, an heirloom to his son, Frederick Adolphus, and a gift of a pony and trap to his daughter. [72]Fred's final estate was valued at only 221 pounds and 15 shillings.[73]

The involvement of Fred's new family at first glance suggests he was buried and mourned only by them, but he was laid to rest in the Wombwell family burial ground at St Michaels Churchyard Coxwold, in the North Riding of Yorkshire.[74] Fred was an important part of Wombwell heritage. Fred's grandson Philip (the son of Marie's first child, Frederick) was the successor of the Wombwell baronetcy and the present baronet is Philip's son.

Almina was 13 when Fred died, yet his absence would have made little impact on her since her parents had been estranged throughout her childhood. For Marie, Fred's death was an opportunity to ally herself with Alfred de Rothschild, and the riches and influence in his command. Thus Alfred became Almina's guardian of sorts, her father figure. Together, Alfred and Marie mapped out a prosperous future for the child.

Almina, the debutante

On 9 May 1893 Almina Wombwell was presented at Court by Lady Julia Wombwell, her aunt (her mother's sister-in-law). Julia was of the old school that firmly believed that birth and breeding, not wealth, were the passports to admission into the inner circles of Society. Julia's involvement in the process of Almina's Court introduction points to her being considered a part of the Wombwell family.

The Lord Chamberlain's officials stated that the May Court of 1893 was the largest presentation in the Queen's reign, "with over 500 debutantes and 50,000 people cheering from The Mall".[75] Queen Victoria traditionally presided over these Court occasions in the afternoon. The Prince of Wales was present and also the Dukes of York and Connaught. The Queen took up her position in the Throne Room at three o'clock, whereupon Miss Almina Wombwell was presented to Her Majesty. She performed a curtsey to her sovereign without fault. Aged only 17, Almina was 'out' in London Society, and it didn't take long for Marie and Alfred's dreams of a handsome match to materialise. Just two months later, at the Queen's State Ball, held at Buckingham Palace on 10 July 1893, Almina caught the eye of Lord Carnarvon – the man who would become her husband. [76]

George Edward Stanhope Molyneux Herbert
5th Earl of Carnarvon
Co-discoverer with Howard Carter of the Tomb of
Tutankhamun in 1922

Almina as a child　　　　**Alfred de Rothschild**

**Marie Boyer, Mrs Frederick Wombwell
Almina's Mother**

Chapter 2
1893–1895
The Marriage of Convenience
A mother's wisdom

George Edward Stanhope Molyneux Herbert, the heir to the Earldom of Carnarvon, was born on 26 June 1866 in his parents' London townhouse at 66 Grosvenor Street. He was named after his maternal grandfather but was initially known – as are all Carnarvon heirs – by the Viscount's title of Lord Porchester (Porchey[77] for short).

The Carnarvon family[78] is a cadet branch of the House of Herbert, descended from the Earls of Pembroke and Montgomery, whose family seat is at Highclere Castle, Hampshire. George's father, Henry, the 4th Earl of Carnarvon, was a smart, wealthy, landowning English peer who was appointed Secretary of the Colonies in Lord Derby's government in 1866, a post requiring an understanding of over 50 dependencies in different parts of the globe.

George's mother was Lady Evelyn Stanhope, daughter of George Stanhope (1805–1866), 6th Earl of Chesterfield of Bretby Park near Burton-on-Trent – a famed follower of the turf who died a few weeks before George's birth. George was Lady Evelyn's second child: her daughter Winifred was born in 1864, Margaret followed George in 1870 and Victoria (Vera) followed in 1875.

Lady Evelyn was a strong character, and a powerful influence on her husband and children. According to the writer and hostess Lady Dorothy Nevill (1826–1913), it was Evelyn who helped write the 4th Earl's most successful political speeches, and it was she who vetoed, with the "the strongest possible objections"[79], a proposed marriage between her mother, Lady Anne Chesterfield, and the widower Benjamin Disraeli, a regular face at Bretby Park.[80]

Along with his sisters, Porchey enjoyed "a dreamily carefree childhood doing the usual things that all boys find to do for fun and mischief"[81], but then tragedy struck. Lady Evelyn contracted puerperal fever, and in January 1875, following the birth of her last child, she died.[82] George was nine when he was ushered into a chapel to look upon his mother's frozen form in her coffin. "Tears and sobbings told how heavy was the trial that had to be borne."[83]

Evelyn had known she was dying, and she left a sharp warning to her son in her last will and testament. It was as though she could see what George would become in the years to follow. She feared he would be too like her own father, who was once described as "fashionable, spoilt, and a wastrel".[84] In addition to inheriting Highclere Castle, with its Hampshire estates, the boy was ultimately destined to own the Chesterfield Estates in Derbyshire and Nottinghamshire, as well as the family seat and hall at Bretby Park. Evelyn's will begged the boy to look upon the family estates "as a solemn trust, to be used not for his own gratification or pleasure but for the glory of God and the honour of those who have gone before him".[85]

Porchey adored his mother, but, as we shall see, he outgrew the memory of the stern advice she offered from beyond the grave.

New mothers

Following his death in 1923, Lady Winifred, Porchey's older sister, compiled a moving portrait of her brother. Allowing for the time internal between the events recalled and the writing of them, with some papering over of the cracks, this text gives an interesting, but insight into Porchey's early life. [86]

Health wise, Porchey was by all accounts a fragile little boy.[87] Winifred says the Herbert children were by necessity close, on account of losing one parent and the other being a busy public figure. The children were constantly boarded-out between the Carnarvon homes, even before Lady Evelyn's death.

Two women, his father's sisters, became mother substitutes to Porchey: Lady Gwendolen Herbert, who was unmarried, "a delicate invalid around whose sofa young and old clustered, secure of sympathy in sorrow or in joy"[88] and "a vegetarian", and Lady Eveline Alicia Juliana Herbert, mistress of Eggesford House, " a pioneer in many phases of work and thought, and... a strenuous advocate of open air"[89] , who was married to Isaac Newton Wallop, the 5th Earl of Portsmouth, a collateral relative of the famous philosopher Isaac Newton. (In later years the Wallop family also provided Jean, Lady Porchester, the wife for Henry, 7th Earl of Carnarvon, Almina's beloved grandson). One record of this surrogate child-rearing, with its consequential impact on Porchey and his sisters, suggests that it " entailed all sorts of complications, because Lady Gwendolen, good natured and indulgent allowed almost everything, and Lady Portsmouth unyielding and strict, forbade almost everything"[90].

In addition, although omitted in Winifred's account, Porchey's last surviving grandparent, Lady Anne Elizabeth Forester Stanhope, 6th Countess of Chesterfield, was also a close influence in trying to maintain the well being of George and his sisters.

In 1878 the heir to the Carnarvon and the Chesterfield lands acquired a step- mother, Elisabeth (Elsie) Catherine Howard (1856–1929) of Greystoke Castle, Cumberland.[91] George was 12 years old and never warmed to her. Later came two half-brothers Aubrey, the renowned Albanian figurehead, traveller and adventurer, and Mervyn, who was a great sportsman and diplomat. Neither of them (like other Herbert men) was ever in good health or lived long.[92]

Lord Porchester's education

Whilst George's father was a classical scholar, Porchey was anything but: he was given to being lax and lazy about his studies. So when private schooling failed to improve Porchey, like his father and both grandfathers before him, he was enrolled at Eton.

In the Schools Census for 1880 the Michaelmas list for Eton indicates that amongst the boarders were a duke, a marquis, eighteen lords (including George), a prince, three counts, four baronets and forty-three honourables. Amongst Porchey's Eton contemporaries in his house, under tutor Arthur Coleridge James[93], were Francis Denzil Edward Baring, later 5th Baron Ashburton, from a family of merchant bankers; John Douglas-Scott-Montagu, later 2nd Lord Montagu of Beaulieu, one of the early motorists; Ralph Nevill, whose family were courtiers; and Prince Victor Duleep[94] Singh, the eldest son of the displaced Maharajah Duleep Singh of Lahore.[95]

Some of his fellow Etonians remained Carnarvon's lifelong friends, sharing his gentleman's passions for shooting, gambling[96], horse racing and motoring[97]–particularly Prince Victor Duleep Singh.

But whilst Porchester succeeded at forging alliances at Eton, he failed miserably at the academic side of life at the school. Thus his father was forced to remove him, and for a time he was tutored by Robert William Frederick Harrison (1858–1945), who went on to study law and was later a notable member of the Royal Society of London.[98]

27

Finally, Porchester was enrolled in Trinity College, Cambridge, where his marks continued to be no better than appalling. His father, who'd earned a first at Oxford, chastised his son severely for spending too much time on the racecourse and frittering money away on art and loafing. But Porchey found an ally in his grandmother, Lady Anne, who had tolerated Porchey's grandfather's excesses for sport, especially the turf, at the expense of matrimony and, good housekeeping and learning. Anne knew that a man's passion for horse racing could not compete with anything else. But even her support had its limits: in 1883, when Porchey was expected to accompany his father and stepmother to Canada, he turned to his grandmother to appeal his case. She knew Porchey was being bullied, but she would not defy the 4th Earl. On 27 July 1885 Anne, who had been a trustworthy but ultimately ineffective mentor "and always so kind",[99] passed away at the age of 82.

At university, Porchey is recorded as achieving no better than fourth class, and he left Cambridge without taking a degree. Although he had previously sat an examination for entering the army, a history of poor health in his developmental years precluded this course. So instead, he drifted.

An early globetrotter

In June 1885 Lord Salisbury, a lifelong friend of the 4th Earl, appointed Porchey's father Lord Lieutenant of Ireland. But the Earl was not always at ease in the political arena. A pen picture by Mary Jeune, Lady St Helier, in her reminiscences *Memories of Fifty Years*, suggests that despite his abilities Henry was a shy, modest man, someone who was at his best with the people who knew him. She declares that he was "temperamentally ill-suited to the hurly-burly of political life" [100]. Thus, after the return of William Gladstone as Prime Minister, Carnarvon effectively retired from public service on the grounds of ill health.

Lady Winifred (always her father's favourite) found a first husband during her father's time in Ireland. Captain Hon. Alfred Byng, aide-de-camp to the 4th Earl, died the same year they married in 1887. The Byngs lived briefly together at Bretby Park, suggesting that on coming of age, at 21, Porchey was prevented from occupying the property of Bretby Hall, inherited from his deceased mother, Lady Evelyn.

But whilst Winifred was flying the nest, George was increasingly in need of supervision, for the heir's pursuit of gentlemanly pleasures was gaining him something of a reputation. [101] So his solo antics were systematically curtailed as he was brought under his high churchman, powerful Freemason father's ever-watchful eye. During the 4th Earl's time as Lord Lieutenant of Ireland, Porchey was obliged to constantly and reluctantly shadow him, along with his stepmother and his stepmother's brother, Esme William Howard (later Lord Howard of Penrith 1863–1939), who was appointed to Lord Carnarvon's staff in June 1885, largely at the request of Lady Carnarvon. Porchey was forced to endure attendance at endless dinners, the divine services at the Royal Hibernian Military School, and meaningless and dreary presentations and ceremonies at the Vice Regal Lodge, Dublin. His only retreat was to escape to rural Ireland to enjoy cycling (which proved as accident prone a recreation as his later love of motor car driving). He also spent time in Galway salmon fishing. Surprisingly, he was given permission to travel to America in the August of 1886, where he visited New York and indulged in sailing, gambling and entertaining, in the company of his old Eton and Cambridge pal, Prince Victor Duleep Singh.

Back home in January 1887 Porchey spent some weeks suffering from bronchitis made better by a stay at the family's villa at Porto Fino, near Genoa in Italy. Later in 1887 he was elected as a member of the Royal Yacht Squadron at Cowes, Isle of Wight, allowing a love of sailing to peak. Local gambling trips to Monte Carlo and Ostend were made more accessible by acquiring the latest, fastest steam yacht, ensuring this other love was satisfied too, with no regard for the expense incurred.

In June 1887 Porchey turned 21, but the celebrations were dampened by his father's year-long run of acute bad health. In July it was announced George would accompany his parents on a trip to Australia, via South Africa, a voyage recommended for improving his father's health. The 4th Earl had many contacts in the Colonies; he had also made some shrewd overseas investments in property. He was warmly welcomed in Cape Town and in Australian cities by diplomats, old colonials and his fellow Freemasons. The trip held less appeal for Porchey, but he enjoyed the horse racing and the theatre.

Eventually, Porchey's father cut him some slack, but not without issuing some frank warnings. On 29 September 1887 George left

Cowes on his yacht *Aphrodite*, bound for Lisbon and Madeira. The plan was to proceed to the West Indies. Come November, Mrs E Caws, wife of Captain Caws of the *Aphrodite*, received a letter from her husband from Tenerife (dated 16 November) saying that they were making for St Vincent and the Cape de Verd Islands on their way to Barbados. One story is that Porchey instigated a strict rule of 'no ladies' and 'no black shoes' on board the yacht. Carnarvon was the champion of male bonding and wearing brown shoes.[102]

It was in February 1889 that Porchey first visited Egypt[103], where he developed an interest in ancient art and photography. The climate also suited his fragile health: he was never strong and was a victim of congenital lung disease. One commentator of the time made an illuminating remark: "We believe that this trip has been decided on in order to keep the young nobleman out of temptation."[104] But the visit was hardly going to do that; in fact, it fed his libertine habits.

Egyptian gaming houses were rife, with private establishments such as the Turf Club and the Khedival Club, Cairo, with its "real bath, haircut and shave and fizz in magnums iced"[105] blossoming in the era of the Royal Baccarat scandal in England.[106] Porchey spent large sums on art, and lost plenty gambling at the tables. He forfeited other sums with high stakes in horse racing and betting, all compulsive habits he shared with Victor Duleep Singh. The two were textbook gamblers, fulfilling the very definitions of gambling: "playing extravagantly for money" (Samuel Johnson) and "an enchanting witchery gotten between idleness and avarice" (Cotton in *The Compleat Gambler*).

The American socialite Julian Osgood-Field observed that Victor led Porchey into "wild ways".[107] This almost certainly included frequenting Cairo sin spots, dope and smoking dens and numerous whorehouses, where Arab boys and girls were available for money. They had also both "drunk of the sweet waters of Paris rather too deeply, and... began a life of gaiety rather too early to suit the view of their very sedate, quiet and hard working papa(s)" [108]

In a country riddled with sexually spread diseases, the two young men ran a high risk of contracting a crippling venereal disease that would blight the chances of a healthy, sexually satisfying relationship in marriage, with children. Yet that did not deter Porchester in his amorous advances. According to the respected American newspaper The Washington Post, Porchester was cited on two occasions prior to his accession to the earldom as being "about to contract an American matrimonial alliance".109 He was subsequently forced to retract promises, with exposure to high costs in reparations.

As the decade closed Porchey indulged in further overseas travel, always with his valet George Fernside but surprisingly without Victor 110, to South Africa, New Zealand, Australia and Japan. In 1890, when Porchey returned to England to be presented at Court, it was after a meandering journey through Australia and the Far East, then the West Coast of the United States and through the Rockies to the East Coast ports. He had succeeded in being dubbed one of the early globetrotters, as this extract from another American newspaper reveals.

Lord Porchester and valet of England arrived on the steamer City of Rio de Janeiro yesterday from Hong Kong and is registered at a down town hotel...He is making a tour of the world for pleasure only ...He is an amateur hunter and is anxious to try his hand on some of the larger American game in the Rockies.[111]

On the afternoon of 16 June 1890 George's feet touched the ground long enough to be introduced by Viscount Lascelles at the levee held by the Prince of Wales on behalf of Queen Victoria at St James Palace. Less than two weeks later, on 29 June 1890, George's father lost his battle with cancer, and Porchey earned the title 5th Earl of Carnarvon.

Becoming Lord Carnarvon

The new Earl of Carnarvon had been spared the full agonies of his father's death from liver cancer, but it had caused great suffering for the family, especially his stepmother Elsie. She was left to take comfort from the obituaries of her husband, which revealed a great respect for the highly principled Earl, who was, said one, "high minded, accomplished, sincere, kindly, a devout member of the Church of England and an eminently good man."[112]

One of Porchey's first duties as Earl was communicating details of his father's funeral to the great and good who had known the old statesman, including his father's lifelong friend, the 3rd Marquis of Salisbury (1830–1903) who was then Prime Minister and represented the Cabinet at the funeral at Highclere.[113] In the 4th Earl's final years he and Lord Salisbury had been torn on the Irish question, but the two men had reached "a reconciliation after temporary estrangement".[114]

Carnarvon's stepmother Elsie formally left Highclere on Wednesday 30 July 1890 accompanied by her two young sons Aubrey and Mervyn and travelled to Greystoke Castle, Cumberland. The *Hampshire Telegraph* records the extent of her permanent removal: "Lady Carnarvon took away her horses and carriages, several of her old servants, and an immense quantity of heavy luggage."[115]

The 4th Earl's will was revealed in November 1890. He made provision for his widow to retain a life interest in Pixton Park, Somerset. All the children were provided for, as were the 4th Earl's sisters. The new Earl inherited the entailed lands, but he already owned Bretby. Lady Carnarvon could not take up residence at Pixton Park, as the property was let. She retained the family house in London (now at Portman Square, which was sold) and the villa (at Porto Fino) near Genoa, which had been built in 1874 as a family retreat by the 4th Earl. This "Italian Highclere, "Altachiara", rose upon the cliffs overlooking the little land-locked harbour of Portofino".[116]

As a widow, Elsie Howard, Lady Carnarvon, dressed only in black. [117] She saw herself as the new protector of the family's moral high ground. She used her pen to do this on several occasions, including taking over the editing of the biography of the 4th Earl from his friend Sir Arthur Hardinge (1859–1933). Hardinge's obituary writer in *The Times* of 29 December 1933 comments that: *"Life of Carnarvon*, a task which he had undertaken for friendship's sake was, we believe, much altered by another's hand before its publication." [118]

Elsie also stepped up as George's moral compass. She warned her stepson in stern terms, echoing the advice given him by his own long-deceased mother, that with the titles and land came a legacy of a good name and a noble character, and that must shape his future conduct.

Perhaps unsurprisingly, Carnarvon struggled to come to terms with his role as the Earl of Carnarvon. Some local tasks required him to follow almost immediately in his father's footsteps, such as attending a meeting of the Newbury Corporation to elect him Lord High Steward of the borough. George was only content or at ease with

Victor and those who understood him, and he disliked being under watchful eyes, such as those of his brother-in-law Herbert Gardner (later Lord Burghclere) who had married Lady Winifred after the death of her first husband.

As Elsie had disposed of the family's London home another property was required, so Carnarvon bought 13 Berkeley Square as his London townhouse in 1891. He fell ill again during August, and his sister Winifred Burghclere stayed to give him support, but she was later persuaded to leave her brother to Victor to raise his morale and aid recovery. He was well enough by October to attend the funeral of his uncle, the Earl of Portsmouth, and then he spent the winter of early 1892 back in Egypt, arriving home at the end of March.

In May 1892 he fell seriously ill from a malady picked up in Egypt and almost died. [119] One bulletin was ominous: "Lord Carnarvon who is lying dangerously ill at Berkeley Square, London passed a fair night and is on the whole better." [120] On the 13th of May the report was more favourable: "Invalids – Lord Carnarvon: A fair night. Better today." A few days later the Pall Mall Gazette stated that "Lord Carnarvon continues to improve". On 25 June 1892 another statement was made: "The Earl of Carnarvon, having partially recovered from his long illness, has left town and gone to the seaside to recruit his strength."[121]

Carnarvon was clearly not a supreme figure of manhood to assure the bloodline would successfully continue. The affects of poor genes, illness and self-injury scarred his body. There were abuses too from Victor's enforced leadership that they must prove their manhood.

With debts trapping him from making any forward plans and a failed attempt to sell the Bretby Park estate to John Gretton (later Lord Gretton, 1867–1947) for a rumoured 400,000 pounds,[122] he was forced to seriously consider his future. With his poor health, his financial situation and his looks (harsh attacks of measles and smallpox and abuse had left his (one time handsome[123]) face ravished with deep disturbances consistent with a venereal disease of the skin and facial surgery),[124] George was not a prize specimen to present himself to a virgin bride. However, he had one thing that was highly desirable: he was an Earl in the peerage of Great Britain.

Alfred de Rothschild plays Cupid

It is inconceivable that Almina and George had not happened upon each other *before* their formal introduction at Buckingham Palace in July 1893. They were, after all, neighbours in Mayfair: Almina's mother Marie lived at 20 Bruton Street, and the Carnarvons had a house at 16 Bruton Street, and later, from 1891, at nearby 13 Berkeley Square. But now, with Almina of a marriageable age, Alfred de Rothschild was quick to spot the opportunity to secure her entry into the British peerage.

The courtship between Lord Carnarvon and Almina was over in less than a few months, but far from being a whirlwind romance, it was an arrangement of convenience and pragmatism architected by Alfred. [125] Carnarvon, ten years Almina's senior, was aristocratic enough to suit Alfred and Marie's aspirations for Almina: the Herberts were well connected to the nation's notable families. Yes, George possessed far from an ideal personality, but Alfred had known Porchey's wasteful grandfather, George Chesterfield, and envisaged that Almina would eventually learn to handle him as Lady Anne had done her spouse.

Almina's access to the Rothschild's wealth made the 5th Earl's decision simple enough in respect of the terms of the deal. In *No Regrets*, the 6th Earl's memoirs, George's son suggests that his father struck up a hard bargain with Alfred in negotiating the size of the marriage settlement. If this is true, it is an unflattering but an invariably accurate reflection on how Carnarvon saw Almina's assets of youthful charm, petite French beauty and feminine allure. [126]

The approval of the families was, of course, essential to the success of the match, so Alfred was careful to sound them out. Both families were reluctant, but acquiesced. Alfred de Rothschild was pleased with the deal; he considered it an exceptional gift to Marie Wombwell.

Almina was happy enough at the match, but was under no delusions that she could expect a fairytale happy ever after. Her husband-to-be was far from being the dashing, romantic, young lord of women's fantasies in magazines of the day; he appeared prematurely old, crumpled and boorish. Not overlooked was a vein of madness in the Wallop family[127] (later a concern for Almina, coupled with the closeness of the blood tie, when her grandson Henry wanted to marry a Wallop in 1956), and the Herbert men's propensity for illness and early death. Moreover, Porchey remained too close to Victor Duleep Singh and "addicted to associations which had caused his own father much anxiety".[128] And then there were the character flaws: he could be stubborn, reckless and neglectful, especially about carrying out any repetitive responsibilities of birth, and his devotion to satisfying himself made him a selfish, self-interested man. [129]

But for Almina, the one thing he offered outweighed the apparent flaws in George as a suitor: a place in the aristocratic elite, the chance to become, at the tender age of 19, a countess.

Preparing for the wedding of the season

In late October 1894, several newspapers carried details of the engagement: "A marriage is arranged between the Earl of Carnarvon and Miss Almina Wombwell, only daughter of the late Mr Frederick Wombwell, and niece of Sir George Orby Wombwell." [130] The newspapers were generally polite in describing Marie as having "a connection of some members of the Rothschild family".[131] The statement followed Alfred de Rothschild's announcement that he was settling the "generous sum of 300,000 pounds on Almina as a marriage portion".[132]

In fact, the dowry from Alfred was variously described as falling between 300,000 and 500,000 pounds, a colossal sum for its time. The settlement made George's true motive for the marriage abundantly clear to Society onlookers, who saw Porchester as a "black sheep, never-do-well, idler, spendthrift, and gambler".[133] One commentator remarked that "the 5th Earl married the daughter of Alfred de Rothschild's mistress principally to induce solvency".[134]

With the engagement announced, the families moved on to setting a date – Wednesday 26 June 1895, Lord Carnarvon's 29th birthday – and arguing over the technicalities of the event. Far from wielding a position of power as mother-of-the-bride in the arrangement of the nuptials, the Wombwell and Rothschild matriarchs snubbed Marie, and she had to contend with hostility from the equally uncompromising Herbert, Stanhope and Wallop groupings. A flurry of correspondence between Porchey's stepmother, Elsie, and the Stanhopes and Wallops reveals they had a particular gripe: they were aghast that Marie, whom they described as "unpopular in London Society"[135], was proposing to host the celebratory breakfast on Almina's wedding day at her house at 20 Bruton Street. They argued that the proper person to host this was her aunt, Lady Julia Wombwell, and she had already sounded out her daughter, Lady Cremorne, in London, who was standing by to provide a safe haven.

Porchey would not allow interference from his own side, especially with so much money at stake. For his financial freedom, he desperately needed the union to go smoothly. The problem was finally resolved by Marie herself, when she called in a favour from her old friend the American millionaire William Waldorf Astor (such were her social contacts) and arranged the reception at Lansdowne House, an Adam building that had been occupied by four Prime Ministers over the years.[136]

To help ease her nerves and give Almina a chance to see what her own wedding event would be like, she acted as a bridesmaid to her friend Millicent Wilson on 10 June 1895. [137]

With just days to go before his wedding the reluctant but determined groom made it back from Paris. His stag night consisted of a dinner party at 13 Berkeley Square where Miss Marie Tempest sang, and Miss Cissie Loftus, imitated, and a group known as the Sisters Hengler danced with grace. This was Carnarvon at his best: as a voyeur with women in a passive role. Like Alfred de Rothschild, George enjoyed gazing upon the unattainable.

Here comes the Countess

It was headlined as one of the weddings of the season: the tall, slim, bachelor Earl marrying the lovely, barely five-feet-high half-French "Pocket Venus".[138]

The ceremony took place at St Margaret's Church, Westminster in front of a large congregation and choir. Lord Carnarvon's cousin, Reverend Hugh Rycroft, officiated, assisted by Reverend Herbert Moore and Reverend Canon Troutbeck of Westminster, once personal chaplain to Lord Carnarvon's father. Amongst those gathered were Almina's brother, Frederick Wombwell,[139] and the former Prime Minister Lord Rosebery (whose mother was a Stanhope and whose wife was Hannah Rothschild, 1851–1890, Alfred's cousin) and Madame Adelina Patti (the goddess of song, whom Alfred showered with jewels).[140] There was also a large contingent of Rothschilds and Lord Carnarvon's Eton contemporary

George William Coventry, Viscount Deerhurst, with his new American wife. And of course there was Marie's and Almina's chaperone, Alfred de Rothschild: the rich friend who had funded the bride and groom's coupling. Alfred had to be satisfied with being guest of honour in the church rather than giving Almina away: Victorian society was not geared up for such a blatant display condoning illegitimacy or creating a bridge between religious divides.

Prince Victor Duleep Singh was best man, and there were eight bridesmaids, including Ladies Margaret and Victoria Herbert (the bridegroom's sisters) and Victor's sister, Princess Sophie. The bridesmaid's costumes were cream mousseline-de-soie over white satin skirts, trimmed with bows of blue silk ribbon, with hats of cream coloured straw adorned with white feathers and pale blue ribbons. The bridegroom's half-brother, Hon. Mervyn Herbert and Lord Arthur Hay, son of the Marquis of Tweeddale, acted as pages to the bride, dressed in Louis XV costumes of white and silver brocaded satin, with hats to match. (Lord Hay's connection to the family was later cemented: he was killed in action in 1914 at the age of 25 whilst serving as a Captain in the Irish Guards, and his widow later married Robert Leatham, father of Michael Leatham, who married Almina's granddaughter, Patricia Evelyn Beauchamp.)

Almina entered the church shortly after half-past two, and made her journey down the aisle on Sir George Wombwell's arm. Her dress was of white satin duchesse with a full court train, draped with a priceless veil of beautiful Brussels lace, caught up on the shoulder, which was a gift from her mother. The bodice was trimmed with natural orange blossom and magnificent old lace, courtesy of the bridegroom – his gift to his bride had also included the Carnarvon jewels, including a diamond and emerald tiara, a necklace of pearls and diamonds, an emerald and diamond bracelet, a pearl and diamond ring and an emerald ring. The bride's attire was completed with a tulle veil covering a coronet of natural orange flowers, delicately offsetting the palms, lilies and tinted peonies that decorated the church.[141]

The service ended with the hymn 'Now Thank We All Our God' and whilst the newlyweds signed the registers Thome's 'Andante Religioso' was played. Then Almina and George left the church as man and wife to the bridal march from *Lohengrin.*

Almina's mother, Marie, hosted the wedding feast at Lansdowne House.[142] She was adorned in the most magnificent jewels: a talking point in itself. [143] Afterwards the new Earl and Countess of Carnarvon left by special train from Paddington for Newbury and then a carriage took them to Highclere Castle for the first part of their honeymoon. Highclere's staff reached to the heavens to welcome the Earl and the new Countess. There were large-scale demonstrations of affection by the house and estate workers, under J.A. Rutherford, the Estate Steward with the finest woodland displays by Mr Storie, the head forester, and seasonal flowers by Mr Pope, the head gardener.

Lord Carnarvon was a shy man amongst any crowd, and he wished he were elsewhere. But he made a short speech:

I thank you very, very much for your kind reception. I never expected anything half so pretty as has been today. I shall never forget this greatest pleasure. I thank you, not for myself but my wife begs me to thank you very much indeed. Again I thank you.[144]

Photographs of the bride and groom appeared in the public arena in the magazine *Black and White* of 29 June 1895, taken respectively by Walery and Edward Passingham. On the same date *The Penny Illustrated Times* carried Almina's full-length photograph by Miss Alice Hughes of Gower Street, with the 5th Earl's study by Passingham.

At Bretby Park the celebrations continued, with numerous wedding gifts from the tenants on the Carnarvon estates. But the festivities were cut short late afternoon by a huge storm, which was spoken of as being "without parallel for many years"[145]: a deluge of rain that flooded numerous buildings accompanied by a thunderstorm and incessant lightning. The 1,200 employees and tenants were forced to abandon their tents and the feast laid out within.

The preliminaries over, on Saturday 7 July 1895 Almina and Lord Carnarvon left Highclere for the Continent on the second leg of their honeymoon, and a chance to get to know each other. For although their match had been declared by those who arranged it to be "love at first sight",[146] the truth was that Lord and Lady Carnarvon barely knew each other. They were strangers locked into a loveless marriage, which would endure for the next 22 years.

**Anne, Lady Chesterfield
And daughter Evelyn**

George, Earl of Chesterfield

Henry, 4ᵗʰEarl

Elsie, 4ᵗʰ Countess

Chapter 3
1895–1902

The New Earl and Countess Step Out

A warm welcome at Bretby

For Lord Carnarvon, the jewel in the crown of the Carnarvon estates was undoubtedly Bretby Park. The name Bretby is of Danish origin, and means "farm of the Britons". This was an ideal sanctuary of an ancient hall nestled amongst mature trees, a deer park, a chain of ornamental lakes and a clutch of dairy farms. Bretby Hall had once been home to the Chesterfields, and was the scene of the famous murder [147] of Lady Elizabeth Butler, the wife of the 2nd Earl of Chesterfield, who had his wife poisoned following (untrue) allegations of infidelity.

This Derbyshire home was Carnarvon's own personal haven. It was here that Lady Anne, his beloved Chesterfield grandmother, had once showered him with attention, and after his father's death he had used Bretby to provide much needed breathing space from the invidious demands imposed by life as the new Earl at Highclere and London. For George, Bretby held happy memories of shooting and race meetings, and socialising with his lifelong confidante Prince Victor Duleep Singh, who had practically moved into the Hall before his marriage.

Following their wedding, Almina had high hopes for making changes across the Carnarvon properties to suit her own style and taste for the Parisian palace and parlour. She was determined to see Bretby, but for the first months of their marriage the Earl was in no hurry to share this precious haven. The issue was addressed on their return to Highclere from a grouse-shooting holiday, with Victor, in Scotland at Delnadamph Lodge, Strathdon, Aberdeenshire.[148] Finally, George acquiesced. He fitted in two days of game shooting at Pixton Park, his stepmother's estate near Dulverton, famed for its deer park, before joining Almina to travel with her by train to Repton.

On Sunday 15 September 1895 the Carnarvons received a warm welcome at Bretby. The village was decorated for the occasion with evergreen banners and triumphal arches, and the Bretby Colliery Band played 'Home Sweet Home'. Throngs of tenants, miners and school children turned out to welcome the new incumbents at the Hall. The local community was, after all, dependent on the Carnarvons for their existence, and the Earl had earned respect by maintaining relief funds for victims of coal-mining accidents at Bretby and other local coalfields, and acting as vice president of the Midland District Miners' Fatal Accident Relief Society, directed by the 8th Duke of Devonshire. Everyone was provided with hospitality in the servant's hall and the steward's room. The gathering was brief, and the Earl failed to give a speech, but he did express his gratitude after the event in a bulletin to the local press:

> To the tenants and employees on the Bretby Estate and to the men employed in Bretby Colliery – Gentlemen: On behalf of my wife and myself I beg to thank you most cordially for the very kind and hearty manner in which you have received us this day on our arrival at Bretby. Our reception being quite unexpected was all the more pleasant and agreeable to us and will always afford a most delightful reminiscence to us both. Believe me, yours faithfully, CARNARVON.[149]

The Earl planned to entertain regularly at Bretby and their other homes, and Almina was happy to oblige: playing hostess kept her busy. Early guests included Victor Duleep Singh and Lord Ashburton, two of Carnarvon's inner circle.

In October the Carnarvons spent time in Paris at the Hotel Continental, and they planned another visit there for the same month. These frequent trips to Paris would continue throughout the following years. The French capital was to Almina what Bretby was to her husband: a haven, a home from home. Trips to Paris therefore became the price George paid to keep her happy and spending money: a nice substitute for marital relations.

Come November, they returned to Bretby. Almina busied herself making plans for an overhaul of the interior of the hall, whilst Carnarvon shot at Bingham.

Bertie, Prince of Wales, visits Highclere Castle

At Highclere the pre-occupation for the latter months of 1895 was the forthcoming visit of Albert (Bertie), Prince of Wales, the future King Edward VII, who was ostensibly coming to shoot, but was also keen to see the new Countess of Carnarvon in action. Almina could not have been tested as a hostess to any greater extent than this in her first year of marriage.

To ensure the quality of game over the winter fields a dry run was staged by Carnarvon on 26, 27 and 29 November. Over the course of the three days, shooters Princes Victor and Frederick Duleep Singh, Lord de Grey[150], Lord Ashburton, Lord Carnarvon and Henry Chaplin (the man who had destroyed Fred Wombwell's friend, the Marquis of Hastings) quite literally made a killing: 16 partridges, 5,671 pheasants, 43 hares, 5,033 rabbits, four woodcock, two wildfowl and 38 other birds. This extraordinary shooting spree took place over the Beeches, Highclere Wood and Grotto beats. The other preserves were kept intact for the Royal visit. ;[151]

The housekeeping preparations were left to Almina. A room at Highclere (The Stanhope bedroom) was suitably decorated with new panels and tapestries for the Prince, with some general refurbishment undertaken, including additional stabling. It is recorded by one of Almina's intimates that Lord Carnarvon was "quite firm"[152] with his wife and that "a great deal of prompting went on before the actual stay".[153] Almina was naturally apprehensive about the visit and meeting Bertie. As he, too, was a friend of Alfred de Rothschild, Almina wanted to ensure she impressed her future monarch.

Shortly after five o'clock on 17 December Bertie left Marlborough House, attended by Commander Hon. Seymour Fortescue, and drove to Paddington railway station and from there took the train to Highclere. The Princess of Wales stayed behind in London with her daughters at Marlborough House in the company of Prince Nicholas of Greece. The Royal Family had just commemorated the 34th anniversary of the death of Prince Albert (1819–1861) on 14 December, and on the 16th had celebrated the arrival of a new baby for the Duke and Duchess of York: George, who would one day be crowned King George VI.[154]

Bertie's reputation was that of an august sportsman, but he was recovering from a painful eye caused when some grains of powder were blown into his right eye during an earlier shoot at Hall Barn, Buckinghamshire. But these distractions did not affect Bertie's plans, although the weather took its toll. On 18 December the Prince and a large party shot over Highclere's Bigg's beat and the Warrens. The short hours and the dull damp weather cut back the day's programme, which was abandoned after a downpour of rain.

Carnarvon had gone to a great deal of trouble to ensure his coverts were stocked with 20,000 pheasants that were brought in at some expense from a Hampshire game farm. The Prince and his party succeeded in bringing down about 11,000 of the birds.

Amongst those invited to join the shoot as guests were the Earl and Countess of Westmoreland, Lord and Lady Burghclere, Viscount Chelsea MP, Viscountess Chelsea, the Earl and Countess Howe, Lady Dorothy Nevill, Hon. Mrs Lowther, Sir Edward and Lady Colebrooke, the Russian Ambassador and the Brazilian Minister.[155]

The dining was of a high standard, but Almina was astonished that the Prince preferred drumsticks of chicken to best breast meat. The menu was submitted personally to the Prince daily for approval, and Almina learned that her future king preferred small, choice dinners to elaborate banquets.[156]

Carnarvon engaged a number of personalities to amuse the Prince and his party, including the leading professional billiard exhibition player Eugene Carter. There were Indian jugglers and conjurers, songsters of the Yvette Guilbert type from Paris and a dramatic troupe from London, as well as music from the Gottlieb band.[157]

At the end of his stay, on the 19th, the Prince expressed himself as being highly pleased with the whole visit. His Royal Highness returned to London by special train and spent Christmas with the rest of the Royal Family at Sandringham.

The Carnarvons were pleased with themselves. They had passed their first vital test and gained a Royal blessing from their future king.

1896

It soon became clear to Almina's that her marriage would be a lonely one. Carnarvon had not consummated the marriage, and he had his own interests to pursue that seldom included her. Almina had to content herself with mastering her role as mistress of a large English country house and estate.

Although Almina had little experience of managing a household, she was used to managing staff – a housekeeper in attendance, with a butler, footmen, cook and performing maids as servants, in keeping with the style in which her mother Marie lived at her Mayfair home.[158] Almina organised and delegated well, and she was well supported as several of Carnarvon's relatives occupied Highclere's house and estate staff were old hands.

But Almina was soon given a break from her duties as mistress, as the Carnarvons returned to their beloved Paris in January 1896, remaining there until the middle of March. They stayed at the Hotel de Paris in Monte Carlo, and the Hotel de Provence, Cannes. In February they arrived at the Hotel de Paris, Monte Carlo, where they were joined by Victor, who was on his way back to England from visiting his late mother's relations in Cairo, Egypt. Alfred de Rothschild also paid them a visit; he was cruising the area on board one of the Rothschild yachts, the *Rona*.[159]

The Riviera was at its best: the weather was superb. One report referred to "immense crowds of well dressed people, many in summer costumes walking and driving in every direction. All the hotels and restaurants are thronged with visitors."[160] The Carnarvons shared the dining rooms at the Hotel de Paris with the Emperor of Austria, the Duchess of Devonshire[161], Prince Soltykoff[162] and the Lords and Ladies Wolverton and Coke. News had filtered through the ranks of the Carnarvons successfully hosting the Prince of Wales' visit to Highclere during the previous December, and the couple had gained social standing after the rumours about the artificiality of their union.

The Carnarvons returned to London to be back at Highclere for Easter time. A further trip to Paris was taken whilst extensive improvements were carried out at Highclere on Almina's insistence. The work, for which Alfred Rothschild footed the bill, included electricity being installed in the castle and stables and a considerable portion of the interior of the Castle being redecorated. During the renovations Ladies Victoria and Margaret Herbert, Carnarvon's sisters, were re-housed at Milford House, a beautiful structure on the shore of the lake at Highclere, later preferred to the Castle by the 7th Earl and Countess as a home.[163]

Milford House was at the disposal of the family's personal friends and visitors during the summer, when large parties were given at Highclere. The public was also allowed to visit the picturesque park on Wednesdays and Saturdays. Almina urged Carnarvon to throw open the beautiful woodland walks on the same days during June.

Besides that Beacon Hill, adjoining Highclere Park, was open and a favourite rendezvous place during the summer months.

On 10 June 1896 it was time for Almina to once more journey to Buckingham Palace. Elsie (the 4th Countess) presented Almina at Court as the new Countess of Carnarvon to Her Royal Highness the Princess of Wales, who was standing in for Queen Victoria. The Dowager Countess of Carnarvon carried out the honours, by way of a peace gesture, and in recognition of Almina's success as the new Countess. Soon after, on Monday 22 June 1896, Carnarvon took his seat in Parliament for the first time in the session. Almina watched the proceedings from the Peeresses' Gallery.

Thereafter, Alfred de Rothschild invited the Carnarvons to his country estate at Halton House, but the time there was interrupted by Carnarvon being taken "seriously ill"[164], requiring medical attendance by one of Alfred's gaggle of physicians, Alfred (later Sir Alfred) Cooper.[165] (Rothschild was a hypochondriac who feared death – he had a doctor on hand at Halton and in London at all times of the day and night.) Victor Duleep Singh was on hand to offer his special brand of comfort and friendship to Lord Carnarvon, and to increase his personal, intimate kindness and thoughtfulness to Almina. Victor had particular skills for handling women that were lacking and even loathed by Carnarvon.

Whilst they were in London for a state concert at Buckingham Palace held on 29 June 1896, Victor offered his services again. He agreed to accompany Almina to a gathering on Wednesday 1 July 1896. This let Carnarvon, who found functions dreadfully dull, off the hook.

Every corner of the gentry attended the event, a dance at 12 Grosvenor Crescent held by Captain Quinton Dick of County Galway to introduce the Grand Duke Michael of Russia and Countess Torby to London Society. It was a glittering affair with throngs of the British peerage lining up to meet and greet the visiting dignitaries. There, Almina was reacquainted with her Wombwell relations Sir George and Lady Julia, as well as Highclere regulars the Nevills.

During her stay in London Almina made time to catch up with her mother, with whom she had always been close, at Bruton Street. Then the Carnarvons were reunited for a brief cruise off the coast of

Guernsey, in a hired yacht, *The Iolanthe*, owned by Sir Donald Currie.

In September 1896 Lord Carnarvon was taken ill again with a severe chill and was forced to rest. Victor substituted for him again, this time in leading a shooting party at Bretby.[166] But later in the month he was able to fulfil a commitment to partridge shoot with Victor and Lord Ashburton at Highclere. He was also well enough to shoot on Victor's estate at Hockwold in Norfolk.

On 20 September Almina persuaded Carnarvon to return to Highclere, where her guest was regular companion Princess Sophia Duleep Singh (1876–1948), Victor's sister. During Sophia's later visit to Bretby Park an incident occurred that would be inspirational in the Princess developing a political stance. The two friends were out driving in a pony carriage in Burton on Trent when an overzealous police sergeant observed that the Princess was holding a small Pomeranian dog that was not muzzled, contrary to the law, resulting in Sophia being fined 12 shillings in the Swadlincote petty sessions. Sophia later became a leading suffragette and a member of the Women's Tax Resistance League. Taking a stand on the principle that there should be no taxation without representation, she recalled the experience of this first law breach several times, refusing to pay similar licence fees, which resulted in the authorities seizing her property and jewels.

The climax of that year's shooting season took place at Highclere on Monday 19 October 1896 when Carnarvon and Duleep Singh slaughtered 3,000 rabbits, some 600 in the first hour, one creature every six seconds. The rabbits were specially arranged for the occasion. One commentator said that the Prince "ought to go to Chicago; they are constantly killing live stock there".[167]

In November and December 1896, following the Derby races, the Carnarvons welcomed Lord and Lady Ashburton as guests at Highclere, and there they celebrated their second Christmas as man and wife.

In this first full year of marriage Almina and Carnarvon had surrounded themselves by people, and put on an excellent show as a united couple. But there was no sign of Almina producing an heir, and tongues began wagging of the Earl's incapacity and the Countess's increasing unease.

The Carnarvons were at Highclere for the start of the New Year and spent two weeks receiving a number of guests. They escaped to Paris and Cannes in the middle of February 1897, where they accepted various invitations to social functions.[168] It was announced they would be away for a month to six weeks, and then they were in Paris again at Easter time. Having installed themselves at the Hotel du Rhin, they dined in the company of other members of the British peerage, including the Earls and Countesses of Dudley and Essex and Lord and Lady Wolverton.

Almina mooted that their personal relationship could benefit from time spent away from the usual gazes at Highclere, Bretby and London. So in May 1897 they decided to live temporarily in Paris. They took a rented property for the start of the June season there, but the couple continued to pursue their own pleasures. At the time of Queen Victoria's 78th birthday a celebration was given in Paris by the British Ambassador Sir Edmund Monson. Lord Carnavon attended, but there is no indication that Almina was present.

From Paris the Carnarvons spent time at Monte Carlo. On their return to Paris they attended the Grand Prix de Paris at Longchamps and at Deauville. The latter was described as "the most important race meeting in France after Longchamps and Chantilly".[169] Almina and the 5th Earl were amongst those who made the racecourse popular with the English aristocracy.

Back in England, Almina's attentions switched to making alterations at the Carnarvon's London home at 13 Berkeley Square. Whilst news of the refurbishment seemed to signal the Carnarvons were adding a nursery wing, the truth was that Almina had requested building changes only to suit her own preferences. There was hardly a time when she did not want something done to the inside of the many houses she occupied during her lifetime.

That June saw two national days of celebration for the Queen: the 20th, when she had inherited the crown from her uncle King William IV in 1837, and the 28th, when she had been crowned at Westminster Abbey in 1838. The Carnarvons organised their own celebrations at Highclere on 22 June 1897. School children from London and local urchins were invited to spend the day at the Castle. Four special trains brought the children and their teachers from London to Highclere station, where they were joined by the local children. There were displays by the Royal Berks Yeomanry Cavalry Rifle Volunteers, the fire brigade and other bodies, and then the children were organised into a procession of immense length and marched to the Castle to loud musical accompaniment from the Newbury and Wickham bands. Up at the Castle a large tea was provided and Carnarvon made a rousing speech about Queen Victoria's illustrious reign. Great cheering followed, with the Mayor of Newbury thanking Carnarvon and Almina for arranging such a happy day. In the evening bonfires were lit on Beacon Hill and on Cottington Hill, Kingclere.

The celebrations continued in London, at the Queen's Jubilee Garden Party on 28 June, which saw a huge attendance of the gentry including the Carnarvons and the Dowager Countess. But one of the highlights of the 1897 season was the Jubilee Ball at Devonshire House on Friday 2 July, which the Carnarvons attended together. It had been 23 years since a grand ball on the same scale had been given (the last had been on 22 July 1874 at Marlborough House). [170] The Duchess of Devonshire's invitation indicated that guests should appear "in an allegorical or historical costume dated earlier than 1820".[171] Prince Victor Duleep Singh's elaborate Muslim costume (of Mogul Emperor, Akbar [172]) brought him high praise and much attention.[173]

At the end of August Almina sought refuge at the spa at Schwabach, Germany[174], and then she returned to England. Carnarvon enjoyed shooting with the Singh brothers at Hockwold with a record kill for three guns on 23 September 1897 of 1161 partridges.[175] In October Lord Carnarvon left Almina at Highclere whilst he travelled to the Continent; they were subsequently reunited in Paris. Then the Carnarvons joined Elsie, the Dowager Countess, at Wiesbaden and installed themselves at the Villa Montana, where they stayed over Christmas, before speeding back to England before the New Year to participate in the wedding of Lady Anne Coventry and Prince Victor Duleep Singh, lifelong friend of the Carnarvons.

1898

A marriage and a baby

Prince Duleep Singh (1866–1918) was always a favourite companion of Lord Carnarvon from the time they were Eton schoolboys together aged 13. But there was sometimes an underlying tension between the two. This created a rivalry of sorts as may exist between male siblings. Victor was two weeks younger than Carnarvon, born 10 July, with Carnarvon's birthday falling on 26 June. This should have given Carnarvon the psychological edge, but Victor frequently seized this. He forever played the role of the more dominant, predatory male.

Born and reared in England, Victor had the manners of an English gentleman but despite his mother's attempts at guiding him, he had followed in the footsteps of his temperamental, domineering father, the Maharajah, in developing an eye for the ladies and an incurable passion for gambling. He had a caddish approach also to his financial dealings and a scandalous track record with women, including being cited as a party in a divorce involving an actress, Mrs Kettlewell.[176]

Despite his obvious flaws, Almina took a shine to the charismatic, though portly Indian Prince. He had the right social standing to earn her respect: Victor walked in Court circles and dined regularly with Queen Victoria, his godmother, whom he was named after. [177] Almina was wise enough to tolerate his history and respect the sincerity of his attachment to Lord Carnarvon.

Lady Anne Blanche Coventry (1874–1956), daughter of the 9th Earl and Coventry and sister of an old school contemporary, Viscount Deerhurst, had caught Victor's eye. Anne, "a tall, fair beauty" [178] was quite a catch for Victor: she was a dashing horsewoman and much loved by the Coventry tenants in Malvern and Worcester, where she had spent her childhood years at the family seat of Croome Court, Severn End. (Interestingly, in his youth Lord Coventry had taken part in shooting and Derby horse racing with the Marquis of Hastings, Lord Carnarvon's grandfather Lord Chesterfield and Frederick Wombwell.)

The love match between Victor and Anne set London society agog. It was not without opposition. Race, colour and religion were cited as being incompatible; and there were rumours that the origins of the

Singh dynasty were less than satisfactory in terms of Royal blood. [179] Plus, Victor was struggling to convince the Earl of Coventry of his financial stability (indeed, he was quietly raiding the family treasure chests to fend off his creditors), and was forced to write to Queen Victoria asking her to oblige the India Office to give assurances about his allowance.

But this was the romance that could not be stopped, not by Anne's parents, nor her brother Viscount Deerhurst, and not even by Queen Victoria, who was not amused by the match. Against the odds, Victor's marriage was blessed, but only after Lady Anne made an extraordinary promise to Queen Victoria. In his book on the Duleep Singh family, Peter Bance[180] explains that Lady Anne swore, on the Queen's request, that she would never fall pregnant with Victor's child. She later stated she kept that promise, which, if true, suggests that for the next 20 years, until Victor's death in 1918, Victor had no carnal knowledge of his wife.[181]

But it is unclear when Victor was made aware of his fiancée's promise, and before the wedding he certainly continued to act the playboy Prince. He was regularly sighted in Cannes, Monte Carlo, Wildbad and Baden Baden, and when necessary Carnarvon gave him money and allowed him to lie low at Pixton Park, Bretby and Highclere. Almina had no objections: she encouraged Victor to visit and stay. For his last socialising as a free man, Victor enjoyed his stag night with Carnarvon and Alfred de Rothschild in London. Alfred had known Victor's father for years, since his own introduction to London Society at the Guards' Ball of 1863.

On Tuesday 4 January 1898 the wedding ceremony took place at St Peter's Church, Eton Square, London. Lord Coventry gave his daughter away, and Victor's brother Prince Frederick was his best man. Amongst the six bridesmaids were two of the bridegroom's sisters and Carnarvon's sister, Lady Victoria Herbert. Conspicuously absent was Viscount Deerhurst, who refused to attend [182].

Almina's French influence on the bride's outfit was obvious. The dress of ivory satin was adjoined to "a bodice finished with a Marie Antoinette fichu of white mousseline de soie, edged with full frills".[183] Precisely what Victor wore on his wedding day is not completely established. One report, in *The World*[184] states he was dressed in full native costume with headdress, that he had famously worn at the previous year's Devonshire House Ball. However, Peter Bance comments "the Devonshire Ball costume is a Muslim outfit as he was dressed as Akbar so I doubt he would dress as a Muslim on his wedding." [185]

The stunning jewels given by Victor to his bride included "a crown of stars in diamonds, a large diamond bow with an enormous sapphire in the centre". The Singh diamonds were legendry: Victor's late father (the last Singh Maharajah) had been dispossessed as a child and his state taken over by the British, who had confiscated the family's famous 186-carat Koh-i-Noor diamond. The Maharajah had once sought the jewel's return, but Queen Victoria refused.[186] The fabled jewel (meaning *"mountain of light"*) was always prized by Queen Victoria and later British monarchs; it is "still locked up in the Tower of London and adorns its monarchs on special occasions".[187]

One record suggests that Victor wanted to take his new wife to India for the honeymoon, but all the affected governments and officials resisted this, for fear that it would start a race war. Therefore the new Prince and Princess Duleep Singh travelled to Monte Carlo for the first part of their honeymoon, and then moved on to Cairo in early February 1898, the cooler temperatures making this the height of the Egyptian tourist season. There, the Carnarvons joined them. [188] And it was during this time in Egypt that the 22-year-old Almina became pregnant with her first baby.

A paternity question, again

In the period leading up to the conception of her first child, Almina may *not* have lost her virginity to the 5th Earl. Moreover, he is almost certainly *not* the father of her child. Casting echoes into her own past, the paternity of Almina's child is riddled with doubt. Some questions must persist without ever being resolved. Was Almina seduced or set up? Was there some warped conspiracy or pact between either one of the Carnarvons and the progenitor to attempt to deliver a Herbert family heir, or did the Countess simply rebel against Carnarvon's display of marital coldness?

It seems the 5th Earl was slow to do his duty as a husband, and Almina admitted to having a fling (Lady Chatterley style) with a gardener at Highclere, though his name and the time of the affair are unclear. An informant says she "would stand away from her desk at the window in one of the drawing rooms [at Highclere] and summon him". [189] But if Almina engaged in an affair at this time it was clandestine, the details are expunged or suppressed. She was not by nature a serial adulteress, but as we shall see in later chapters, as a more mature woman she developed a remarkable skill for controlling, manipulating and even possessing the men she was intimate with in her life.

However, an informant has given stark, convincing reason to believe that the identity of the father of Almina's first baby is at least "a grey area".[190] Highclere Archives may hold further proof or clarity of the family's posturings in Almina's papers and private correspondence. [191] Unfortunately, the author has been unable to gain access to the Archives[192], but it is known that they contain numerous legal documents relating to the Countess and Highclere over many years.[193] Here lie too the findings of an earlier biographer's research into Almina's life [194], a retrospective apparently abandoned upon the discovery, by accident, of the true identity of the father of her first child.[195] (See also the Epilogue to this book.)

The 5th Earl was not impotent; he just did not find Almina attractive. His wife had a similar revulsion, and she "was always afraid" of him.[196]

Two and a half years into their marriage did practicality win out over romance? The couple needed to beget an heir. Judging from Lord Carnarvon's later acquiescence to the coupling between Almina and Colonel Ian Dennistoun from 1921 onwards, and the testimony of Alice Butler, the Dennistoun's maid, that they conducted a close liaison *with the Earl's consent*, the surrender of Almina's virginity was almost certainly contracted along similar terms. There was at best a surrogacy arrangement rather than a long passionate love affair between the parties, sustainable more as the end justifying the means. [197]

The Earl's devoted friend Prince Victor Duleep Singh had an uncompromising spouse who kept her distance in the bedroom.[198] Years later Victor and Lady Anne were dubbed "the odd couple"[199], a title that was already applicable to George Herbert and Almina Wombwell, the 5th Earl and Countess of Carnarvon.

A Carnarvon heir

The Carnarvons were back at Highclere for Easter, having returned from Cairo via Monte Carlo and the Riviera. The newly married Prince and Princess Victor Duleep Singh arrived back in London in the middle of May. By then, the news of Almina's pregnancy had been revealed. In July the Carnarvons ventured from Highclere to London for the remaining days of the season, no doubt holding their heads high amongst those who had once wondered at the security of the childless couple.

During much of the next few months Dr Marcus Johnston [200], Lord Carnarvon's own personal physician, medically supervised Almina. "Dr Johnnie", as he was always known as in the Carnarvon family, recommended a change of air for his favourite patients, but a Continental trip was discouraged for the mother-to-be. Thus in August the Carnarvons, along with Lady Margaret Herbert, spent time relaxing at the West Cliff Hotel at Folkstone. The Continental ban not applying to Carnarvon, he promptly deserted his wife and sister for a short trip to Deauville for the races and regatta.

Indeed, George wasn't one to hover, and he had no qualms about leaving his pregnant wife to her own devices. During September Almina rested at Highclere, enjoying a visit from Victor and Anne Duleep Singh and managing a short visit to Elsie, the Dowager Countess of Carnarvon, at Pixton Park. Her husband floated on and off the scene, visiting the Duleep Singhs at their home at Hockwold Hall, hosting a shooting party at Bingham, staying at the Hotel Chatham in Paris and answering a summons for "furious driving"[201] at Newbury, one of many naming and shaming of his indulgence in early automobiles.

Finally, with her pregnancy advancing and upon Dr Johnnie's recommendation, the decision was made to move Almina to their London home. Almina was far from happy at the move. Being small of stature, she expected a difficult delivery, and she was terrified of having the child at 13 Berkeley Square, seeing the number 13 as a bad omen. But there was more to Almina's anxiety: she was worried that the child she was bearing would take after his real father. Prepared for any scandal, Almina rented Lady Dorchester's house as a safe refuge.[202]

Finally, Almina's child, a boy, was born on 7 November 1898. Any alarm was over. The boy would be accepted as the Carnarvon heir: he would take the title of Lord Porchester and would, upon the 5th Earl's death, become the 6th Earl. A few days later Carnarvon cavorted with Alfred de Rothschild and others at the theatre, celebrating the news that the Carnarvons had an heir-apparent. *The World* reported under "Invalids" that "Lady Carnarvon is doing capitally". [203]

The new Lord Porchester was brought home to the family seat at Highclere. There were grand celebrations inside the Castle and on all the Carnarvon estates for many days. The baptism of Porchester took place in the Chapel Royal, St James Palace on 12 December. The Reverand Edgar Sheppard, Sub Dean of the Chapels Royal, conducted the ceremony and water brought from the River Jordon was used in the rite. The child received the names Henry George Alfred Marius Victor Francis. His godparents were Prince Victor Duleep Singh, Lord Ashburton, Alfred de Rothschild, Lady Winifred Burghclere and Marie Wombwell.[204]

The 1898 Christmas festivities at Highclere, Lord Porchester's first, saw Victor and his wife in attendance along with Lord Ashburton. Additional guests included old friend of Alfred de Rothschild, Alfred Cooper, with his notable Society wife, the three times married Lady Agnes Cooper.[205]

1899

The New Year of 1899 was celebrated in typical Carnarvon style at Highclere. Whilst the baby snoozed in the nursery, tended to by a troupe of nursemaids and a nanny (as he would be throughout his childhood, always kept at arm's length from his parents), the new parents played their roles as bright, welcoming host and hostess. A conjurer and ventriloquist from London named Hercat provided amusement, aptly accompanied on the piano by none other than Victor Singh, who came to the rescue when the pianist missed his train.[206]

January was also hunting time, and Lord Carnarvon shocked Newbury's country families by attending the local hunts in his latest new-fangled automobile. One of the pioneers of the new automobile age, George kept several cars at Highclere and sung praises of their development, although he did raise concerns that the horse could be replaced and thus create unemployment for those in the horse and carriage industries. Almina enjoyed being ferried around, but preferred the elegance of the horse and carriage. Yet she soon came around to the idea of automotive travel. It was, after all, the latest fashion.

In the months following the birth of Lord Porchester, Almina decided that she needed a complete break. So the Carnarvons headed to the south of Europe in the mid-winter of 1899, arriving back at Highclere for Easter. Then Almina's focus turned to her social standing. Having been isolated by her pregnancy and then away on the Continent, it was time for Almina to return to the London scene. Her pedigree was revisited by a number of newspapers and journals:

> Lady Carnarvon was a Miss Wombwell, and is good-looking in rather a French style, and generally wears Parisian clothes. She has very beautiful jewels, and has done some gorgeous entertaining at Highclere, where on one occasion the Prince of Wales was one of the guests and Parisian artistes were brought over to England in his honour.[207]

Almina's public appearances included Lady Lansdowne's reception at Lansdowne House in late May. She was also one of twenty-seven stallholders at the Royal Albert Hall in early June that year eager to raise money for the Charing Cross Hospital. [208]

Almina was also amongst the peerage at the June Court of 1899 in front of the Princess of Wales. Her dress of all white orchids was admired enough to be reported on in the press.

A summer tea party with royalty was an ideal additional opportunity to hobnob with the gentry. She appeared at a garden party at Kensington Palace held by Princess Louise. Always the fashion trend setter, Almina's dress was again reported on, along with those of other leading women of the day. But there was increasingly tough competition; she was now a mother and already yesterday's news:

> The young Duchess of Marlborough looked very slim and girlish in her soft white muslin frock with shady black hat; Georgiana, Lady Dudley looked quite beautiful in mauve; Lady Carnarvon was very smart in white muslin with incrustations of fine lace; and no one looked lovelier than Lady Helen Vincent in picturesque attire.[209]

A musical party given by Lord and Lady Rothschild brought a more praiseworthy review of Almina's choice of dress: "Lady Carnarvon was gorgeous in terra-cotta satin with a pearl and diamond necklace, with big pendant pearls."[210] This was also a night for mingling with some of the period's established and rising stars, with Lord Kitchener and Winston Churchill amongst the guests.

Meanwhile Lord Carnarvon was enjoying hearing about and occasionally seeing his horses run at various race meetings across England. In the world of horseracing the Earl first registered his colours in 1896 and became a Member of the Jockey Club in 1919. He was also a founder member of the Thoroughbred Breeders' Association. The best horses to run for him included Robert le Diable (which won the Doncaster Cup) and Mauvezin (winner of the Stewards' Cup).

Ascot in June was ablaze with fashion, albeit the weather was cold and wintry. Almina appeared "in a bright cherry-coloured cloth".[211] But the reports included a briefing about Carnarvon that once again alluded to illness: "Lord Carnarvon has now quite recovered from his severe illness, and every one was glad to see him at Ascot."[212] A further shadow over the year came with the loss of the Countess of Effingham, Marie Wombwell's sister and Almina's aunt, who died suddenly at Boulogne in France whilst on holiday, which brought with it much sadness. Of the three Boyer sisters, Almina's mother was now the lone survivor.

By August it was time to instigate a curious Highclere custom in honour of the infant Porchester: the brewing and casking of 500 gallons of beer, to remain unopened until the heir came of age. A Newbury cooper was commissioned to make the cask from oak grown at Highclere, hooped with brass and bearing a coronet with an inscription plate. The inspiration said: "May Highclere Flourish: This cask of ale, containing 500 gallons, was brewed in commemoration of the birth of Lord Porchester born November 7 1898. Albert Strefield Butler, Highclere Castle 1899."[213]

These were prosperous times for the Carnarvons. The Earl's finances were better than they had been for years. He indulged his passion for speed by ordering the construction of a new motorcar "to cost considerably more than 1,000 pounds",[214] and he was even able to decline offers of upwards of 8,000 pounds to rent the shooting over the Highclere estate. But while the coffers were healthy, George was anything but. And so on 17 July 1899, under advisement, Lord Carnarvon left London for Germany to stay at Bad Homberg – once a favourite gambling den for Carnarvon and Victor in their wasteful youth – under the supervision of a specialist. Almina stayed behind to attend at Mrs D'Arcy's concert in which Nellie Melba, Alfred de Rothschild's great friend, was expected to perform (in the end Melba was replaced with songsters Plaucon, Saleza, Mademoiselle de Lussau, Ysaye and Madame Rejane), and then travelled to Bad Homberg to join Carnarvon. Almina knew the German town and had taken the waters of its renowned spa.

The couple returned to Highclere on 11 September 1899. Victor Duleep Singh was on hand with his wife to speed the invalid's recovery with good cheer, freeing Almina to fill up her social calendar. On Wednesday 4 October she attended a Rothschild wedding with Alfred, where at the reception at 19 Grosvenor Square she was described as "looking very smart and pretty".[215] Then, in the middle of October, it was announced that Almina was going to stay at her flat in Paris, and that Lord Carnarvon's health was much improved. Victor persuaded Carnarvon to continue his recuperation at his home at Hockwold Hall, Norfolk. By the end of the year George was fit enough to organise a shooting party at Bingham, whilst Almina returned alone to Highclere from Paris.

1900

Almina began the following year stepping out in the style to which she had become accustomed. On Thursday 22 February 1900 she sat with Alfred de Rothschild in his box at the Royal Opera House in Covent Garden, enjoying the flowers and vast box of bonbons proffered by her benefactor and watching artistes such as Madam Adelina Patti perform. It was a glittering concert organised by Lady Lansdowne and her committee in aid of charitable funds for the Officers' Wives and Families Fund, raising over 11,000 pounds for victims of the war in South Africa. After the concert, supper was served in the Crush Room. Almina headed one of the supper tables, and Rothschild and the Prince and Princess of Wales were at adjoining tables. Alfred and Bertie were mutually appreciative that Lady Lansdowne had secured "the services of a dozen extremely pretty young ladies, who were smartly dressed as vivandieres".[216]

But Almina's planned social networking in the 1900 season was frustrated as Carnarvon's ill health returned again. In March it was announced that the couple would "not be settled in town until early in May, as Lord Carnarvon has just left for Egypt for his health".[217] Carnarvon had been suffering breathing problems and the damp English climate made matters worse, so his doctor Marcus Johnston advised a stay in Egypt, whose acrid climate from the months of November through to April would offer some relief.

By May Almina had extricated herself from her matrimonial duties and was at their home at Berkeley Square. On Friday 11 May 1900 she was able to attend Court for the first of the Queen's Drawing Rooms, which drew large crowds in the neighbourhood of Buckingham Palace, Marlborough House and St James Palace. She also fitted in a trip to the north of England, visiting Penrith to see Elsie, the Dowager Countess, and supervised a sweet meat shop at the National Bazaar held at the Royal Palace Hotel, London, in the aid of sufferers from the Boer War. Alfred de Rothschild topped up Almina's stall with his contribution; he was inclined to do this for several other stallholders' year on year for good causes.

When Carnarvon finally landed at Marseilles after a voyage from Port Said Almina joined him at the port, and a return to normal duties ensued. The Carnarvons took a short let of The Mount, the residence of the Dowager Marchioness of Conyngham, for the race week at Ascot. Then, at the invitation of Alfred de Rothschild, they joined a gathering at Hertford House to view the Wallace Collection. Alfred was one of the patrons of this establishment, as well as a trustee of the National Gallery.

The following weeks saw Carnarvon in a good mood (his horse Baldur had come home third in the Chester Cup), and the couple maintained a cheery air at a state concert, with the Dowager Countess, at the Queen's Garden Party at Buckingham Palace. At the end of July they threw a Saturday till Monday party at Highclere. There was just enough time to see Lord Porchester before his dutiful nanny took him in mid-July to spend a few weeks at Westgate-on-Sea.

In August Carnarvon was on the Continent, at Trouville. His unremarkable role in local military operations (with the Boer War in progress) was to present a new rifle range at Beacon Hill for use of the N Company of the Hampshire Rifle Volunteers. There was time enough left in the month for the couple to take a yachting cruise[218], before returning to Highclere in September to host a shooting party. This was followed by a visit to Mr and Mrs John Menzies at Escrick

House near York as part of a larger party gathering for the Doncaster races, where a number of Carnarvon's horses were in the field, including Inchmurran (ridden by J.H. Martin), and the two-year-old Kunstler and Voie Laetee and three-year-old Killarue (all ridden by Carnarvon's regular jockey, G. Chaloner).

Carnarvon joined Victor at Hockwold Hall for shooting in mid September, and then left for the Continent. Returning from Paris, Victor called on the Carnarvons in London. By early December 1900, Almina was pregnant again. By this juncture the Earl had despite a myriad of health conditions, miraculously consummated his marriage, precluding (it would seem) any challenge that another party had obliged. The baby expected was George and Almina's: their offspring, Lady Evelyn Herbert.[219]

1901

Death overshadowed the beginning of 1901: Queen Victoria died at Osborne, Isle of Wight on 22 January. The new monarch was King Edward VII, and as High Steward of Newbury, Carnarvon presented a silver loving cup to the borough as a token of his good will to the town to commemorate the accession of the new King.

As the excitement of the changes in the monarchy died down, Almina was entering her third month of pregnancy and declared that she needed rest and warmth. So the Carnarvons left England to spend two weeks together visiting Constantinople. They returned via Paris (where they stayed at The Ritz hotel[220]) and attended the horse racing at Longchamps.

As Almina struggled with the burden of pregnancy, her husband turned to the turf for escape, with Victor. The two old friends were still betting heavily together. They were at the first day of the Newmarket Spring Meeting on 30 April 1901, which included the " 2000 Guineas". Carnarvon's three-year-old horse Yellow Bird ran at Kempton in a selling race, which Carnarvon witnessed, again with Prince Victor. The Earl's horse Dark David came second at Newmarket on 14 May, with the American jockey Danny Maher riding one of his mounts for Carnarvon. Then Yellow Bird came in third at York in a field of ten runners on 22 May.

That summer it was Almina's mother Marie who was Alfred's companion at events such as a private recital by Nellie Melba at Baron and Baroness de Meyer's home at Cadogan Gardens and a soirée at Seamore Place where she mingled with musical celebrities such as Nellie Melba, Madame Rejano and Monsieur Coquelin. But Almina did manage an evening out on Saturday 15 June 1901 with Victor and Alfred de Rothschild to watch a performance of *Othello* at Covent Garden, and on 18 June she and her husband stepped out at Ascot: the only public sighting of Lord and Lady Carnarvon together for the duration of Almina's pregnancy. It was a less than brilliant meeting, overshadowed by an extended period of Court mourning and the fallout from the Boer War.

Almina joined her husband for the Ascot meeting. On 19 June Lord Carnarvon's Irish-bred three-year horse The Solicitor ran unplaced in the Royal Hunt Cup. His lordship purchased a brown filly by Loved One – Flora McIvor – for 170 guineas in a sale of the Benham Stud yearlings. Carnarvon's horses also ran at Epsom, Newmarket and Doncaster and other courses throughout the year, with at least one horse, Mauvezin, being well fancied. His horses did better later in the season at Longcamps, in September, when Londres won the Prix Glatigny. Victor joined the Earl at Kempton Park in October.

But it is hoped that the whirlwind of socialising and horse racing paled into comparison against the pleasure afforded by the birth of Lord Carnarvon's legitimate daughter on 15 August 1901. They named the baby Evelyn Leonora Almina Herbert.

1902

In early February 1902 the Carnarvons left London for Egypt, by train via Paris. Once back in England, they returned to the turf, their shared passion, making an appearance together at Newmarket for the spring meeting with their attention on the 2000 Guineas. The King was present, as was Prince Victor Duleep Sigh and his wife.

Carnarvon was set to continue running more horses in the 1902 season, and this year marked the commencement of the Highclere stud. The stars of the stable were The Solicitor and Mauvezin, the latter having won the Steward's Cup at Goodwood. The tally for the year was 11 winners amounting to a return of 5,300 pounds.

The Carnarvons attended the May Court before the new King and Queen at Buckingham Palace on Friday 16 May, as did the Duleep Singhs.[221] Then Carnarvon travelled to Paris for the French Derby at Chantilly on 1 June, while Almina attended a dinner hosted by her brother- and sister-in-law, Lord and Lady Burghclere, at their home in Charles Street for the Crown Prince of Sweden.

In July 1902 Lord Carnarvon's illnesses took a turn for the worst and he had to undergo an operation. He spent time recuperating in London at 13 Berkeley Square, his recovery no doubt was assisted by the happy news that Mauvezin had won at the first day of Goodwood on 29 July 1902. Almina's spirits were also lifted by a description of her in *The London Reader.* [222]

In August the Earl and Countess celebrated, along with the rest of the nation, the belated coronation of King Edward VII (it had been delayed by illness, requiring an emergency appendectomy). There followed more shooting at Highclere, attendance by both Carnarvon and Almina at the Doncaster races and some recuperation for Carnarvon at Bretby Park.

Keeping up with the trends, in November Almina joined the women wearing sables for the Derby races in her husband's pavilion. The Bretby party comprised Lady Grey Egerton, Lady Leucha Warner, Lord Effingham (Almina's cousin – his mother was Marie Wombwell's sister Victoria), Mrs Arthur Paget and Lord and Lady Marcus Beresford. The same month Almina was a talking point amongst her friends and family when little over a year after her delivery of Lady Evelyn she appeared on the front cover of the magazine *Country Life*[223] with her petite figure fully restored.

The Great Jewel Robbery

In December of 1902 the Carnarvons fell victim to a crime on their return journey to London following a stay in Paris. The incident received huge publicity in Britain, Europe and America, dubbed by the press "The Great Jewel Robbery".

On Sunday 21 December the Carnarvons left their hotel (The Ritz) in Paris bound for the Gare du Nord. Their luggage contained jewellery worth 5,000 pounds, set in a small green tray packed in a dress basket, which was locked. At the station the luggage was duly registered and handed over to the railway authorities, and the

Carnarvons travelled by train to Calais before transferring to a ship to cross the Channel to Dover. They arrived at Victoria railway station at seven o' clock in the evening, and then drove to their townhouse at Berkeley Square. It was then the theft was discovered.

Some jewels, packed at the bottom of the basket, remained, but plenty of Almina's jewellery, to which she had sentimental attachment, was gone. The haul including twelve rings, eight gold bangles, ten brooches, two ladies' watches and several charms and other trinkets, all set with diamonds and other precious stones. One of the most notable articles was a cross-over ring set with a single pearl weighing 30 grains and a diamond of over three carats. The ring alone was valued at 800 pounds.

Almina was understandably upset. Sympathetic editors referred to her having "very pretty hands" and said:

> She always wears a quantity of the most beautiful rings, and amongst those she has lost are a very beautiful pearl ring which was her engagement ring and a magnificent diamond one, which was given to her by Lord Carnarvon on their wedding day.[224]

One editor took the opportunity to pass comment on the Carnarvon's relationship, declaring that these items fell into the category of "tokens of friendship".[225]

There had been other jewel robberies in the period including offences against the Marquis of Anglesey and the Duchess of Sutherland. A gang was thought to be behind them. The wealthy were constantly travelling between London and the Continent of Europe, and several and conmen (and women) preyed on them. The favoured routes to plunder were Calais to Paris, Paris to Marseilles and along the Riviera coast between Marseilles and Monte Carlo. All these were Carnarvon haunts.

Detective Inspector Drew of Scotland Yard was appointed to the case, and Lord Carnarvon offered a reward for recovery of the jewels. The London police were not confident of getting any of the jewels back as there was, according to commentators, "reason to believe that the jewels were stolen between Paris and Calais"[226]. Another report mentioned that the police believed a trio of foreign thieves had been aboard the train.[227] The story disappeared from the news headlines after the first few days of reporting, but was released worldwide. A full description of each missing item was published and circulated. Despite all these efforts, the pieces were never seen again (they were probably broken up and disposed of on the Continent). [228]

Christmas at Highclere

On Christmas Eve Almina travelled from London to Highclere, where Carnarvon was expected to join her and the family for the festive holidays. As 1903 approached the Carnarvons could reflect that they had been married more than five years, and produced two Herbert children. Almina had put her own mark on her title of Countess of Carnarvon, and Carnarvon had began to be known in the racing world, securing several wins and increasing his winnings almost sevenfold in two years from 819 pounds in 1901 to 5,370 pounds in 1902.

Carnarvon looked forward to the New Year with good cheer, for in January the family would begin a lengthy stay in the United States of America; a holiday that would no doubt be good for his health and full of the usual pleasures. But it was to be a trip that altered the course of Carnarvon history for ever, for a chance encounter would draw the Earl into a world of Egyptian heritage, and ultimately his own demise.

Chapter 4
1903–1914
Years of Uselessness

The Carnarvons visit the USA

In January 1903 the Carnarvons travelled to North America. The Earl had visited the country twice before; in his playboy days, as Lord Porchester, he had gained praise there for his ability as a yachtsman. This latest trip was intended to improve his failing health and provide rest, though it seemed to consist more of amusement, with planned activities including a motoring tour, fishing expeditions to mountain lakes, horse racing and observing buffalo hunting in the Rockies. It was Almina's first time in America, as it was for Marcus Johnson[229] (Dr Johnnie), the Earl's tireless physician. Only George Fernside, Carnarvon's faithful 37-year-old valet, had accompanied his master on a surfeit of similar sojourning around the world, including the past trips to 'Yankeedom'.

The visit to America almost never happened. The party was forced to forfeit the ship's passage booked on the *Celtic* out of Liverpool on 14 January 1903 when four-year-old Henry, Lord Porchester, the Carnarvon heir apparent, was struck down by a high fever. As soon as the boy rallied, they left him to Nanny Moss's care and made the connecting train from Euston railway station, boarding the *Oceanic* on 28 January. The *Oceanic* – the second ship so-named by the famed White Star Line – was a modern vessel complete with the comfort of electric lighting and refrigeration, and she was built for speed. Embarrassingly for White Star Line, though, she arrived a day later than scheduled when she was slowed by head winds and heavy seas. The *New York Times* cheekily reported that the real reason for the delay was "a heavy cargo of titled foreigners".

On board, travelling in the saloon, the Carnarvons were reacquainted with their Wiltshire neighbours Jacob and Julian Pleydell-Bouverie, the 6th Earl and Countess of Radnor. [230] Carnarvon greatly admired the 5th Earl Radnor's horse stud, which had been dispersed on his death in 1900. Julian, Countess of Radnor, the daughter of a clergyman, had founded the Wiltshire Nursing Association and was a stalwart figure in the Women's Institute, organisations that would later attract Almina.

Arriving in New York on 5 February, Almina's first impressions of the US were less than favourable. First she was made to endure a cross-examination by a custom official before disembarking, and then she had to witness the vulgar scene of Rosalind, Lady Chetwynd, being photographed and declared in her home city of New York "the most beautiful woman in the ship" [231]. But she was somewhat appeased when a newspaper announced the arrival of "more bearers of English titles including the Countess of Carnarvon, a very pretty young woman, small and piquante" [232].

Almina disliked America on sight; she felt she had entered hell. Particularly irksome were America's womenfolk, with whom she found no affinity. She was irritated that Society women in England felt it essential to spend winters in New York and thought the opposite was true: it was American maids and matrons who craved drawing room acquaintance with desirable persons such as herself from the smart worlds of Paris and London.

The fashionable folk of Gotham, Newport and Washington Society included her in several social gatherings, but as they clamoured over Almina she thought herself more like a zoo exhibit than an honoured guest. These meetings were mostly luncheon parties where only females were present, and this was not Almina's idea of enjoyment. She was also less than charmed by a ridiculous ball given by one East Coast hostess, Mamie Stuyversant Fish [233], and her accomplice, a jester named Harry Lehr[234] , well known for his practical jokes. Mrs Fish's was in social competition with the notable American Madames Astor and Vanderbilt, and owned a grand white residence named Crossways, in the style of "a large framed Colonial Revival" [235] . More folly followed. During a dance night at 78th Street and Madison Avenue, the ladies were expected to "lead guinea-pigs on their arms whilst dancing with their male escorts" [236]. Almina recalled this as being "hilarious and disastrous; the small creatures screeched with fear and then began to soil the dance floor" [237].

The Carnarvons stayed briefly at the Waldorf Astoria, New York, and dined with Countess Cassini[238] , niece of the Russian ambassador. Almina was unimpressed when the Countess bragged of her friendship with the Roosevelts and of having set the Puritans of Washington alight by organising her Sunday frivolities. Almina was pleased to point out that London were well ahead on that score. Lord Carnarvon's Pembroke cousin, Sir Michael Herbert[239] , sent them a warm greeting; he was the newly appointed Ambassador to the

British Embassy in Washington. (His tenure was brief. In common with Lord Carnarvon, Herbert suffered from perpetual medical problems; he died a few months later, the cruel consequence of consumption.)

Eventually the East Coast lost its appeal, and the party moved westward by railroad from Chicago to California, where his Lordship favoured the milder climate. They arrived in Los Angeles on the *Golden State Limited* on 26 February 1903, barely a year after this great train's first inauguration, glimpsing en route Kansas City, El Paso and southern Arizona. In San Francisco, Alfred de Rothschild had arranged for them to meet a banker friend and former mayor of the city, William Alvord[240], whom they both found charming. Almina and Carnarvon each wrote to Alvord afterwards with their grateful thanks. They were shocked by his death only a few months later.

Back home the Earl was increasing his racing stable at Highclere Stud, so he was on the lookout for New World bloodstock. He had his first taste of Californian racing at the famous Oakland track, where he was the guest of Richard McCreary, a local socialite, of Burlingame. Later, the Earl and his wife were invited to a dinner with McCreary hosted by maverick Irish-American Jeremiah 'Jere' Lynch [241] at his Bohemian Club in San Francisco. Almina enjoyed the evening's extravaganza in the quaintly named Owl Room of the Bohemian Club. Normally an all-male bastion, the confirmed bachelor Lynch assembled 15 friends, including several ladies, from the "crème de la crème among the Oakland sect" [242]. The Bohemian's decorations were wonderfully lavish:

> Apple and orange blossoms were arranged in a large bowl in the centre of the table. Candelabra with yellow silk shades added a soft glow to the scene. Clusters of foliage also decorated the walls and were hung over pictures making it a most charming effect. [243]

Lynch enjoyed a busy life as a former senator and gold prospector in the rush to the Klondike of 1898. He also travelled in Egypt and had written a book, *Egyptian Sketches*[244], all about these experiences. He even owned a female mummy, a figure wrapped in a shroud that stood at the foot of the Club's inner staircase.

Carnarvon already had an interest in Egyptology. After all, his father, the 4th Earl, had been attracted to the ancient sites on the

Nile more than 20 years before, and he had been one of the founder members of a society to conduct excavations in the Delta as a contribution to archaeology. So Jeremiah Lynch, the long-standing lover of Egypt and its tombs, intrigued Carnarvon with tantalising tales of Egyptian tombs and mummies in the rocks at Deir-el-Bahari. How puzzling, expounded Lynch, that so comparatively few notable Egyptian mummies of the wealthier kind had ever been recovered.

Lynch undoubtedly stirred Lord Carnarvon's interest towards seeing Egypt as a haven for antiquities, a passion that would be his undoing one day. He went on to remove additional mummies from Egypt following the loss of his mummy in a fire [245], probably enlisting Caranaron's help in getting permission to do so from Lord Kitchener[246], always a close friend of Almina and Lord Carnarvon. Lynch died in 1917, and he has since remained forgotten in the King Tut tale.

After his fateful evening with Lynch, Carnarvon continued to please himself – meeting friends and Herbert family acquaintances and exploring the city sights of San Francisco by day and night, George Fernside on hand, his camera documenting the actresses of a touring opera company and the down-town ghettos of the Latin and Chinese quarters[247]. Left to her own devices, lonely Almina turned to the ever-dependable Dr Johnnie, the "dear little man" [248]who would remain a confidante throughout her difficult marriage to Lord Carnarvon. They risked a public scandal of being intimately matched, but this was not London, so Almina requested that Johnnie take hold of her arm at all times in public. He did just that, and they promenaded together around the hotel and gardens. They caused heads to turn on the restaurant veranda by ordering drinks of "scotch whisky and soda" [249], setting the trend for other guests who would insist they sample the same cocktail as the Countess. And as ever, Almina's fashion sense attracted a flutter of attention. She must have been delighted that newspapers praised her choice of eveningwear made from black lace, with syndicated pieces describing her pretty gowns and individual style and commenting on her "piquant French type of beauty" [250].

But though she may have appreciated their admiration, Almina was far from fond of the people of the New World. She considered their language, their manners and their attitudes to be sloppy, rude and rough. Where else on earth would a liftboy at a hotel spit out his chewing gum at her feet ?[251] The original plan had been to stay in

America for six months. The speedier return – after only three months – suggests that Almina called time. To her towering relief, the Carnarvons left New York on 8 April, once again on the *Oceanic*, and arrived back in Liverpool on 15 April. [252] Almina never set foot in America again.

The Countess was no doubt delighted to be on home soil, but back at their town house at 13 Berkeley Square, London, where they would spend a few days before returning to Highclere to see the children, the Carnarvons were met with sad news. Whilst they had been away one of the Earl's favourite horses, the four-year-old Etrusean, had won at Hurst Park and then dropped dead at the finishing post. Even more shocking was the fatal accident of a footman named Charles McKinley employed by the family at Berkeley Square. An inquest into the matter heard that he had "met his death by falling through a sky light". [253]

Carnarvon flaunts the law

Carnarvon was a famed motorcar pioneer from his early days. One history says he was with Mr C. S. Rolls, one of the first converts to automobilism. He enjoyed speed and owned a range of cars of between 24 and 70-horse power. He also prided himself on fashion extras of motor scarves and scarf pins, items that long survived in Almina's possession and, as her godson Tony Leadbetter recalls, that she gave away as gifts in later years [254]. Clad in his long white coat, Carnarvon frequently dashed along through Hyde Park looking like Herne the Hunter.

It's no surprise then that the Earl was among the 10,000 people who gathered for the first meeting of the Brooklands Automobile Racing Club on Saturday 6 July 1907; indeed, his Lordship and his wife had pride of place in the new club. But the Earl's love of speed would soon land him in trouble.

On 25 July 1903 Carnarvon was fined £10 for speeding when motoring to the historic Bibury racecourse for a race, and he earned a further £5 fine on 11 August, cited as amongst a dozen law-breakers that year who were motoring too fast[255] The Earl was a frequent offender on the roads en route to Bibury, and he had a whale of a time evading fines. [256]Once Carnarvon turned up a side road and drove the car through a farmyard and a river to escape a police officer who was trying to pull him over, but unfortunately for the Lord, his distinctive goggles and mask made him easily recognisable.

During the hearing of a later charge heard by West London Police Court, after Carnarvon was caught speeding at Gunnersbury in 1903, the explanation from his Lordship was that he thought he was "going slowly because he was overtaken by an electric car, and so he put on speed a little, but unfortunately changed at that moment to enter the sacred strip of road marked out by the police and so fell a victim to the inspector" [257]. His solicitor, Mr Pierron, admitted the offence and asked the magistrates to be lenient in view of the Motor Car Bill relating to the speed of motor cars that was before Parliament, going as far to say that the police should have turned a blind eye. The magistrates thought it a "most unconstitutional"[258] suggestion that the police should suspend the execution of the law because of a measure that had not yet become law, and thus another fine of £5 was imposed. Carnarvon was delighted when later that year the Motor Car Act raised the speed limit to 20 miles per hour.

Consoling and caring

As was their custom, Almina and Carnarvon's enjoyed an active social life for the rest of 1903. The couple held a house party at Highclere, and stayed at Bretby Park for the Derby races. The London scene was awash with celebrations and luncheon parties at restaurants, marking the beginning and end of the racing seasons. At one of these Almina dressed in dark blue, with a short pleated skirt to lunch at the Carlton Hotel.

But aside from the frivolities, Almina made time to care for others. Her mother, Marie Wombwell, was mourning the passing of her brother, Jules Boyer, who died in his native Paris. [259]Worried about the strain on her mother, Almina travelled to Cromer where Marie had joined her two-year-old granddaughter, Lady Evelyn Herbert, and Nanny Moss on holiday. Cheered by her daughter's support – the two women were always close – Marie then felt able to travel to Paris where she stayed at The Ritz, dining with English gentry and local dignitaries.

Meanwhile, there was high drama at Highclere. Victor's brother, the unmarried Prince Frederick Duleep Singh[260], had been staying there when he suddenly fell ill. Almina insisted on nursing him personally throughout his indisposition: an early excursion into nursing that perhaps influenced her later path in life. Frederick remained at Highclere until the Christmas season.

1904

Having wintered in Egypt, and enquiries made about digging rights, in early 1904 Carnarvon and Prince Victor Duleep Singh were busy planning a big game hunting trip to India, Ceylon and the Far East. As well as being a jolly jaunt for the Earl, the idea was no doubt to bolster the spirits of Victor, who had fallen on hard times. Years of gambling, stock market speculations and carefree spending had plunged Victor into bankruptcy (though the Prince also blamed an inadequate allowance from the India Office). Yet despite Victor's misfortune, he remained Carnarvon's "great friend".

However, this pleasure trip was postponed. Carnarvon's health was erratic, and he was advised by Dr Johnnie to set aside all travel and social plans in favour of a complete rest.

Almina, meanwhile, attended the funeral of Mabel Baring, Lady Ashburton, wife of one of Carnarvon's regular shooting coterie, the 5th Baron Ashburton. After ailing for months, Mabel left a young family when she died aged 37. Her admirer, King Edward VII, gave his permission for a memorial service at the Chapel Royal, St James's Palace. Carnarvon was absent as he was ill again, this time with flu. Lord Ashburton later remarried to some controversy, and the envy of his shooting coterie, his second wife was a chorus girl from New York City.[261]

The subject of politics reared its head about this time; not an area that usually much concerned Almina or her husband. She coaxed Carnarvon into accepting an invitation to dine at Wimborne House, Arlington Street, at a reception given in the presence of some of the era's political names: the Devonshires, Lord Rosebery, the Harcourts and Henry Campbell Bannerman, a Liberal who was later British Prime Minister from 1905–1908. Those attending were advocates of free trade.

Furthering their public profile, a profile of Highclere Castle and the Carnarvons featured in the Society journal *The Sketch*. Under the article's title of 'Beautiful Homes and their Owners'[262], the Earl and Countess were featured with photographs. The resulting exposure was met with raised eyebrows among their peers who wondered whether letting riff-raff journalists into one's stately home was in good taste. But the Carnarvons had no qualms about their actions, they were keen to use the media to their advantage to gain attention, whether it was Almina displaying the latest Parisian fashion craze or the Earl promoting himself as a successful race horse owner of the English turf. In the 20 years that followed, photographs of the Earl and Countess of Carnarvon often appeared in the pictorial newspapers, capturing their highs, lows, fads and fancies, yet they were rarely photographed together.[263]

Almina became unwell during the summer, and she was confined to Highclere, but by mid-August was improving. She took a motor car tour for the benefit of her health and later spent time with Carnarvon in Dublin for their usual attendance at the horse racing and sales. In September she was cheered that they were to spend time in her beloved city of Paris.

On Saturday 10 September 1904, Elsie, the Dowager Countess, hosted the wedding of her step-daughter, Carnarvon's sister, Lady Margaret Herbert, to George Duckworth (1868–1934) at Dulverton, Somerset. George Duckworth – private secretary to Austen Chamberlain, Chancellor of the Exchequer – was a wretch. Half-brother of the writer Virginia Woolf (1882–1941), after Woolf's mother died when she was 13, George, 14 years her senior, had molested her and their sister, Vanessa. [264] This sexual abuse continued until Virginia reached her early 20s and "only stopped when she had a nervous breakdown after her father died and the household was broken up" [265]. Duckworth's female conquests extended to older women too. He was on intimate terms with his new wife's stepmother: he was regularly seen with Elsie, the Dowager Countess, at the Opera, and Virginia once heard them embracing behind a pillar. [266]

Almina remained in Paris, but Carnarvon travelled from Constantinople, where he was recuperating and exploring, to give Lady Margaret away at the wedding, and he made Highclere and Bretby available to the couple for their honeymoon. Five-year-old Porchey acted as trainbearer and page, dressed in a court suit of blue velvet and white satin. Austen Chamberlain was the best man and the wedding gifts included a diamond brooch from Alfred de Rothschild.

When Almina returned from Paris she went on retreat to Scotland. Then, as Christmas 1904 loomed, she left for the Continent again, before returning to spend the festive period at Highclere to ensure that the Earl's gaggle of house guests were entertained and that her mother would be welcomed to spend time with the children.

1905

The Carnarvons were in Egypt for early winter 1905. The *Egyptian Gazette* reported that they were staying at Shepherd's Hotel, Cairo, and a popular rendezvous for the English abroad in the season.

It was during this trip that Carnarvon first met Howard Carter[267] through Sir Gaston Maspero, Director of Antiquities at the Cairo Museum. Carter had been an inspector of antiquities at Luxor for several years and had worked in the Valley of the Kings for Theodore M. Davis, an American excavator who owned the concession for the Valley until June 1914. However, in 1905 Carter was reduced to selling watercolours to visitors at the Winter Palace Hotel. By this point, one chronology describes that all Carnarvon had found in tomb digging was a large mummified cat[268], and he could well use the services of an experienced Egyptologist such as Carter.

Back from Egypt in mid April, Almina and her mother attended Nellie Melba's birthday concert. The event was full of Society folk, and Almina sat with her mother's friend Nellie Needham, 3rd Countess of Kilmorey, for a midnight supper. Marie Wombwell was ranked by the *Daily Mail* amongst the "more important personages" present. Soon after, Marie joined the Carnarvons in Alfred's box at Covent Garden, in the presence of the King and Queen, for a concert (including Melba and Caruso) in honour of a state visit by King Alfonso of Spain. It was a grand occasion, with beefeaters lining the walls of the theatre staircases.

While his wife was toeing the line in polite society, Lord Carnarvon was doing anything but. Often vociferous (as Almina could attest), he led a protest campaign through the governing body of racing, the Jockey Club, against the extortionate charges imposed by railway companies for conveying racehorses to and from race meetings. Although Carnarvon was not a member of the Jockey Club, he hoped the protest would endear him to his fellow horse owners and improve his chances of membership of this much-coveted clique.

Then, on Wednesday 28 June 1905, it was three-year-old Lady Evelyn Herbert's turn to make an impact at her social debut under the guardianship of her six-year-old brother. The occasion was a children's party given at Charles Street by their aunt Winifred Burghclere for three of her own daughters. Grown-ups present included Lady Dorothy Nevill, Lady Jersey and Lady Victoria Manners. This was followed by another children's party organised by Almina at her mother's house.

As the tenth anniversary of her marriage fell at the same time, Almina arranged to keep up appearances with an evening dinner at 13 Berkeley Square and a second dinner party and supper served at round tables charmingly decorated with flowers. Guests included Marie Wombwell, The Burghcleres, the Kilmoreys, Lord Ashburton, Sir John French, Arthur Portman and many others. [269]

Away from their London rituals and travel, horse racing dominated. On Saturday 14 October 1905 the Carnarvons were at Kempton Park races. Almina was among the newcomers in the stewards stand. The Earl strolled about with old chums Lord Westbury [270] and Lord Charles Montagu[271]. Then, as November drew close, they stayed at Bretby from where Lord Carnarvon led a cheery party to the Derby races, though he was experiencing a spell of bad luck on the turf.

1906

As the New Year dawned, the postponed trip of 1904 to India, Ceylon and the Far East was back on the agenda. On 8 January 1906 the Carnarvons left Highclere Castle for Berkeley Square and on 11 January they set out for Marseilles. From there they connected to the P&O mail steamer making for the Straits Settlement, arriving in Colombo in early February, along with Prince Victor Duleep Singh and his wife, Carnarvon's valet Fernside and, of course, Dr Johnnie. They next travelled to the Federated Malay Straits and Malacca and then on to Singapore. On 15 February Almina paid a visit by motor car (with another traveller, the Countess of Lanesborough[272]) to a mine at Tambun, with its amazing hot springs, whilst Lord Carnarvon and Victor went big game hunting. Then on 26 February the party arrived at Singapore, where they stayed at Raffles' Hotel.[273] There they attended a reception in honour of Prince Arthur of Connaught (1883–1938) given by the governor, Sir John Anderson. [274] In early March Sir John joined the Carnarvons and the Duleep

Singhs on board the *SS City of Delhi* as they journeyed back to England [275], arriving home in early April to see the children, whom Marie Wombwell, in their absence, had been entertaining as a dedicated grandmother. For Victor, April 1906 also saw the end reached (unsuccessfully) to a long running appeal by his trustee in bankruptcy against the Secretary of State for India for compensation. [276]

As the racing season commenced, Carnarvon was much more interested in climbing the social ladder in the horse-racing arena. He relished his position as President of the Racehorse Owners' Association and hoped it would bring membership of the coveted Jockey Club, and he was delighted when the King took a keen interest in his stable. At the Newmarket races it was announced that "the King will visit Newbury Races to-day, and afterwards, His Majesty will go on to Highclere Castle for the week-end, as the guest of Lord Carnarvon", and a photograph in the *Daily Mirror* showed the monarch and the Earl together with Lord Westbury at Doncaster. Carnarvon's horse stud had a fairly successful year, winning 12 races, but it fell short of his achievements in 1904, when he had secured 20 wins, earning prize money of £12,143. [277]

The July edition of *The Bystander* magazine captures a rare picture of The Earl, Countess, Marie Wombwell, Victor Duleep Singh and other Highclere regulars together during a weekend of shooting and entertainment. [278]

Another family death lowered the mood in early October. After a shooting party at Highclere with Victor and Lord Ashburton, Carnarvon was saddened by the death of his aunt, Lady Eveline Alicia Juliana Herbert, the Dowager Countess of Portsmouth. She had been one of Carnarvon's minders after his mother's death in 1875.

1907

Almina and her husband are cited as being in Egypt in March of 1907. [279] Carnarvon had started the year ill again, this time from influenza, but on return to England he had recovered for a highly successful race meeting at Brighton. He appeared in the *Daily Mirror* of 27 May 1907 leaving the enclosure leading in his horse, Malvina, which won the Laughton Plates with a prize of 200 sovereigns. A house party at Highclere for the Newbury races was followed by Goodwood, which marked the end of the London season. Carnarvon also fitted in a reunion with Victor at the opera, who was spending more time abroad (according to a later report, Victor and Anne were usually now residing in Paris).

Meanwhile, Almina was alarmed when her mother fell seriously ill, but she recovered to travel to Folkstone to recuperate, leaving Almina free to work on her public image. She appeared on the front cover of *The Bystander* of 9 October 1907 in a full-length white dress, with train, tiara and rows of pearls; reviews described her as "beautiful".

The Christmas of 1907 was spent Bretby Park, and once more the guest of honour was Marie Wombwell. No doubt the children – Henry and Evelyn – were thankful for their doting grandmother's presence. Alfred and Elsie were never as affectionate, and the 6th Earl remarks in his memoirs that during his childhood he spent more time with nannies and Marie than he ever did with his parents.

1908

In early 1908 Carnarvon reverted to his voyeuristic nature by escaping with his racing friend Lord Westbury to the Palace Theatre for a special afternoon performance by the daring Canadian actress Maud Allan, whose performances of Salome in 1918 would cause furore and a libel case in which the Earl and Aubrey Herbert were cited. [280]

In April the Carnarvons returned from Egypt. The Earl had secured new rights for Howard Carter, the Egyptian antiquities expert he'd met in Cairo in 1905, to excavate at Thebes. Thus their friendship was cemented. Several people warned Carnarvon that Carter was a fanatic with a quick, uncompromising temperament. Ironically such traits as these were reflected in the opinion that each man ultimately had of the other in their relationship of the next decade and more. Carter stood up to his patron and could be condescending [281]; but Carnarvon, as pay master, had the last word. In the following years the pair would shift between mutual admiration and disagreement. They were not equals, socially or intellectually, but they were similar in that both were highly strung emotionally and had very few friends of either sex. Almina never knew whether she liked Carter, and in her customary aloofness of " never lowering herself to anyone:

treated him as a mere employee" [282]; but it was her daughter who would seemingly develop a greater affection for the man[283].

As a host, Alfred de Rothschild invited into his homes many notable and powerful men from the era's national and international scene. Almina was frequently invited to attend dinner parties at Seamore Place, with and without her husband, to meet Alfred's coterie of friends and associates from Royal and diplomatic circles and the financial world. She was favourite dinner companion, it seems, of the American banker, John Pierpont Morgan, a regular guest of Alfred and who was another insatiable collector of art. [284]

The final day of the Ascot meeting on 19 June, with the King and Prince of Wales in attendance, brought praise for both the Earl and Countess. Carnarvon saw his horse Bembo win the Hardwicke Stakes, to great surprise, whilst Almina was described as being " as usual exquisitely dressed." [285]

Almina continued to foster her reputation as a delicate beauty and a loving mother. She appeared in a full length photograph on the cover of *The Bystander* of 1 July 1908 in her latest Parisian finery and "dainty figure and face", and she took her daughter to a children's party at Buckingham Palace on Monday 6 July, where she was delighted that Queen Alexandra talked and played with the little guests. Then, in early December, the Carnarvons were in London on their way from Bretby Park to Highclere for the festive period, and one report recorded that "Lady Carnarvon... entertains children delightfully". Behind closed doors, though, Almina was far from a virtue of patience. In his memoirs Porchey recalls being "kicked" and subjected to "bread and milk" for two days following an incident at Court when Almina judged the boy had disgraced her in front of royalty [286].

Christmas was held at Highclere, and included a hunt that brought down a fox. The fox's mazard was presented to Lord Porchester and the brush to Lady Evelyn.

1909

The summer of 1909 brought with it another wedding: this time the marriage, on 6 July, of Almina's brother Captain Wombwell to Mary (May) Harrison Smith, eldest daughter of Alfred Harrison Smith

(1845–1925) and Fanny Wardle (b. 1846) of Carlton Hall, near Worksop, Nottinghamshire. Harrison Smith was the owner of the Don Brewery of Sheffield, which was later absorbed by Tennents. Marie was delighted that her son was finally settling down, after all her efforts to get him seen in the right circles and noticed by the right women. The reception was held at Carlton Hall and the newly-weds went to London and the Continent for the honeymoon, before returning to live in Doncaster.

Not long afterwards disaster struck the Carnarvons when, in August 1909, the Earl was involved in a serious motor car accident, an event that is as often recorded in texts as the infamous mosquito bite of 1923. Writers usually place this accident (and its influence) several years *before* it actually happened, incorrectly citing it as the reason why Carnarvon first turned his attention to study Egypt's antiquities when in fact at the time of this accident, in 1909, Lord Carnarvon had long been fostering his interests. [287]

The most authoritative version of the accident, which occurred when the Earl was *en route* to meet Almina in Germany, is Winifred Burghclere's posthumous tribute to her brother:

> It was on a journey through Germany that disaster overtook Carnarvon. He and his devoted chauffeur Edward Trotman, who accompanied him on all his expeditions for eight and twenty years, had been flying for many miles along an empty road, ruled with Roman precision through an interminable Teutonic forest, towards Schalbach, where Lady Carnarvon was awaiting their arrival. Before them, as behind, the highway still stretched out, when, suddenly as they crested a rise, they were confronted by an unexpected dip in the ground, so steep as to be invisible up to within 20 yards, and at the bottom, right across the road, were drawn up two bullock carts. Carnarvon did the only thing possible. Trusting to win past, he put the car at the grass margin, but a heap of stones caught the wheel, two tyres burst, the car turned a complete somersault and fell on the driver, while Trotman was flung clear some feet away.

Carnarvon suffered concussion of the brain. Victor left London on Saturday 28 August to rush to his best friend's bed, and to give support to Almina. At the end of August the telegrams from Germany reported that the Earl was progressing satisfactorily and that doctors were quite satisfied with his condition. A further bulletin on 1 September stated that he was continuing to make progress.

When he was able to return, Carnarvon went to Highclere. In the middle of September a report said he was "still slightly indisposed from the effects of his recent motor accident"[288] and "had postponed his departure from town"[289] . The remainder of 1909 was blighted by the Earl's recovery from the accident, which required much rest. But ill health or not, Almina gave a grand party at Highclere as a warm up for the Newbury Races. [290] As the year ended Carnarvon was determined to resume his arrangements with Carter in Egypt.

1910

The Carnarvons left London on 21 January 1910 aboard the Orient liner *Otranto* that was making its return trip via Gibraltar, Marseilles and Port Said. The Earl was very unwell and easily fatigued, but hoped the warmth of Egypt would help, which it did.

Back in England, the country mourned the passing of King Edward VII. The Carnarvons paid their respects at the funeral at Westminster Abbey on 20 May 1910. A happier occasion followed with the wedding of Carnarvon's half-brother Aubrey to Mary Vesey at St James's, Piccadilly in October. Mary was the daughter of Evelyn, Viscountess de Vesci, and a granddaughter of the Earl of Wemyss, who gave her away. Nine-year-old Lady Evelyn Herbert was a bridesmaid along with Winifred Burghclere's daughter, Alethea Gardner. Aubrey's half-brother Mervyn was best man. Carnarvon placed Highclere at the disposal of the couple for the honeymoon. Notable among the wedding gifts was an Irish jaunting car and a harness given by the people of Abbeyleix, the de Vesci estate in Queen's County.

Both Lord and Lady Carnarvon were keen to support the development of flying, and the year 1910 is also notable in Almina's history as the year she established a branch of the Women's Aerial League at Newbury. Gertrude Bacon (1874–1949) was the Honourable Secretary; she was a writer and balloonist who, on 29 August 1909, had been the first British woman to fly in an aeroplane.

1911

In July 1911 *The Scotsman* reported that Bretby Hall, the family seat in Derbyshire, was up for sale, but the offer was withdrawn. Both the Carnarvons were by now accustomed to spending freely, but this was the first indication of money problems. Alfred, ever a soft touch in meeting both Lord and Lady Carnarvon's debts and demands, consented to increase his support.

By November Almina's stirring political interest was piqued when her brother-in-law, Aubrey Herbert (1880–1923), tried his luck for a third time in contesting South Somerset for a seat in Parliament. He was considered a strong candidate not only because of the local influence of the Herbert and Wallop families but because he was a man of ability. Almina was roused to give support as Lord Carnarvon was poorly and laid up in bed; the Countess didn't mind a jot for she simply adored (and secretly loved) Aubrey. [291]

To the Carnarvons' delight, Aubrey won. He entered Parliament as "the very independent" conservative Member for the Southern division of Somerset (later Yeovil), having polled 148 votes more than his Liberal opponent, Henry Vivian. It was a historic victory for the Conservatives, who had held the seat since it was created in 1885 [292].

This was at the high water point of David Lloyd George's reforms as Chancellor of the Exchequer. The threat from "the common herd" (Almina's description of the masses[293]) hit hard at the gentry. Asquith's government's controversial People's Budget imposed taxes on the wealthy: a super tax for those on the highest incomes; an increase in death duties on the estates of the rich; and heavy taxes on profits gained from the ownership and sale of property.

On 4 May 1911 Lloyd George had introduced the National Insurance Bill, which included both health and unemployment insurance, and it received the Royal Assent in December. Almina found this the act of a scoundrel, and she organised protest meetings. One of these was at the Corn Exchange, Newbury on 8 December 1911. There, before 2,000 people and supported by Aubrey and his fellow MPs, she made a speech, a part of which survives:

> Seldom has the country been so stirred, and small wonder, for the Insurance Bill, while imposing a tremendous burden upon the national finances, leaves out in the cold those who most need a helping hand from the State – the ill paid and those whose livelihood is precarious. Insult had been added to injury, for Parliament had been throttled and all discussion had been smothered by gagging the representatives of the people. The result of this and of the many amendments was the imperfect ill-considered jumble of discordant clauses and amendments. The country was bewildered, and the feeling against the Bill was spreading every hour. If they valued their freedom their duty was clear and imperative. They must protest, sign petitions, and urge their friends to do likewise. Let them spread the truth about the Bill, and thus save national insurance from the evil result of haste. The course followed by the Government was

not legislation, but despotic government on the lines of the most bureaucratic tyranny[294].

It is clear that Almina could have been a strong politician. She was certainly a reluctant admirer of Nancy Astor (1879–1964), the first woman to be elected as an MP in Britain. The Earl, on the contrary, was never a political man. He claimed he was "too honest [295] " for politics, and he left Aubrey to follow in their father's footsteps in a political career, which he did as an MP until his death in 1923.

At the end of December thoughts turned to the Egyptian season of 1912, and the Carnarvons entertained Dr Budge[296], the Keeper of Egyptian Antiquities in the British Museum, at Highclere. Then they travelled to Monte Carlo for the Christmas and New Year holidays, before heading to Cairo.

1912

As the Cairo season got underway false rumours of cholera and plague reduced visitors. Royal visitors, including Louise, the Princess Royal, and her husband, the Duke of Fife, had braved the risk of sickness. The tales did not frighten away the Carnarvons either, and although Almina did fall ill, it wasn't with a serious illness.

The news in Cairo wasn't overly encouraging, though. Carter, unfortunately, had not been very successful. The excavations undertaken from 1907–1908 onwards had produced only items of minor significance, with nothing of any great importance. Undeterred, Carnarvon and Carter planned to publish an illustrated volume of the previous five years of excavations at Thebes.

Worse news followed: Almina's brother, Captain Frederick Adolphus Wombwell, had died on Saturday 17 February at the age of 42. He was survived by one son, Frederick Philip Alfred William Wombwell (1910–1977), who later inherited the family baronetcy. Frederick was buried at Carlton Cemetery, Worksop, and his sister missed the funeral. [297](His widow, Gertrude Mary (May) Harrison Smith, later remarried, becoming Mrs Stamford Booth.)

In March it was announced that: "Lord and Lady Carnarvon will return from Cairo soon after Easter. Lady Carnarvon has been very unwell, and had to undergo a slight operation [298]. " It's unclear exactly what was wrong with Almina, but the couple were indeed back at Berkeley Square in April. Before heading to Highclere, Almina saw her grieving, ailing mother and tried to distract her from her mourning by persuading her to help in the matter of her eight-year-old granddaughter, Lady Evelyn, being a bridesmaid at the wedding of Lady Eileen Butler. This was one of the season's grand weddings: Eileen, daughter of the Earl and Countess of Lanesborough, married the Marquis of Stafford, the elder son of the Duke of Sutherland. With these tasks fulfilled, and Marie's morale and health restored, Almina retreated to Highclere.

The 6th Earl portrays his grandmother Marie as a lonely figure in her last years. Porchester was only 13 when she died, the same age as Almina upon Fred Wombwell's death in 1889. The 6th Earl could not know the depth of tragedy Marie suffered in losing her only son Frederick, having lost her brother (Jules) and two sisters Victoria (Lady Effingham) and Eleanor (Mrs Lethbridge) also in the few years before. However, Marie was still travelling, dining out and attending the theatre whenever she could. In May 1912 she was with Almina and Lady Nellie Kilmorey at the International Flower Show at Chelsea Hospital.

Carnarvon had returned to the turf, but he was with Almina at Buckingham Palace for the State Ball on Friday 19 June 1912, where their friends Victor and Anne Duleep Singh were also present. Almina attended the Duchess of Devonshire's Ball, which was graced with the presence of Queen Mary, and the August wedding of the Marquess of Anglesley to Lady Marjorie Manners. Interestingly, she is also cited with other titled Ladies as a member of the Committee of the Queen Alexandra and Jubilee Nurses, which met at Marlborough House and raised funds for the Jubilee Institute – an early example of Almina's support for nursing causes.

1913

On Saturday 4 January the annual children's tea party was held at Highclere for Lord Porchester and Lady Evelyn. The houseguests who were in residence over the holidays included Lady Burghclere, her daughters, Prince Frederick Duleep Singh, Arthur Portman, Mr Serocold and Marie Wombwell[299] , all joined in the fun and festivities. Sadly, this was to be Marie's last Christmas and New Year. The entertainment included "coon songs and a cinematograph show... the guests numbered 500 and included junior members of the leading families of the district." [300]

The Carnarvons then spent a long period of the winter in Egypt, languishing by the Nile at the Palace Hotel. The news was that "the excavations near Luxor had been more than ordinarily successful [301] ". Almina endured the social side of a particularly brilliant Cairo season, attending several balls and dinners. The Egyptologist Arthur Weigall (1880–1934)[302] recorded her flirtatious nature that season: "Lady Carnarvon gave me her photo and kissed her hand to me when I left – so startling, as she and I have always been rather stiff and formal with one another."[303]

In March the writer, hostess and Highclere regular Lady Dorothy Nevill died just a few days short of her 87th year. Lady Nevill had attended the Prince of Wales's visit at Highclere in 1895 and Victor's wedding in 1898, and had hovered at many of Almina's social events in her two decades as the Countess of Carnarvon. Yet while the Burghcleres and the Duleep Singhs sent funeral wreaths, those from the Carnarvons and Alfred de Rothschild were conspicuously absent. Dorothy had once had a fling with Disraeli – Alfred's great friend – which may have lost her their respect.

Meanwhile, Marie Wombwell's health was failing. She had left Paris, where she had held her last dinner party at The Ritz hotel, and spent some time at Highclere during April and May of 1913 being cared for by Dr Johnnie. She then returned to her own home at 20 Bruton Street to prepare for a further trip to Paris, but she relapsed and was forced to remain in England.

In mid June 1913 the Carnarvons held a large party at Highclere before Newbury Races.[304] There were celebrations when Carnarvon's horse Rivoli came second in the Newbury Summer Cup. Then Ascot, also in June, saw the Carnarvons in the royal enclosure with Victor Duleep Singh in white ducks and attended to by a bearer of a parasol. Rivoli won the coveted Ascot Stakes. The Earl spent the night with Victor rejoicing at Datchet whilst Almina returned home to Highclere Castle.

July saw the local annual show at Highclere Park, in its 23rd year, bringing together the parishes of Highclere, Burghclere, Newtown, Crux-Easton and Woodcott for exhibitions and competitions of their " home and garden industry".[305] Almina's contribution was a " very fine sample of sweet peas of the waved spencer type." [306]

Memorial Window For Almina's Brother

Also during July 1913 Almina dedicated a memorial stain glass window at St Michael and All Angels Church, Highclere " in loving memory of Frederick A Wombwell, Captain 16th Lancers" [307] as a gift of " his sister, Almina Carnarvon." [308]

The end of an era

Marie Wombwell's health was fading. At the end of the London season she had gone to Vernet-les-Baines, a spa town in the Pyrenees, but whilst there she became very unwell. Her yearning to return to Paris was never fulfilled. The London *Daily Mail* of 1 October 1913 announced the death[309] of Almina's mother at the age of 66:

> Mrs F C Wombwell, the mother of Lady Carnarvon has died. The latter has been with her mother since she was taken ill in France six weeks ago. Mrs Wombwell entertained a good deal at Bruton Street up to the time of her illness. She will be interred in the family vault in Paris.

Almina was with her mother when she passed away. A memorial service was held for Marie at the Catholic church of Notre Dame de France in Leicester Place, London. [310]

Further sadness followed for Almina when her uncle, Sir George Wombwell, died a few days later in his 82nd year. 'Sir Jarge', the old squire, Newburgh Priory's incumbent for 60 years, had been well known on the London scene in his clubs and a model landlord with loyal tenants. Almina's uncle Harry (Fred Wombwell's best man in 1868) became the new Baronet.

In November the extraordinary contents of Marie Wombwell's last will and testament, made on her deathbed on 24 September 1913, were revealed[311]. The will named Alfred de Rothschild, Lord Carnarvon and Marie's nephew (her late sister's son) Walter Lethbridge as executors. It detailed a number of possessions Marie had bequeathed, including *objets d'art* for Alfred de Rothschild and his brother Leopold, whilst some personal items went to her grandchildren. Marie's estate was valued at gross £86,326, net £72,252. After payment of a number of modest legacies (including annuities to her nephew, Walter Lethbridge, and her maid, Sylvia

Purchase), Almina was left only £1,000, with the will instructing that the balance of the estate, which was to be invested, be left to Almina "in trust" . Almina was entitled to receive the interest on the investment, which after her death was to revert to her children, Marie's grandchildren, Porchey and Lady Evelyn.

Part of the residuary estate comprised the freehold of 20 Bruton Street, which was sold on 1 January 1914 for £4,000. When the proceeds were realised, Alfred was "informed and advised that it should be invested and the income only [the interest] paid[312] " to Almina for life. However, Almina was not impressed by her mother's apparent lack of faith in her prudence in financial matters, and she insisted that the capital should be paid to her. Alfred unilaterally agreed this course. Later, he was concerned enough at Almina's prima facie defalcation to issue an indemnity to his co-trustees. A document in the Rothschild Archives records:

> In consideration of your concurring with me in allowing the purchase money Four thousand pounds of No 20, Bruton Street to be paid to the Countess of Carnarvon instead of being retained as part of the Trust Fund, I hereby agree to indemnify you against any claim that may be made by Lord and Lady Carnarvon's children or either of them in respect of such payment and generally to hold you harmless in connection with the above mentioned transaction [313] .

Marie's death marked the end of an era for Almina: the termination of what she described as her "years of uselessness [314] ". The Countess craved a more exacting role beyond that of being a show wife at race meetings, of attending balls and functions run with military precision and of sitting like the Sphinx on the baking desert floor in Egypt. A turning point was near: in 1914 Almina would launch herself as one of the Society ladies who rose to their country's call when World War was declared.

Chapter 5
1914–1918
The Years of Usefulness

Enjoying a brief respite in England

In 1914 Almina was aged 38. She had long tired of the year-on-year winters in Egypt. She cringed at the wretched balls of the Cairo residency and the enforced greetings to the less-than-weighty Society figures of the world who drifted through its portals, all seeking their own glimpse of the arid country's ancient monuments. Besides this, there was little of interest in Lord Carnarvon's desert campaign with Howard Carter apart from sitting under inadequate parasols in the aching sun and rubble. Almina was therefore happy to return from Egypt in April 1914; and when the season ended she was consoled that Carter and Carnarvon's archeological work would be halted if war broke out.[315]

Back in England, the start of the horse racing season provided an opportunity for the Earl to spend some time with his son. Carnarvon and his son Henry (Porchey) were never close. The 6th Earl's memoirs echo with resentful memories of being harshly beaten for laziness and otherwise ignored by the man he called his father. Yet the two men shared a passion for horse racing, and in early 1914, with Porchey approaching his 16th birthday, Lord Carnarvon gave him his first real taste of the turf. The Alexandra Park meeting saw several of the Highclere horses run. However, even the legendry jockey Steve Donoghue riding Maggie could only achieve third place and Namur, with E. Huxley, a mere second.

Sadly, this proved too short a spring for the Earl and his heir: the quickening pace of events in Europe put an end to their bonding. By the time the Great War was over, Porchey would be his own man – an experienced cavalry officer – and the Earl would have disappeared to Egypt to spend his last years shadowed by his daughter, Lady Evelyn.

War preparations

The assassination of Archduke Franz Ferdinand, heir-apparent to the thrones of Austria and Hungary, on June 28 1914 plunged Europe into a diplomatic crisis that would quickly evolve into the

Great War. The gloomy black cloud of Britain's impending entry into the war permeated into the highest levels of society.

In mid July the Carnarvons hosted a high level gathering at Highclere[316]. Ostensibly, this was a country house weekend party, following the racing at Newmarket and Sandown Park and the annual horse sales in Ireland. But there was more to the event than frivolity and socialising: those at Hichclere were assembled to make their individual and collective preparations to weather the storm of the encroaching war.

The guests were luminaries drawn from the civil and military elite, including army men Lieutenant General Sir John Maxwell (1859–1929) and Major General Sir John Cowans (1862–1921), "the greatest quarter-master since Moses" [317] ; from the legal profession, the advocate Sir Edward Marshall Hall KC (1858–1927), the country's leading defence barrister; from Egypt, Carnarvon's right-hand man Howard Carter (1874–1939); and from the court circle, Viscount Lascelles (1882–1947) (who later married King George and Queen Mary's daughter, Princess Mary). The 5th Earl's half-brother, Aubrey Herbert, was also there, and among the female guests were influential and wealthy wives, countesses and baronesses. Almina invited her cousin, the American Blanche Lethbridge, and Dr Marcus Johnston was also present. (Ten years later several of these figures, notably Cowans and Marshall Hall, would be caught up in a cause célèbre with Almina that would have devastating consequences.)

The only key figure missing was Horatio Herbert Kitchener (1850–1916), a close friend of the Carnarvons and the most talked about figure of the day, having conquered and excelled during his past exploits in the Sudan, India and Egypt. Following the Archduke's assassination, Kitchener had risen up the ranks: he was made an Earl and Prime Minister Herbert Asquith "requested that he stay in England, pending the outcome of the July 'crisis' in Europe [318]" (after the declaration of war, he would become Secretary of State for War). Although he was unable to attend the Highclere gathering, Kitchener met with the Carnarvons at the State Ball at Buckingham Palace that month, and he briefed them on the prospect of war.

Two weeks later, at the closing night of the season at Covent Garden on 1 August, Queen Alexandra, the Queen Mother, sat in the royal box, dressed sombrely and appropriately in black and wearing simple jewels of single stones set in a diamond chain. Her daughter, Louise, the Princess Royal, and grandchildren Princess Maud and Prince Arthur of Connaught were, like her, distracted by the events unfolding in Europe. Royalty throughout Europe was praying that there would be a last minute back down by their German relatives.

Alfred de Rothschild was entertaining the Carnarvons at the same event. Seated in his usual box, next to the stage and close to the royals, Alfred's mind was preoccupied too. He had taken a desperate step earlier that day to attempt to stop the war: he had sent the Kaiser, an old friend from his days as the Austro-Hungarian Consul General in London, a telegram[319] appealing for peace. The Kaiser received the telegram but did not respond, and the telegraph lines to and from Europe were suddenly severed.

Whilst others in political and diplomatic circles were also urgently trying for peace, it was all to no avail. On 4 August 1914 Britain declared war on Germany, and the country entered into the greatest and bloodiest war in history.

Setting up a hospital at Highclere

After almost 20 years in an artificial marriage, Almina was tired of being merely a show wife and of spending her life hosting needless shooting parties, lavishly entertaining at country house weekends, attending dull receptions and balls and enduring endless, exhausting trips abroad. The Countess wanted to do something of worth; something that would make a difference. She found the serious role she was seeking in nursing.

Almina had supported nursing causes, but she had no direct experience of nursing except for the rare occasions when she had attended the children or wiped the brow of guests taken ill whilst staying with the Carnarvons. Nursing Lord Carnarvon had never featured in her marital duties; that task was left to others. But Almina was determined to do her bit for the war effort, and she was stirred by Kitchener to put proposals to the War Office for a hospital within the Carnarvon seat at Highclere.

The Earl thought the idea "quite mad[320]". He declared facetiously to Kitchener, "In future, my dear K, our telegraphic address will have to be AMPUTATE, HIGHCLERE. [321]" But the Earl was appeased when Alfred de Rothschild agreed to give the cause financial support, and agreed to Almina's plans. Alfred's experience and wealth made him an ideal backer: he was Treasurer of Queen Charlotte's Hospital, he knew all the right people and his family was already involved in providing medical aid for the conflict, his brother, Lord Rothschild, was President of the Red Cross.

The War Office approved Almina's proposals, and Highclere Military Hospital opened its doors almost as soon as the first major British casualties were sustained.

Almina was just one of scores of aristocratic women across Britain who opened up their stately homes to treat the wounded. An American newspaper carrying a photograph of Almina reading to a wounded soldier remarked: "England's titled women are busy with the wounded, the most famous society leaders having forsaken drawing rooms for the hospital tents. ... Lady Carnarvon is one of the leaders of the titled nurses. [322] "

Millicent, Countess of Sutherland, and her sister, Lady Angela Forbes, reached out to all ranks in the grim battlefield hospitals in Northern France, at Etaples, where 'tents' were the norm. Elsie, the Dowager Countess of Carnarvon, made her contribution to the war in Egypt, at Alexandra, by organising nursing for victims of the fighting in Turkey and Greece. [323] Carnarvon's spinster sister Victoria (Vera) Herbert (1874–1957) helped old soldiers, especially during the winter, with their rents, medical treatment, fuel, warm clothing, blankets and a Christmas dinner. [324] Carnarvon's elder sister Winifred was involved in providing aid for British prisoners; in her case, those held in Turkey, and "many a miserable man had reason to bless her for the fund which bore her name [325]".

But as well as doing their patriotic duty, such work had a secondary benefit for British society. In post-Edwardian Britain socialism already rife and the gentry were being pushed into a corner by politicians like Lloyd George taxing them to the hilt, in life and death. The efforts of wealthy women during the war successfully turned around simmering discontent against the House of Lords and aristocracy.

Administering the Highclere hospital

Almina's hospital at Highclere could take upwards of 18 men at any one time.[326] Only the best would do when it came to equipment, and Almina appointed Marcus Johnson (Dr Johnnie), the family's physician and close confidante, to the post of Medical Director. The Countess generously carved out space in her home for the patients: the wards were initially allocated on the second floor, a bedroom was designated as the operating theatre, the library was turned into a dayroom and an adjoining room was given over to a dining area. The wooded grounds of the Highclere Estate provided an ideal space for recreation and recuperation.

Almina brought her own style to the task of running a hospital. She had no medical qualifications of course, but she took it upon herself to act as the hospital's commander-in-chief-cum-matron. Her team of nurses were issued with a uniform of woven cotton dyed a fuchsia colour, which was specially ordered.[327] She allowed the nurses to apply a little makeup, which made all the difference to wounded men recovering their faculties. [328]

Almina tends the wounded

The wounded were driven to Highclere in vehicles from Southampton, where they arrived off hospital ships. The military authorities in field hospitals and at the embarkation ports in France, including Almina's life-long friend Major General P.H. Henderson, RAMC [329] often tagged the cases meriting referral directly into her care.

One survivor of Gallipoli, Lieutenant (later Captain) David Campbell, MC of the 6th Royal Irish Rifles, was referred to Highclere. Campbell's diary[330] indicates that Almina welcomed him on arrival there.

> The Countess of Carnarvon met us at the front door of her beautiful castle and greeted us with the kindest and most welcoming words. By the time we had reached our respective rooms we felt that, in truth, we had come to a haven of rest, to a veritable paradise.

Campbell vividly describes Almina's hands-on approach:

> Later on came Lady Carnarvon and the doctor to inspect my injuries. She did the undressing and later the dressing of my wounds. She told me she

was going to nurse me herself, personally. Then I learned that she had decided to take on as her own patient the first Irishman that arrived and I was the lucky man. She, apparently, had a penchant for the Irish and all the nurses and doctors were of that nationality.

Another patient was a familiar face. Aubrey Herbert, Carnarvon's half-brother, was in the Special Reserve Corps as an interpreter, but when war came he volunteered for the Irish Guards, despite being semi-blind. He was suffered near fatal injuries in the battle for Mons, and once back in England, in order to take in the country air, he went to Highclere to convalesce. [331]

Aubrey was allocated a bed in a ward on the second floor where young and attractive nurses cared for him and his injured comrades. Sometimes that 'care' went beyond the call of duty. Indeed, in the bed next to Aubrey was an officer from the Scots Guards[332] who had the good fortune to receive the attentions of "a delicious young, auburn-haired nurse" [333]. One evening when Almina was doing her rounds she caught the couple in bed, and was forced to reprimand her nurse because "that sort of thing must have put a great strain on the patient's heart and he might well have died as a result[334].

Aubrey must have thoroughly enjoyed his convalescence, and Almina his company, for he was a colourful character. (Indeed, Aubrey's later exploits with Colonel T.E. Lawrence inspired fiction writer John Buchan's heroic character Sandy Arbuthnot in the book *Greenmantle.* [335])

Almina raises morale

In April 1915, a long report of a speech by Almina to the Newbury Congregational Church (where she was distributing prizes) provides a glorious tribute to her powers as an orator and for raising local morale in time of war.

The short extract below (reported in the Newbury Weekly News[336]) also draws on Almina's fall back upon her Christian faith and her belief in good overcoming evil.

Almina had also been involved in heralding Kitchener's call for volunteers:

It was not so many months ago that she (the Countess) was present at a meeting in Newbury, the principal object of which was to encourage the young men to go forth and join the ranks of those that had gone forth and set a great example in which they were all anxious to participate.

They might ask how weak women could take any part in this great and awful struggle. It was her object to point out how, individually and collectively, each one had been given a great task, a duty that they could only perform by asking the help of Almighty God. Many of them had dear or near ones fighting for their country for the freedom of the people, for the protection of their homes, fighting for the freedom of great Britain. They had gone forth prepared to lay down their lives leaving all that were near and dear, and for their sakes they must not be regretful, but be cheered by that wonderful inspiration, that wonderful courage, that wonderful faith and, especially in the time of tribulation by offering their prayers to God, beseeching Him to send that peace, that comfort, that strength and that courage that He alone could give.

Her Ladyship said that reference was made to her hospital at Highclere and she proceeded to give some interesting details of the work, with which she and her husband had been associated. She paid a tribute to the resident medical officer, the nurses and her own household staff, all of whom had taken a keen interest in the needs of the wounded officers. For herself, she could not describe the joy and pride, which she felt at being able to take part in this war. She was only one of hundreds who had done exactly the same thing by placing their homes at the disposal of the brave men who had been disabled. So they all individually and collectively, could do something for their country, bear the cross nobly and bravely, because they placed their reliance on the one and only source of strength. To Him they would pray for that comfort and help which they knew He would give.

The hospital relocates

However, the 5th Earl's lukewarm attitude to his life being disturbed[337] by a hospital was quickly replaced by mounting irritation. Carnarvon was already struggling – he missed the relief the Egyptian climate gave his failing lungs, and his passion, horse racing, was hard hit by the war. But Almina's hospital was pushing his patience too far. The hospital "turned sumptuous salons and an art gallery into a casualty ward [338]", and Almina was running up high costs, not least for the travel expenses of the visitors and the consultants summoned from London for serious cases. And as the number of beds increased, food shortages became a factor:

> As another floor at Highclere was converted to take more of the wounded, Almina and her nurses were kept very busy. Even with many Estate workers serving away in the war, food supplies and provisioning was acute, a fear of food shortage became a vital part of the future planning [339].

Carnarvon wanted his castle back, and to appease her husband Almina was persuaded to relocate to larger premises in the capital. At least there the wounded would have better access to specialist and pioneering medical experts. [340]

At the end of 1915 Almina happily abandoned her husband in favour of the wounded, and began relocating her centre of nursing activity to rented premises in London, leased to Almina by her friends Lord and Lady Lovat[341] . Her new hospital at 48 Bryanston Square opened its doors with a reception on Tuesday 4 January 1916 under the watchful, if not admiring, gaze of military VIPs, notably Lord Kitchener, Sir John French (1852–1925) and Sir Ian Hamilton (1853–1947). Accommodation for 24 officers was provided and patients were admitted immediately. [342]

Setting high standards

Almina endeavoured to provide the best possible care by purchasing the latest medical equipment and bringing in highly esteemed medical staff. She charmed and befriended a number of eminent medical men who offered their services to her hospital.

Her anaesthetist at Bryanston Square (and at Highclere) was 'Cocky' Boyle, Henry Edmund Gaskin Boyle (1875–1941), an eminent and indefatigable pioneer of new procedures who excelled in tackling the heavy workloads brought on by the casualty crisis in the war hospital circuit. Boyle's career in the operating theatre had begun when chloroform was being replaced by ether; he left his own legacy behind in Boyle's nitrous oxide-oxygen-ether apparatus. He became an institution at St Bartholomew's Hospital, London, where to this day a department is named after him.

Word of Almina's superior hospital facilities spread and she soon secured the patronage and services of the consulting surgeon to the British Expeditionary Force, Sir Berkeley Moynihan (1865–1936), later Lord Moynihan. One of England's leading medical experts, the proud Yorkshire man was Professor of Surgery at Leeds University and based at its Royal Infirmary. He occasionally travelled by train to London if Almina expressed concerns over a particular case. (Years later, long after the war had ended, Almina would call upon his services again, this time in opening Alfred House, her nursing home at Portland Place.)

The collaboration between Almina and Moynihan saved lives, not least her husband's when in early 1918[343] he developed a perforated appendix at Highclere. Almina, accompanied by doctors and nurses, rushed down and carried Carnarvon off to her hospital in London where Moynihan promptly operated. Lady Burghclere later recalled that it was a close call.[344] Moynihan reported that he "had only given him [Carnarvon] another three-quarters of an hour to live"[345]. The Earl ascribed his resulting recovery to "his wife's resource and exertions and to the skill and devotion with which she surrounded him"[346] A short time after this near-death experience, Lord Carnarvon drew up a last will and testament, still considerably shaken, but feeling grateful to be alive, rewarding Almina (whom he describes in the document as "my dear wife") with the majority of his wealth.[347]

Berkeley Moynihan spent many hours in conversation with the Countess. He taught Almina much about medicine and surgery, and relied on her advice based on her growing medical experience. The pair developed a close relationship, one of several Almina would have with brilliant, exceptional and charismatic men (which Carnarvon was not), and it did not stop short of spilling over into marital infidelity.[348]

In time Almina's hospital began to handle victims of terrible burns (from crashed aircraft; British pilots were not issued with parachutes), which brought Almina into contact with the pioneers of plastic surgery, including Harold Gillies, a mentor of the legendry Archibald McIndoe of the later Guinea Pig Club of the Second World War. Gillies (later Sir Harold) was a New Zealander by birth who had trained at St Bartholomew's. As well as being an ambitious surgeon, he was an accomplished golfer in his university days at Cambridge.

As the war raged and the numbers of serious casualties climbed ever-upwards Almina found herself involved in raising funds directly from the public. During 1915 her name headed a campaign, on behalf of the Royal Free Hospital in London, called 'Comforts for the Wounded Soldier'[349]. Gifts and cheques were requested for clothes, wheelchairs, wicker chairs, cushions, Bovril, cocoa, tobacco, jam, soap and scarlet blankets. The link with the Royal Free Hospital brought Almina into contact with Cecil Augustus Joll MS, MD, FRCS (c. 1886–1945), a senior surgeon there who was full of new ideas about procedures and patient care.

Her years as the perfect hostess and Society lady stood her in good stead when it came to networking. And her hard work would pay off in the long term as well, for the doctors whom Almina charmed during the war would later work with her in the nursing homes she set up.

Praise for Almina's work

Mary Francis Billington (1862–1925), a pioneering journalist with the *Daily Graphic*, compiled a roll-call of serving women who established private hospitals. Billington emphasised that:

> The duties of maintaining such hospitals are not evaded by those who have assumed them. They have been undertaken with the fixed purpose of giving the best skill and care to the men who have obeyed so willingly and cheerfully their country's call [350].

Almina certainly took to her heart the cause of delivering the best skill and care. The luxury afforded the wounded at Bryanston Square was in complete contrast to the bleak wards of the military hospitals, and at times it seemed to those convalescing that they were being treated more like a guest in a top hotel than a patient in a nursing home.

An early arrival at Almina's hospital in London was a man from one of the Empire's outposts, Major F.W.W. Fane of Vegreville, near Lethbridge, Canada. [351] A former Canadian Mounted Policeman, Fane commanded the 3rd Mounted Rifles [352] and was badly wounded on December 1915. He arrived at Lady Carnarvon's hospital as it opened its doors at Bryanston Square with a fractured left leg, right foot and collar bone, and a splintered hip. Settled in the comfort of Almina's hospital, Fane was jovial, saying: "I've really no right to be alive at all. They hardly thought I was worth picking up at first, but I am feeling fine now with the exception of these few trifles.[353]"

Similarly, the grandson of Lord Tennyson, Lionel Tennyson (1889–1951), who was twice admitted to Bryanston Square, had nothing but praise for the hospital, recording in his autobiography *From Verse to Worse* :

On my way back [from the Western Front] I was wounded for the third time, and was immediately evacuated to England, where I was sent to Lady Carnarvon's hospital in Bryanston Square. ... I was lucky to be able to recover under such care and supervision. No attention was too much trouble, the nursing was wonderful, and the food given us exquisitely cooked and served. [354]

Another patient, Sydney Roberts – commissioned into the Suffolk Regiment, wounded at Ypres in 1917 and later Master of Pembroke College, recalls in his memoirs *Adventures with Authors* :

After about a week, I received the welcome news that I was on one of the convoys for home. Again my luck held. I was one of the few stretcher cases and the M. O. at Calais affixed a label to me and said 'I'm marking you for Lady Carnarvon's Hospital. They like good surgical cases there.' So, about 1am., I was carried up the stairs of a house in Bryanston Square. I woke to find a dignified butler bearing my breakfast tray. 'Good morning', I said. 'Good morning to you sir.' Behind him was a footman, who asked not whether I would like a paper, but which morning paper I would like, It was the beginning of a delectable month. Lady Carnarvon was active and friendly and her staff was entirely civilian – and Irish; so there were few dull moments. The surgeon in charge, for instance, when he took you downstairs for an X-Ray examination would turn a number of switches on and off with an experimental air and then turn round and say: 'The whole place will probably blow up. You don't mind, do you? [355]

As word of Almina's successful hospital with its medical specialities and special pampering spread, gaining entry required a certain amount of string-pulling. [356] Major Vivian Nickalls, one of England's greatest pre-war oarsmen who in 1915 had given up a position as a rowing coach at the University of Pennsylvania to join his country's call, served as a battery commander in France, where he was wounded. He recalls in his memoirs, *Oars, Wars and Horses*[357] :

After about a fortnight I was lucky enough owing to the good offices of a great friend of mine, Captain Ernest Courage, to be sent to Lady Carnarvon's Hospital until I was discharged as convalescent at the end of November. Lady Carnarvon was a most charming commandant and ran, I suppose, the most efficient and pleasant hospital in London...

48 Bryanston Square, Mayfair also gained a prized reputation for dealing with orthopaedic cases, in particular following arm or leg amputation. [358]

Another of Almina's notable charges was Captain David Fallon, a 30-year-old Officer in the Oxfordshire and Buckinghamshire Light

Infantry who was seriously wounded in France. He was one of several Oxfordshire and Buckinghamshire soldiers who found their way into Almina's care thanks to the Rothschild family's links with the regiments. Fallon describes his time at the hospital in his book *The Big Fight* :

> Arrangements for our reception at Southampton were as smoothly efficient and kindly as had been our transportation and treatment in France. Individually, good fortune was attending every little distance in my journey. Taken to London I found myself billeted in the home of Lady Carnarvon in Bryanston Square. She had turned her beautiful residence into a hospital and there I was quartered in a spacious apartment with Lieutenant McDonald of a Lancashire Regiment who had a smashed leg and Captain Fred Monk MC, who had also a smashed leg and lost an arm.
>
> But he (Monk) was very cheerful regarding the situation and so was McDonald. On the train for the wounded and also abroad the Caledonia you hardly heard any talk of war. Everybody was sick of it. They wanted to talk about anything but war. But here at Lady Carnarvon's in the days that followed, naturally our memories came crowding back. And we went over our hardships, the thrills we had experienced and then inevitably the panorama would sweep our vision of the sections of No Man's Land we had seen with its piled and distorted dead and one of us without feeling the necessity of telling the others of what he was thinking would as inevitably say "Well, we are very lucky beggars after all."
>
> These would usually be the thoughts in the twilight hour and then in would walk our smiling rosy-cheeked Irish tease of a nurse Miss Anne O'Laughlin – all the nurses at Lady Carnarvon's were Irish and therefore for me the more charming – preceding an orderly with tea things. She'd sit and smile and jest and make an hour or more dash by so pleasantly that – well, we very well knew at those times that we were very lucky beggars indeed. [359]

Another of Almina's patients, Major Sir Ralph Furse (1887–1973), an old Etonian and a tireless colonial administrator who served in France and Italy, reveals in his recollections *Aucuparius* [360] that he "kept as fit as a fiddle as long as the fighting lasted and went down the day after it ended [361]", suffering from "a sharpish attack[362] " (Spanish influenza[363]). He spent a "month in the lavishly appointed hospital which Lady Carnarvon had provided out of her private purse" [364]

In addition to her patients' praise, Almina gained recognition from the King himself in 1916 when he sent a total of 120 bottles of port, sherry, claret and burgundy as part of a gift package sent to each military hospital. She was honoured and very grateful on the behalf of her patients:

> Lady Carnarvon presents her compliments to the Master of the Household and begs to offer her most humble thanks to the King for the kind present of wine which his Majesty has been so gracious as to send to her hospital and for which Lady Carnarvon and her patients are deeply grateful [365].

News of Almina and other women's work in assisting casualties was admired by Royal Family, and the following year, on 15 February, the King and Queen paid a personal visit to Bryanston Square.

The War Office also acknowledged the splendid, courageous work done in the war hospitals at home by producing lists of those "ladies brought to the notice of the Secretary of State for War for valuable services rendered in connection with the war[366] ". The list from 1917 includes:

> War Office, London 3 March 1917 – MACKEN, M, Head Sister, Lady Carnarvon's Hospital for Officers, 48, Bryanston Square.
>
> HUTCHINSON, M., Nurse, Lady Carnarvon's Hospital for Officers, 48, Bryanston Square.

Almina was also mentioned in the list published by the War Office on 29 January 1918:

> The names of the following ladies have been brought to the notice of the Secretary of State for valuable services rendered in connection with the establishment, maintenance and administration of hospitals
>
> CARNARVON, Countess of Carnarvon Hosp, 48, Bryanston Square

Almina was also delighted when she opened her copy of *The Times* on 25 January 1917, in which the King had recognised the important work of the people in the various medical services. Among the awards were the names of two of Almina's close medical allies at Bryanston Square who had been given Companions of the Bath, in connection with services rendered by them in the war.

> Temp Lt Col Sir William Arbuthnot Lane Bt, MB, FRCS, RAMC
> Temp Lt Col Sir Berkeley George Andrew Moynihan MB, FRCS, RAMC.

Old pals network

Almina's life-long friend General Sir John Cowans, Quartermaster General of the British Army, whose organization fed and clothed the services at home and in the battlefields provided supreme assistance to the Countess ensuring she never went short of essential requisitions.[367] Where necessary, Almina bought directly from the black market, paying well over the odds simply to keep up standards. Alfred de Rothschild was another key part of the *"old pals network"* for Almina and the other titled women operating hospitals for officers in London.[368]

Dealing with criticism

As a tenant, Almina was entitled to use the enclosed garden area in the middle of Bryanston Square. As part of Almina's recovery programme she instructed staff to take convalescing servicemen out to the green space in wheelchairs and beds.

All went well until Almina attempted to erect toilet sheds for the convenience of her patients behind shrubs and well-chosen trees. When the other residents of the Square realised what was going on many of them objected loudly, and the more influential were prepared to stop Lady Carnarvon at all costs. Almina consulted lawyers and put up a fight, but even with her connections in the military and royal household, opposition was too strong.

Instead, Almina suggested that staff take patients up to the roof of the nursing home during the summer months for some fresh air. But this practice stoked the fire of her critics further when one morning an invalid was found dead on the roof, having been forgotten and left up there all night.

An initiative was needed to help counter the critical comments from residents received by some tenants opening up their London squares to soldiers and sailors. In Bryanston Square alone there were at least two Royal Flying Corps hospitals, Almina's at number 48 and Lady Tredegar's at number 37. After much discussion a plan was hatched: a social club for flying officers, with recreational facilities, a lounge and a dining hall furnished in the Jacobean style, was opened in premises at Bruton Street off Berkeley Square.[369]

Lord Carnarvon: A lonely figure

The Carnarvons' roles had reversed: while Almina had blossomed and found meaning to her life outside her marriage, the Earl's poor health meant he was not able to participate in the action[370] or continue his excavations. He was a figure without real purpose, and he idled away the war years.

It was a lonely time for Carnarvon, with Almina tending the wounded in London, his son away with the 7th Queens Own Hussars in Sandhurst, Ireland and then India, and his daughter, Lady Evelyn Herbert, still at school. The Earl found no refuge in seeking out his siblings or half-siblings for company for they were engaged in making their own contribution to the war. Only his younger sister, Lady Margaret, wife of George Duckworth, "played little or no part in public life" [371], but she was raising her young family in West Sussex, which of course kept Carnarvon away.

Constantly frustrated, Carnarvon turned to his old love of horse racing. But many of his friends from the turf were officers in the battlefields, fighting or already dead, and stable lads across the racing fraternity had responded to Kitchener's call, depleting the ranks of those who rode for or waited upon the rich and elderly race horse owners, whose officer sons had also gone off to fight. Disillusioned and depressed, Carnarvon avoided race meetings altogether for short period. However, his passion soon brought him back to the racing circuit.

The 1914–1915 winter season was limited, deserted and lack-lustre. By 1916 his two well-served jockeys, Danny Maher and Frank Wootton, had retired and the Irish jockey Stephen Donoghue headed the league table of winning riders. In the restricted racing season up to 17 July Carnarvon won four races with two horses and gained only modest winnings. Also, in 1916, he was pleased to facilitate the wedding arrangements of his Irish-born horse trainer, Richard Cecil Dawson, by providing The Lake House at Highclere for the honeymoon. [372] This was the year that Dawson's horses won the war time Derby and Oaks. [373]

During the war years the Earl returned as Chairman of the Racehorse Owners, Breeders and Trainers Association and achieved a burning ambition to be elected to the Jockey Club. This at least gave him some direction and a sense of importance. During 1917, when the Government decided to prohibit racing, Carnarvon was involved in proposing a compromise for some continuance of racing for the improvement of the breed, which, he argued, was vitally necessary for military and other national purposes, and under the Jockey Club's rules this could still be carried out during war time with a maximum of 600 horses in training.

Carnarvon also found solace in another pastime – photography, which allowed him to indulge his voyeuristic tendencies. [374] Being a wealthy man with a wealthy wife, the Earl could afford the latest equipment, and his studies were highly regarded in Society circles and were considered worthy of display in a number of photographic exhibitions, including those held at the Camera Club in London, of which Carnarvon became President.

Of the 55 pictures[375] exhibited in one exhibition most were of a tamely erotic nature, studying the poses and expressions of beautiful young women, many of them actresses. The images recalled the freedom enjoyed by Carnarvon in his pre-marital days on his travels with Victor Duleep Singh. Besides nude and semi-nudes[376] his photographic collection included many scenes from his exploits in Egypt, and these photos were exhibited at the Salon of Photography in Pall Mall during 1916. One reviewer commented: "The Earl of Carnarvon exhibits a decoratively conceived and attractive 'Portrait' and another work of a high order particularly the 'Dust of Ages' an imaginative rendering of the excavations at Thebes….'[377] After Lord Carnarvon's death his loyal valet, George Fernside, destroyed the photographs of the nudes[378].

The prospect of peace

Eventually, after years of bloodshed, a series of armistices brought an end to the fighting. With peace a real prospect, the Carnarvons were able to entertain again; as usual, inviting prominent people to their gatherings. The influential (but indiscreet[379]) *Times* and *Morning Post* war correspondent Lieutenant Colonel Charles à Court Repington (1858–1925) records in his diaries :

> 16 August 1918: Dined with Lady Carnarvon at 48 Bryanston Square: the Arthur Portmans, the young Duchess of Sutherland, Mr Lygon, Colonel Lucas, General Hutchison and his wife, Lady C's daughter, Lady Massereene and several others. A pleasant party. The house is a hospital, and Lady C is famous for her dressings in difficult cases.

> Oct 1918: I dined with the Carnarvons at 48, Bryanston Square on the 23rd, meeting Lady Robertson, the Arthur Portmans, General and Mrs Hutchison, Sir Marshall Hall and some others. [380]

The dinner table talk was about effects of the war but also about the final operations and the difficulties that were certain to prevail at the peace settlement to come.

Almina was disappointed at the prospect of peace. With this change she would be plunged back into uselessness, but she was in her prime, aged only 42.

Counting the costs

Almina had gained much during the war: a newfound sense of herself and her skills, extensive medical knowledge and lasting contacts in the medical profession that would benefit her in the years to come. But she and her husband had to contend with great losses.

The Carnarvons' friend Kitchener met his fate during a voyage on *HMS Hampshire* in 1916. On the way to Russia the ship was sunk after striking a mine and he drowned along with most of the crew and his secretary, Lieutenant O.A.G. Fitzgerald. Almina travelled by train to Eastbourne for the funeral of Lieutenant Fitzgerald, and then on 13 June she joined the Earl at the memorial service for Kitchener at St Paul's Cathedral.

Another sad death was that of Prince Victor Duleep Singh, who died in Monte Carlo in June 1918 [381]. Victor had been Carnarvon's closest friend for 40 years, as much too a friend of Almina in years gone by and the godfather of her only son, whose name he carried.

But the most important loss for Almina – in terms of her own feelings and the Carnarvon bank balance – was the passing of Alfred de Rothschild in 1918. The Baron had been laid low by the death of his two brothers, and he died in London in January after a short illness[382]. The death of Alfred de Rothschild was, of course, sad for the Carnarvons, but his legacy ultimately saved them from the bankruptcy courts.

By 1918, Almina was completely starved for cash. Her war work in running the nursing homes had been entirely funded by her resources, and she had spent £125,000[383] on equipping and maintaining her hospitals at Highclere and 48 Bryanston Square. Almina was not good with money; nor was she an efficient bookkeeper. As the war ended evidence from the Rothschild Archives reveals her need for money to repay debts had reached crisis point. A letter from solicitors Freere & Co to Alfred de Rothschild's executors, dated 6 December 1918, states: "Her Ladyship has also incurred very heavy liabilities in connection with her Officers' Hospital and she requires some money. [384]"

Over the course of their marriage Almina and Carnarvon had constantly importuned Alfred for handouts. It was common for Almina to ask him for five, ten or twenty thousand pounds, which Alfred granted with a twinkle in his eye: "Oh, puss-cat, I gave you ten thousand pounds only last week. Whatever have you done with it, my darling child? [385] " Almina always had an explanation, and Alfred always wrote the next cheque. In the case of maintaining her war hospital, Alfred's banker instinct came to the fore: "Oh my darling, you are terribly extravagant. Do try and be more careful. I know it is all in a very good cause [386]." But Almina was always able to charm him into parting with his money. So much so that Alfred was remembered by one observer as " all gilt and plush and glamour, a sort of ascetic Jew Suss, who used to pay…" [387]

Throughout his life Alfred, "the joyless lonely bachelor" [388] had cared for " the importunate and extravagant" [389] Almina emotionally and financially; now in death he sought to ensure that this security would last her lifetime. The Baron left much of his wealth[390] to Almina, including his magnificent London home at 1 Seamore Place, with its priceless artwork and furniture worth several hundred thousand pounds[391] . In addition, he left her £50,000 in cash and declared that "the covenant he had entered into on the marriage of the Earl and Countess of Carnarvon for the payment of £500,000 to the trustees of their marriage settlement remained in full force"[392]. Only his estate at Halton remained within his family, inherited by his nephew Lionel de Rothschild (1880–1942)[393].

Until probate was granted, the Carnarvons needed to boost the coffers. They adopted Seamore Place as their new London residence[394], and sold 13 Berkeley Square. [395] They also commissioned Christies to sell off 147 lots of Chesterfield artefacts[396] (raising some £16,447) from the Bretby estate[397] (which had been used as a prisoner of war camp during the war). Almina also sold some valuable items from Seamore Place, though she'd later regret her rash clearout. For example, she sold the small Titian 'An Allegory of Prudence' for 25 guineas to art collector Francis Howard. On Howard's death in 1956 the picture was valued at £11,000 and when it was donated by the Dutchman David M. Koetser to the National Gallery in 1966 it was valued at £175,000[398].

A return to normalcy?

With the end of the war life gradually returned to a semblance of normality. In 1919 Lady Carnarvon's hospital, which had nursed scores of service men back to health, closed its doors after the last of the patients went home or rejoined their respective units. With little fanfare *The Times* announced: "The Countess of Carnarvon having closed her hospital at 48, Bryanston Square, all letters should be addressed to 1, Seamore Place, Mayfair W." [399] The Earl, meanwhile, whose health was poor, had been bolstered by an inheritance of £25,000 from Alfred, and he busied himself with planning a trip to Egypt where his colleague, Howard Carter, was pottering about in the Valley of the Kings[400].

Almina was expected to return now to her previous incarnation as a lady of high society whose biggest responsibility was choosing her outfit for the latest soirée. But her experience running a hospital had transformed her, and it would not be easy to let go of the aspirations she had built. [401]

Almina at War 1914-18   **1920s**

At Eastmore, Isle of Wight 1937   **1920s**

The Faces of Almina, Countess of Carnarvon

Chapter 6
1919–1922
Paving the Way for Change
A quiet year: 1919

With Alfred de Rothschild's legacy, the Earl was in a position to guarantee his colleague Howard Carter further seasons in Egypt, and he invested the money on implements and an army of native diggers. According to the late Thomas Hoving, in his book *Tutankhamun: The Untold Story*, Howard Carter had resumed his excavations in Egypt in the autumn of 1917, but it wasn't until March 1919 that the Carnarvons were in a position to travel to the Valley of the Kings.

Back in England for the summer, in July the Carnarvons attended the wedding of Sir John Maxwell's daughter, Helena Philae, and the American Clifford Carver at St Paul's, Knightsbridge. (Maxwell, a legendry soldier of the Great War with a reputation for zero tolerance[402], was held in esteem by Carnarvon and later represented Almina in championing her cause for new digging rights with the Egyptian authorities after the Earl's death.) Approaching the age of 18, the Carnarvons decided this would be the season for their daughter to be introduced to high society, so the debutante accompanied her parents to the high-profile wedding.

Next attention shifted to the Carnarvon heir, Henry, who turned 21 in November 1919. Lord Porchester's coming of age was celebrated at Highclere Castle and on the family estates. The festivities included the opening of the cask of ale that had been brewed when he was born.

Henry had a good deal to celebrate. He had survived the war: whereas numerous heirs of great families had been butchered in France and at the Western Front, Porchey had served in India and Mesopotamia and had never been in the firing line. In addition, Porchester had inherited £25,000 from Alfred de Rothschild (as had his sister), and a handsome square-cut sapphire ring from Prince Victor Duleep Singh.

Starting the new decade in style

In February 1920 Porchester was first across the finish line to cheering and applause at Kempton Park on the horse Gracious Gift.

Meanwhile, Almina, Carnarvon and Lady Evelyn were installed at the Winter Palace, Luxor[403], which had been returned to its former grandeur after being used as a convalescent home for officers during the war. In this season's digging, they were encountering excitement of their own:

> In one small area they discovered thirteen alabaster jars ... This was the nearest thing to a discovery of any significance in almost two years. It was exciting, particularly to Lady Carnarvon, who had removed the spectacular objects from the parched soil with her own hands[404].

Exhilarating as it was to finally unearth artefacts of interest, this would be the last decent find until 1922, and Carnarvon would be forced to doubt that any great find would ever be achieved. He considered (no doubt influenced or even directed by Almina) putting part of the already established collection of Egyptian antiquities gathered over previous years on display at 1 Seamore Place. The Egyptians claimed first ownership of finds, so much of this collection had been purchased, with Carter acting as the Earl's agent. Interesting though it would have been, the exhibition was not to be. The Earl was too easily distracted by his other passions in life, of which horse racing was king.

Carnarvon had by now gained the honoured status of a being a member of the Jockey Club, and he was at long last counted as one of racing's inner set. At the May meeting at Kempton Park he delighted in counting among his company Lord Lonsdale, Lord Cholmondeley, Lord Coventry, Lord Dalmeny, Mr Arthur Portman, Sir Charles Hartopp and Lord Westbury, and he was honoured to take part in a dinner party given by the King for members of the Jockey Club at Epsom Races on 2 June. The Earl was later seen at almost all the classic racing occasions of the year, but he attended alone for his wife was occupied elsewhere.

Lady Evelyn Herbert's second coming-out year meant that Almina was required to show some interest in hosting parties at Highclere and London. There were rumours that Lady Evelyn and Howard Carter were matched, but no romance between them was workable; their friendship was more simply based on a mutual appreciation for Egypt. [405] Almina was determined to show her daughter off to the crème de la crème of English society, and in doing so hope she would catch the attention of suitable young men.

First, Almina organised what was billed as "a most important event [406]," at Alfred de Rothschild's old house at 1 Seamore Place on Wednesday 2 June. She had just had the house, now the family's London town house, "thoroughly done up[407] " at huge expense. On taking over the house Almina had found it in a state of ill repair inside and out, and had sought (after complaining bitterly) reimbursement of additional expenses for refurbishment from Alfred de Rothschild's dumb-struck executors, none of whom was willing to challenge Almina when at the height of her demands.

By the end of the 1920 London season Almina had given two lavish balls for her 19-year-old daughter, who it was said had a most enjoyable season. Lady Evelyn had also accepted invitations, which Almina chaperoned. And, of course, the Countess kept up her own social engagements and regularly attended concerts, piano recitals and receptions graced by royal princesses and foreign crown heads.

In August the Carnarvons left Seamore Place and returned to Highclere. Carnarvon is cited as a member of the Duke of Newcastle's party at Clumber for a wedding there in September. The Carnarvons entertained Aleksander Stamboliyski, the Bulgarian Prime Minister[408] at Highclere in October. At the same time Lord Porchester was at a house party at Doncaster Races. The heir to the Carnarvon title was already well established as a rider, punter and tipster on the turf circuit. He was also a playboy and Casanova with an incautious interest in the post-war glut of single, widowed and married women.

In the autumn of 1920 Lord and Lady Carnarvon's friend Sir John Cowans fell ill. Cowans had been Quartermaster General to the Forces during the war, in charge of finding food, clothing, equipment and a reserve for the army in the field as well as the regiments being raised in Britain. Almina was indebted to Cowans and his staff for their personal help in fast-tracking the provision of key supplies during the conflict which had allowed her to maintain her high standards for dressings, food and transportation in her wartime hospitals.

Now, Lady Carnarvon rushed to Sir John's bedside to provide him with support. It was here, on 29 November 1920, that she first met the woman who would become her nemesis, Dorothy Muriel Dennistoun – a woman who would cost Almina tens of thousands of pounds and almost lose her the much heralded place she had established in Society circles; and a woman whose husband, Ian, Almina would soon marry.

Dorothy and Ian Dennistoun

Until the two women met across a bed in Sir John's nursing home, Dorothy was only known to Almina by gossip. It was no secret throughout London and Paris Society that Dorothy was the mistress of Sir John Cowans. It was also common knowledge that Sir John had helped accelerate the army career of Dorothy's husband, Lieutenant Colonel Ian Onslow Dennistoun (the circumstances surrounding that deed were to fuel legal proceedings in which Almina and Dorothy became embroiled during 1924 and 1925).

Dorothy was born Dorothy Muriel Webster in 1888, the daughter of Geoffrey Seymour William Webster (1864–1888) and Ada Mary Paget (d. 1947). She was descended on her father's side from Elizabeth Vassal (later Lady Holland; 1770–1845) who famously deserted her husband for Henry Richard Vassal-Fox, the third Lord Holland. Dorothy's father Geoffrey died before she was born, and her mother remarried several times.

Interestingly, it seems litigation ran in Dorothy's veins. Her twice divorced mother Ada had been previously at the centre of court proceedings in the 1890s against her own father, Francis Henry Paget, said to be "a lunatic ... living a fast life [409]". The Court decided that whilst Paget wasn't mad he was incapable of looking after himself.

Dorothy's early years were spent growing up at Maunby Hall, Yorkshire (the seat of her step-father, Gerald Walker). As a teenager she met many eminent people in the racing world through the orbit of her next step-father, Sir John Miller. But in 1910, aged 22, she chose a husband from her suitors: 31-year-old Ian Onslow Dennistoun who was serving in the Grenadier Guards.

Ian was born on 29 April 1879, of Scottish roots. After some time at Eton he ran away to South Africa, where he was for a short time in the Rhodesian Volunteers and Cape Police. He was bought out [410] and later obtained a commission in the militia. He joined the army in February 1900 and was gazetted as a 2nd Lieutenant, serving briefly in the South African War, and later joined the royal household attached to Windsor Castle. For his services to the Queen, Ian was an early recipient of the MVO (Member of the Victorian Order).

After struggling with his examinations Ian was promoted to Captain in 1910, the year he married Dorothy. He waited a long time for that promotion, after several attempts and representations. At the State Ball given on 5 July 1912 at Buckingham Palace he was the officer in charge of the Guard of Honour of the soldiers mounted in the Quadrangle of the Palace. Elsie, the Dowager Countess of Carnarvon, also attended that event.

Dorothy had brought a substantial sum of money into the marriage settlement and Ian's father, John Dennistoun, a wealthy merchant banker in Dennistoun Cross and Co., provided the couple with an annual allowance. But when John Dennistoun's finances began to crumble in 1912, the allowance was ended and the Dennistouns fell on hard times. The couple were accustomed to spending money, but Ian had no visible means of supporting Dorothy other than his army pay. Ian spoke of resigning his commission and trying his hand at a business venture, but Dorothy objected and suggested instead that she should contact General Cowans, whom she had known as a child.

Dorothy explained:

> We were in a desperate state. ... I was in this frame of mind when one day I met General Sir John Cowans at a party. I had known him as a girl. It was at that meeting that he requested another meeting. My husband at the time was a Captain. The renewed friendship between Sir John Cowans and myself resulted in my procuring for my husband the position of Secretary to the Governor of Jamaica.
>
> In October 1914 we returned to England from Jamaica and again through the influence of Sir John Cowans my husband received a staff appointment while I became a nurse in St John's Ambulance Brigade.
>
> In 1916 my husband was given an appointment to Gibraltar where he remained for three months and where I joined them. In April of that year I returned to London and took a flat at Queensgate. In the autumn Colonel Dennistoun was given an appointment in France and ultimately through my influence with Sir John Cowans he became a member of the Supreme War Council (at Versailles). He remained in France after the end of the War. By this time relations between us had become strained; not much affection was left.[411]

As the work of the Supreme War Council diminished, Ian was released from service on 31 December 1919 and retired from the army on 15 July 1920. Dorothy and Ian were by then leading separate lives. Ian complained to Dorothy of struggling with his finances, conceded that she could not live with him and pressed her to return to England and "do the best she could [412]". He remained in France, trying his luck in a few commercial enterprises including selling wine. Dorothy, meanwhile, had been conducting an adulterous relationship with Sir John Cowans since 1916.

But their relationship soured. When Dorothy pulled some strings for Ian and gave him money, he wrote to her on 14 November 1919 saying, "You are a darling, doing such a lot for me. Bless you."[413] He enquired of Dorothy asking whether "the General had been nasty again". [414] For Sir John was becoming more demanding, and Dorothy wasn't helping matters by flirting with several men whom she had met at the General's side. One of these, a Spanish diplomat named Bolin, became the new object of Dorothy's affections, and she callously cast the General aside. Cowans was naturally embittered by Dorothy's snub, and relations between the former lovers became strained.

Almina did not know the exact state of play in Dorothy and the General's relationship when she broke the news to Dorothy that Sir John was terminally ill, just a few days after the two women first met at Cowans' bedside. Recalling later, in 1925, exactly how Dorothy took the news of Cowans being *in extremis*, Almina said:

> It took me five days to break the news to her. Mrs Dennistoun was very calm when I told her. It took her a few minutes to understand. I was in a state of nerves, and it was the real deuce to find what to say, because Mrs Dennistoun seemed callous about it. She said "Don't think me hard, but the General has killed the love I had for him a long time ago". As a nurse I said "Don't let him know it, as he has a short time to live and we must do all we can. Life is everything." [415]

Thereafter the two women "wrote little notes to each other in respect of the General's health [416]".

Also in November 1920, Ian (who, like Dorothy, had engaged in several affairs whilst they remained husband and wife) made his position clear about Dorothy's latest lover, the Spaniard, Bolin. In a letter of 14 November 1920 to his wife he wrote:

> Dear Old Darling: Your letter received. Well now it is the end, and we must treat it as such. Pack up what you can, and I will try and arrange

for where they are to be sent. I must ask you girl to give way in certain things. I want my wedding presents back when you finally leave me to go to this other man. I am not inclined that he should profit by my loss. I hate the whole race of Spaniards, however many nice individual ones there may be. Remember girl he has got to be responsible for you. I have given way to you rightly or wrongly. You loved some one else within a few months of our marriage, and took him to our home while I was away. When I knew you ceased to care I had to look to for a woman to go to [417].

The Dennistoun divorce in the following year was inevitable.

Returning to Egypt

The Scotsman of 8 January 1921 reported that amongst the passengers on board P&O's steamship *Narkunda*, which had sailed the previous day from London bound for Bombay, were the Earl and Countess of Carnarvon and Lady Evelyn Herbert, who were en route to Egypt. Sir John Cowans was also present, suggesting that Almina had persuaded the dying old soldier – who had been under Almina's nursing care at 1 Seamore Place from December 1920 onwards – to take a final sea voyage. Also aboard were Robert Baden Powell and his wife, on their way to India where Baden Powell was planning to co-ordinate and reconstruct the work of the Boy Scouts.

This year marked the first real revival of Egyptian season since 1914 and the wartime restrictions imposed. Between overseeing excavation works that were disappointingly fruitless, the Carnarvons found time to mingle on the social scene. *The Times* of 17 March 1921 records that: "At the Hotel Continental are Lord and Lady Carnarvon, who have concluded their excavations at Luxor for this year, Lady Evelyn Herbert, Sir George and Lady Cooper and Lady Ruffer." A few days later they were guests of Lord and Lady Allenby at an event held for Winston Churchill.

Mr Churchill's Diversions: Cairo 19 March: During the past week the High Commissioner and Lady Allenby have been given a series of dinner and luncheon parties on the occasion of the presence in Cairo of members of the conference summoned by Mr Churchill. In addition to the Colonial Secretary and Mrs Churchill, the guests have included the Earl and Countess of Carnarvon, Sir Percy and Lady Cox, the Earl and Countess of Ossory, Sir Hugo and Lady Fitzherbert, Sir Geoffrey Archer, General Sir Walter Congreve, VC and Lady Congreve Major Dodds, Mrs Forbes and Major General ER Kenyon[418].

In the wake of Cowans' death

The news on Sir John Cowans' health was now seriously grim. But despite being at death's door, his feelings for Dorothy were unforgiving. In a jealous rage over Dorothy's affair with Bolin, he summoned her to explain herself. Dorothy refused to see him and the General sent several "very unpleasant" letters cursing his former mistress. When Almina later saw the letters, their cruel tone shocked her. She remarked: "I knew the dreadful illness from which he died but I was terribly hurt that somebody I had been so fond of had been so ungallant to a lady who had been a friend of his for so long. [419]"

By March Cowans was at Mentone, in the South of France, when his condition deteriorated. He was tended to by his wife, Lady Cowans [420], who showed extraordinary strength in tolerating her husband's serial adultery of many years standing. *The Times* of Monday 18 April 1921 finally reported: "We regret that General Sir John Cowans died at Mentone shortly after 5 o'clock on Saturday morning, aged 59." His body was conveyed back to Britain where it lay in state at Westminster Abbey, and he was subsequently given a full public military funeral with honours, the costs fully covered by the War Office in recognition of Cowans' contribution to the First World War. This was to the huge relief of Cowans' widow, for Sir John had died impoverished, with debts far exceeding the value of his estate.

Dorothy was more interested in what she could gain from her lover's death than his loss. Sir John had promised Dorothy a motorcar; however, on his deathbed his anger towards his mistress had driven him to instruct the garage housing the motorcar not to make it available to Dorothy because she had been "very negligent".

Dorothy consulted Almina over Cowans' actions. The Countess was sympathetic over her legal rights about the possible repossession of Cowans' car. She wasted no time in arranging for Dorothy to consult Sir Edward Marshall Hall, Almina's great barrister friend; even offering to pay his fee. [421] Dorothy went to see Marshall Hall with her lover Bolin. The barrister's advice was that as Dorothy and Bolin were contemplating marriage it was "hardly worth advertising to the world" that she had been Sir John Cowans' mistress for many years, especially for the sake of the car worth only £350. In addition, Cowans' executors, who were administering a bankrupt estate, were unlikely to see Dorothy's point of view. Thus Dorothy abandoned the fight, focusing instead on clearing a path to being able to marry Bolin, whose baby she was secretly carrying.

Almina, meanwhile, was happy with her blossoming friendship with Dorothy, who had come to mean a great deal to the Carnarvon family.

> I may say that this was the true foundation of the friendship and the affection, and what I thought possibly, the love that had been created between Mrs Dennistoun and me. She is a peculiarly fascinating person, attractive to the last degree. There was never anyone else who entered our home who so captivated the hearts of my family [422].

In April of 1921 the Dennistouns began divorce proceedings in France, where Ian was now domiciled. Despite wrongdoing on both sides, Ian gave way to Dorothy in order that she could claim the grounds for the divorce of "desertion and misconduct"[423]. One letter captured Ian's feelings: "Sorry for all the trouble I have caused you. We were never suited for one another, and that is why I left you. [424]" Knowing that Ian was penniless, Dorothy did not demand alimony. Thereafter Dorothy even sent various small sums to her former husband including the proceeds of some silver that had been given to them when first married.

Back in London Dorothy had been staying with her great friend Baroness de Forrest. When the Baroness was unable to continue to provide a room for her, giving the excuse that she lacked sufficient servants, Almina stepped in to help Dorothy, and even sent a car to meet her at the railway station. According to Almina, Dorothy shared the Carnarvons' homes from May 1921 until either the end of February or the beginning of March, 1923.

For the Carnarvons, the rest of 1921 was very much business as usual. In May the Carnarvons supported the Earl's sister Winifred, Lady Burghclere, at the memorial service for her husband, Herbert Gardner (1846–1921), a Cabinet Minister, actor, playwright, novelist and father of four daughters. In June, the Earl's half brother Mervyn was married in Spain. [425] July brought a pleasant duty when Carnarvon, in his capacity as one of the Vice Presidents of the Egypt Exploration Society, opened an exhibition of Egyptian antiquities at the Society of Antiquaries, Burlington House, which represented the Society's labours at Tell-el-Amarna from 1919. In September Almina and Evelyn were at Doncaster races for the St Leger, and then in

October Carnarvon showed Lady Evelyn off at the racing at Kempton Park.

Good companions

As time passed Almina and Dorothy developed an extraordinarily close friendship. At this time Dorothy's income was very small and "it was a matter of great relief and comfort to her that she had such kind, rich friends".[426] Almina provided food, clothes and comfort for Dorothy; the Countess declared in 1925, "Mrs Dennistoun had nothing in the house that was not the best." [427] This was a source of tension for young Porchey, who disliked Dorothy for her habit of flirting outrageously with several of his male friends. But the two women were inseparable, for their relationship was mutually beneficial. While it suited Dorothy to live in great comfort, it also suited Almina to keep Dorothy near at hand so she could preserve the untainted memory of Sir John Cowans at least from anything adverse leaking into the public domain.

As their friendship grew, Dorothy confided the history of her affair with General Cowans to her companion, but Almina would later insist that Dorothy never disclosed any involvement by Ian in seeking favour from the General. It was Almina's belief (albeit later fully exposed as untrue by Ian's letters to Dorothy produced in court) that he never knew of or encouraged Dorothy's advances towards the General.

In their discussions of affairs of the heart, Dorothy sought Almina's advice about her relationship with Bolin. Almina persuaded Dorothy to cast the Spaniard aside, not least because of the disparity of their ages (Bolin was in his 20s, Dorothy, her 30s). By August 1921 Almina had successfully convinced Dorothy to regard her lover as irksome. She may even have arranged or assisted in the termination of the Bolin foetus that Dorothy was carrying. An intimate of Almina has advised that she had once mentioned the horrific scene of finding Dorothy attempting to "flush a foetus down the toilet"[428] following either a miscarriage or an attempted abortion.

Almina meets Ian Dennistoun

In December 1921 came an important turning point, the first meeting of Almina and Ian Dennistoun. Almina recalled of Ian that Dorothy would "...often talk about him. She always referred to him as

'Tiger'. She said he was an awfully sweet man, very kind, a great gentleman, too hopelessly weak for words, but an absolute – excuse the vulgar expression – 'wash-out'." [429] Now Dorothy deemed it time for her friend to meet her former husband, and she orchestrated a meeting.

Almina was planning a trip to her beloved Paris. Dorothy told her she had left some belongings in a hotel in Paris where she had previously stayed, and Almina agreed to go and fetch these belongings. Dorothy asked Ian to go to this hotel and hand over the items to Almina. Thus the couple first made each other's acquaintance.

When she was later pushed away by Almina, Dorothy's accusation was that Ian began a love affair with Almina during the lifetime of the 5th Earl. Dorothy's words were that this meeting:

> ... started an acquaintance which ripened into love between Lady Carnarvon and my former husband. He wrote to me of Almina that "she is overwhelmingly kind to me, and she has now proceeded to buy me a country cottage". This was while Lord Carnarvon was alive. [430]

This scenario does not prove Almina's adultery. During her lifetime (when she still had a sizable degree of wealth) Lady Carnarvon bought property for several male friends; it was a way of hooking her prey but equally it was born of an inherent kindness she displayed at times which often had no rationality or hidden motive. However, Almina was a vulnerable woman at times, and she was attracted to passive, needy men, which Ian certainly was.

The question remains, why did Dorothy push her former husband and her companion together? An intimate of Almina's highlights the Dennistouns' capacity for scheming and artfulness, both jointly and separately. Could it be that they saw a window of opportunity – or at least Dorothy did when she met Almina beside Cowans' deathbed? Did Dorothy anticipate that she and Ian could put themselves in a position to take advantage of Almina's weaknesses? If so, it follows that an entire conspiracy was formed between Dorothy and Ian Dennistoun to exploit Almina, and the subsequent death of the 5th Earl allowed the scheming pair to take their plans further.

Almina said that when she first met Colonel Dennistoun in Paris his condition was "lamentable": "He looked like death. He was emaciated. His clothes were shiny and he apparently hadn't had food enough to keep body and soul together." [431] If there was an element of contrivance by either Dorothy or Ian to deliberately draw Almina into the Colonel's life, the staging of quite such a state of destitution would be proof.

During Almina's time in Paris Ian was ill with neuritis and sciatica. She visited him in his spartan attic space which had no fireplace, and no hot or cold water. She immediately lavished money on Ian to improve his quality of life, and she agreed to help him further, if he would do her the odd favour in return.

For far from being an innocent taken in by a conman and his ex-wife, Almina had a plan of her own. Following in the footsteps of Alfred de Rothschild, she was looking to hire, on her own terms, a suitable male companion whom she would own by showering him with affection, attention, gifts and money. This arrangement was not about love or love-making for Almina, but about providing a sense of control and company to assuage her loneliness. Though they enjoyed a frivolousness bordering on romance, probably no sexual advances were made at this time. This was purely a business arrangement, as Almina described later: "He honoured me with a most wonderful, straight, loyal and clean friendship." [432]

But Almina also realised that she could make use of her new acquaintance to iron out some complexities in her financial affairs. She had sold jewels and three works of art (Gainsboroughs [433]) which she had inherited from Alfred de Rothschild, and her lawyers had advised her to look to delay (though not, of course, avoid) paying estate and legacy duties. A perfect solution for Almina seemed to be Ian's barren bank account, which she could use to hide the sale proceeds from the tax authorities. This scheme of laundering funds amounted to upwards of £100,000 in less than 12 months during 1922–1923. Later, Almina's official version of the reasons for passing her money through the Colonel's account was as follows:

> I asked him to mind it for my use for my own personal reasons. At that time my Solicitor and also one of my trustees Mr Boscawen of the Bank of England were worried, knowing that at the time I was not prepared to pay the duty on these things to Somerset House [the Inland Revenue]. [434]

Family affairs

By this time, Almina and Lord Carnarvon were living separate lives and Lady Evelyn had long assumed the role of her father's companion. But Almina did take the time to spend the winter with Carnarvon and Evelyn in Egypt, accompanied by Dorothy, who was recovering from losing her baby. Howard Carter also joined the party, of course, having spent some weeks enjoying Almina's nursing at 1 Seamore Place while recovering from an operation.

The winter season of 1921–1922 in Egypt was heralded as having "a gaiety unusual here for years [435]". News on the Carnarvons whereabouts was in the Society columns: "The Earl and Countess of Carnarvon with Lady Evelyn Herbert, spent a few days in Lower Egypt before proceeding up the river, where Lord Carnarvon is to resume his archaeological work. [436]" Later the Carnarvons caught up with their great friends, the Cunliffe-Owens. Dorothy's health returned, and she was introduced to people who became new friends in Cairo and Luxor.

Auguste Wild, an international hotelier, comments on Almina's "beauty" and the lack of charm of the 5th Earl in his memoirs *Mixed Grill in Cairo* :

> I was often called upon by Lady Carnarvon and Lady de Walden to arrange functions for them to help raise money for the troops. Lady Carnarvon was beautiful, the most caring and generous of philanthropists. I knew and liked Howard Carter, but (Lord) Carnarvon was not so approachable, I never saw him smile. When staying in Cairo at hotels where I was present he would insist during a meal that the whole joint of ham or other meat being served, be placed on the table in front of him, so that he might carve it himself. [437]

Lord Northcliffe (1865–1922), the newspaper proprietor of the *Daily Mail*, was on a tour of Egypt, and he lunched with the Carnarvons at Cairo in early February. T.G.H.James records in his biography of Howard Carter that Carnarvon arrived in the Valley of the Kings on 7 February 1922.

Back in London by early summer, the Carnarvons, with Lady Evelyn, attended a dance and supper given by the Duke and Duchess of Buccleuch, with Princess Mary and Viscount Lascelles present, at 2 Grosvenor Place on 26 May. In the same week Almina and Lady Evelyn attended a dance given by Lady Knaresborough for her daughters at the Hyde Park Hotel. Then, on 3 July 1922, Carnarvon opened an exhibition of ancient Egyptian life at the Society of Antiquaries, Burlington House. This represented the work of C.L. Woolley at Tell el-Amarna, 150 miles south of Cairo.

By now, the issue of Lord Porchester's wedding to an American, Anne Catherine Wendell, was dominating the family's inner sanctum. Matchmakers at Court had mooted that Henry, Lord Porchester, heir to the Earl of Carnarvon and his parent's legacies from Alfred Rothschild, might make a suitable husband for Princess Mary, the only daughter of King George V and Queen Mary. It is recorded that Porchester "dodged the honour" [438], but it is more likely that his precise credentials were found flawed by the inner circle of royal scrutinisers and advisers, who opted for the safer Viscount Lascelles. Porchey may have seen himself in the role and resented that part of his failure lay with his parent's profile: the 5th Earl and Countess were an unconventional couple, even without the truth being revealed of his true paternity.

Instead of a pursuing a royal marriage, Porchester followed the popular fashion of the time of finding an American wife. He certainly had his pick of the American ladies, with the *Pittsburgh Post Gazette* calling him one of the "greatest matrimonial catches in England". He decided on Anne Catherine Wendell, whom he'd been seeing in secret for some time.

Catherine was born 20 November 1900, the daughter of the deceased Jacob II (Jack) Wendell, a New York commission merchant, and Marian Fendall Wendell (d. 1949), who was from a prominent Virginian family. On the death of her father in 1911 Catherine, together with her two brothers, had come to England to live at Sandridgebury, Sandridge, Hertfordshire.

The Times of 1 June 1922 announced the engagement of Catherine and Porchester, but evidence suggests that Henry had not discussed the matter much with the Earl and Countess in advance of the declaration. When the news of her son's would-be wife's background reached Almina, she was far from enthusiastic. Catherine Wendell had been "out" in London for two seasons, and had been engaged to marry Francis Collingwood Drake of the 10th Hussars, whose father was the High Sheriff of Hertfordshire. In his memoirs Porchester reveals that on first meeting Catherine his father was in favour, despite her being an American (suggesting that Lord Carnarvon's

dislike for his contemporaries across the pond equalled Almina's).
However, Porchey's father was also concerned about the full extent
of the Wendell financial coffers, which were not vast. Carnarvon
thought Catherine good-looking, but cautioned that if she was poor
his son should more mindful of that failing.

Almina was perturbed enough by her son's actions that, according to
an intimate, she made a special trip to Paris to confront him over his
would-be bride.[439] But the Countess, at least, eventually warmed to
Catherine when the young woman presented her fiancé's mother
with violets, the flower symbolising modesty. Almina withdrew her
opposition, and held a dance at 1 Seamore Place jointly for Catherine
and Lady Evelyn a few days after the announcement. There were 500
guests, including Prince George, later Duke of Kent.

Porchester married Catherine at St Margaret's, Westminster on 17
July 1922, with Tommy Frost as best man and a guest list drawn
from London and New York circles. Prince George graced the
Carnarvons with his presence, along with Lord Louis Mountbatten
and Miss Edwina Ashley, who married the very next day. The
Carnarvons attended the Mountbatten wedding with Lady Evelyn.

Later that month Almina attended a reception given by the Duke and
Duchess of Westminster at Grosvenor House, and then the
Carnarvons were together at Chesterfield House for a reception
given by Princess Mary. In August Carnarvon and Lady Evelyn were
at the races at Deauville, in the company of the Aga Khan. On 9
September Almina attended the funeral of the surgeon Sir Charles
Ryall, one of her medical friends from the Great War. For much of
the rest of the autumn Almina was at Highclere. Then in late
September she was Newbury Races with Lord and Lady Porchester,
before they left Britain for the East.

The legendary Egyptian discovery

On 4 November 1922 Carnarvon's optimism, Carter's instincts and
Alfred's money paid off at long last. In the Valley of the Kings
Carter's team unearthed steps leading to the tomb of Tutankhamun,
the heretic king of the 18th dynasty. Inside, awaiting the awe of the
world, were riches beyond belief, "golden beds and couches of state,
golden caskets, chariots, candlesticks, furniture, statues, clothes,
weapons, and a magnificent throne, encrusted with gold, silver and
jewels" [440].

Reuters' man Valentine Williams saw ahead of the find and reported back to England – before the excavators had left the tomb. Williams claimed that it was his report in the *London Evening Standard* that was sent across the world and was the first seen by Almina, setting out the "crowning of her husband's hopes".[441]

As the news of the historic find broke, Lord Carnarvon and Lady Evelyn were at Highclere, Almina was in Paris and Lord and Lady Porchester were in India. The Earl and his daughter set out quickly for Egypt, arriving in Cairo on 20 November. Almina stayed put to publicise the treasures awaiting description, writing an article for the *Weekly Dispatch* on "The Great Egyptian Treasure Fields". Then she left London for Paris on 4 December 1922. Her intention was to meet Carnarvon and Lady Evelyn on their successful return from Egypt.

Carnarvon submitted a long article to *The Times*, describing his first impressions of the interior of the great tomb, which was published on 11 December 1922.[442] He dutifully recorded regret that Almina was not present at his moment of triumph:

> My only regret is that my wife who has been with me during all my excavations, and has shared with me what, I am sorry to say, have been nearly always been disappointments, was, owing to indisposition unable to make the journey to Egypt.

On his arrival back in London on 18 December all the newspapers reported Carnarvon's personal description of what was discovered inside the tombs. Lord Carnarvon negotiated a deal with *The Times* for exclusive rights over the press reporting of the great King Tut discovery. This brought huge criticism from many sides, including Howard Carter, who believed that the treasures of Tutankhamun belonged to the world. The Egyptians, meanwhile, thought the tomb and its contents only belonged to them. Some local authorities felt the two Englishmen were nothing less than grave robbers, the equivalent of two Egyptian excavators breaking into the royal tombs at Westminster Abbey or Windsor Castle. Moreover there was a lack of trust in the various factions on the ground in Egypt and rumours that Carter and Carnarvon had already smuggled items away from the tomb in the dead of night.

Journalist Valentine Williams thought the Earl "the very reincarnation of a certain type of 18th century peer." [443] He wrote that Carnarvon was

> ... unaffected in manner and simple in his mode of life he had, nevertheless all the arrogance of his class in his approach to his fellow men, particularly the Egyptians, who he frankly despised and was at no pains to conceal it – at Luxor the natives always spoke of him as "El Lord" of "Lordy" with respect, with fear, even, but without affection. [444]

Almina's feelings for her husband were similar. She wisely retreated when his " half kindly, half malicious smile" [445] was put on.

Another curt portrayal is that Carnarvon was:

> Highly cultured, with a wide knowledge and appreciation of art, he had the inquiring mind of the dilettante. Spiritualism interested him profoundly. He was the type of nobleman who in another age would have had one of those cabinets of curiosities in which Pepys so delighted.
>
> I used to see him as we sat together after dinner in the smoke room of the *Adriatic*, with his rather sleep air, his eternal cigarette, which he smoked out of a quill holder, and the old brown cardigan he wore over his evening waistcoat as a precaution against draughts. [446]

The *Daily Express* called the treasures "appalling in their magnificence". The mummy was enclosed in a solid gold coffin, which was enclosed in two outer shells of wood. The three coffins were in an enormous sarcophagus of quartzite which was hidden within four ornate wooden shrines. The pharaoh's head and shoulders were masked with enamelled gold, an enamelled gold necklace hung round his neck and his waist was enclosed with a gold belt. The tomb itself had four rooms filled with ancient beds, chairs, alabaster cups and plates, musical instruments, religious symbols, weapons and all the bejewelled and gilt trappings of royalty. Impressed by the find, on 22 December 1922 the King gave Carnarvon an audience at Buckingham Palace.

The family (and Dorothy) were reunited at Highclere to spend Christmas together and discuss plans for a return to Egypt in early 1923. Almina wrote a (somewhat overly-familiar) letter to Howard Carter, offering him good luck for the clear-out of the tomb that lay ahead. A reference to this letter (which is in the Metropolitan Museum Collection, New York) is quoted by T.G.H. James in his biography of Carter:

Lady Carnarvon... on Boxing Day writes "My dear Howard, This line is to send you my love and every blessing in the coming year" After four pages of news and congratulations, she ends "With much love and every good wish for the New Year. Yrs affly [affectionately] Almina Carnarvon.[447]

It was the very best of times for Lord Carnarvon, but his elation would be short lived. In just four months he would be dead, the victim, some say, of the curse of Tutankhamun.

Chapter 7
1923–1924
Losing a husband, gaining a husband

The final return to Egypt

In the New Year Lord Carnarvon and Lady Evelyn Herbert returned to Egypt, arriving at Alexandra on the *SS Adriatic* on 25 January. For this trip to assess the Tutankhamun treasures, Carnarvon was happier to have his devoted daughter, rather than his estranged wife, at his side. Lady Evelyn was her father's constant companion, and to his joy she had inherited Carnarvon's fascination with Egyptology. Between the two existed a deep love and mutual admiration. One journalist, Valentine Williams, described a "tender friendship between them, delightful to watch" [448]. Evelyn wanted to be by her father's side at the moment of his triumph.

The world, and in particular the world's reporters, awaited the official opening of the tomb. Carnarvon cracked under the pressure from the constant presence of unhelpful Egyptian officials [449] and had a huge row with Carter (partly over his exclusive deal with *The Times*) that would only fully be resolved on Carnarvon's deathbed. But the pair put aside their differences on 16 February 1923 when the boy king's tomb was exposed to the world for the first time in 3,000 years. The following day, *The Times* printed a full account of the "magnificent spectacle" at the opening of the tomb of Tutankhamun.

Almina had a right to be present too for this moment of glory – after all, it was her benefactor Alfred's money that had funded much of the 14 years of digging. But Almina's absence on the trip was no snub; she was content for father and daughter to enjoy the glory. Besides, she and Lord Carnarvon were hardly a close couple [450], and Almina was caught up in her relationship with Colonel Ian Dennistoun and her deteriorating friendship with his former wife, Dorothy. The pair's relationship was breaking down due to them sharing the same lover, Tommy Frost, who was a friend of both Almina's husband and her son; indeed, he had been Porchester's best man at his wedding.

A friend of Tommy Frost recalled:

> I remember Almina as small and frankly no beauty. Despite this, a much
> older friend of mine, Thomas Frost, now long deceased, was reputed to
> have had an affair with her. The story goes that having been a close friend
> of her son, Porchey Carnarvon, following the affair, Porchey would never
> speak to Tommy again! [451]

Dorothy had fallen heads over heels in love with Frost, and marriage
remained an option. But the detestation felt by Almina's son over
Dorothy's liaison with his best friend was unbearable. It created an
unhealable wound in his mother too, since she had brought Dorothy
into the family's circle. Thus in February/March of 1923 Dorothy
resumed residence in her own flat; though whether Almina had
evicted her former friend or Dorothy had left voluntarily remains
unclear.

The mosquito bite

In Egypt, after weeks of Tutankhamun mania, Almina's husband
was dealing with a different drama of his own. Concern began when
Evelyn ordered the Earl to his bed in the hotel at Assouan with
suspected flu. With his daughter at his side, the stricken Carnarvon
returned to Cairo on 14 March, but paid little attention to the matter
of an insect bite he'd sustained. Then, on 18 March Lady Evelyn
wrote Carter, describing her father as:

> ... very very seedy... and incapable of doing anything. You know that
> mosquito bite on his cheek that was worrying him at Luxor, well
> yesterday quite suddenly all the glands in his neck started swelling and
> last night he had a high temperature and still has today. He feels just too
> rotten for words. [452]

Poisoning from the innocent-seeming bite had set in and spread,
affecting Carnarvon's tonsils. His temperature rose to 104 degrees
and his condition gave everyone cause to fear for his life. Doctors
succeeded in bring his temperature down to around 102, but the
Earl's condition remained serious.

Accordingly, Lady Evelyn informed Almina by cablegram in London
on 19 March of Carnarvon's perilous situation and that the following
24 hours were critical. Porchester, who was in India, was also made

aware by telegram, probably by Lady Evelyn, of their father's plight.[453]

On Tuesday 20 March 1923 it was widely reported in the press that Lord Carnarvon had been bitten on the face by a mosquito. When Carter arrived at his colleague's bedside the following day, it was clear that his patron's life was hanging in the balance.[454]

Almina flies to Carnarvon's side

Some writers suggest that when news of Lord Carnarvon's condition reached Almina she was annoyed at having to go to his bedside. It is insinuated that she was at the time cavorting with Colonel Dennistoun in Paris. Such reports are inaccurate[455]. As soon as Almina got word in London of her husband's ill health, on Monday 19 March, she declared that she was determined "to lose no time in reaching Egypt". Her statement continued, "I am a nurse myself and my place is at my husband's side. I'm going on by air today. [456]"

Air travel was by far the fastest way to bridge the 2,700-mile gap between Almina and her husband. Almina had never flown before, but on the very day she received the telegram with its worrying news she arranged with Daimler Airway a special three-seater De Havilland aeroplane, and the services of a Harley Street specialist.

Almina left Croydon Airport in the De Havilland biplane, piloted by Captain F.L. Barnard.[457] But whilst in the air she was taken ill and the plane had to land 30 kilometres from Paris at Beauvais, from a descent of 3,000 feet at night. Almina eventually made it to Paris, where she consulted an official of the Daimler Airway about the prospects of being able to continue the flight in the biplane. She was advised not to attempt it, but to try to charter a hydroplane at Marseilles and to break the journey at Naples before going on to Athens and Cairo. But Almina's efforts to requisition a hydroplane from Marseilles were unsuccessful, forcing her to take a train from Paris to Lyons.

At Lyons Lady Carnarvon received news that Carnarvon's condition was improved, on the strength of which the medical specialist accompanying her returned to London. Almina continued her journey on board the liner *Lotus* from Marseilles to Egypt.

On 26 March Carter recorded in his diary Carnarvon's deterioration and Almina's arrival at her husband's bedside. "Ld. C. developed pneumonia. Lady Carnarvon arrived." Lady Evelyn met Almina at Alexandra; the Egyptian State Railways put a saloon carriage at their disposal.

Carnarvon suffered a relapse on 29 March and his condition became grave. The news about Porchester was that he and Catherine had already sailed from India.

In addition to Dr Johnnie, four other doctors attended Carnarvon: Professor Fletcher Barrett, Colonel Charles Turner, Frank Madden and the leading French doctor in Cairo, Dr Louis Roeder. Almina and Evelyn kept night vigils in the sickroom. But the team of doctors eventually informed Almina that there was no hope of recovery. The family members who were present gathered round Carnarvon's bedside. He died peacefully at 2am on Thursday 5 April 1923.

Reactions to the death

During the remainder of the day of her husband's death, Almina, who occupied suites on the second floor of the Continental Hotel, was left undisturbed to mourn the 5th Earl's loss. Condolences soon poured in from around the world.

Two flags flew at half-mast over the Continental Hotel, Cairo and a special book of condolences was placed at the entrance. King Fuad sent his Grand Chamberlain to convey his regrets.

A telegram from King George V and Queen Mary was received by Porchester.

> The Queen and I have learned with great regret of the death of your father, especially after the splendid fight which he made for his life. We offer you and your dear mother and family our sincere sympathy in your great loss. GEORGE, R.L.

Almina received a telegram from Queen Alexandra:

> I offer you and your family my heart felt sympathy in the terrible sorrow you have sustained in the death of your husband, whose name will be remembered with pride by his fellow countrymen.

The Egyptian High Commissioner Lord Allenby and his wife were the first official representatives of King George V to express their personal sympathy to Almina and her family. They were invited to stay at their residence until they had arranged for a departure date back to England.

The numerous obituaries on Lord Carnarvon were mostly complimentary and sympathetic, paying special tribute to his character and munificence and his unparalleled work in the cause of Egyptian archaeology. With regard to the sensational discoveries with Carter at Luxor, one commentator spoke for everyone when he recorded that they had been assured perpetual remembrance. Noteworthy amongst the pair's other important finds besides Tutankhamun were two limestone slabs containing an account of King Kames; a number of lines of the version of the precepts of Ptahhetep; two ruined temples of Rameses IV; an unfinished temple of Hatshepsut; a 12th dynasty cemetery; tombs of the period between the 12th and 18th dynasties; and a tomb with a sarcophagus of yellow crystalline limestone, prepared for Queen Hatshepsut.

The consensus among the doctors was that Lord Carnarvon's death was due to blood poisoning from the proboscis of the insect or from dust penetrating his wound. The *Daily News* gave prominence to a suggestion of medical experts that the bite was followed by a tick, a tiny spider-like creature, that caused the fatal condition of 'tick fever'. It is true that the Valley of the Kings was an unhealthy place for an individual, infested with vermin including wolves, jackals, wildcats, foxes, snakes, lizards, scorpions, vultures and insects. The heat of the day attracted plagues of flies.

But some of those reporting on the death found more sinister meaning behind the Earl's demise, attributing the death to a curse. One bulletin said:

> The Curse: Fears of further retribution, it is suggested, may deter Egyptians from touching the tomb again, but Sir Ernest Alfred Thompson Wallis Budge, keeper of Egyptian antiquities in the British Museum scoffed at this idea, saying that If the excavation enterprise continues to be financed he Is sure there will be no trouble in procuring native labour, as "the most powerful influence in the life of the modern Egyptian worker is money".[458]

Another was more cautious, but considered Carnarvon and Carter's violations of the tomb.

> They caused that hidden and sealed outer entrance to be broken through. They excavated the stairway. They entered through the second sealed wall. They forced their way through the passage and into the outer chamber. They stopped not at the sealed wall of masonry into the chamber containing the royal catafalque. They even opened the doors of the outer case. And then they stopped – because of reverence for a dead Pharaoh? Not at all. They stopped because they could not go further into the catafalque without destroying it [459].

Later casualties would fuel rumours of a curse, and Lord Carnarvon would perhaps become more famous for his death by King Tut's curse than his life.

Almina, meanwhile, was determined to comply with her dead husband's wishes to see the work in Egypt continue. She gave her full blessing to Carter recommencing work in sorting out the pharaoh's tomb. In an interview on 9 April 1923 Almina went as far as to proclaim that she would "dedicate her life to the completion of the work of Lord Carnarvon, who left no diary, but who did leave considerable manuscript from which I will complete his memoirs". [460] Later, the 5th Earl's private papers were largely destroyed in the Blitz, or even discarded long before this time. [461]

One brief extract from the countless obituaries on Carnarvon summed the state of affairs up eloquently:

> Lord Carnarvon, is dead, deserving regret and honor. He spent well, for the education of the world, part of the great fortune that old Rothschild left to Lady Carnarvon. Rothschild's adopted daughter. Romance attends such a death, and breaks out in various ways. The native Egyptians are afraid to go near the tomb now, to continue their work. They think ancient poisons are there to kill intruders. Money will restore their courage. [462]

In a public statement by the authorities Almina was duly "authorized to continue the clearance of the tomb of Tut-ankn-amon which she wishes to complete in memory of Lord Carnarvon". [463]

Laying Carnarvon to rest

Lord and Lady Porchester, now the 6th Earl and Countess of Carnarvon, along with Lady Evelyn Herbert, left Egypt before Almina, on board a ship for Marseilles on Monday 9 April.

Albert B. Armitage was a Captain with the P&O Steam Navigation Company, and a member of Captain Scott's famed *Discovery* expedition. In his recollections *Cadet to Commodore*, Armitage "broke regulations and turned two hospital cabins into passenger cabins[464] " in order to accommodate the new Earl and Countess and Lady Evelyn on their trip back to England. He described the scene at their leaving:

> Almina, Countess of Carnarvon, came to Port Said to see them off. She was one of the most pathetic figures I have ever seen as, clad in deep mourning, she tightly clutched my arm when I led her from my cabin to the gangway [465].

For the days following Almina was a captive in Cairo, awaiting news that the embalmers had completed their task, whilst Dr Johnnie and Howard Carter endeavoured to make the arrangements for the final grim formalities.

Finally, on Saturday 14 April 1923, Almina left Egypt with her dead husband's body accompanied by Marcus Johnson. The utmost secrecy was maintained. The official bulletin said that they were to take the afternoon train from Cairo to Port Said; in fact, they left on a special train at 11pm in the evening. Howard Carter, who had been under great nervous strain, returned the same evening to Luxor.

On 21 April Almina and Dr Johnnie arrived at Marseilles on board the liner *Malwa*. They then travelled on that ship to Gibraltar and finally England. The arrangements were for the body to be landed at Plymouth and taken by special train to Highclere. Lady Evelyn met her mother at Plymouth and travelled with her on the train. The 6th Earl met them on arrival.

Lord Carnarvon was laid to rest on Monday 30 April 1923. As stipulated in his last wishes, his grave was simple, cut into the chalk on the summit of Beacon Hill, facing Whitchurch. Rehearsals had taken place to ensure that an ascent could be made. In the end a Red Cross ambulance was found most suitable as a hearse, coupled to a Fordson for the last part of the ascent.

At noon Almina, Lady Evelyn, Catherine, the new Countess, Lady Burghclere, George Duckworth and his wife Lady Margaret, Lady Victoria Herbert and Mervyn Herbert left Highclere Castle in four large cars. A walking procession of mourners travelled to the grave with the officiating clergymen, and included Dr Marcus Johnson, Major Rutherford (Highclere's Chief Estate Agent) and a number of old servants: Streatfield (house steward), Fernside (valet), Grove (butler) and others.

The ordinary burial service was used and there were no hymns. A hallowing service was held on the site by the Rector of Burghclere. A memorial service was also held in Highclere Church and another at St Margaret's, Westminster, conducted by the Dean of Westminster. Among those attending in London was Dorothy Dennistoun. A memorial service also took place at the same time in Cairo, attended by Carter.

After the ceremony only Almina was left to mourn beside the grave. It was said she maintained her vigil until late in the afternoon. The *Daily Express* [466]was criticised for publishing a picture they claimed was of Almina, clad in black, sitting beside the open grave of her husband on the wind-swept top of Beacon Hill.

Almina follows her own path

Twenty-four-year-old Henry, Lord Porchester, was now Earl of Carnarvon, the 17th Lord of the Manor in succession from the time of Hunferth, Bishop of Winchester, in the year AD 749. But Henry resented the control that Almina yielded over the 5th Earl's legacies in the will drawn up in 1919, with two later codicils, which the 6th Earl was advised not to challenge. [467]

The 5th Earl left £500 to Howard Carter but all his Egyptian relics went to Almina and a codicil in his will dealt with the private antiquity collections: "I suggest the nation... be given the first refusal... otherwise, I suggest that the collection be offered to the Metropolitan, New York." (The word 'suggest' made all the difference between these antiquities being retained in Britain and the collection going to America; this matter later reached a head in 1927.)

In the immediate aftermath of the 5th Earl's death, Almina ensured that a smaller bequest of a single piece to the British Museum and the Metropolitan Museum of New York, set out in the will, was fulfilled. The British Museum took custody of "a very beautiful wooden figure of a high official who was connected with the services performed in chapels of the Pyramids at Ghizah about 3500 BC". [468]In addition, Almina presented them with "a wonderfully fine example of a small grey granite pot of the pre-dynastic period, with castings of gold". The Metropolitan received "a portion of a very wonderful glass vessel made under the 18th dynasty". [469]

On 2 May 1923 the Court Circular of *The Times* carried this historic announcement:

> The widow of the late Earl of Carnarvon wishes it to be known that she will be called henceforth Almina Countess of Carnarvon. She wishes also to thank her many kind friends for their affectionate messages of sympathy, which she hopes in time to acknowledge personally.

Almina was determined that her husband's death wouldn't see her lose the position she'd built in Society circles – a position built on the title of countess that had now, strictly speaking, passed to her son's wife. For Almina, her husband's death was an opportunity to reinvent herself, and what better start than with an impressive title?

With the succession of her son to the title of Earl of Carnarvon had passed the family seat at Highclere. The new Countess of Carnarvon quickly took over Almina's once beloved home, confidently removing her mother-in-law's favoured decor. A *Daily Mirror* journalist recorded: "Young Lady Carnarvon does not share the passion of her Mother in law for relics of Marie Antoinette and is modernizing her own particular rooms. The great hall is used as a living room...."

Almina decided she needed a place of her own and purchased the Alvie Lodge estate situated at Kincraig, Kingussie, Inverness-shire from Sir Robert Boville (Bertie) Whitehead (whose grandfather invented the torpedo). The Alvie Lodge estate comprised a "commodious mansion", Alvie Lodge, and 7,000 acres of land described as "very extensive, and provid[ing] fishing grouse shooting, deer-stalking and covert shooting" [470].

Almina made extensive renovations to Alvie Lodge, and set up at Balchurn (Home Farm) a model dairy farm. She also invested large sums in grouse shooting. The sums involved were greatly frowned on by the 6th Earl; in his memoirs he says his wasteful mother spent £150,000.

But Almina was not concerned by her expenditures to make her new home comfortable. This was the first residence she had owned herself, and it was a true home, a refuge. It was here that she ensconced herself after the unpleasant business of firing her chauffeur, Mr S. Cox. Almina's reasoning was simply that she was "forced to reduce staff at 1 Seamore Place", but it may have been the case that Cox was attempting to blackmail Almina over the disposal of Alfred's legacy; her pre-marital involvement with Colonel Dennistoun; her relationship with Dorothy; or (and this is a suggestion made by an intimate of Almina) the accusation that during the War she had obtained foodstuffs and fuel from unconventional marketeering sources.

A few months later, Almina was once again mourning the passing of family: this time, Aubrey Herbert, her dearest brother-in-law whom she deeply admired, secretly loved and would have preferred as a husband.[471] Aubrey died in London on 26 September 1923 aged 43. His death followed from blood poisoning after being rashly persuaded that his sight could be restored if he had all his teeth removed. [472] The 5th Earl's adventurous, heroic half-brother was described in many circles as being another victim of the King Tut curse. Although Aubrey was not superstitious, he had been anxious about the activities at Luxor, believing it unwise to interfere with the tombs of the dead. [473] He had famously remarked: "Something dreadful will surely happen in our family." [474]

The Carnarvons gathered for Aubrey's funeral at Brushford, Somerset. The coffin was draped in a Union Jack and was brought on a farm cart from Aubrey's seat at Pixton Park. His widow, Mary, their two daughters, his mother, Elsie, and his nephew, the 6th Earl, headed the mourners. Aubrey was remembered fondly as a maverick, an eccentric and a brilliant linguist and negotiator. Among Aubrey's finest hours was his gigantic feat during the First World War in Mesopotamia of arranging the exchange of a number of prisoners and the liberation of all badly wounded British soldiers to enable their return for medical care in India. Later the Canadian sculptor Cecil Howard produced a memorial tribute to him in stone in his last resting place near Pixton.

Soon, Almina returned to business as usual: installing Colonel Dennistoun in an expensive, fully furnished apartment in the West End of London at Sackville Street, and selling some pearls on behalf of Dorothy, who was pleading poverty. September also brought an opportunity to catch up with Howard Carter. Almina prepared the invitation list and was present in Oxford for the first of a number of lectures by Carter in the years that followed on his discoveries in Egypt. A similar event was held in London. [475] The lectures offered much-needed breathing space for Carter, as he was facing difficulties in Egypt with several authorities regarding access and clearance of the tomb. He went on to give further lectures in New York, where he was "celebrated and adulated like a star".[476]

Lady Evelyn Herbert's wedding

The Times of 16 July 1923 had announced the engagement of Lady Evelyn Herbert to Brograve Campbell Beauchamp (1897–1976) of the First Life Guards, the only surviving son of Sir Edward and Lady Beauchamp of 26 Grosvenor Place, London. The couple had wooed at a great distance – he in England, she in Egypt – and many in the Carnarvon family had worried that Captain Beauchamp would be put off by the curse of the Tutankhamun; after all, he had visited, with his parents, the tomb of Tutankhamun before the 5th Earl's fatal illness. But Brograve had not the faintest inclination of going back on his word. Brograve's sincerity was born of old-fashioned English gentlemen's charm and valour:

> If there is anything to this Pharaoh's curse my place is by your side to do all I can to protect you from danger; or, if worst comes to worst, to share it with you. And if it is all poppycock, why you need me just the same to keep you from being worried about the wild imaginings of a lot of slaves of superstition [477].

Lady Evelyn chose to stay with her Aunt Mary, Mrs Aubrey Herbert, and not with her mother at Seamore Place, during the time she arranged the matter of her trousseau. Almina was inanycase living away from London, she was bent on spending time gathering her thoughts in the Highlands of Scotland.[478]

The marriage took place on Monday 8 October 1923 at 2pm at St Margaret's, Westminster, which was decorated with standards of pale mauve chrysanthemums and Michaelmas daisies. The ceremony was conducted by Dr Pollock, the Bishop of Norwich, and the 6th Earl gave his sister away. The bride wore a draped gown of soft ivory charmeuse and, hanging from her shoulders, a train of the same material with a deep border of old Italian guipure lace. The full tulle veil was held by a Russian diadem of orange blossoms. Her bouquet comprised real orange-blossoms and a Brussels lace handkerchief. Her sole ornament was a diamond cross, which hung low over the corsage of her gown. She was attended to by 11 children. Hon. Bruce Ogilvy, an equerry to the Prince of Wales and the brother of the Earl of Airlie, was best man. Almina (who was dressed in a draped white gown with a long coat of ermine and a black feathered hat) hosted the reception at 1 Seamore Place.

Dorothy Dennistoun was a guest at the wedding – as was her ex-husband, the Colonel. When Almina was asked in Court whether she saw Dorothy at Evelyn's wedding she replied, "I saw her; she extended her hand and I took it." [479]

Keeping Dorothy at bay

Dorothy was complaining of being out in the cold. Despite being divorced for almost two years, she met Ian several times during 1923 and begged him to help her financially. Ian was torn: he very much needed to keep Almina onside because his comfortable lifestyle was all her doing; but he was still fond of his former wife.

Almina could see her companion's struggle. She later said, "I never realized that it was possible for any man to love a woman as he (the Colonel) loved Mrs Dennistoun." [480] Asked whether Ian's affection was infatuation, she replied, "Madly." [481] Almina authorised Ian to pay Dorothy £500 (from her own coffers), and the Colonel added a further £100 the following week towards repayment of advances she had made to him. But the payment was not enough. On 28 September 1923 Dorothy wrote to Ian:

> TIGER: For God's sake give me help I don't even ask to see you. if you don't it is only making things worse for both of us. I am desperate now. It is more urgent than you realise. All I ask of you is to speak to me as soon as you received this. I do not wish to annoy Almina or you I wish you all happiness ... I must have my affairs settled. [482]

The words "I do not wish to annoy Almina" would later be construed by Edward Marshall Hall as an attempt at blackmail.

Ian did not reply to Dorothy's pleas for any further assistance. On 2 October 1923 Dorothy wrote again:

> It is humiliating for me to ring you at your flat constantly and when I ask for you to be given an excuse. If you cannot help me it will mean me leaving the country, as I am down and out. I have £550 a year and cannot leave England on that...
>
> ...
>
> I am all alone. I have not a soul to fight for me. I have lost my two best friends through you, I have fought for you in the past. I know you have suffered and had bad times but I am a woman and have had a hard time and am suffering still more. I could not marry the man I liked through you. I cannot face life much longer. I have nothing to live for. I cannot leave it to the day of reckoning.[483]

Almina forbade the Colonel from offering any further support to Dorothy. Lawyers were brought in by all sides. Ian's tailored response was plain.

> Dear Dorothy: I have your letters and I am sorry to hear you are in such trouble. I am very busy and cannot see you or speak to you now. My solicitor has my affairs in hand and if you get your lawyer to communicate with him I am quite sure he will do all that is possible with regard to settlement. Since you divorced me I regarded the settlements as dead. At any rate the important point is that our lives are definitely severed and any communication you may wish to make to me must be through my solicitor. Yours, Tiger. [484]

Almina marries Dennistoun

A meeting took place on 10 October 1923 between Almina's solicitor Alfred Fryzer and Sir George Lewis, who was acting for Dorothy Dennistoun. Lewis had been charged by his client to establish when Almina and the Colonel intended to marry, going as far as to imply that they may have already married. Fryzer said he did not know and could not answer this. Later in court in 1925, Sir George denied that any questions were ever asked about Almina's proposed wedding to the Colonel.

Almina and the Colonel married in London soon after this meeting, on 19 December 1923. The notice of their intention to marry made headline news, and the speed at which Almina had buried one husband and so soon acquired another gave the gossip mongers rich pickings. The ceremony was conducted in a registry office in Princes Row, with barely a handful of onlookers. One report records:

> Lady Evelyn Beauchamp accompanied her mother to the office, and both were wrapped in velvet and fur coats, as the morning was cold. In addition to Lady Evelyn... the witnesses were Mr Alfred W Fryzer, solicitor, and Mr E R Frere.[485]

After the ceremony, the newlyweds travelled to Sidmouth, where they spent their honeymoon.

Almina's son, the 6th Earl, was horrified by his mother's remarriage. The Colonel was considered high maintenance, and the new Earl of Carnarvon was in financial peril as he attempted to hold on to his single family legacy, Highclere Castle. In his memoirs he describes his determination to keep Highclere going at all costs.

Dorothy was also unimpressed by the union, though she recognised what Ian's access to Almina's money could mean for her. She wrote a letter to Ian on 23 December 1923 that would later prove important. In the letter, she inferred that Almina had committed adultery with Ian in Lord Carnarvon's lifetime.

> You cannot imagine how difficult it is for me to write as I am doing. With regard to Almina I propose to say nothing. She was my friend and I valued her friendship intensely. Through you I lost it when you became her lover.[486]

This letter, which Dorothy showed to Sir George Lewis, was much debated in court in 1925. The implication that Almina and the Colonel were lovers before their marriage, or before the death of Lord Carnarvon, is not proven. However, some years afterwards Alice Butler, Almina's housekeeper for eight years including the period straddling the death of the Colonel in 1938, said she was told by Almina that "she had an affair with the Colonel with the full permission of the 5th Earl" [487].

Dorothy's accusing letter went on to refer to Colonel Dennistoun living in the lap of luxury, and demanding that he could afford to keep his financial promises to her, and quickly.

Almina's view was that Dorothy's correspondence was a blackmailing letter. There was now no alternative but to put the whole matter in the hands of the law. It was not a pleasant way to begin married life.

Almina was determined to keep up appearances, and that month she was one of a number of notable women who rallied to the call of Princess Louise, Duchess of Argyll, when she opened a sale at the Central Hall, Westminster in aid of the Church Army. Amongst the stallholders were the Duchess of Rutland, the Countess of Cromer, the Countess Annesley and the Marchioness Townsend.

Settling into married life

As the New Year dawned, Almina's mind was on money. On 28 January 1924 Dorothy Dennistoun issued a writ (through her solicitors Sir George Lewis of Lewis and Lewis) against her former husband for £13,035.18, as well as the elements of support she said Ian had promised her in April 1921, in lieu of her not seeking alimony in the French courts. Almina had no intention of settling the writ from Dorothy. However, Dorothy's legal action did give impetus to her plans to straighten out some financial matters.

The Colonel's finances from the funds transferred by the Countess were especially vulnerable to the legal process that Dorothy had begun. Almina immediately required Ian to close his deposit account at the London and Westminster Bank. At the same time she sought to turn a variety of her assets into cash, to settle other pressing matters.

Wherever Almina turned, bills were mounting. She faced demands from the Inland Revenue for legacy duty[488] on the money from Ian's bank account – which was actually the proceeds of Almina's art sales through the art dealer Joseph Duveen[489] and Christies of Alfred's Rothschild's prized Gainsboroughs. She was still financially committed to continuing the 5th Earl's concession (now reissued by the Egyptian authorities in her own name), with Howard Carter acting on the ground at Luxor to clear and catalogue the contents of Tutankhamun's tomb, and costs were mounting due to Carter's tantrums with the Egyptian authorities and some tough legal wrangles. There were also large scale renovations to pay for at Alvie Lodge in Scotland.

A sale was therefore arranged of the Carnarvon pearls and what Christies called "some fine French furniture from the collection of the late Mr Alfred de Rothschild now being sold as the property of a lady of title"[490]. The proceeds of this sale, together with the disposal of Alfred's portrait of Lady Hamilton for £17,000 on 29 February 1924[491], produced enough ready cash for Carter's running costs and making Alvie ready for occupation if and when a safe haven was needed for the Colonel to protect him from Dorothy's demands.

Almina was completely exhausted, and so her new husband took her on a cruise to South Africa for some much needed respite. The couple arrived back in England on Monday 21 April 1924 on the *Arundel Castle*. This trip had constituted their second honeymoon, an escape from the horrors of Egypt and Dorothy Dennistoun's increasing instability. However, the cost was that Almina missed her first grandchild's christening at Highclere Castle, an event which could have postponed but was not, suggesting it a hostile act by the 6th Earl towards his mother and stepfather. In Almina's place, Catherine's mother Mrs Wendell acted as godmother. A stunning photograph of Catherine, with her baby son appeared in the edition of *Country Life* for Saturday, 26 April 1924.

On 13 May Almina attended a musical soiree given at 18 Belgrave Square for members of the Vienna State Opera. On 21 May her mother-in-law, Mrs Dennistoun, presented her at Court to King George V and Queen Mary at Buckingham Palace. Then Almina and the Colonel travelled to Paris, spending time at The Ritz hotel, before heading to Alvie Lodge in Scotland, where the couple planned a long stay.

At Alvie Almina and her husband entertained a succession of guests, and enjoyed the shooting. One report said: "Shooting over Lady Carnarvon's Alvie Moors, Colonel Dennistoun bagged six and a half brace grouse in a couple of hours" [492]. In the nearby villages of Kincraig and Kingussie Almina became known with the locals, and she was much in demand for opening sales in aid of good causes. Today, more than 80 years later, Almina is remembered by a surviving member of the Williamson family who bought Alvie in 1927:

> The Countess of Carnarvon used to frequent Smith's General Store in our local village Kincraig where she used the phone. Mr Smith claimed to be shocked at the way she sat on his desk and swung her legs in what could have been considered a provocative manner....[493]

In September Ian's father, John Dennistoun, died, leaving the Colonel £10,000. It was the first decent sum of money he had in his own right that had not been given to him by Almina. The inheritance incensed Dorothy, and it seems extraordinary that Ian (now wealthy in his own right) failed to pay her off. Almina's resistance ruled that decision.

The wedding of the new Countess of Carnarvon's sister Philippa Wendell to the Earl of Galloway on 14 October 1924 at St Margaret's, Westminster brought some cheer, but no appearance by Almina and the Colonel. Almina did, however, attend a Herbert wedding in November at St James Church, Spanish Place when Conte Robert Lucchesi Palli, Duca della Grazia, eldest son of Prince and Princess di Campofranco, married Lady Hermione Herbert, the only daughter of the Earl and Countess of Powis.

Preparing for battle

As 1925 loomed it was clear that Dorothy's legal suit would have to proceed to a full hearing in court. She believed she had been forced to such lengths by Almina and the Colonel and their lawyers, since they would not give in to what they deemed was nothing less than blackmail. Dorothy was ready to draw blood.

Lady Helen Cunliffe-Owen, a great friend of the Carnarvons and also a friend of Dorothy, did everything she could to stop the matter from spilling over into open court; but her efforts were to no avail. Dorothy told Lady Cunliffe-Owen that she would be surprised if Almina fought the suit because whatever happened the Colonel must get the worst of it in terms of public humiliation and discredit.

In the later proceedings Dorothy denied that she had also told this same mutual friend that Almina would pay £100,000 to prevent the case coming into court.

1960s

1920s

1930s

1950s

The Faces of Almina, Countess of Carnarvon

1950s

1960s

1900s

The Faces of Almina, Countess of Carnarvon

Almina in the 1960s

The Faces of Almina, Countess of Carnarvon

Chapter 8
1925
Dennistoun v. Dennistoun: The Dustbin Case[494]

A scandalous law suit

By mid January of 1925 Howard Carter resumed work on the tomb of Tutankhamun (which had been closed since February 1924[495]) under a new Egyptian agreement granted to Almina with "a choice of duplicates of objects found there"[496] . Whilst this removed one pressure from the Dowager Countess of Carnarvon's life, another hung over her, and her husband, the Colonel, like the great Sword of Damocles: that of the impending court case of Dorothy Dennistoun versus Ian Dennistoun.

In early February Sir Hugo and Lady Helen Cunliffe-Owen, mutual friends of Almina and Dorothy Dennistoun[497], met (at the Hotel Metropole, Brighton) Sir Ellis Hume-Williams, the barrister briefed to act for Dorothy in her forthcoming litigation. In a final effort to avoid a public slanging match, Hugo and Helen Cunliffe-Owen sought a way out of the legal wrangling for Almina and her new husband. But their appeals made no difference, and in the weeks that followed both sides grimly prepared to fight out their differences in open court.

For while Ian would have settled the case privately out of court, by this point Almina and Dorothy were set upon a public airing of their grievances. For Dorothy, this case was not only about money, but also about revenge: Almina had cost her dearly in her coffers and her relationship with Ian; and in court she would brand her former friend "a love thief"[498]. And for Almina, compromise with this woman was simply not an option, and she was prepared to go to any lengths – including having her name dragged through the mire in public – not to concede a penny to her former friend.

Thus the London Law List – curiously labelled 'The Warned List' – included the suit of Dennistoun v Dennistoun with the first day's hearing scheduled for 3 March 1925. Almina attempted to delay proceedings and buy time for her husband's defence team by announcing she was suffering from influenza, but even her formidable charm and skills in manipulation couldn't stand in the way of the legal process. The case was opened as scheduled and the Dennistouns and their barristers made their way to the High Court of Justice, to resolve matters before the Special Jury in the King Bench Division.

As plaintiff, Dorothy's case was simple: that Ian had failed to provide for her despite having promised to do so. She claimed that Ian had entered into a verbal agreement to provide for her when his means permitted in consideration of her not seeking alimony in the French courts in 1921. She chose as her barrister Sir Ellis Hume-Williams, KC, who was a mastermind of contested divorce cases and a regular opponent of the Colonel's barrister, Sir Edward Marshall Hall, KC.

Marshall Hall was the obvious choice for Almina and Ian: he was the greatest criminal defence barrister of the era and they had long been friends (he had been one of Alfred de Rothschild's executors). Though the legendary lawman was not on best form because he was suffering from phlebitis of the leg "which made him irritable and prone to lose his temper" [499], he had excellent support from his defence team, particularly from up and coming barrister Norman Birkett, KC. Marshall Hall's defence on Ian's part was clear cut: that after Dorothy had rowed with Ian over his failure to provide for her, she had planned a relentless blackmail campaign to extract money.

Dorothy and Ian's "strange marriage"

Sir Ellis Hume-Williams began the case by setting the scene of Dorothy and Ian Dennistoun's "strange marriage"[500]. Sitting demurely in the witness box in a fashionable sealskin coat and turban, Dorothy claimed that her former husband had forced her into intimacy with a respected general in the British Army, effectively selling her for favours and money – an accusation that created a frisson of excitement in the room: who was this general? Finally, the judge ruled that in order to dispel suspicion on others, and because the general was deceased, his name could be given in open court, and Dorothy named her enforced lover as General Sir John Cowans, the renowned Quarter Master General of the British Army in the Great War, and Ian's former commanding officer. Dorothy was plain: "I am afraid that the price the General paid was that he obtained preferment for my husband. The price I paid was to become his mistress."[501]

In his defence, the Colonel denied Dorothy's claims that he had forced her adultery with Cowans and had used his wife's hold on Cowans to secure advancement. He declared:

I had no control over her whether she went to General Cowans or any other man. She was undoubtedly in love with him. She told me in Gibraltar that she made herself pretty for General Cowans. That was her mentality.

The Colonel maintained his position even in the face of letters purporting to have been written by him in which he orchestrated how best to retain Cowans' affections (conveniently, whilst Ian's letters were read to exhaustion, it emerged that Dorothy had destroyed all of her letters to him). The letters were clearly damning evidence in indicating Ian's own co-operation in Dorothy's affair. In one he declared: "Oh girlie darling. I hate you using that lovely body of yours as a gift"[502]; and in another:

> Now, darling, don't be depressed about the future. All will be well. I feel it. Don't bother about JC. The less you worry about him the longer you will keep him. The fact of your not always trying to keep him is quite sufficient to make him stick to you. ... Don't worry precious. It does not help and we have been in far tighter corners, and, after all we have gambled nothing away...[503]

The Colonel answered the charge under Birkett's steer that he could not do anything to stop Dorothy falling into Cowans' arms. The defence portrayed Ian as a victim of an adulterous Jezebel of a wife, rather than a co-conspirator in her affair. And to strengthen their case against Dorothy – particularly their argument that if an agreement to pay maintenance ever existed it would have had an implied term that Mrs Dennistoun should lead a chaste life – the defence called forth evidence that Cowans had not been the first nor the last of Dorothy's lovers.

The evidence, gleaned by detectives hired by Almina for the princely sum of £12,000 who had followed Dorothy around Europe for the past two years, was compelling. It was shown that she was involved with a variety of men during trips to Geneva, Madrid, Barcelona, Lisbon and Budapest. However innocent these associations may have been (and they certainly weren't all platonic relationships), it was clear that Dorothy's life was dominated by many male friends. To gasps in court Marshall Hall offered to read a list containing the names of "many other alleged admirers of Mrs Dennistoun"[504], but Mr Justice McCardie stopped him, remarking that "the alphabet had been heavily taxed in designating the men concerning Mrs Dennistoun"[505].

Ian's team demonstrated their client's helplessness in the fact of his wife's roving eye, and his benevolence in forgiving her adultery. While describing her affair with a young soldier, Oscar Senhouse[506], Colonel Dennistoun said:

> She never hesitated to tell me what she had done, and once she told me that if she wanted to make love to Senhouse I could not stop her. And when he was killed she cried for hours on my shoulder. I had no control over her morals at all.

The defence did their utmost to cast Dorothy as cold and manipulative, while she continued to play the role of a wronged woman, as this heated exchange between Dorothy and Marshall Hall illustrates:

> Marshall Hall: You heard the terms in which Sir Ellis spoke of your husband.
> Dorothy: Yes.
> Marshall Hall: You heard the condemnation that he thought fit to utter of him.
> Dorothy: Well, he said I suppose what most people would say.
> Marshall Hall: Did you hear the specific charge that he had forfeited the right, if he ever had it, to call himself a gentleman, and had lived on your immoral earnings?
> Dorothy: I heard it said.
> Marshall Hall: Do you approve of it?
> Dorothy: I think it is a very unfair question.
> Marshall Hall: Madam, fair or unfair, I propose to repeat it: do you approve of that charge?
> Dorothy: I was fond of my husband.
> Marshall Hall: How much do you think a woman who loved her husband would pay not to have this case in open court?
> Dorothy: It is a great deal harder for me than my husband thinks. I am a woman alone, and he is a man.
> Marshall Hall: A woman alone?
> Dorothy: I am a woman alone.
> Marshall Hall: Is that true?
> Dorothy: Absolutely and entirely.

The world watches

Following these first days of the hearing, on 6 March 1925 the King's private secretary wrote to the Lord Chancellor:

> Dear Lord Chancellor, The King feels sure that you will share his feelings of disgust and shame at the daily published discreditable and nauseating evidence in the Dennistoun case. His Majesty asks you whether it would not have been possible to prevent the case coming into Court either by refusal of the Judge to try it, or by the joint insistence of the respective Counsels to come to an arrangement, especially when, apparently the question at issue was one of minor importance? The King deplores the disastrous and far reaching effects throughout all classes and on all ranks of the Army of the wholesale Press advertisement of this disgraceful story. Yours very truly, Stamfordham. [507]

But even the King himself couldn't halt the public spectacle unfolding. As events unfolded in court, Britain became fiendishly excited by Dennistoun v Dennistoun, and the case was also given top billing in newspapers for several weeks in America, Canada, Australia and on the Continent. One commentator said the case was "of no more real importance than the conduct of two or three dogs in the gutter"[508]. Yet despite that remark, the court proceedings held a curiosity that extended to thousands of people (mostly women) who wanted to know every detail of the law suit. In consequence, the Dennistouns became the hot topic of conversation at dinner parties, London clubs and social gatherings, especially among the gentry and at Court. The attraction? The racy undercurrent of sex and blackmail, and the many skeletons unearthed during the proceedings.

Soon long queues of sensation seekers appeared outside the court. One report said: "more than two score of women waited outside the doors of the law courts. Some had equipped themselves with blankets and flasks of hot tea, for the day was bitterly cold."[509] Each day the Court "was crammed with mink and orchids"[510]. Judge McCardie, well known for his spark and wit on the bench, complained that he was being treated like a Mayfair hostess. He was overwhelmed by the requests from peers and peeresses for seats. Court officials were forced to ban the use of opera glasses in court by those who were able to be seated but who craved a closer look at the parties.

After years of working to make a name for herself among the English gentry, Almina had finally succeeded – but at what cost?

The Colonel under attack

When Ian took his place in the witness box, Almina looked on anxiously with her son Henry beside her for moral support. Colonel Dennistoun's examination was interrupted for several days because of illness (a Harley Street specialist gave evidence of the Colonel's ragged state of health), which gave the defence team time for a reorganisation: now Birkett stepped to the fore to allow the increasingly ill Marshall Hall to rest.

The Colonel was portrayed as an innocent, but the prosecution were quick to probe the validly of this image. They exposed Ian's adultery with two French women between 1918 and 1920, and an unnamed American woman (details of this affair would explode later), and questioned Ian's purported helplessness in the face of Dorothy's relationship with Cowans. When Hume-Williams enquired why Ian had done nothing about the affair, Ian said he had wanted to protect Dorothy:

> Colonel Dennistoun: I did not want everyone to know that my wife was an adulteress.
> Hume-Williams: But surely Colonel Dennistoun you could have protected her without telling everyone that your wife was an adulteress?
> Colonel Dennistoun: What would you do?
> Hume-Williams: What would I do?
> Colonel Dennistoun: Yes.
> Hume-Williams: I would have told my wife that if she did it again I would divorce her. I would have gone up to London and assaulted General Cowans – and to hell with my career!

As to his military appointments, these, said Birkett, were unremarkable but "not a single thing that the Colonel got that he would not have got in the ordinary turn of events"[511]. But in a later exchange with Birkett Ian admitted to Cowans' influence:

> Birkett: Did you know when you came back from Gibraltar that you were to get a better appointment?
> Colonel Dennistoun: I knew that before I went.
> Birkett: Through Sir John Cowans?
> Colonel Dennistoun: Yes, they were all due to him.

His adultery and Cowans' favour now apparent, Ian nonetheless strongly maintained the other key argument in his case, denying that he had ever made any promise to Dorothy to provide support following their divorce.

Almina had been present for some of the case, and had displayed emotional reactions at times. At the reading aloud of one of Ian and Dorothy's love letters, Almina became "quite distressed, covering her face with her hands and wept, but recovered after taking a drink of water"[512]. Then when the court heard that Dorothy's friendship with Almina had ended when Ian became "her lover", "Dowager Countess Carnarvon bowed trembling shoulders and covered her face as the letter was read" [513], and then "buried her head in her arms for fully five minutes before she regained control of herself"[514]. How much such displays represented genuine emotion and how much attempts to create sympathy is open to interpretation.

The day Almina was called as a witness she was elegant and sombre in a black dress and black cloche hat. She gripped the rail of the box with the fingers of her left hand on which two wedding rings were plainly visible. She spoke with deliberation.

After explaining how she had met Dorothy[515] and come to meet the Colonel and set him up in a luxurious flat during the 5th Earl's lifetime, she threw further light on the large sums of money paid into the Colonel's bank account from the sale of pictures – explaining that the money was not his. She was later reduced to weeping after admitting that she had given this "second hand husband" over £100,000 to "uphold his dignity"[516].

She went on to describe the attacks on Ian as "wicked and abominable"[517]. She exclaimed: "He is a simple soul and that describes him absolutely. He was a tool in Mrs Dennistoun's hands; absolute putty. He had no will; he was a mere rag." [518] She then declared: "I love him with all my heart, soul and body." [519] An ensuing episode of near-swooning, with Almina dramatically recovering her composure with the aid of smelling salts, brought the questioning – to some parties' surprise – to an end.

Closing speeches

Various other witnesses having been called, the barristers were finally ready to give their closing speeches.

The plaintiff's barrister said that in the early days of the action, before it reached court, Dorothy might have accepted a small sum, but the position had changed. Hume-Williams blasted the Colonel's camp: "But now how many thousands could compensate her for her ordeal in the witness-box for several days, for charges made against here, for the mud thrown, for being charged with being a liar and a blackmailer?" [520]

In repudiating Birkett's allegations of blackmail further Sir Hume-Williams declared that the word was merely a parrot-cry and that in fact the whole defence had been built up with the purpose of frightening Dorothy Dennistoun out of court. At this juncture Almina (who was sitting with the Colonel at his solicitor's table) commented quietly but in a voice audible throughout the courtroom " It's a lie." [521]

Norman Birkett was briefed to close the defence. (It was considered that Marshall Hall had lost credibility with the jury over a number of legal gaffes, not least in revealing information obtained under client confidentiality over the matter of the Dorothy–Cowans motor car affair). Birkett referred to "the unspeakable anguish" [522] undergone during the proceedings by the Colonel and Almina. They had been forced to spend more money than would satisfy Dorothy rather than submit to accusations that were entirely unfounded. Birkett postulated that the jury might perhaps think that now Colonel Dennistoun had money, he might well give some to Dorothy, as she had none. He cautioned:

> Remember, Lady Carnarvon had married the Colonel and was in love with him. Was it natural for her to say "I give you the money, you give it to the woman who divorced you." No, that was repugnant to morals, common sense and decency.

On the accusation of blackmail from Dorothy's side Birkett was at his best:

> Blackmail is a hideous term. It takes many forms, but perhaps it is most hideous in the form of such an action like this. Let the jury think of the torture this has meant for Colonel Dennistoun. He has faced it, knowing what it would mean, because of one dastardly phrase in a letter from his former wife: "since you and Almina, Countess of Carnarvon, became lovers." [523]

Judge's summing up

Dorothy arrived at almost exactly the same time as Almina and the Colonel to hear the judge's summing up. Dorothy was dressed in a black fur coat and black velvet hat, and Almina carried a bouquet of violets and wore a sprig of white heather.

Judge McCardie began by declaring that "cases like this do not in any way represent the general life of the well-to-do people of England" [524]. McCardie was careful to point out that Ian and Dorothy's divorce was legitimate, and that in consequence the marriage of Almina and Colonel Dennistoun was "binding". At this pronouncement a pleased smile passed over Almina's face, and she pressed Ian's hand as she glanced up towards the press box.

The judge made clear that the jury should try to "find what was a fair compensation" [525] to Dorothy. For the purposes of assessing damages the jury were warned that they must not consider material the conduct of the Colonel in permitting his wife's liaison with General Cowans. They should also disregard the moral character of Dorothy in the past or the future.

In conclusion the judge added: "Whatever Mrs Dennistoun's character may be she does seem to have helped her husband readily. But the question is not whether she helped him readily and generously or not, but whether the claims are legal against him." [526]

The jury retired.

The verdict and judgment

On 24 March 1925 the final scenes began to unfold. Many unemployed men lined up at daybreak to sell their places in the queue for high prices to those whose liveried chauffeurs drove them to court in costly cars. Inside, neither Almina nor the Colonel were present to hear the jury's verdict; only Dorothy sat and waited, in "absolute composure"[527]. Finally, after fifteen days of sensational revelations, the world's news services telegraphed the verdict delivered by the jury after three hours of deliberations: an apparent win for Dorothy with damages awarded of £5,000.

The jury accepted that the Colonel had made a verbal agreement to assist his former wife from time to time, albeit he had not (they viewed) made the agreement set out in Dorothy's plaint. But they tempered their verdict by adding (in answer to one of many questions put to them by Judge McCardie) that the Colonel was not bound to support Dorothy if she became the wife or mistress of her lover Bolin, the Spaniard, or the wife of another man. Yet they found that the Colonel had, before the issue of the writ in the case, been financially able to support his former wife and decided that the sums she had advanced him, which he claimed were gifts, before their divorce were in fact loans which must be repaid.

But before Dorothy could celebrate victory, the judge delivered a "reserved judgment" in which he dismissed the jury's findings, ruling that the alleged agreement between Ian and Dorothy was void and could not be enforced by law. There was, he said, "no binding agreement to support her". He accordingly denied Dorothy the £5,000 in damages awarded by the jury. He only accepted that Dorothy was entitled to recover certain sums loaned by her to her former husband, a total of £472.18.

It was estimated that the trial cost over £40,000, much of which fell later on Almina. The case was a national joke: the magazine *Punch* published a full-page cartoon satirising what it dubbed "The Dustbin Case". The ailing Marshall-Hall had done himself no favours in agreeing to take the case due to his friendship with Almina, which Hume-Williams would later unkindly say had "warped his independence and I think his judgement"[528]. There was only one true winner in the case: Norman Birkett, who had made a name for himself in the legal world.

The case of Dennistoun v Dennistoun would not fade fast from public memory, due in part to the deaths, in the following few years, of several key players in the case, which led to mutterings of some curse associated with it. Marshall Hall had been ailing for some time, and his death aged 68 in February 1927 wasn't a huge shock. But then, in August of 1927, Dorothy Dennistoun's solicitor, Sir George Lewis, died at Territet in Switzerland having been knocked down by an express train. Whether he had slipped and fallen or committed suicide was hotly debated. In April 1933, Justice McCardie committed suicide by shooting himself. Finally, in January 1934, Lady Helen Cunliffe-Owen, who had tried to broker a deal between Almina and Dorothy, died aged 37. [529] In retrospect, it seems clear that nothing sinister connected these deaths; but with Almina already associated with the legend of the curse of King Tut, gossipmongers were bound to enjoy finding meaning in such a mortality rate.

The aftermath of the Dennistoun case

The Dennistoun court case was among the last high profile cases in which spouses washed their dirty laundry in public. Despite a strong protest campaign by the press itself, Parliament passed the Judicial Proceedings (Regulation of Reports) Act in 1926 prohibiting the detailed reporting of divorce cases in newspapers.[530]

But for Colonel Dennistoun, the damage was done. At 46 Colonel Dennistoun remained a soldier, due for recall until he reached the age of 55. He had been retired to pension in 1920, but following the case the Army was quick to review its position. The internal report dated 8 April 1925 in Dennistoun's surviving service file urged condemnation:

> As a general rule the Army Council are opposed to interfering in purely domestic matters, such as a divorce case, but in the present case it seems... that this officer's conduct during the period under review has been such as not only to bring disgrace upon himself but also upon the Army. ... [T]here can be no doubt from the evidence given or admitted by Dennistoun that he was aware that his wife was the mistress of the late General Cowans, that far from taking steps to put a stop to this, he actually accepted money from her whilst this state of affairs existed to his knowledge and further that he received during that period at least one appointment through the influence of the officer whose mistress his wife was.[531]

The recommendation was that a letter be sent to the Colonel referring to the state of affairs following the court proceedings. The letter would say that before any decision was taken "as to why he should not be removed from the Army for misconduct" [532], the Army Council were prepared "to consider any statement he may desire to offer." [533]

The Colonel anticipated the Army would come down on him. On 4 May 1925 (before the Army's own letter was issued) he wrote to the Secretary of State from 1 Seamore Place, London:

> Having regard to the reports that have appeared in the public press of the case Dennistoun v Dennistoun in which I was defendant I feel I should be acting in the best interests of the army if I asked as I now do that His Majesty be graciously pleased to accept my resignation of my commission

as one of His Reserve of Officers. I desire to add that I have been greatly misrepresented both in the reports and comments that have appeared in the Press and that I have been attacked upon insufficient and misrepresented material. Under the circumstances however I feel that I am taking the right course and if His Majesty is graciously pleased to ascent to my request I am prepared to waive any claim I have to a pension. [534]

When the Colonel received the Army's letter (also of 4 May) he acknowledged it and referred to his own offer to resign. The King readily approved Dennistoun's resignation on 7 May, and two days later the Army wrote to the Colonel approving the resignation of his commission, which it said would appear in the *London Gazette*. His retired pay was suspended. Although Dennistoun's army file made it clear that he "retained no rank"[535] after his resignation, he used the title of Colonel or Lieutenant Colonel for the remainder of his life, without ever being challenged.[536]

Despite the Colonel's public humiliation, it was Almina who suffered the most after Dennistoun v Dennistoun, both in money and in mind. All she had to compensate her for the painful humiliations of the case was a widespread sympathy for her loyalty to the Colonel. But the higher ranks of British society were not so generous. The daily revelations and insinuations had caused many people to break off their friendships with Almina. And before the Countess could catch her breath, yet another scandal about her husband erupted.

The Lois Meredith scandal

Lois Meredith was an American film actress[537] with whom the Colonel had enjoyed a brief intimate relationship at some point between his divorce from Dorothy in 1921 and his subsequent marriage to Almina in 1923. Ian had been flattered to have a pin-up as a girlfriend, and had showered the actress with gifts and promises – including an offer of marriage. During the affair Ian wrote Lois over a hundred letters, and it was this evidence that Lois's American lawyers were ready to produce in a claim against the Colonel for breach of promise and defamation – a magnificently well-timed suit right after the Dennistoun v Dennistoun judgment.

In the light of the costly and disastrous decision to go all the way on Dennistoun v Dennistoun, and with the Colonel's confession that the letters were both sleazy and incriminating, this time Almina ordered her lawyers to arrange an urgent out-of-court deal. A flurry of newspaper headlines in America and in Paris [538] culminated in a financial settlement being agreed by Almina's lawyers to heal Lois's "broken heart and injured feelings"[539]. A condition of the settlement was that the original letters written by the Colonel and any copies were to be "consigned to the flames"[540] in the presence of Almina's lawyers.

Luckily for Almina, the British press failed to get wind of the scandal. But nevertheless this was the last straw for the Countess and she was livid at the ordeal she had been through that year. Thus far her new marriage had been on a rocky footing: although the marriage was one of convenience to suit Almina's financial dealings, she probably did love Ian and yearned for happiness with him. But her husband had brought little in the way of security for the future, and now she was faced with the great challenge of generating funds to cover the costs of litigation of not one but two of her husband's former lovers.

Chapter 9
1925–1929
Getting Back to Status Quo Ante Bellum

The sale of the century

After all the mud-raking and costly litigation, Almina and the Colonel decided to keep their distance from London and retreated to their estate at Alvie, Scotland in April 1925. They remained self-exiled here even when another grandchild, Lady Anne Penelope Marian Herbert (1925–1990), the only daughter of the 6th Earl and Catherine Wendell, was christened at Highclere Church on 12 April 1925.[541]

The 6th Earl may well have preferred his mother out of his way for this happy occasion. He was angry with Almina over her marriage to Ian and her dire financial state which, as far as Henry saw it, had been caused by her pouring good money into bad reputations for no other reason than her stubborn refusal to settle with Dorothy. And while his mother was squandering the family's money, the 6th Earl was crumbling under financial pressure himself and faced the threat of losing his beloved home, Highclere.

Backed into a corner, the Carnarvons had little choice but to raise capital by selling possessions: for Lord Carnarvon, some prized family portraits by Gainsborough [542]; for Almina, more of Alfred's legacy. And so it was that mother and son put their differences aside to arrange a joint auction at Christies to be held over four days from 19 to 22 May 1925.

It was the most remarkable event of its kind for the array of lots on offer, and the sale captured the imagination of the collecting world. Even Queen Mary attended a preview showing of the items.[543] For the first time in history, the last day of the sale was broadcast on radio, from a microphone at the side of the auctioneer.[544] The buyers sat at two long tables in front of the auctioneer, and green-coated attendants brought the lots to them for examination – on the first three days, a choice collection of objets d'art, porcelain and furniture, and on the last day, important pictures and drawings.[545]

Parting with several items was a wrench for Almina, but there was no time for sentimentality . A much-loved miniature cabinet, just over eight inches high and overlaid with flower sprays in rubies, emeralds and diamonds, raised £862 – more than £100 an inch. *A Book of Hours*, a tiny French manuscript dating from 1532 [546] in a remarkable jewelled binding that had been a wedding gift from Alfred de Rothschild, made 2,000 guineas. [547] *The Raphael Missell*, Alfred's legacy to Lord Carnarvon, (in which he expressed " the hope that he will regard it strictly an heirloom" [548]was simply sold off to the highest bidder.

In all, (according to *The Times*) £129,398 was realised. This sale was augmented by another at Christies on 1 July 1925 featuring further possessions of Almina and the Colonel, which at last reduced the financial pressures upon the couple. [549] On 10 July 1925 Almina's solicitors paid over a cheque to Inland Revenue for £90,000 arrears of legacy duty.[550]

Following the Christies sale, Almina was delighted by the announcement of the safe arrival of a new grandchild on 11 July – Patricia Evelyn Beauchamp born to her daughter, Lady Evelyn Beauchamp. Lady Evelyn's pregnancy had been difficult, and the stress of the Dennistoun case had not helped matters – indeed, Lady Evelyn's husband Sir Brograve was by now furious by his mother-in-law's conduct, which had damaged his own reputation by association, and was doing all he could to stand separate from her in social circles.

By August 1925 Almina had reached the end of her tolerance for being at the heart of conflict and blame, and she sought sanctuary and respite in the spas of Germany and Austria. Notably, she travelled alone.[551] Although she must have revelled in the freedom and peace of a life away from her family and England, she returned home in October to attend her new granddaughter Patricia's christening at St Margaret's, Westminster. Almina mourned the passing of the Queen Mother, Queen Alexandra, the widow of King Edward VII, who had died at Sandringham in November 1925. [552]

1926

Almina and the Colonel continued to hide out at Alvie for much of 1926. She whiled away the time studying horse racing. She retained ownership of several race horses including Mothersyll, whose profile is recorded in horse-breeding records. The 6th Earl points out in his memoirs that whilst he inherited the horse stud at Highclere, Almina owned the bloodstock. This was a further irritant, since the stud's future depended on its successful breeding record. Instead of joining forces with his mother, Henry sought, at further cost he could ill afford, to make arrangements with other owners of bloodstock to sire the next generation of Highclere's horses.

While Almina lay low, her daughter-in-law Catherine Wendell, the 6th Countess of Carnarvon, did her best to keep the family name upheld. She was often photographed in fashionable outfits on her husband's arm at the racing events they regularly attended[553] (they both enjoyed horse racing, and also both bet heavily on the horses, often making large losses). She also carved a name for herself as a devoted mother, "one of the younger matrons of London's noble Society set" [554], through frequent coverage in newspapers and journals, especially in her native America, showing her out and about with her children, Lord Porchester and Lady Penelope[555].

But behind closed doors, Catherine was far from the happy mother and wife she pretended to be. The 6th Earl was not easy to live with; he had a roaming eye for the opposite sex. He treated Catherine much like one of his horses, and she felt constantly controlled. The 6th Earl's cruelty extended to taunting her about the poor extent of her pedigree, reducing her to a "housewife Countess"[556]. This made Catherine feel worthless, and she sought relief in the consumption of alcohol. In December 1926 Catherine had an abdominal operation purportedly for appendicitis (a common Society euphemism for an abortion) performed in a Leeds nursing home by Almina's close medical friend Sir Berkeley Moynihan. [557]

Almina snubs the British Museum

In February of the following year, 1927, Almina was involved in a motor car accident on the Albert Embankment. She was slightly hurt, but her doctors were satisfied of her condition after a "restless night"[558]. She was soon back on her feet and arranging yet another sale of property that would plump her purse: her deceased first husband's Egyptian artefacts. On 21 February 1927 it was announced that the Metropolitan Museum of Art in New York had acquired the 5th Earl of Carnarvon's private Egyptian collection, comprising over 1,400 pieces, valued at over £50,000. This collection was the rakings of excavations and Carter's purchases before the discovery of Tutankhamun.[559]

The sale was highly controversial. In the 5th Earl's will he had "suggested" that the nation (namely the British Museum) be given first refusal of the Collection at £20,000. The use of "suggest" made all the difference between the items being retained in Britain and them going elsewhere. One commentator remarked: "If instead of the word 'suggest' Lord Carnarvon had written 'direct' Almina, Lady Carnarvon would have had no discretion in the matter." [560] As it was Almina, as owner, had a perfect right to do as she thought fit and sell it to the highest bidder.

Sir Frederick Kenyon (1863–1952), director of the British Museum, told the press: "This is a tragedy... the Collection was not offered to us."[561] Kenyon continued, "Of course Lady Carnarvon is a free agent, but it is a great loss to the country."[562] Howard Carter was equally appalled by the sale, but Almina was resolute: there was no room for sentimentalism where money was concerned. Only the 6th Earl was supportive: after all, he hadn't enjoyed storing the artefacts at Highclere given the King Tut curse.[563]

Alfred House

Almina's sale of the 5th Earl's Egyptian collection was about more than just raising funds to pay off debts: now, Almina had a new aim: to return to nursing and the one time in her life she had felt she had a purpose by setting up her own nursing home, Alfred House, as a tribute to Alfred de Rothschild. This was a quest that gave Almina *joie de vivre*, and she was prepared to go to great lengths to fund her dream. Thus she put her estate: "of forest and moor, salmon and trout fishing and one of the best mansions at Alvie, near Kingussie in the Highlands of Scotland, with 7650 acres" [564]up for sale. Almina was only too happy to sell the estate, which she considered increasingly inhospitable to the ailing Colonel Dennistoun, who was in declining health and needed specialist nursing care. In truth, Almina was keen to get back to living in London.

Not everyone was jubilant about Alfred House. The Colonel's view of his wife's further ambitions is not clear, but he knew he had to be loyal: Almina was paying for his nursing care (not providing it herself, we may note; indeed, although they were far from being strangers, they had no fixed abode together for any length of time).[565] The 6th Earl considered Alfred House (as the 5th Earl had viewed Almina's wartime hospitals) with consternation. As for the professional critics of Alfred House, the *British Journal of Nursing* of November 1926 declared:

> The astounding announcement has been made in an evening paper that Almina, Countess of Carnarvon (whose devotion to the dictates of Eros cost her the loss of fabulous treasures) will view with "Sister Agnes" and open a Nursing Home with the support of a celebrated surgeon[566] – who, as a Member of the council of the College of Nursing Ltd, should surely have ere now denied the soft impeachment if it was not true. ... It is high time an Act of Parliament was in force for the Registration of Nursing Homes, making such ridiculous proposals impossible.

As usual undeterred by criticism, Almina steamed ahead with her plans and hired a team of over 300 workmen under the direction of architect James Naylor to rebuild 7–9 Portland Place[567], London, which would be home to Alfred House. The conversion involved adapting two old houses, originally built by Nash, and cost tens of thousands of pounds.

On Saturday 2 July 1927 Almina threw a party for her workmen at a fashionable restaurant in Holborn. Colonel Dennistoun joined Almina for the celebrations. The Countess addressed the men and told them how much she appreciated the way they had executed their work. She was frequently interrupted by cheers. She shook hands with each man after dinner and they rose up and gathered around her for autographs. One report states:

> Lady Carnarvon complied with the request [for autographs] until her hand ached so much that she could write no more and she took the remaining menu cards, with the names and addresses of the owners, promising to autograph them at a more leisurely moment and forward them by post. [568]

Then, on 11 July, the day of the grand opening arrived. Almina wore a flowered chiffon dress with a fashionable hat and greeted her guests warmly. Among the large number attending were Sir Ernest Hatch, Chairman of University College Hospital, Almina's son and Lady Evelyn Beauchamp, Lady Burrell (1885–1966) and her daughter Dreda (later Lady Tryon; 1909–2002).

Comments about the home were complimentary, and showed that the Countess had spared no expense:

Nurses in cheery red and white uniforms greeted the visitors who were allowed the privilege of looking over the home, which has been planned on the lines of the highest scientific efficiency combined with home life.[569]

One of the most luxurious of such institutions in the world... [570]

It is equipped with every conceivable amenity of modern civilisation. Each room has, of course double windows and electric heating, doors and lifts are noiseless. No sharp corners exist to harbour dust. [571]

Other reviews commented on Almina's personal input. The 'As I See Life' column of the *Daily Mirror* remarked:

She [Almina] works very much indeed in the nursing home and almost any time of the day you find her there dressed in matron's garb directing the organisation of the home. She wears pretty dresses of dainty pasted shades especially mauve and wears a cap like all her nurses, who by the way are more than ordinary good looking.

Lady Carnarvon recently gave a dance at her home in Mayfair and among the most attractive guests were her nurses.

"Who is that gorgeous looking creature?" I heard a man ask her and Lady Carnarvon was able to confess that the beautiful woman in gold lame low backed dress with magnificently coiffured hair was one of her best nurses.

One testimony sums up the luxury of Alfred House as seen by a visitor, and illuminates further on Almina's role:

Gran is in a nursing home in Portland Place. I thought I'd wandered into the Berkeley (Hotel) when I arrived and was confronted by a Hall Porter in Medals and uniform. It's the home kept by Lady Carnarvon who sweeps among the sick in pure white with a nurses cap upon her head; such an angel of mercy, what she knows of illnesses I can't think... [572]

Almina recruited nurses from Ireland, just as she had done in the Great War. One of these was Eileen Lovett, of Clifden, Galway, who recalled:

I went to an exclusive nursing home for lords and ladies in the West End of London, run by Lady Carnarvon. You had to be easy on the eye to get a job in a place like that. I'd a gorgeous pink crimplene uniform and the food was magnificent, but we only got a pound a week.[573]

Another Irish nurse of note was Miss Mary Gentles, originally from Jamaica, who worked at Alfred House for two and half years. [574]

Speaking in 1939, after returning to Jamaica, Mary's memory of Almina was of " a very kind and generous woman, she is much beloved by all who come in contact with her. The patrons of this hospital are mostly members of royalty and aristocrats. I left Prince Paul of Yugoslavia there recovering from a recent illness." [575]

Almina had fulfilled a dream – a personal tribute to her benefactor Alfred de Rothschild. And it was Alfred House that would ultimately restore her reputation in London Society.

Beneficent Almina

With Alfred House now up and running, Almina launched into another public relations exercise. Having installed the Colonel with a nurse at Seamore Place, she toured her remaining leased lands in Devon, on the Pixton Estate, which was property left to her in the 5th Earl's will. In August she dazzled and charmed 250 of her West Somerset and Exmoor tenants at a lunch at Brushford. Responding to a toast of her health and a reference to the 5th Earl Almina was outwardly loyal:

> Nobody in the world loved Lord Carnarvon more than I did. His life was just sacred to me and all he wanted and would have wanted for his dear people in the future I am trying to put into execution, though I feel it is in a very humble way.[576]

The following year, 1928, Almina decided that the Colonel needed further rehabilitation and a change of scene. He still craved a place where he could shoot, fish and play golf. Accordingly Almina took a let on The Barracks, Rannoch, Perthshire, a homestead at the far end of Loch Rannoch, which boasted some of the best fishing in the Highlands.[577] The advantage over Alvie (which was sold in 1927) was that the London train went directly via Rannoch station. [578] This meant she could safely leave the Colonel to convalesce in more appealing surrounds, and travel back and forth as necessary.

In her new hometown, news of the Countess's beneficence spread fast, largely for her generous tips of ten shillings (and often more) to station porters and station masters during her regular trips by train. Henry Keown-Boyd, the author of *The Lion and the Sphinx: The Rise and Fall of the British in Egypt 1882–1956*, whose parents spent much of their lives in Egypt and knew the Carnarvons well (Keown-Boyd's godfather was Almina's unfriendly son-in-law Sir Brograve Beauchamp), remembered Almina as "a small, vivacious and (over) generous person". He affectionately recalls being at the receiving end of Almina's tips:

> As a boy I knew her quite well as she was a great friend of my parents. In fact I was born in her nursing home in London. When I was about eighteen I remember driving us from our home in Herefordshire to catch the London train at Newport. A First Class compartment had been booked for her and on arrival at the station we were greeted by the Station Master and a porter. As she was handed onto the train she turned and gave a pound to the Station Master, ten bob to the Porter and ten bob to me. Noblesse oblige! [579]

Then tragedy struck at Highclere on 15 July 1928, when Reginald Lee Wendell, Catherine's brother, died suddenly of a meningeal haemorrhage while playing tennis. He was just 29. Almina attended the funeral at Newbury on the 19th July, keen to show how much she truly cared about her daughter-in-law, and to mend what bridges she could with her son, who was still furious with his mother for her carefree spend, spend, spend philosophy and the disgrace she had brought on the family, as he saw it, by marrying Dennistoun. But Almina's efforts were to little avail. Still, the 6th Earl copied his mother's example of maintaining a cheerful demeanour in public.[580] Leaving his wife at home to grieve and drink herself into oblivion, he stepped out to race meetings such as Kempton Park with his sister, Lady Evelyn.

Admired once more

Meanwhile, Almina busied herself flitting building up an active social life to soothe the ruffled feathers of Society spectators and to outdo her nemesis Dorothy Dennistoun, (who was by now remarried) and stepped out in all the smart dances clubs, gaining praise from the gossip columns for her fashion sense; and managing her beloved Alfred House. The Countess took an exceptional level of interest in the goings-on at her nursing home: never a lady with a faint heart, she even took to helping out in the operating theatre:

> Lady Carnarvon had no training in medicine or surgery at all, but in every case where Moynihan operated she came into the operating theatre gowned up. It was her job to pick the swabs off the floor and hang them up; she was a great talker, but she kept her mouth shut in the theatre. ... Lady Carnarvon was a really kind person. [581]

Occasionally there was a medical man who did not always appreciate Almina's assertive approach or her busy-body role in the theatre. She had a difficult professional relationship with one surgeon, lecturer, academic and respected physiologist, Wilfred Trotter (1872-1930).[582] He was renowned for having a harsh temper in the operating theatre and raising his voice; Almina disliked him intensely, and with good reason. She often found herself on the receiving end of his tantrums during which he would throw medical instruments and bloody swabs in all directions - sometimes aiming them directly at her. [583]

But Almina's very personal, hands-on approach gave many of her charges extra confidence in surrendering themselves to treatment. One reporter commented: "Almina, Lady Carnarvon's small bird like, white clad form may be seen flittering constantly about the corridors." [584] Another added:

> Almina Countess of Carnarvon is rarely late in arriving at her nursing home in Portland Place in the morning, no matter how much she entertains the evening before. Sometimes her own dances do not end before 4 am, but by nine o'clock she is fresh and apparently unwearied at her nursing home. [585]

Her enthusiasm for her nursing work sometimes overtook Almina's social obligations, but she remained a notable Society hostess of the era and did her best to blend both sides of her life. Her elegant appearance belied the hard work she put in at Alfred House: Daphne Fielding (Marchioness of Bath, sometime Viscountess Weymouth; 1904–1997) recalled seeing Lady Carnarvon during her convalescence at the nursing home: "A most attractive woman, Lady Carnarvon was looking particularly beautiful that day, dressed in one of the pastel-coloured, short sleeved silk dresses she always wore, which reminded one of the tennis courts rather than the operating theatre." [586]

Part of the work of arranging Almina's guest list was left to her social secretaries. One of the women who performed this task during the mid to late 1920s was Dorothy Wilde, the niece of Oscar. Dorothy's cousin Vyvyan Holland (Oscar's son) recalls in his book *Time Remembered After Père Lachaise*:

> My cousin Dorothy (Dolly) Wilde, the daughter of Willie Wilde, Oscar's brother, became social secretary to Almina, Lady Carnarvon in the twenties. To be social secretary was no sinecure. At her house in Seamore Place at the end of Curzon Street... she would give impromptu parties. On one wet Sunday she asked Dolly to arrange a dance for that night. Dolly set to and collected about 40 people to dinner, with a further 40 to come in after dinner to dance. [587]

Dolly Wilde was one of the era's bohemians, a witty lesbian, and for a time another of Almina's adoptees. Almina gave her money and support when she was in personal despair. Dolly's health and mental state were very often unstable but she was, like Almina, someone "who understood the joys and miseries of the human heart". According to *Truly Wilde*, Joan Schenkar's candid biography of Dolly, Almina "assumed financial responsibility for Dolly's expensive nursing care" and paid for the ball gowns she wore at Seamore Place. But eventually, Almina tired of Dolly's costs. She was a hopeless depressive, who made several attempts of suicide, swallowing bottles of pills and administering self-mutilations, requiring long spells of treatment and recovery in sanatoriums. In the end Dolly suffered terminal breast cancer, but the fact that she had taken an excessive number of pills in her final hours points to the suspicion that she may have taken her own life.

It helped Almina's public image greatly that in October 1928 Alfred House admitted a royal patient: Princess Elisabeth of Romania, (1894–1956), the exiled Queen of the Hellenes (Greece), who needed an operation to remove her appendix. On 31 October Princess Victoria Eugenie of Battenberg (1887–1969), the Queen of Spain, arrived in London accompanied by two of her daughters, Infanta Beatrice and the Infanta Maria Christina, and they hastened to Alfred House to see the exiled Queen.

The visit opened the door for a new alliance. On Sunday 4 November 1928 the exiled King George of the Hellenes (1890–1947), attended by Major N Levidis (1891–1964), his liaison officer with the British Royal Court, accepted an invitation to lunch with Almina and the Colonel at 1 Seamore Place. The following month, the recovered Queen and her husband were guests of honour at a dinner at Seamore Place for 400 of Society's elite, including several foreign ambassadors, courtiers like the Knollys, old Highclere friends like the Cunliffe-Owens, racing friend Arthur Portman and his wife and Almina's children and their spouses.

Almina quickly followed this grand event with a New Year's party and dance at 1 Seamore Place for staff and doctors and a good many of the former patients of Alfred House. No expense was spared: "Beautiful spring flowers from the Riviera decorated the staircase and the corners of the drawing room."[588] Almina had much to celebrate at the party, not least the announcement that her friend and surgeon at Alfred House Sir Berkeley Moynihan had been made a Baron in the King's New Year's Honours List.

Almina basked in admiration from all sides for her unswerving dedication to nursing. The grandson of the poet Lord Tennyson, Lionel Tennyson, the 3rd Baron, who had been treated as a war casualty at Bryanston Square, remarks in his autobiography *From Verse to Worse*: "I wonder how much gratitude and affection she has won in the course of her life – much more than falls to the lot of most people, I am sure!" [589]

A year of loss

1929 was a tragic year that saw the death of General Sir John Maxwell, one of the 5th Earl's greatest personal friends and an executor to his estate. The General had also been of tireless assistance to Almina in the aftermath of Carnarvon's death and the battle (stirred up by Carter's irritating feud with the Egyptians) over new digging rights.   Maxwell had died in South Africa, where he developed a cold, which turned to pleurisy.   Almina attended his memorial service in London, with Lady Evelyn Beauchamp. The General's widow, Louise, died from heart failure later in the same year, at her home in London at 4 Queen's Gate place, and Almina and Lady Evelyn were among the mourners at the funeral. [590]

The death of Elisabeth (Elsie) the previous Dowager Countess of Carnarvon on 1 February 1929, aged 72, marked the end of an era too. She had survived the 4th Earl by 39 years. In her last years Elsie had lived for a time in Albania where she established hospitals, schools, anti-malaria clinics and a village for refugees that she named Herbert after her elder son Aubrey. She died at Porto Fino soon after a visit to her beloved Albania, where she came to be known by the people simply as "Mother".[591] Almina and her former mother-in-law had never been close.[592] Their paths did not cross much, since the 4th Countess frequently lived abroad (avoiding any possible clash as Elsie was also a famed nurse and hostess). At a large gathering of the Herbert, Beauchamp, Wallop and Fry wings of the family, Almina was careful to ensure she paid her last respects by sending flowers, but she is not listed as attending either the burial at Highclere on 8 February or the memorial service at St Margaret's, Westminster.[593]

To Almina's horror, several newspapers published photographs of her, instead of Elsie, in the obituaries, causing acute embarrassment, which the 6th Earl was accused of perpetrating out of mischief.[594]

Death follows death, and soon after news broke that Elsie's last surviving son Mervyn had passed away at the British Embassy in Rome on 26 May at the age of 46 having eventually succumbed to pneumonia. He was buried on Saturday 1 June at Kingston near Taunton, with a memorial service in London at St James, Piccadilly. After some contact with him as a child (he was page boy at her wedding), Almina hardly knew Mervyn, although he was close to his niece, Almina's daughter, Lady Evelyn Beauchamp[595], who attended the funeral with her brother, the 6th Earl, and two of their Herbert aunts. [596]

Back home in June, Alfred House was continuing its great work and winning her praise from all quarters. In 1929 the nursing home was the centre of huge publicity over the admittance of actress Lady Diane Duff Cooper (famed daughter of the Duke of Rutland) to deliver her child.[597] Under Almina's personal management and the supreme care of the physicians the child was born safe and well despite a difficult birth completed by caesarean section. [598]

But now Almina faced a difficult choice: the running costs of Alfred House were vast, and to raise funds she needed to once more let go of property – in this case, 1 Seamore Place. But despite putting the house on the market, Almina was unable to attract a buyer, and the house would not be disposed of until several years later. Still, Almina could not manage the combined staff and maintenance costs of both 1 Seamore Place and the nursing home, so she stripped out and abandoned Seamore Place, Alfred de Rothschild's remarkable bequest, selling off more antiques, and borrowing money on the strength of an imminent settlement with the Egyptian government over the 5th Earl's excavation costs.

One notable death at Alfred House on 13 May 1929 was that of the Society hostess and benefactor Evelyn (Evie) James (1868-1929) formerly of West Dean , Chichester, where Evie (and her first husband, Willie James) lavishly entertained guests for the horse racing at Goodwood. Evie was a favourite of King Edward VII, and may have been his daughter. [599] The wonderfully eccentric Evie, mother of four, three daughters, and a son was once asked by the family's nanny which child she wanted to accompany her to church. Evie replied " the one that goes best with my blue dress!" [600]

Evie's son, Edward Frank Willis James (1907-1984), married Tilly Losch, who later went on (after a messy divorce action with James) to marry Almina's son, Henry, 6th Earl of Carnarvon.

For July and August of 1929 Almina rented from the first Lord Mottistone[601] his family home of Mottistone Manor on the Isle of Wight. This paved the way for a plan to purchase a property on the island, but this was not to reach fruition until a few years later. Instead, an announcement in *The Times* of 12 December 1929 advised the Countess of Carnarvon and Colonel Dennistoun had "arrived at Temple Dinsley, Hitchen, which is now their permanent address". [602]

Sunset in Egypt

In April of 1929 Almina had travelled to Egypt[603] with the Colonel on holiday and had taken the opportunity to catch up with Howard Carter, who was still in her employ.[604] Carter had completed all his remaining tasks in the Valley of the Kings the previous winter, and with the abandonment of any claim to the contents of the tomb by Almina, the Carnarvon executors or Carter, only the restitution of the cost of the 5th Earl's excavations remained unresolved. That matter, along with the issue of offering duplicates (where there were copies of artefacts), was before the Egyptian government.

Now, as 1929 drew to a close, Howard Carter was effectively embargoed by the Egyptians from any further close involvement in the tomb of Tutankhamun – he was forced to "surrender the keys to the local Inspector of Antiquities, and not enter the Tomb without the latter's permission". [605]

Egypt, it was clear, had benefitted enormously from Carnarvon and Carter's discovery of the only royal mummy ever to have been found unplundered in its sarcophagus. From its opening in 1924 an estimated 10,000 people had visited the tomb and many more had visited Cairo Museum to wonder at the artefacts housed there. Now, diplomats in Cairo and London hoped the protracted negotiations over the claims by the 5th Earl's executors (and Almina) would end in a full and final settlement using the British Museum as an intermediary. That way some element of the settlement could include the acceptance by the Museum of any duplicate items in the tomb; thus benefiting the home nation of those who had discovered the tomb. It was, however, decided by those representing the Carnarvon heirs (directed by Almina) to reject this approach in favour of a one-off payment.

Almina had been badgering for the repayment of her late husband's expenses for several years. A two-page typed letter written by Almina in September 1924 to His Excellency Morcos Hanna Pasha, Minister of Public Works in Cairo gives an estimate of these expenses:

> My late husband spent 10 years in Research work in the Valley of the Kings and... he carried out this work year after year, in spite of many disappointments, entirely at his own expense, the total of which Mr Harold [sic] Carter places at approximately £45,000. [606]

That Almina had abandoned the campaign for duplicates disappointed the British Museum authorities. Once again Almina, who was as usual in dire need of money, snubbed the British Museum's aspirations. A brief was prepared for the *Egyptian Gazette* making clear the hope that the British Museum might still be offered first refusal in the event of the Egyptian government making duplicates "available for exhibition outside Egypt". Moreover, a somewhat damning indictment of her is to be found in a telegram from the HM High Commissioner, Cairo to the Secretary of State in London:

> I am not aware how closely if at all British Museum and other authorities in England have been following the negotiations. I am on the other hand well aware of the serious difficulties of status and character with which any attempt at dealing with Dowager Countess Carnarvon must necessarily be faced. I may therefore well be completely at fault when I express my apprehension lest we as a nation are losing opportunity to secure some permanent share in Lord Carnarvon's discovery.
>
> Legally Carnarvon interest is entitled to all duplicates although in practice that term might be very rigidly defined. As a matter of gratitude for immense wealth conferred both directly and indirectly on Egypt by Lord Carnarvon's discovery there seems also a case for expecting something more than duplicates. I am informed that Egyptian Government have decided to surrender no objects whatsoever to Lady Carnarvon in the certain belief that they will at once be sold to the highest bidder. [607]

Almina's previous track record of cashing in on Alfred de Rothschild's immense legacy and then her disposal to the highest bidder of the 5th Earl's Egyptian collection showed her loyalties lay with money, not sentiment. With her nursing home commitments at near breaking point, the Colonel's fragile health (he was still in decline from years of chronic back and neck pain, which greatly affected his mobility, and with it came the increasing onslaught of mental health problems), and the unsuccessful sale of 1 Seamore Place, Almina played the shrewd businesswoman in negotiating the best financial settlement for her husband's investment in the excavations: £35,867, of which Almina would pass just under 25 per cent to Carter.[608] Soon, Egypt was a distant memory for Almina.

Henry, 7ᵗʰ Earl of Carnarvon Prince Victor Duleep Singh

Sir George Wombwell   Henry, 6ᵗʰ Earl of Carnarvon

PRINCE VICTOR DULEEP SINGH

Almina   **Prince Victor Duleep Singh**

George, 5th Earl and Prince Victor   Colonel Dennistoun

Chapter 10
1930–1939
The Rise and Demise of Dreams

Balancing work and play

The year 1930 was an uneventful one for Almina, consisting merely of ensuring Alfred House was ticking along nicely and attending social engagements. Sometimes maintaining her public image demanded attendance at sombre Society events, such as the funeral at Westminster Cathedral in April of Commander Ronald Egerton Balfour[609], who had died in a motor car accident and whose father, Brigadier-General Sir Alfred Balfour (1858-1936), was one of Almina's committed colleagues during the Great War as the Commandant of the military port of Southampton, administering war-wounded soldiers. But other occasions were altogether more fun and frivolous – such as the dinner the Countess hosted at The Ritz hotel in May for guests including her family and Colonel Dennistoun. According to the 6th Earl's memoirs, by now the Colonel Dennistoun was being attended by two nurses. Although the Colonel was often unwell, he was far from being immobile or helpless and he appeared at several social events in the late 1920s and early 1930s.

At this time Almina was leasing a small house at 26 Charles Street, Mayfair, which gave her a base when in the capital, and she became firm friends with one of her neighbours, Lady Downshire.[610] They attended functions together including the Christmas Ball at Grosvenor House for the Canning Town Woman's Settlement, always one of Almina's pet causes. Almina was also a member of the committee that organised a subsequent ball at Grosvenor House for the League of Mercy, and on this occasion the Prince of Wales graced guests with his presence.

Fees at Alfred House were twenty to twenty five guineas a week. [611] Yet while working hard to raise funds for charitable causes, behind the scenes Almina was also still doing what she could to support Alfred House in its considerable running expenses in her usual manner: by selling off her possessions. Thus on Tuesday 8 July 1930 Christies sold four lots belonging to Almina including a 26-inch-high Lois XV clock in an ormolu case made by C Balthaser of Paris, making 290 guineas. [612]

A month later, Almina and the Colonel set out for the Isle of Wight – a place they had fallen in love with the previous summer. At the Cowes Regatta[613] on Tuesday 5 August 1930 they looked on amid a crowd of spectators resplendent in bright yellow oilskins rather than the traditional navy blue or white yachting clothes as bad weather marred the activities.[614]

The following year, 1931, began with the death in Paris of Almina's last maternal cousin, Walter Alexander Charles Lethbridge,[615] to be followed by an unpleasant court case. Mr Charles Gillam, the night porter at Alfred House, was prosecuted for theft of £150 from a patient "in order to gratify his vanity".[616] Gillam's wages were two pounds and ten shillings per week with food and substantial tips, a not insubstantial sum for the day. But in his greed he had helped himself to the contents of a registered letter containing £150 for a Mr Sharples, a patient of Almina's who was in a serious condition. When the money disappeared Almina had personally launched enquiries on a par with Miss Marple. Consequently Gillam was watched and his extravagant living – riding in taxicabs, taking girls to expensive entertainments, spending a lot of time at hairdressers and having his photograph taken at expensive studios – proved to be his undoing. Gillam confessed in court and was sentenced to three months in prison.

The serious mood continued that year with more funerals of soldiers involved in the First World War. On 3 July Almina attended St Margaret's, Westminster for the memorial service to General Sir Alexander Cobbe VC (1870–1931) who had died in her care at Alfred House. Cobbe was "a fighting soldier" who had distinguished himself by winning the Victoria Cross in Somaliland in 1902. [617]Another memorial service attended by Almina later that year was for Lady (Morgan) Crofton at the Church of All Saints, Ennismore Gardens on 15 December. Almina was given a top listing among the mourners. The deceased was Adele Donaldson, who had died in Paris after an operation. She and her husband were regular race goers and guests at Almina's frequent gala dinners at Seamore Place.

Almina's patients at Alfred House ranged from millionaires[618] to her social contacts and those recommended to her.[619] But the year 1931 is most notable for the admission into Alfred House of Almina's most prominent patient yet: the Duke of Gloucester, on 21 August 1931, for an operation for appendicitis next day. Almina allocated one of her very best nurses, Nurse Jean Robertson, to ensure the Duke received the maximum care and attention and pampering. [620]

On 24 August the King visited his son and stayed at his bedside for 40 minutes.[621] Court physicians Albert James Walton and Maurice Cassidy were both in attendance. The Duke of Gloucester was in Almina's tender care for the following two weeks, and she managed his care with a firm hand to the point of banning the Duke's dogs from having visiting rights[622] and harshly regulating his alcohol intake. [623] At the Duke's attempt to persuade her otherwise, she simply illustrated that her word was law by recounting the tale of her stopping Winston Churchill going into the operating theatre with a lighted cigar.[624] One abiding memory of Almina by the Duke of Gloucester was that he found her choice of scent " overpowering" [625].

Outside of her work and her social life, Lady Carnarvon's interest was piqued in her daughter following in her footsteps and taking an interest in politics. Almina's son-in-law Sir Brograve Beauchamp stood for Parliament as the National Government candidate for East Walthamstow in 1931, and Lady Evelyn vigorously supported his campaign. She organised an effective method of canvassing known as "mass canvassing", in which a band of women supporters, under Lady Evelyn's leadership, went door to door and when the householder appeared Sir Brogrove was introduced with beaming pride. Sir Brogrove went on to win the seat and sat as an MP until he retired from Parliament in 1945.

The following January, after attendance with Lady Evelyn at the marriage of the Earl of Jersey to Patricia Richards, saw Almina and her husband embarked on a seven-week cruise on board the Canadian Pacific liner *Duchess of Richmond* via Trinidad, Jamaica, Bahamas, Barbados and Gibraltar. On this small British ship, built on the Clyde, luxury and pampering were assured: indeed, there were only first class cabins. The trip gave Almina to break from the pressures of creditors and the day by day rattle of bedpans. The Colonel, whose general health was rapidly failing, was much boosted by the cruise[626], which was a form of coming home for him – he had, after all, lived in Jamaica with Dorothy in 1913–1914. In an interview the Colonel said he was delighted to be back after an absence of 20 years, and was looking forward to visiting some of the "old beauty spots". [627]

The couple were back in England in March, and Almina resumed business as usual, juggling social engagements and running her nursing home. The spring had brought another eminent patient to Alfred House: "Kerry", the 6th Marquis of Lansdowne,[628] (son of a famous Indian Viceroy), soldier and former MP, who had become seriously ill, and Almina was on hand to ensure her patient benefitted from the best possible care. Then, on Wednesday 20 July 1932, Almina held a dinner at The Ritz hotel to meet the Duchess of Aosta, a member of Italian royal family. Colonel Dennistoun also attended.

Almina's secretive service

Almina was the soul of discretion, and as an independent woman herself, believed in free choice for women when it came to pregnancy. Thus in 1933 a steady trickle of well-to-do female patients were checking in to Alfred House, ostensibly there to have their wisdom teeth or appendix removed but in fact benefiting from Almina's hush-hush abortion service.

The cartoonist Osbert Lancaster hinted at the abortion provision in his memoirs *With an Eye to the Future*, in his description of "the immensely chic but slightly wayward nursing home run by Almina, Lady Carnarvon".[629] Almina's nephew,[630] the writer Evelyn Waugh (1903–1966), was altogether more direct, referring in a letter to "Almina's abortionist parlour".[631]

Newspaper columns in the popular papers like the *Daily Express* and *Daily Mirror* covered the comings and goings of numerous actresses. An example of one shotgun abortion was when the marriage of the movie star Douglas Fairbanks to Mary Pickford failed because he fell head over heels in love with Lady Sylvia Ashley. Fairbanks "rushed to London"[632] from the USA when Lady Sylvia was admitted to Alfred House for "an operation" [633]. Fairbanks was cited in the Ashley divorce a year later.

The notable writer and doctor A.J. Cronin, who stripped away the medical profession's hypocrisy for making money from the idle, healthy rich, parodied Almina as Ida Sherrington in his famous novel *The Citadel*:

> Ida Sherrington's nursing home was the most fashionable in London. Half the Peerage had been to Ida, society women, racing men, famous barristers, and diplomats. You had only to pick up the morning's paper

to read that yet another bright young person famous on stage or screen had left her appendix safely in Ida's motherly hands. She dressed all her nurses in a delicate shade of mauve, paid her wine butler two hundred pounds and her chef twice that sum a year... forty guineas for a room each week... and on top of that extras. But when argued with Ida had one answer, which she often adorned with a free and easy adjective. She had her own worries, with cuts and percentages to be paid out, and often felt it was she who was being bled.[634]

Almina's secret abortion service demonstrates her ability to be deceptive when she deemed this necessary, and her genuine sympathy for her patients. Never was this more apparent than when a patient was terminally ill. When Noel Coward's brother Erik (Eric) Vidal Coward (1905–1933) was admitted to Alfred House, Moynihan was quick to realise he had terminal cancer. Coward held Almina in high regard (he was also a patient at Alfred House, receiving treatment for piles), describing her as "that remarkable woman Almina Carnarvon, whose well-known efficiency was only equalled by her kindness". [635]Thus to spare the dying man anguish, Noel and Almina conspired to tell him that he was suffering from a lesser ailment. [636]

Also in 1933 Almina's daughter-in-law Catherine, the 6th Countess, was admitted to Alfred House. Almina saw to it that an announcement was made stating that Catherine was being treated for a suspected damaged spine. In truth, Catherine was suffering from a complete nervous breakdown and acute alcoholism.[637] Porchey's wife of 11 years was growing weary of her husband's serial adultery. But it was of course in Almina's best interests to maintain complete discretion and safeguard the family reputation.

A run of deaths

In February 1933 Almina attended the funeral and memorial service at Westminster Abbey of Field Marshall Sir William Robertson (1860–1933), another veteran of the First World War and a close colleague of her great friend Sir John Cowans.

Then, in May, one of the leading British racing drivers of the era, Sir Henry 'Tim' Birkin (1896–1933), was admitted to Alfred House as an emergency case after a freak accident during the Tripoli Grand Prix on 7 May. Birkin had burnt his arm whilst refuelling, but had carried on with the race and secured third place. But later in London he relapsed, as the burn became septic and blood poisoning set in.

Almina's doctor on the case, Joseph Dudley Benjafield (1887–1957) – himself a passionate racing driver – was unable to save Birkin's life.[638]

The death of the older sister of the 5th Earl, Lady Winifred Burghclere, was a major family event. She died suddenly in London on 28 September, from heart failure. A tribute records "She was bookish, but never authorish; most sociably bookish[639]... she loved talk and had the gift of making people talk who had something to say". Almina said her sister-in-law "always disapproved of her" [640], and although she did not attend the funeral at Bishop's Stortford, she was present for Winifred's memorial service held in London.[641]

The Countess did attend the December funeral of Robert Pugh Rowlands, FRCS (1874–1933), a senior surgeon at Guy's Hospital and vice president of the Royal College of Surgeons. A Welshman by descent, Almina knew his work as an abdominal expert.

The year was not all doom and gloom, however. In May Almina attended a dinner at the Savoy Hotel in aid of the Sunshine Convalescent Home for the Invalid and Crippled Children's society, presided over by her old charge the Duke of Gloucester; and in November she and Colonel Dennistoun gave a luncheon party at The Ritz hotel in honour of Princess Helen of Serbia, with several notable guests from royal circles in the shape of the Marquis and Marchioness of Carisbrooke and actors Douglas Fairbanks and Gertrude Lawrence.

Almina attended the funeral of Lt Colonel Neil Stewart-Richardson, DSO, at St Mark's, North Audley Street, on 27 February 1934. Stewart-Richardson, a soldier in the South African War and the Great War had died of pneumonia at Alfred House.

The treatment received and the surgical operations performed at Alfred House on some of its notable patients feature in several autobiographies and biographies. [642] Tony Leadbetter remarks that Almina's nursing homes were in fact hospitals, since they each had an operating theatre. [643]

Hobnobbing with the gentry

When a closer look is taken at some of those who attended Almina's wedding to Lord Carnarvon in 1895, one British peer who stands out is John Spencer Churchill (1871–1934), known as Sonny, the 9th Duke of Marlborough who famously married two American dames.[644] Almina and the Duke enjoyed a singular friendship on account of them both being small in height. They fought a common cause as both thought that they were misjudged on being diminutive, leading to them being "misunderstood by many people". [645]

Towards the end of the 9th Duke's life he was ailing from cancer, and converted to a Roman Catholic. He had completely given up on public life. To raise his spirits, Almina persuaded him to come to London to attend one of her Society luncheons at The Ritz hotel, in honour of the Queen of Greece. It was a glittering affair demonstrating Almina's social pull. In the light of her reputation for lavish parties and nursing home clientele singing her praises, she had many satisfied and would-be customers who responded to the call. Those holding court on this occasion included diplomats, peers and peeresses and the military. Names also on the list of guests again include the stage actress Gertrude Lawrence, who was at the peak of her career, and the American film actor Douglas Fairbanks Jnr, both of whom had been among Almina's charges at Alfred House.[646]

Sonny found comfort in Almina's tender loving care, but a little over six months later the 9th Duke of Marlborough was dead. She attended his Catholic funeral, which moved her (Almina, like Sonny, was a late convert to the Roman Catholic faith, 30 years later).

Almina and the Colonel were also well acquainted with John, the new 10th Duke of Marlborough, who had been the Marquis of Blandford. He attended a dinner at The Ritz on 27 June 1934 jointly hosted by Almina and the Colonel. This was Almina's finest hour, with 800 guests dancing to Ambrose's band after a sumptuous dinner. The guest list included Prince George of Greece and Prince and Princess Arthur of Connaught, several former Alfred House patients including Lady Diana Cooper and Viscountess Weymouth, and royal intermediaries including the Marquis and Marchioness of Carisbrooke and Viscount and Viscountess Knollys. Lord Moynihan was also present.

Almina and Lady Evelyn Beauchamp were also friends with the 10th Duchess of Marlborough, Hon. Mary Cadogan (1900–1961). Almina shared a passion with Mary for nursing and medical charities. They were both involved in establishing hospitals in the pioneering days before (and after) the National Health Service came into being.[647]

Soon after Almina joined another old friend, the eminent surgeon Sir Willie Arbuthnot Lane, and his wife Charlotte at a cocktail party at the Dorchester Hotel to celebrate their golden wedding anniversary, and attended a luncheon given by Mrs Gordon Moore – wife of Dr Charles Gordon Moore[648] (who had referred wounded officers to Almina's wartime hospital). Princess Beatrice (1857–1944), youngest daughter of Queen Victoria, was the guest of honour. Almina and the Princess would later become good friends through being neighbours on the Isle of Wight, where Beatrice was governor and constable, and the Princess's daughter Eugenia (Ena) 1887–1969), the exiled Queen of Spain, would be another of Almina's patients at Alfred House.[649]

Selling up and moving to the Isle of Wight

During 1935 Almina continued to appear at social functions, though the Colonel was no longer well enough to accompany her. A planned trip to Ireland was cancelled because the Colonel was not fit to travel.

The couple had ceased being happy living in Temple Dinsley. They weren't very popular among the villagers. One local historical retrospective describes the Countess as "a somewhat eccentric lady [who] frightened the villagers by asking them to mount Tutankamen [sic] relics on black velvet [apparently for an ornamental display inside the house] which, naturally, they refused to do".[650] There was talk of a curse on the inhabitants of Temple Dinsley arising from Almina's time in the village.[651]

Almina decided a change was in order, and *The Times* reported a sale "By Order of Almina, Countess of Carnarvon" of the "remaining contents of Temple Dinsley" [652]on 10–11 July 1935. The couple soon found a property they deemed ideal on the west side of the Isle of Wight named Eastmore, and an adjoining property, Eastmora, situated near the town of Yarmouth. In addition, a summer house was commissioned for the Colonel to inhabit close to the sight of boats on the Solent.[653] In addition, the Almina rented a small house (The Red House [654], later one of her nursing homes) as another retreat in Hove, nearer to London.

For Eastmore, Almina needed to hire a housekeeper, but without a large population finding one of the island was a challenge. Fortunately, at the premier of the film *The Guv'nor* at the New

Gallery Cinema in London in December of 1935 Almina ran into an old horse racing contact, Mrs Sofer (Tiddles) Whitburn, who knew of a capable woman who had worked for her[655] whose family roots were on the Isle of Wight. Consequently Alice Butler was interviewed and hired.

While his wife took care of business, the Colonel was delighted by the move because it allowed him to pursue his hobby of model yachting.[656] The model boat racing fraternity on the Isle of Wight, a respected group, welcomed the Colonel's patronage. The *Daily Mirror* of 16 August 1935 printed a photograph of the Colonel at Hove in a motorised "easy chair", with a long pole to help him push the model yachts around a large marina, and the caption:

> Lieut Colonel I O Dennistoun sending off one of his model racing yachts on Hove lagoon. Being an invalid, he cannot sail full size craft, but by having models specially built for him he is able to enjoy a good imitation of the real thing which gives scope for his skilful seamanship.

Crisis in the family

A family crisis arose in the early summer of 1935. Catherine, the 6th Countess, suffered a further nervous breakdown. Since her illness the previous year the 6th Earl had continued to play the field with other women – there was plenty of female company on offer in racing circles and he put as much physical effort into that sport as he did with his racing ventures and horse stud. Consequently, rumours circulated that he and Catherine were to divorce. To subdue speculation Catherine's mother said "she could neither confirm nor deny published reports that the Countess had instituted divorce proceedings against Lord Carnarvon".[657]

By June 1935 Catherine's condition was described as "greatly improved"[658]. A rest under Almina's personal care at Alfred House brought Catherine to her senses, and she stirred Society circles with an announcement that a divorce suit would be filed.

No sooner had the family began to come to terms with this news than another crisis arose. In July 1935 Almina's daughter, Lady Evelyn, suffered back injuries in a motor car accident while driving to the Newmarket races. She was admitted to Alfred House for specialist care, and made a good recovery.[659]

Pleasing royalty

In November 1935 Buckingham Palace wrote to advise Almina that because she had been awarded the insignia of Officer of the Chilean Order of Merit, for her medical services to Chilean residents in London, the King "has been graciously pleased to give you Restricted Permission to wear the insignia"[660]. Almina was glowing with pride that Christmas when she attended a ball given by the Prince of Wales at Grosvenor House on behalf of Canning Town Woman's Settlement.

Almina's services to members of the Royal Family in Britain and Europe, as well as to some of their particular friends, were exemplary. A collection of over 100 letters in the Royal Archives[661] offers a unique insight into a few of Almina's important contacts and distinguished patients at Alfred House during the mid 1930s. Queen Marie of Romania (1875–1938) and her daughters, Marie of Yugoslavia (1900–1961) and Princess Ileana, Archduchess of Austria (1909–1991), feature prominently in the correspondence.

A close friendship clearly existed between Almina and Queen Marie. One letter in 1934 describes the option of an operation at Alfred House for Princess Marie, and the Queen asked Almina to send a nurse to help Ileana at the birth of her third child. Almina duly provided the services of Mrs MacLean, one of her Irish nurses, in 1935 to attend the Archduchess of Austria and look after her two other children.[662]

King George V and Queen Mary of England were also well-acquainted with Almina's work at Alfred House. They each took a special interest in the admittance in 1935 into Almina's care of Lord Tweedmouth, one of the King's Lords in Waiting. [663]Almina also kept the royals informed of Lady Carisbrooke's recovery after an operation.[664] Lady Carisbrooke's was the wife of the Marquis of Carisbrooke, a grandson of Queen Victoria, and Queen Mary made a personal visit to the house to check in on the patient. Almina wrote later in thanks: "[Lady Carisbrooke] was greatly cheered by Her Majesty's kind visit. Lady Carisbrooke is now able to lie about on the roof balcony and will shortly, I hope, be able to go for a drive." [665]

Almina did her utmost to please her royal patients and their relatives, to the point of offering services for free to "guests". When Sybil Cochrane, a mutual friend of Almina and Princess Beatrice

(Lady Carisbrooke's mother-in-law), required an operation on her feet, Almina persuaded Sybil to go into Alfred House.[666]

Godmother Almina

The following year, 1936, began with a sad death: that of King George V on 20 January 1936 after a reign of 25 years. and Almina wrote immediately to Queen Mary with her deep condolences. Following a trip with the Colonel to South America, in March Almina attended the funeral of a former patient, the 6th Marquis of Lansdowne, at St Margaret's, Westminster. Then, in April new life followed death and Almina attended the christening of David Henry Anthony Babington, the infant son of Captain Geoffrey Babington of the 16th/5th Lancers and Lady Anne Babington. Almina was named a godmother, and the Duke of Gloucester was godfather.[667]

Over the years Almina also became godmother to a number of children born on the Highclere Estate, and although being mostly based in London she still attempted to attend special events taking place in Newbury and district during the 1920s and 1930s. [668]

Despite the pressures of running Alfred House and the constant worry over the Colonel's health, Almina managed to escape to attend the 1936 Derby at Epsom on 27 May. She was news again for the fashion writers: "Almina, Countess of Carnarvon had a long cape of silver fox over her printed crepe dress in black and white. Her small black cap had a transparent crown held by a band of ribbon." [669]

At race courses Almina picked up gossip too. Her nursing home at Portland Place and Miss Jean Jacomb's reign as matron at the rival London Clinic[670], in the 1930s, practically swept in all the high life celebrities at one time or another, from both sides of the Atlantic. Almina took an interest in anyone in the public gaze whom she knew to be ill, finding time to send them a kind greeting or making a telephone call.

Showing supreme solidarity with her daughter-in-law Catherine, who was about to divorce the 6th Earl, Almina joined her at a large reception given on 9 July by Mme Edwards, the wife of the Chilean Ambassador at 3 Hamilton Place. Lady Evelyn Beauchamp was also present, well recovered from her perilous motor accident.

Then came the memorial service for another of Almina's patients, thirty-three- year old Mary, Lady Alington, who had died after an operation for acute appendicitis. The next tragedy was even more heartbreaking for Almina: the loss of her old friend and most treasured medical colleague Lord Moynihan. Almina attended the funeral in Leeds, and the following year she presented the surgical instruments that Lord Moynihan had used at Portland Place to the Council of the Royal College of Surgeons. [671]

Good news was to follow: finally, a buyer for 1 Seamore Place. Almina announced in *The Times* of 10 November 1936 that she had sold 1 Seamore Place, (it was purchased by Westminster City Council as part of a road widening scheme of Park Lane and Curzon Street) and asked that all letters and communications be in future addressed to her at Alfred House.

A doomed romance

In 1936 the marriage of the 6th Earl and Catherine Tredick Wendell, Countess of Carnarvon, was formally ended in court, with Catherine taking custody of the two children, aged 12 and 11. The 6th Earl's misconduct was cited as the reason for the divorce; he admitted adultery with a woman called Jean Cooper. In his memoirs he takes most of the blame for the failure of the marriage, but he admits that there was wrong doing on both sides – indeed, it is alleged that Catherine had an affair with the bisexual Prince George, Duke of Kent, the fourth son of King George V and Queen Mary, who was an intimate friend of hers before and during her marriage to Porchey.[672] The rumour circulated that Henry, 7th Earl of Carnarvon, was possibly George's son, albeit the child was born eighteen months after the Porchesters' wedding day.[673] The Duke, the boy's godfather, attended Henry's christening celebrations at Highclere Church on 20 April 1924.[674] Catherine remarried in 1938. [675]

Porchey was indefatigable following the divorce. At once he threw himself into the pursuit of finding the next Countess of Carnarvon: a cad of Victor's match for conquering women. He quickly became engaged in the USA to Tanis Eva Bulkeley Guinness (1908–1993), one of the "Guinness crowd" and an heiress to a fortune made by her father as a lawyer in Pittsburgh, USA. Almina was too busy ensuring that the Colonel was properly nursed to keep constant track of her son's love life. She was, however, told to expect a new "Countess" daughter-in-law.

But the match was not to be. First Lord Carnarvon and Tanis agreed to elope from New York City to Harrison, New York State (a sort of American Gretna Green), but Tanis changed her mind and returned to New York. Then, having alleviated the bride's qualms, they set a date to marry in Baltimore on 4 November 1936. The Earl booked the bridal suite on a luxury liner to take them back to England. But Tanis stood him up, and the ceremony failed to take place. Neither would discuss their shattered romance. Both headed for New York, insisting on separate departures back to Europe. Tanis sought refuge from reporters in her regal suite at the St Regis Hotel. At the same time, whilst his valet packed his luggage to return to England, Porchey was cursing her dead in his rooms at The Ritz. Attempts at further reconciliation failed. Only Porchey boarded the ship, *Europa*, bound for England. In Southampton, Almina was waiting to greet the happy couple in her Rolls Royce, but instead she was met with disappointment. The *Daily Express* featured a photograph of the mother and son reunion, and reported that Porchey had said: "The marriage is definitely off. It is not a postponement. Everything is washed up. That is all. What else can I say?"

1937

The year 1937 appears to have been largely an uneventful year for Almina. However, her attendance in January at the memorial service for a minor diplomat, Ralph Wigram[676] (1890–1936), who was later acknowledged as an important insider who informed Churchill of Germany's increasing rearmament, suggests an involvement by Almina in the nursing care of Wigram's child, Charles, who was born disabled. Almina also knew Wigram and his wife, Ava[677], from past British Embassy receptions in Paris.

In March she requested Messrs Jackson Stops and Staff (of Curzon Street) to dispose of the lease of Dewlish House, near Dorchester, with its shooting over 1,000 acres. She had acquired this property for the Colonel but his state of health was far from satisfactory. He was increasingly inactive, but his mobility was improved by the use of a wheelchair. Later that year, in April, the Colonel joined Almina and her children at the memorial service for Lord Londesborough at St Mary Abbot's Kensington; and in November Almina attended a special performance of *Macbeth* at the Old Vic theatre in aid of the

Centenary Fund of King's College Hospital, in the presence of Queen Mary.

Testimony of one of Almina's domestic staff

As well as the nursing staff at Alfred House being fairly treated, Almina is remembered by one surviving member of her domestic staff as a kind employer. Margaret Sharp (later Mrs Margaret Lawson), now a sprightly nonagenarian, recalls working six days a week at Alfred House, between 1937 and 1939, for 2 pounds, and 10 shillings a month. Margaret says "I lived in a four bedroom flat with three other domestic staff. The flat was even cleaned for us. We worked at the nursing home each day until 5pm." [678]Almina is also remembered fondly by Margaret as the Countess arranged for her to receive medical treatment at Alfred House. "I had suffered for some years with tonsils. Lady Carnarvon got a surgeon called Mr Brown to come from Harley Street to do my operation. I was looked after so well and have been grateful all these years since." [679]

Loss of another husband

By the middle of 1938 Almina's marriage to Ian Dennistoun was drawing to a close. The time at Eastmore, Isle of Wight, had prolonged his quality of life. The house was filled with Ian's precious and elaborate collection of model toy soldiers [680] , and Almina had even uplifted the prized fireplaces from Temple Dinsley, which Ian much admired. The previous summer they had been able to entertain in a limited way, enjoying a last glorious season together in the company of several intimate friends at Eastmore.

But now, facing little prospect of a recovery, Almina moved Ian to London. The Countess had never failed to provide for any part of Ian's medical well-being, comfort and fads. But theirs was a strange match. With her contacts and great wealth Almina could have married other men, wiser men, stronger men, richer men than the rakish Dennistoun. There is no doubt she loved him of sorts, but he was not the love of her life: she used him to her own end, and paid dearly for it. As we shall see later, during the marriage and at the height of Ian's bad health, in a state of chaos over her mounting debts, she revived at least one long love affair with another man she had come to know well during the Great War.

Tragedy struck the relative calm in the family with the death, on 22 May 1938, of Colonel Ian Dennistoun at the age of 59. The Colonel passed away in a London nursing home, having suffered heart and breathing complications during his last weeks. Almina was devastated. She and Ian had been married for nearly 15 years, and he had been so much more of a companion to her than her first husband. Now, aged 62, Almina was alone once more. Replying to the Queen of Spain's letter of condolence, she said: "I am utterly heartbroken. Ian was just all in all to me[681] and the thought of facing life without him is almost beyond endurance."[682] To Queen Mary, who had sent condolences through her Private Secretary[683], she wrote of her "aching heart" and her "great sorrow" and repeated "Ian was all in all to me".[684]

Struggling to come to terms with her loss, Almina did what she could to delay laying Ian to rest. *The Guardian* of 26 May recorded that Almina intended to have Ian buried in the grounds of Eastmore. According to an intimate of Almina, she had him embalmed (in the same manner as the 5th Earl), and Alice Butler, Almina's housekeeper at Eastmore, recounted that the Colonel was kept in a sitting room on the property for a considerable time after his death. This was achieved by Almina "adopting" an undertaker, paying over large sums and treats[685] to him to provide her with more time to consider what she finally wanted to do over laying Ian to rest. It may well have been Ian's wish to be buried at Eastmore. A remarkable heart-shaped piece of granite in the grounds, still on display but removed from its original location, may have once marked the spot where Ian's remains are interred.[686]

By July Almina had sufficiently recovered to attend the memorial service in London for her great friend Queen Marie of Rumania, held at the Greek Cathedral of St Sophia, Moscow Road, Bayswater. She was also one of the mourners at All Soul's Langham Place in September for the funeral of Lancelot Burrell, FRCS, an old medical crony and an expert on the treatment of tuberculosis.

Moving on

In 1939[687] Almina made the difficult decision to sell Eastmore and move from the Isle of Wight. The death of her husband and, in March 1939, of Howard Carter[688], who died peacefully at his London home aged 65, had brought home her advancing age, and it seemed now that life was too short to sit still. Thus *The Times* of 6 June 1939 declared:

> Almina, Lady Carnarvon has requested Messrs Harrods Estate Offices (Brompton Road) to sell Eastmore, 13 acres and Eastmora, an adjoining property of three acres, and 10 acres of freehold pasture, on the Solent at Yarmouth, in the Isle of Wight. Eight views of the properties are given in illustrated details, prepared by Mr Frank D James. The principal house, Eastmore has a white cement elevation and the accommodation includes a music room 45ft by nearly 25ft. The inner hall is even larger. The grounds slope to the foreshore, and are mainly laid out in the Italian style. The summerhouse, an elaborate building, overlooks the Solent. Over £40,000 has been spent on the property which can be bought on favourable terms.

As Princess Beatrice, once Almina's royal neighbour at Carisbrooke Castle, said in a letter dated 7 May 1939: "I dare say you could not face continuing living there alone." [689]But Almina's motives in the sale were also financial in light of the continued burden of running Alfred House. A sale of English and French furniture, tapestry and objets d'art from Eastmore realised a total of £4,752 at a sale at Christies on Thursday 22 June 1939, but this was still not enough capital to keep the nursing home afloat, and so Almina was forced to dispose of her interest in Alfred de Rothschild's £500,000 fund, which provided her an income of £2,400 a year. She sold this interest for £62,000 to her own family, with the 6th Earl and Lady Evelyn splitting the interest 50-50.[690]

Meanwhile, marriage was once more on the cards for the 6th Earl. At first, there was some concern over his fiancée, Tilly Losch, an international stage dancer of the era [691], dragging her heels and memories of the Tanis debacle resurfaced. But a wedding did follow, and Almina dubbed Tilly "the dancing Countess" (later "the bitch").[692] The union was disastrous. Tilly was unhappy and soon deserted her husband, to return to her adopted country, the USA.

The start of war and the end of Alfred House

In the spring of 1939 Almina took a lease interest in 32 Avenue Road, Regent's Park[693] , intending this as her main London home in succession to Charles Street, Mayfair. Then events on the international scene began to loom large over her plans, and she began to face the strong possibility that her country would go to war once again.

When the time came, in September, Almina reacted speedily to the outbreak of war. As Alfred House was close to the BBC building, it was considered a primary target for enemy bombing; and in any case, Almina later admitted that she was unable to "obtain the license to nurse officers in the London area". She announced in *The Times* of 8 September 1939: "Owing to present conditions Almina, Countess of Carnarvon has closed Alfred House 7, Portland Place, London and has transferred her nursing home to The Red House, Lansdowne Road, Hove, Sussex." She was right to close the home down: Alfred House was subsequently destroyed by enemy action in 1940. [694]

The Red House was, in Almina's words, only "a small house", but was conveniently placed far enough from London to be safe yet close enough to for the transportation of London causalities. To raise funds for the conversion of the Hove property for her nursing work she obtained a loan of £7,000 from an insurance company on the security of a policy on her life.

A letter dated 18 September 1939 from Almina Carnarvon to Wallis Simpson, the Duchess of Windsor, refers to the announcement that the Chateau de la Croe (the Duke and Duchess of Windsor's home on the French Riviera) was to be converted for the war effort into a military hospital. Almina offered her a contribution of some "theatre equipment, namely the no-shadow Bartlett lamp, the sterilizer complete and the X ray apparatus and table".[695] At the end of this letter she invited the Duke and Duchess to visit her. "I would consider it a great privilege if you and the Duke of Windsor would honour me with a visit at The Red House, as soon as the Home is ready to be opened." [696] The Duchess of Windsor (who had once been a patient of Almina's at Alfred House to have her tonsils removed ...[697]) replied on 25 September thanking Almina and wishing her "every success with the Red House" and added: "I know how hard you will work during these days giving comfort to everyone. Perhaps if I can arrange my house you will come here and see me – just for a little rest." [698] But for Almina there was only hard work ahead, and little rest while the war raged. [699]

Eastmore, Isle of Wight 1930s

Eastmore, Isle of Wight 1930s

Eastmore, Isle of Wight, Today
To the left is the original Music Room building

The heart-shaped stone in the grounds of Eastmore

Highclere Castle

**48, Bryanston Square, London
The site of Almina's Hospital for Wounded Officers
1915-1919**

Almina and the Colonel with their solicitor

**Colonel Dennistoun and Almina
During Dennistoun v Dennistoun**

Mrs Dorothy Dennistoun

General Sir John Cowans   Almina, Countess of Carnarvon

Lt Colonel Ian Onslow Dennistoun

Eastmore, Isle of Wight 1937

Almina, relaxing in France

Chapter 11
1940–1949
Retreat to the Hills

The Glebe

In 1940 Almina poured her heart and her funds into her new nursing home, The Red House in Hove. She was glad to be out of London, and saddened by news of deaths among her acquaintances and intimates – such as Arthur and Mary Portman[700], close friends who were killed in the London Blitz when their house "fell like a pack of cards" [701]during an air raid.

But as the war developed the south coast towns, including Hove, became "prohibited areas", which meant Almina was forced to close down The Red House and end the lease on the property. Undeterred, she wrote letters to her many contacts to gain support in opening up another major nursing home, this time at Monkton Hadley Wood, Barnet in Hertfordshire, from 1941 – an area she knew well from her time living at Temple Dinsley.

And thus The Glebe nursing home was established. Building on the reputation secured at Alfred House, Almina once more enlisted the services of distinguished doctors, in particular distinguished gynaecologists and obstetricians. She ran an advert in *The Times* – and would continue to do so throughout 1941 and 1942 – intended to entice those who wanted to escape from the horrors of London at war: "Situated in peaceful rural surroundings, garden parkland extending 29 acres. All modern equipment and up to date operating theatre. Fees from 8 guineas per week." Later she would add a reference to The Glebe as a "Surgical, Medical and Maternity Nursing Home".

As the opening date of the new nursing home drew near Almina was laid up with an infected knee joint.[702] Queen Mary's Lady in waiting Lady Constance Milnes Gaskell (d.1964) wrote to Almina from Badminton on 25 March 1941 sending the Queen's "best wishes" for the success of the hospital at Monkton Hadley Wood. [703]

The Glebe quickly picked up where Alfred House had left off – providing medical services to the gentry. On 18 December 1941 history was made when a royal prince (William Henry Andrew

Frederick of Gloucester[704]) was born in a private nursing home. The *London Gazette* of 19 December 1941 records:

> Whitehall, 18 December 1941. This afternoon at fifteen minutes after five o'clock Her Royal Highness the Duchess of Gloucester was safely delivered of a Prince at the Carnarvon Nursing Home, Barnet. His Royal Highness the Duke of Gloucester was present. The condition of Her Royal Highness and of the Infant Prince is satisfactory.

The Duchess of Gloucester[705] was most impressed with Almina's nursing home, as a letter from her Lady-in-waiting illustrates:

> Dear Lady Carnarvon, I am desired by Her Royal Highness The Duchess of Gloucester to write and thank you most warmly for all the care and trouble you took for her comfort whilst she was in your Nursing Home.
>
> The Duchess also feels she would like to thank all the sisters and nurses who so kindly helped to contribute to her comfort, and says she could not have been better looked after.[706]

Another eminent patient at The Glebe in 1941, under the charge of physician Sir William Gilliatt, was the youngest of the Mitford girls, Deborah, Duchess of Devonshire[707], who recalls:

> I was twice a patient in the nursing home called after her. She was keenly interested in the patients and once or twice she did visit me. It was through the nurses that I got to know what she was like. The comfort of the place was unsurpassed, the food and the way it was served were worthy of a five star hotel. She used to watch operations, the nurses told me, dressed from head to toe in white. One day they showed me the rows of her white shoes in a cupboard kept for this purpose.[708]

A curious household

By 1942, Almina had made The Glebe her permanent address, but to keep a place in the capital she continued the lease on her London townhouse at 32 Avenue Road, Regent's Park. [709]There, she set up home with her new beau: James Timothy Stocking[710], known as JTS, who would be her constant male companion, and sometime lover over the next 20 years.

Almina had met JTS during the renovations for The Glebe; he had been one of the men working on The Glebe's antiquated heating system. At the time JTS was married with children – two sons and a daughter – but his was an unstable and unhappy marriage. Almina detected male vulnerability in the twinkling of an eye, and she quickly "adopted" him. Almina was approaching 70; JTS was in his early 40s. (This was not her first ensnarement of a much younger man; she had been hopelessly besotted by the undertaker who had done her bidding over the embalming and slow, but eventual, final disposal of Colonel Dennistoun's body on the Isle of Wight. [711])

Having first installed JTS at a flat in London at her expense, once she moved into Avenue Road Almina transferred JTS to live with her. The curious household also comprised JTS's friend named Jack Humphries (who had served with JTS in the army in the Great War[712]) along with Alice Butler, from the Eastmore days on the Isle of Wight, continuing as Almina's housekeeper and lady's maid. [713]

In 1942 Alice invited her sister, Anne Leadbetter, and her four-year-old son, Tony, to visit her at Almina's home. The Butler sisters were close.[714] In the aftermath of the Great Depression Alice's sister Anne had met and married (it seems bigamously) Peter Leadbetter[715], who was 20 years her senior. Leadbetter had a job as a caretaker in a block of flats in Thackeray Court, Elystan Place, Chelsea. A son, Anthony (Tony), was born to Alice and Peter in March 1938. Some time afterwards the relationship faded and they became estranged. Tony recalls spending time with his mother and his father's sister in Staffordshire, long enough for him to acquire a local accent, and later, in the early years of the war, his mother worked as a nursery school teacher in St Albans. It was from there that they went to visit Alice at 32 Avenue Road, Regent's Park. [716]

This was the first time that Tony Leadbetter met Almina; his vivid memories of the Countess extend from this point all the way through to her death in 1969, when he was aged 31. His is a moving and loyal testimony to her existence and influence. Then, in early 1942, Tony recalls sitting in the kitchen in his mother's arms when Almina came in to greet them. The subject of Tony's tea was discussed, and chips were mentioned, to which Almina said indignantly, "Chips? Indeed not. He will have coddled egg." [717]

The final closure

Almina's creditors were moving in on her on all fronts. She announced in *The Times* of 24 March 1942 that she had severed her London ties at 32 Avenue Road, Regent's Park and that her contact address in future was the Carnarvon Nursing Home, Monkton Hadley Common, Barnet, Hertfordshire.

Almina lacked skill in the financial management of her nursing homes. She had no reliable accounting system in any of her homes, and her generosity proved costly. The author Henry Keown-Boyd comments: "I was born in her nursing home in London. I believe it went bust not long after as Almina thought it bad taste to send bills to the less affluent patients." [718]The Countess was loath at times to send a bill, particularly when friends or friends of friends or the royals were involved, even when they were well-off. She saw such a thing as common, a sure admission that she was hard-up and needed the money. The irony was she did: she was heavily in debt. She also had very little left to sell – only The Glebe. [719]

The last patient at The Glebe was Radclyffe Hall, the novelist and well-known lesbian. According to Diana Southami, her biographer[720], the great eccentric (who called herself John) was admitted in April 1943 under the care of surgeon Cecil Joll. Both doctor and patient were suffering from terminal cancer. John stayed seven weeks, but although "Lady Carnarvon herself was kind"[721], "the place had gone to pieces", "it lacked even rudimentary management" and "nursing was non-existent".[722] Almina had completely run out of money, staff had gone elsewhere. [723] Tony Leadbetter recalls of a trip to The Glebe at this time merely empty rooms painted in hospital green paint.

There is evidence in letters that Almina approached a number of her medical associates to try to head off closure of her last nursing home and sell it as a working concern, but to no avail. Harley Street surgeon Mr TJ Phillips wrote in May 1943:

> Although Mr Joll (Cecil Joll, Hunterian Professor, Royal College of Surgeons 1923-1939, died 1945) and myself would have been willing to consider purchasing The Glebe... [we] feel unable to do anything in the matter and several other people I have approached either say it is too far out, or would be after the war, or not big enough and for these reasons would not take any interest in it.[724]

Thomas Pomfret Kilner (1890–1964), a pioneering surgeon in plastic surgery (later Professor of Surgery at Oxford University), wrote from 143 Harley Street on 7 May: "I am very sorry indeed to hear the news about The Glebe. It has been most pleasant working there and your nurses have given excellent attention to my cases. I cannot picture you without Nursing Home activities."[725]

Another mourner of Almina's passing as a hospital proprietor was Sir Maurice Cassidy who had attended King George V and George VI and other members of the Royal Family. Sir Maurice wrote to Almina on 4 May 1943:

> I am very sorry indeed to hear that you are closing the home and realise what this must mean to you. I hope it does not mean that you are leaving London, and that we may meet again before very long, and I hope in happier times. [726]

On 7 June 1943 Maple & Co began a two-day sale of the entire contents of The Glebe. The advert was a harsh in memoriam notice of Almina's long endurance in running her homes.

> By direction of Almina, Countess of Carnarvon. IMPORTANT 4 DAYS SALE THE GLEBE, HADLEY COMMON, BARNET. ANTIQUE and MODERN FURNITURE 450 LOTS Of FINE LINEN, Blankets, RGD Radiogram, Bush and other Radios, Frigidaire and Coldspot Refrigerators, Electric Cooker, SURGICAL and MEDICAL EQUIPMENT, Surgical Linen, Rubber Beds. For SALE by AUCTION June 7th, 8th, 9th and 10th. ON VIEW June 4th and 5th. Catalogues (6d) [727]

On 26 July 1943 Maple & Co wrote to Almina indicating that the sale of the contents of The Glebe had achieved £10,582.11s.6d. With fees and commission Almina received £9,740. [728] And so ended Almina's life as a nursing home proprietor.

Orchard Grove

Disposing of the lease on The Glebe, Almina decided it was high time for a change of scene, challenge and pace. She took to the hills – the Quantocks in Somerset, far from the madding crowd. There, in the village of Bicknoller[729], near Taunton, she set up home in a thatched cottage in Orchard Grove, which she termed her "cabbage patch": six acres with an orchard comprising over 2,000 apple trees and an operational apple-packing station. Always looking for a project with which to busy herself, this time she had settled on market gardening.

Almina's companion in her venture was JTS. She and JTS were already lovers, but they slept in separate bedrooms, as was the gentry's fashion. Almina had "adopted" JTS much as she had done with Colonel Ian Dennistoun, 20 years previously. It's not clear when they became lovers or for how long the sexual side of the relationship endured. But the rest of the household, Alice and Jack Humphries (

albeit he was decamped overnight to digs in the village[730]) , were left in no doubt that JTS was "the boyfriend".[731] He even kept a glass framed photograph of Almina, dressed in her nurses' whites beside his bed.[732]

To make the move easy for JTS, Almina agreed to pay for his daughter, Doreen, to attend a private school in nearby West Quantoxhead and later for Doreen to go to France to spend time with a family Almina knew there, to enhance her knowledge of the French language.

JTS had grand plans to build up the apple-packing business at Orchard Grove. He saw himself as a gentleman farmer; though perhaps some of his enthusiasm for the cabbage patch stemmed from the fact that farmers were free from being drafted into military service.

An interesting element of the move to the cabbage patch is that Almina hid the full truth of her cohabitation from her family. None of the Carnarvons knew about JTS's existence: the family thought Almina was living at Orchard Grove alone with her staff. During any (rare) visit by any member of the Carnarvon family all traces of JTS being in residence at Orchard Grove were completely removed. Clothing was taken out of wardrobes, personal items transferred to the upper quarters and any likely callers or telephone messages stopped. Twice during the war the 6th Earl visited his mother, and neither time did he suspect any mischief afoot. This charade continued for all the 20 years that Almina and JTS lived under the same roof, and points clearly to the relationship being of a close marital nature between them.

Determined to back JTS in his venture, Almina put what money she could into the farming. She still had means: the monies from the disposal of the Rothschild settlement; a sum from the residue of the 5th Earl's Pixton estates in Devon; a monthly allowance from the Carnarvon estate trustees; and occasionally a top-up made by her son. The family solicitor J.F. Fryzer was the intermediary used; Fryzer "seemed to produce extra money when she pleaded".[733] JTS offered to help try to raise sums, but Almina "would not allow it".[734] He was instructed to keep a low profile.

On the ground there was a great amount of work to be done in organising the market gardening. A regular supply of fruit – apples, of course, but also nectarines and a variety of berries – was dispatched to London agents at Covent Garden fruit market in an effort to generate additional household income. In addition, a variety of animals were kept at Orchard Grove, including a herd of pigs and many hens and chickens, which produced a large quantity of eggs. Yet despite the productivity of Orchard Grove, no profit was ever made. The business made a continuous loss on the various apples consignments, and any profit on egg laying was lost when the costs of dispersing the large surplus was taken into account. Almina lost various amounts on these investments only to keep JTS happy. He was a dreamer, constantly imagining himself as a country squire with a family pedigree and unlimited money to match any failure.

However, despite such adversity Almina flourished in turning JTS's would-be business enterprise into a glorified charity. She began by donating surplus eggs to sick friends and local hospitals, and then she began to spread her generosity further. In her years as a matron she had come to know many women who were involved with hospital charities and committees, and she arranged for a parcel of eggs to be sent to each of them regularly. According to Tony Leadbetter: "Egg boxes were specially provided, with special divisions, and the eggs were wrapped in soft tissue paper, with numerous sheets of brown paper." [735] At great personal expense Almina then had the substantial parcels posted off. Remarkably, it seems, the eggs nearly always arrived intact at their required destinations. When the parcels did not arrive (Almina would contact would-be recipients by telephone to say a parcel was on its way) she would phone the local Head Postmaster to demand an immediate enquiry be launched.

Almina was always out of pocket with this egg venture. The only economy that was effected was to suggest the return of the egg boxes for reuse, albeit Almina did not approve of this on account of her concern that her generosity would be seen as a cheap transaction rather than a genuine gift.

A family at war

While his mother packed eggs in boxes, the 6th Earl spent much of his time pining at Highclere for his absent wife, Tilly Losch, who had fled to America. The whole Carnarvon family was united in disgust at Tilly's refusal to be with her husband. All corners of the family offered sympathy and support to the 6th Earl, and Almina sent telegrams[736] to her daughter-in-law, which were ignored. Tilly constantly conceived new excuses – from being stranded because of the war and being concerned for her mother's health to attempting to kick-start her dancing and film career which could only happen in America. The Herberts conspired to gather their own dirt on Tilly, past present and future. There were legal issues around the marriage and divorce proceedings were not without disaster and crippling expense. The whole thing was dragged on until Tilly capitulated in 1947, and Porchey had to pay an allowance towards her keep until she died in 1975. [737]

The 6th Earl was lonely. He was also separated from his regular girlfriend, actress Jeanne Stuart [738], who was working for The Entertainments National Service Association in shows, mostly overseas, to raise troop morale. Based at Salisbury, the 6th Earl worked for some time for Major General Sir Herbert Cole, the originator of the Claims Commission and Inspector of Lands at the War Office, but in general he did little to support the war effort. He spent time at his stable, which continued to function through the war years, training horses for a number of racing peers and peeresses, notably Lavinia, Duchess of Norfolk, wife of the Earl Marshall of England. Shooting also continued at Highclere and a constant stream of guests passed through its portals.

The Beauchamps were similarly detached from the war. In the mid 1940s there were major concerns for Lady Evelyn's husband, Sir Brogrove, after a heart scare, but he recovered under the supervision of royal physician Sir Maurice Cassidy. The couple patronised The Ritz hotel and constantly complained of poor service and its wartime decline without a thought for the struggles the old time establishments were suffering with their key staff on war duties. They were also seen at Highclere, where their daughter Patricia got along famously with her cousin Lady Penelope Herbert, who was a similar age.

Almina was a regular at Highclere too during the war, and enjoyed spending time with her grandchildren, who called her 'Granny'. When not at the family seat she would write to her grandchildren, sharing titbits of her outings. For example, in a letter to her grandson Lord Porchester dated 15 August 1944 Almina writes of her visit to a war hospitals near Taunton in the aftermath of the D-Day landings to "chat with the boys from Normandy". In the same letter Almina says she had not gone to London "since 'Doodlebugs' made their first appearance", adding "not that they intimidate me". She continues:

"Hence the reason I stay put in my cabbage patch, my weekly jaunts consist in a run to Minehead and ditto to Taunton chiefly for household shopping and items of interest do not thrive on these bushes." [739]

But charming as she could be with her grandchildren, Almina's affection did not stretch to holding her tongue when their actions could affect the family name. Almina made no bones of the fact that she did not approve when her granddaughter Penelope (the 6th Earl and Countess's daughter) announced her engagement to Captain Gerrit van der Woude of the Grenadier Guards on 19 February 1945. Nevertheless, the couple were married at St Michael's Church, Highclere on 21 April 1945, and the following month the 6th Earl and his former wife Catherine, with whom he was on civil terms, gave a reception at the Dorchester Hotel to celebrate the marriage.

The reason for Almina's disapproval was something one did not speak of in polite society: Penelope and Gerrit were cousins, sharing a common Wendell great great grandfather, Jacob Wendell of Portsmouth, USA. [740] She warned that no good could come of a union of blood relations; and when, in 1952, the couple's third child, Almina's great-grandchild, was born disabled, the Countess was merciless in her comments. [741] As it was, the child, Catherine, lived to 25 and upon her death the family intimation recorded of "whose happy zest for life charmed." [742]

Almina and the Butler sisters

With the easing of the war time conditions it meant Almina was free to travel once more and escape the stresses and mundanity of her daily life. The South of France was Almina's idea of heaven on earth, and she had a mind to travel there at once. The Countess, JTS and Alice Butler made the journey whilst the innumerable casualties of war were still returning home. It was during this six week holiday at the Hotel du Cap, Eden Roc, Antibes, that JTS began a sexual relationship with Alice.

In September 1945 seven-year-old Tony Leadbetter came to stay at Orchard Grove. Uprooted by the war, his mother Anne was an accomplished knitter and sewer, and Almina took Anne on to tackle some long overdue sewing and to generally help out, thus, with income tight, saving on the hiring of a seamstresses.

About the same time Alice's standing in the household was exposed. Several events prompted this, the key element being Almina's discovery of JTS's affair with her.

JTS was a ladies' man whose matinee idol looks resembled the American singer Bing Crosby. Tony Leadbetter describes JTS as "lecherous" and "a bounder", the same features that were shared by Colonel Ian Dennistoun.

When Almina found out that Alice had been conducting a close relationship with JTS[743] – the couple had even been caught out having sex in the grounds of Orchard Grove – she was furious. She dubbed Alice thereafter "The Rat", corroborating that Almina had, despite the age difference, her own personal aspirations for continuing her marital relationship with JTS. She was appalled that the golden rule of chastity between the man of the house and the staff had been contravened (she conveniently pushed from her mind the fact she, too, had ignored this taboo in the past when it suited her: she told Tony Leadbetter that she had enjoyed, Lady Chatterley style, a romance with one of her first husband's gardeners).

Almina's summary justice was intended to be harsh. She arranged for Alice "The Rat" to be sent away from her sister to Ditchley Park, near Charlbury, Oxfordshire, to work for the proprietor of the grand house and 3,000 acre estate, Ronald Tree (1897–1976). A millionaire and former MP, Tree was an old friend of the Carnarvon family and was happy to help Almina dispose of her traitorous staff member. But ironically, this new employment was the making of Alice Butler. She subsequently went to America with the Trees, and was with them for many years thereafter. She became a close confidante of Ronald's wife Marietta (1917–1991), who was a well-known and respected American political activist and nursemaid to Marietta's daughters, Penelope and Frankie.[744] Despite the rift with Almina, Alice visited her sister Anne throughout the years that followed in the various homes kept by Almina. During these annual pilgrimages back to England, her one time betrayal of trust was remembered but not retried, and Almina tolerated Alice as her sister Anne had become indispensable to the household and her stay at Orchard Grove became a permanent arrangement.

With the abrupt departure of Alice from the household, Anne stepped up to fulfil her sister's role. But another reason that Anne Leadbetter came to live permanently at Orchard Grove was that

Almina discovered that she was an excellent dressmaker. Almina had always had her dresses made for her by the most famed Paris couturiers. As she stood just over four feet in height her clothes and shoes (size three) had always been made specially. She prized her collections of shoes and hats, many of which were handmade for her in the South of France. Tony Leadbetter reports that at one count her collection of shoes alone numbered 76 pairs.

To reward Anne, Almina suggested a holiday away in the South of France. And so it was that young Tony was left in the care of Orchard Grove's animal keeper, Jim Criddle, and his wife, Sally, while his mother accompanied Almina, together with JTS, for a tour of the Countess's beloved places – to Paris, where she had grown up as a child, and to Monte Carlo, where her family friend Prince Victor Duleep Singh was buried. Almina spared no expense for this luxurious trip, staying in exclusive hotels, including the Hotel Metropole at Monte Carlo, and insisting that Anne stay in a guest room adjacent to hers rather than the dingy servants' quarters. The trip cost a colossal £3,000.[745] Anne fell in love with a Belgian chauffeur (named Eugene, whom she wrote to for several years).[746] This attachment ensured, in the short term, at least, that JTS made no improper advances upon Anne.

Over time Almina became fond of Anne, and her young son, and she extended her natural generosity to them when she could. When Anne was taken ill with a diseased ovary the Countess paid for Anne's treatment; and she also footed the bill for Tony to have his tonsils removed in a private nursing home in Fitzroy Square, London. When the young boy was taken suddenly ill with appendicitis and rushed to Bridgewater General Hospital, Almina even donned her whites to assist with the emergency appendectomy, and took great interest in the boy's care, including advising doctors on which drugs he should be given.

In addition, because Anne was not paid wages, Almina would cover the costs of bringing up Tony. She bought up clothing coupons from villagers (who preferred the cash involved) and suits, trousers, jackets, coats, shoes and shirts were ordered from the local high class tailors in Taunton for school and Sunday school. She also took an interest in his education, and would take him to church on a Sunday. The boy was soon serving as one of her regular and close attendants, and in later years he would became her principal chaperone on trips to London and elsewhere.

Although based on genuine affection for her staff, Almina was a controlling employer, and would impose her views on the members of her household. For example, for any ailment Almina would prescribe a dose of cascara, liquid paraffin or syrup of figs to cleanse the colon – essential to good health, in Almina's view; and another tip imparted by the Countess, which she is said to have religiously followed, was never to wear underwear. When Anne's husband Peter came to Orchard Grove to attempt some kind of reconciliation, Almina persuaded Anne to have nothing to do with the man. Tony recalls that his father arrived one evening and was simply gone the next day. He never saw him again. Almina's kindness and personal interest in their lives meant Anne was left unable to leave Almina's service, or to ever go against her employer's directions.

The good life at Orchard Grove

With the war behind them and the drama of the JTS/Alice affair diffused, life settled down for the residents of Orchard Grove. When Almina had moved to there in 1943 she had taken a lease on the property for £325 a year. Now, although she had not entirely given up on returning to nursing in some form, Almina recognised that her advancing age and meagre resources (she was living largely on allowances from the Carnarvon estates, past and present, which amounted to around £6,500 per year) were insufficient. Thus she decided to stay put in her cabbage patch, but in 1947 she bought the cottage, borrowing the £5,250 required from the 6th Earl, creating a permanent home for herself and her 'family' of JTS, Anne and Tony.

Tony Leadbetter offers this vivid description of Orchard Grove, from November 1945:

> Orchard Grove was a most attractive cottage, set in the heart of the Quantock Hills, in the village of Bicknoller. The cottage was thatched, with land of six acres consisting of planned orchards with some two-thousand apple trees and other fruits. There was an apple packing shed, a garage and several outhouses. There was a grape vine and a fruit-cage containing all the usual soft fruits. The garden and lawns were well maintained by a gardener.
>
> Every variety of rose tree surrounded the lawns. The Victoria plum trees were carefully trained around the main windows at the front of the house, which faced south. There was a veranda and French windows on the west side of the house, which led from the parlour. Wisteria was well

established around the honeysuckle and clematis. There was one special tree of nectarines near the veranda.

Inside was small but adequate; the curtains at the windows were lined with wartime black out material. The upstairs consisted of three bedrooms, a bathroom and separate toilet, and various built-in cupboards. The downstairs comprised two main reception rooms, a dining room, a "Glory-hole" with washing and ironing materials, outdoor shoes and coats and storage cupboards. There was a kitchen and pantry, with a dining area for staff. There was also a bedroom, study and bathroom en suite at the back of the house.

The walls were finished in magnolia paint work and the doors and staircase were of polished pine. A Wilton "Donkey Brown" carpet was fitted throughout.

There was also a detached building, a large room made from brick and wood, which Almina called The Wigwam[747]. This was situated in the rear garden and provided additional sleeping accommodation. It was used mainly for storing old furniture. [748]

Tony loved playing in The Wigwam, where Almina stored many of the unsold pieces of furniture, but more interesting to a young boy, left over medical supplies from all of Almina's nursing homes. Free to rummage in medical paraphernalia and fascinated by Almina's tales of her hospitals and homes, Tony naturally gained an early interest in medicine, which led to his own life-long career in nursing.

Though she now lived in a little country cottage with her dogs (including a Labrador from Highclere[749]), vestiges of Almina's previous riches remained all around as reminders of the past. Despite the succession of sales to raise new funds, Almina retained a good deal of furniture, soft furnishings and decorations from her time at Eastmore, London and Hove in her thatched cottage in Somerset. She still cherished her Queen Anne period walnut knee-hole desk, and the collection of cushions of velvet and damask silk material. There was also a series of large watercolour pictures of Chinese subjects, one showing a solitary mandarin on a throne, which she treasured. A Jacobean side-board graced the dining room with a reproduction dining room table and sixteen chairs made of deep red mahogany. Further exquisite examples of Charles II dark oak, carved, cane-backed chairs graced the cottage along with several Queen Anne wing chairs.

In the kitchen shelves were laden with Georgian copper saucepans and steam kettles with the Rothschild monogram and other pieces, including crockery with the Carnarvon crest. Glassware included a collection of 17th-century-style facet-stemmed glassware, which had been a wedding gift from Alfred de Rothschild. These glasses had been superbly copied and comprised wine, claret and champagne flutes together with goblets covered in a pattern of different fruits.

Almina also proudly retained a Royal Lily pattern Worcester tea/dinner service from circa 1790, one of the few examples of family relics she still had from the Carnarvon's Bretby Park estate. The set was brought into use every single Sunday. On this day JTS's daughter, Doreen, would visit Orchard Grove from her nearby school, usually brining along a girlfriend, and Almina would preside over high tea in traditional old English country style, with best silver, best china, best glasses[750] and best frocks.

Among Almina's other prized collections she would never relinquish was a vast number of pure silk scarves. Her particular favourites included those of pure Indian silk that were gifted to her by Prince Victor Duleep Singh and his brother Frederick. She invariably wore these on trips away. She also treasured a number of personally signed photographs, many from ex-patients of Alfred House, including film stars and royalty.

The Countess and JTS always dressed in style for evening dinner at 8pm, preceded by cocktails at 7.30pm. She referred to JTS using the French *"Monsieur"* derived from "Mon" (My) and "Sieur" (Lord), and had everything laid on to please him. [751] With the blight of post-war rationing, Anne's culinary skills were stretched to capacity, but she used up all the glorious bounty that Orchard Grove had to offer. Combining this with the potted, tinned and jarred delicacies in the food hampers from London together with the inexhaustible supplies of eggs, milk, tomatoes, chickens, pork, rabbits[752] and apples, she created a superb range of hors d'oeuvre, main courses and deserts, achieving a standard of fare at the table equal to that any West End hotel. [753] The young seven-year-old Tony Leadbetter learned to crush the ice (from two refrigerators, one inside and one outside the cottage) to make intoxicating sidecar cocktails,[754] always a start to the evening for Almina and JTS.

At weekends Almina and JTS entertained trusted friends from Almina's small circle of retired ex-colonels and local squires. Regular visitors were Bicknoller's vicar, Rev. J. Hamilton-Jones,[755] and husband and wife Mr and Mrs Weston, from Minehead: a solicitor and his French wife with whom Almina enjoyed liberally conversing in her native tongue. JTS had a torrid affair with Mrs Weston, probably unknown to Almina. After dinner Tony's additional task was to set up a card table for playing bridge. When there were no visitors Tony and Anne made up the foursome to play cards.

Outings were also a high point for the residents of Orchard Grove. Almina took responsibility for virtually all the food shopping, and each Friday she would set out at seven-thirty in the morning driven by Ernie Bryant, the local car hire man. A picnic lunch was taken on these excursions, and Almina would often, on a whim, demanded detours. Tony Leadbetter recalls:

> She would just call in at private houses and tip the Butler. Where the owners were away she usually managed to get a viewing of their pictures, silver and furniture. She was also interested in seeing the gardens and architecture. She always left her card before departing. [756]

Life in the Quantock hills was mundane and tedious for Almina at times after the hustle and bustle of London life and running her nursing homes so in an effort to keep herself busy, she organised Christmas and New Year parties at Orchard Grove for the villagers. Harking back 40 years to the days of the 5th Earl shooting at Highclere, rabbit shoots were common. She also had great hams and hampers from Harrods and Fortnum & Mason sent down from London suppliers, making possible grand picnics and lunches at a time when post-war rationing was the norm.

Almina also organised and opened a village summer fete. Vans with loudspeakers attached to them drove around to inform people of events, a giant marquee was erected in case of wet weather and a rifle range was set up in a local quarry (this was favoured by JTS, always a man with a gun, and it would become a permanent feature of village life). Almina won doubters over by agreeing that part of the proceeds from the fete would go to a fund for rebuilding the village hall. Anne Leadbetter made various soft toys to sell and ran a fruit and vegetable stall, with copious produce coming from Orchard Grove, including fresh eggs. Almina helped out on Anne's stall, raising over £70, and afterwards a dance was held for the villagers. The event was a remarkable success, raising some £300 for the village hall fund and the British Legion. The village of Bicknoller had never seen anything like it before. Almina's spark lifted everyone's post-war blues, including her own.

In addition, Almina did not hesitate to act in favour of a villager when someone fell ill or in referring a sick neighbour for specialist help when she detected a medical urgency. Besides this Almina paid out generously for treatment in London for several local children who required to have their tonsils removed or to have a medical condition examined or corrected. [757]

Almina always attended the village church on Sundays, with the young Tony Leadbetter generally acting as her chaperone and bag carrier. This left JTS and Anne alone at Orchard Grove, with Anne faithfully seeing to the preparations for the traditional Sunday lunch. But this assured privacy for JTS and Anne during church going was to lead them behaving unfaithfully behind Almina's back, leading to a relationship of increasingly intimacy between them over time, with lewd undertones. [758]

Visiting London

Almina adored London. Trips from Bicknoller to London were organised weekly by Anne, sometimes by car, but more often by train, from Taunton. Almina adopted a London taxi driver, a Mr Williams, who met her at Paddington Station. Almina called Williams "Nosey" and he drove her about for a nominal fee of £5. When an overnight stay was necessary rooms were taken at The Cumberland Hotel, Marble Arch, usually the same rooms every trip on the second floor. Nosey was always at hand to assist Anne with the heavy luggage, including packing and unpacking. As there was no maid service at the Cumberland Almina adopted one of the chambermaids called Madge, who could always be won over by Almina's charm and kindness, in the event that Anne had stayed behind at Orchard Grove.

Almina was a creature of habit. Merely to be seen in London ensured that news of her existence continued to be relayed amongst those who knew her or knew of her. There were trips to her hairdresser Valentino, and to her chemist Martindales to stock up on her oil and medicines. There was always a call to Tessiers, the Bond Street jewellers, usually with a request for some minor repair to a clock or watch. Presents for weddings and christenings were always purchased at Tessiers, and several unique jewels were sold by them for Almina over the years to provide funds. The directors of the company were amongst her "great trusted friends". [759]

While in London Almina regularly visited her dentist, Cyril Bowdler Henry[760], at Harley Street – dentist to all of Society's most prominent figures. Almina was unflatteringly portrayed by A.J. Cronin in his book *The Citadel* as having "ill-fitting false teeth". Her false teeth troubled Almina for decades, and she would carry an adhesive around with her in a special compartment of her handbag – a pigskin case containing her essential, including her cheque book, pen and blotter. [761]

Although death hit hard at many of Almina's contemporaries, she still enjoyed seeing those old friends that survived in London, albeit mostly by default when dining at Wiltons Restaurant or the Savoy Grill. [762] She readily accepted invitations to weddings and attended funerals, but always resisted attempts by any of those she came into contact with to visit her at Orchard Grove. She continued to appear in all the lists of wedding gifts sent to old English family couplings, such as Almina the "charming wedding present" she sent to Princess Elizabeth on the occasion of her marriage to Prince Philip.[763]

On the rare occasions when JTS was in attendance in London he was never introduced to anyone, which naturally saved on an explanation about his precise role or status. If pressed he was passed over as her associate, driver or secretary. JTS always had a motor car, including a series of Austin saloons, but his pride and joy in later years was a 3.4 Jaguar, from the same vintage as TV's Inspector Morse, albeit JTS's was coloured black.

The Carnarvons sometimes saw Almina in London. Both the 6th Earl and Lady Evelyn Beauchamp favoured staying at The Ritz hotel and met her there for lunch. Evelyn's husband was inclined to absent himself, and if they met he would walk past Almina without acknowledging her. Porchey's wife Tilly Losch was absent – the 6th Earl was in the process of divorcing Tilly and it was rumoured that he intended to marry his long-term girlfriend Jeanne Stuart once he was free to do so.

Almina often returned to Somerset on an evening train, always travelling first class. According to Tony Leadbetter the members of Almina's close family generally only visited her at Orchard Grove, or at any of her later homes, for the purposes of obtaining her signature on a document relating to the Carnarvon family settlement or estates. Catherine, the 6th Countess, was a visitor from time to time as she remained on very good terms with Almina.

A scheming swindler?

Almina always kept up appearances, refusing to admit to her mounting debt. But in 1948 the dark cloud of financial ruin hung over Almina. The result of the complete failure of the business ventures at Orchard Grove with Almina's lavish funding and JTS's naive organisation was a very large overdraft at the bank. Almina had charmed a succession of bank managers into granting her loans that were somewhat unrealistically beyond her means to repay. The mood of the period was glum. But the Countess had always managed to pull off a financial coup when she was in a corner and needed to realise cash, and she held on to this hope.

Up until this point, there had always been things to sell, but now the best of Almina's jewellery was long gone. The woman who had worn some of world's most precious gems[764] was reduced to wearing French paste, with only the best surviving from her collection of "Ciro" of Bond Street. She had a few oddments of silver gilt, including some pins and clasps, but these were not exceptional. Some silver coffee pots, cruets and cutlery were sold. The contents of several picnic hampers that contained silver items also went to auction. But these efforts were merely drops in the ocean, and now Almina faced the fact that Orchard Grove would have to be sold.

Thus in March 1949 Orchard Grove was sold for £9,000 to an aging Colonel named Woodcock and his sister. The proceeds allowed Almina to pay off some debts, but she was not able to repay the sum of £5,250 borrowed from her son for the original purchase. Henry was furious with his mother – she hadn't even told him she was selling the cottage – and accused her of deception. According to the author Victor Winstone: "When he [the 6th Earl] discovered what had happened he wrote to his mother in green ink calling her a scheming swindler."[765] A further letter arrived from the 6th Earl that left Almina feeling "worried and frightened".[766] The heavy tone and threats in the letter was followed up by a writ from the 6th Earl demanding his rightful share of the proceeds of the sale. Almina did not have the money to settle this demand. She decided to play for time, calling her son's bluff.

Move to Higher Hopcott

Despite JTS being no better qualified than being a heating engineer, he convinced Almina that he could be a successful farmer and produce enough profit to provide them all with an additional household income. Almina longed to be nearer to London, but she conceded and looked for a farmhouse or smallholding in the surrounding area to allow JTS to continue his impossible dream.

A frantic search followed by road, with a series of drivers being employed to allow Almina to scour Somerset, Devon and Dorset. Almina took the opportunity to visit her estranged sister-in-law Mary Herbert (widow of Aubrey) at Pixton Park, Dulverton. The two women had not seen each other for many years, but Almina stayed for only a couple of hours.

Eventually a property was located: Higher Hopcott on the Lutterell Estate, near Minehead. In an isolated position on a hill, the property had not been occupied for several years and was in a near-derelict condition. Tony Leadbetter recalls that the only attractive feature was its old water wheel. Still, for Almina the renovation was another challenge to get stuck into. She acquired the property at extraordinary cost, agreeing to a 14-year lease at £600 a year. Then she extravagantly committed between £2,500 and £3,000 to renovating the house of seven bedrooms and outbuildings.

The renovations included a complete new roof and electrical rewiring; a new bathroom, cloakroom, study and pantry; the relocation of the dining room; redecoration throughout; and outside rebuilding of outbuilding, weeding of the overgrown grounds and a new tarmac driveway. New carpet was laid throughout the house, and an AGA and electric cooker were installed in the kitchen. Only the curtains and furniture were carried forth from Orchard Grove.

During the renovations builders worked for many weeks to satisfy Almina's wants, as her instructions seemed to change almost daily. She directed Anne Leadbetter to organise grand picnics for the workers, with hot soups and sandwiches. True to form, Almina insisted on handling any cuts or injuries sustained by the workmen and laid on a first aid table and all manner of dressings and plasters. A supply of brandy was also at hand for any cases of shock.

Finally, the work was done and Almina, JTS, Anne and Tony moved to Higher Hopcott. The plan was to operate the property as a working farm. The smallholding comprised about 100 acres of land for crops and grazing. JTS intended this be worked as a partnership between himself, his brother Alf Stocking and Jim Criddle, who had looked after the animals at Orchard Grove. Farm stock was purchased, including a carthorse named Prince, a herd of young heifers, sheep, pigs, hens, geese and turkeys. The real farmer was Jim Criddle. He worked very hard to make a success of the farm. [767]

The problem was that Almina had little remaining capital left to pay for the final key elements of JTS's project at Higher Hopcott. So in July 1949 she took the quite drastic step of making an absolute assignment of all her remaining interests. The trustees were empowered to mortgage the assets in order to raise £12,000. They were instructed to pay certain outgoings and to apply the surplus to her maintenance.

Regardless of her financial struggles, Almina held her head high at her granddaughter's wedding later that year. Patricia Beauchamp married Major Michael Leatham at St Margaret's, Westminster. The reception was at The Ritz.

As the 1940s ended the ambitious farming venture at Higher Hopcott was in full swing. There had been some successful elements with haymaking, and the production of flowers (mainly daffodils) and large amounts of rhubarb, which were sold at market. But whatever success the business achieved was dwarfed by the outlay cost; and the income made no sizable return or profit. Moreover, the income tax authorities were now homing in on Almina for unpaid duties over a number of years.

Encouraged by JTS, Almina attempted to hide her last pieces of valuable furniture, passing some on to friends and placing others in storage in Bristol, marking many of them "Property of James Timothy Stocks". She continued to sell off possessions too. One painting of Chinese noblewoman was not hard to part with: Almina had just realised it included a small detail of some peacock feathers, which were supposed to bring bad luck, in a corner, which she had hitherto overlooked. Superstitious to the core, Almina thought selling the painting may alleviate her run of misfortune. But the worst of times was still to come.

Chapter 12
1950–1959

A Penniless Countess

The law comes knocking

For many years, Almina had used her charms, ingenuity and willingness to part with assets to keep afloat in the face of financial difficulties. But by 1950, the proud Countess faced total ruin.

In the 40 years since the deaths of her wealth-providers, Marie Wombwell, Alfred de Rothschild and the 5th Earl of Carnarvon, Almina spent a king's ransom. She had used and abused every last vestige of her portfolio of investments, properties, land, antiques, life insurances and loans; every asset was gone. She still received income from the Carnarvon estate, controlled by its trustees, but this dwarfed the debts. She'd sold off assorted collectibles, and now the only possessions the once grand lady had to her name were some furniture and some copper saucepans, crockery, glassware and linen, the last relics of her illustrious past bearing Carnarvon, Dennistoun or Rothschild coats of arms.

Almina couldn't pay the bills on Higher Hopcott Farm. She could barely afford to plan her next meal for fear of eviction. And so it was that 14-year-old Tony Leadbetter was sent to Anne's father and stepmother at Amport, Hampshire, while Almina, JTS and Anne moved into a furnished cottage in the nearby village of Cleeve. It was here that Almina received a bankruptcy summons. Head held high and back ramrod straight in typical Almina fashion, the Dowager Countess of Carnarvon graciously invited the server of the writ from the Inland Revenue "to step inside for a sherry".[768]

Clearly, Almina's personal financial management had brought her to this point; but others had a part to play in her downfall too. Her solicitor, William H. Chitty, had been negligent, mismanaging her accounts and tax returns. He was only saved from blame and referral for professional misconduct by the fact that he was in grave health: Almina would not hear "of the poor man being hounded".[769] But more disturbing is the part Almina's own son played in bringing the law to her door.

The 6th Earl had watched for years, enraged, as his mother frittered away his would-be Carnarvon legacy, and it was only *after* he reported the liabilities to them that the Inland Revenue pursued Almina's tax arrears.[770] He'd first issued an abortive writ for the recovery of monies owed him to drive home a salutary lesson. But the last straw had been Almina selling Orchard Grove for £9,000 whilst failing to repay him the original loan of £5,250 she had taken from her son in order to buy the cabbage patch. On this count he called his mother "a scheming swindler".[771] He heartlessly threatened her over the secret sale, whilst he enjoyed good fortunes himself: on the turf, one horse, Tilloy, bought for £10,000, won several races.[772]

Almina and the 6th Earl at Highclere had engaged in dramatic showdowns before. In the aftermath of the 5th Earl's death in 1923, when the 6th Earl discovered his meagre inheritance after the burden of death duties and virtually everything going to his mother, he shut off one of the Castle's rooms, Almina's favourite, in protest.[773] It was only reopened after the 6th Earl's death in 1987. Whatever assaults took place between them at Highclere in 1951, each was unrepentant: Henry felt justified in sticking in the knife, and Almina appeared stoic and oblivious to her son's poison dart, and the humiliating consequences, remaining aloof and saying she was in no mood to apologise. Of course, inside she must have been hurt by her own son's betrayal, and afraid of how she would cope with the imminent bankruptcy.

Taking to the dock once more

Named and shamed in the *London Gazette*, "Almina Victoria Marie Alexandra (widow), Countess of Carnarvon, Higher Hopcott, Minehead, Somerset", became the subject of a Receiving Order. The petition was filed on 29 June 1951 and the Receiving Order made on 24 July 1951. The first meeting of the creditors took place on 16 August 1951, and her public examination was set for 10.30am on 2 September 1951 in Bristol's Guildhall.

Anne remained at Cleeve, on tenterhooks, whilst Almina's solicitor, William H. Chitty, accompanied his client to the hearing. The bankruptcy proceedings were a concern to Anne's tenure but she cost nothing; she was not paid a wage. Almina had assured her (and JTS) that whilst the future looked uncertain, the Carnarvon estate trustees would fund accommodation and the 6th Earl would demand this be as far away as possible from under his rafters.

In the public examination the Official Receiver announced that Almina owed £22,000 to the Inland Revenue for tax and super tax covering the previous five years, and that her only asset was household furniture valued at £1,000. A statement of affairs showed unsecured liabilities of £30,763.

It had been a quarter of a century since Almina had set foot in a dock. Then, in 1925, she had defending her husband, Colonel Dennistoun, with all her heart and soul. But now, in 1951, the petite, 75-year-old, silver-haired lady was a sombre, lonely figure in the courtroom, peering through her black netted veil at the courtroom as she stood to defend herself.

Questioning Almina was Leonard Ingram, the Official Receiver. Ingram was a polite official, but he did not shrink from doing his job, and he was determined to glean the unvarnished truth about Almina's downfall. Almina, meanwhile, expected to be portrayed as a spendthrift, but had no intention of being seen as a spent force. Her performance was heroic, as the following extract from the examination shows:

> Official Receiver: Shall I use the phrase that you have used in your examination, Lady Carnarvon... that you have been too "extravagant and generous" if you will accept that? Is that right?
> Almina: Well, I suppose so. But it is not up to me to say I am generous. It would be blowing my own trumpet wouldn't it, which I do not intend to do.
> Official Receiver: It was to be fair to you, Lady Carnarvon. Would it be an exaggeration to say you have been a kind of fairy godmother to all and sundry?
> Almina: Yes, I have: I hope I have been.[774]

Being likened to a "fairy godmother" provided the headlines for the newspapers, who said Almina "laughed away" the suggestion that her debts were due to extravagance and generosity. Bristol papers covered the story on the front page; the London *Times* and the Manchester *Guardian* gave it a column, the *Daily Mirror* and *Daily Express* barely an inch or two of space.

Almina struggled to retain her composure with some replies, but she got through the examination, falling on an extraordinary mix of feigned naivety, aristocratic arrogance and self-mockery:

Official Receiver: What has caused your insolvency?
Almina: Not having had sufficient means to meet my liabilities.
Official Receiver: Agreed, but how did the liabilities arise?
Almina: There are always liabilities are there not?
Official Receiver: I note that on three occasions it was necessary for you to raise funds to meet recent liabilities.
Almina: Yes.
Official Receiver: Representations have been made to you of the need for economy?
Almina: Many and often.
Official Receiver: With what result?
Almina: Nil. [775]

The Countess was quick to find reasons to account for her high expenditure, such as her huge telephone bills:

Official Receiver: Did you know your telephone bill for each half-year fluctuated between £90.00 and £150.00?
Almina: Yes.
Official Receiver: That compares with that of a well-known firm in this City [of Bristol] that has *three* lines working. Frankly, do you think that was justified your Ladyship?
Almina: Well I think so. For one thing my children are very scattered. They would reproach me if I did not ring them up. [776]

Ingram conceded that he was confused about the returns submitted by Almina's accountants for the five years 1946 to 1951. The income in round figures was shown as £18,100, £16,900, £15,600, £15,300 and £11,300.

Official Receiver: I should say in fairness to her Ladyship that these figures really give a distorted picture. At the time of the sale to the family of the Half Million Fund in 1939, members of the family covenanted to make up Lady Carnarvon's income to a certain figure and for the purposes of total income and taxation the covenanted figures are grossed up, consequently the actual income is probably not much more than £6,000 a year. [777]

In fact, Almina's income comprised around £6,500 a year from settlements following the 5th Earl's death in 1923, including £2,000 a year from a 1923 deed of covenant, £1,000 a year from an 1895 jointure, £1,000 a year from a settlement from 1874 and £2,500 a year from the Pixton estate, under the will of the 5th Earl. Chitty said that his client's income tax was paid in full. A liability to surtax of over £20,000 remained, albeit this was based on grossed up figures. Almina's surtax (incredibly) was £5,000 a year, a staggering percentage of her total annual income of £6,500. It was this year on year accumulation that had broken Almina's liquidity.

In his examination Ingram went on to pry into all areas of Almina's life and past, which the Countess must have found excruciatingly invasive. Still, she kept her cool demeanour, dismissing questioning of her business dealings at Higher Hopcott Farm as "so minute" that she "did not take a great interest in it". She was also careful to conceal the truth of JTS's status, whose name came up in connection with its regular appearance in Almina's bank statements. In explanation she maintained "he had been a friend for a great number of years, and was a combination of Secretary and Agent". [778]

Finally, the Official Receiver found Almina's Achilles heel. He noted she'd made many gifts over the years, and asked whether she could submit a list of names and addresses of recipients in the two previous years with a view to taking back the gifts. Almina was appalled. These were gifts to old friends; many were wedding presents (newspaper reports show her many contributions to Society nuptials in the 1940s), and there were also thoughtful gifts to former nursing staff who'd served her faithfully. Ingram's action to recover them was devastating. But gone were the tears and fainting spells of the Dennistoun court room drama; now, Almina stood strong and replied that there were so many gifts that she "could not possibly tell" and insisted that "they were not anything of great importance" and "very often a bag or gloves, handkerchiefs, stockings or soap". [779] But Ingram was determined, insisting it was "his duty to recover such gifts given by her" to others. Chitty promised to undertake to provide the information required, and Almina left the proceedings silenced – and officially bankrupt.

The examination was over, but it would be almost a decade before the Inland Revenue stopped investigating Almina because the question of unpaid legacy duty. While it is apparent from Alfred de Rothschild's estate (files in the National Archives, Kew[780]) that Almina paid large amounts of legacy duty in the 1920s when she inherited or sold off the contents of 1 Seamore Place, the Inland Revenue continued to pursue further sums of legacy duty from the later proceeds of antiques, furniture, regarding pictures sold *after* this period, and on items which were exempt from duty until actually sold. In truth, Almina had been party to deception, using private sales to acquire ready cash, and she'd stonewalled the Inland Revenue for years. But finally, concluding that the Countess

wouldn't recover from her permanent state of bankruptcy, in 1960
the Inland Revenue closed the file.

Park Cottage, Cleeve

Almina had acquired her new abode at Park Cottage, Cleeve, by
calling in favours with the Cowlin sisters, Gertrude, Mabel and Rose,
with whom she had once served on nursing committees. The cottage
was the home of their late brother, Sir Francis Cowlin (1868–1945[781])
of William Cowlin & Son, Bristol, a notable firm of builders. After
Sir Francis's death the furnished property had stood unoccupied.
The site stood on a hill, and had served as a vicarage for the
adjoining Holy Trinity Church. It had commanding views of the
landscape, with woodlands, off the main Bristol to Weston-Super-
Mare road.

Tony Leadbetter recalls arriving there for the first time in an old
Austin Eighteen driven by Ernie Bryant, the regular driver used by
Almina. (Alice Butler was home from the USA and accompanied
Tony to see Anne. Despite the animosity over Alice's affair with JTS,
Almina permitted her to stay for short visits, but behind her back she
still referred to her as "The Rat"[782].) Tony paints a vivid picture of
Almina's new home:

> There were two side entrances. The garden was full of evergreens and fir
> trees with a rockery. There were two garden ponds containing oversized
> goldfish and water lilies. A shaped, oak garden seat was inscribed and
> dedicated to Sir William Cowlin at exactly his favourite spot. There was
> also a flagpole, which flew the flag of St George of England. Otherwise
> flowers, with tubs of geraniums in summer, surrounded the area. The
> cottage was covered in spreading ivy, honeysuckle and wisteria, with
> rambler roses at the door porch.
>
> Inside the fittings were mahogany. A collection of Crown Derby porcelain
> was laid out in the alcoves. In the dining room was an early oak dresser
> with a collection of pewter plates, with an oak refractory table and
> matching Windsor chairs.
>
> Ancient calendars hung in the lavatories. A collection of ink drawings of
> local churches lined the main staircase; Cowlin had been responsible for
> restoring many of these old ecclesiastical buildings. All the bedrooms had
> mahogany washstands, with pales, jugs and chamber pots. In the kitchen
> a dresser dominated with a collection of willow-patterned china. [783]

Mabel (May) Cowlin called each Friday to collect the rent of £8.
Almina, the 5th Countess of Carnarvon, who had spent millions of

pounds in her lifetime, was reduced to an impoverished tenant, forced to live in a house surrounded by a dead man's cast-offs.

Death of King George VI

Almina was an enthusiastic royalist. She was concerned for the 56-year-old King, George VI, who'd reigned for sixteen years. With her long-standing medical knowledge she could tell by looking at his face in the newsreels of the doom to come. She sent him loyal and loving wishes, closely following the reports of his weeks of endurance after an operation for the removal of a cancerous growth on a lung. She mourned at the sight of the tired, willowy figure of the "hatness and scarfless"[784] old man who bade farewell to Princess Elizabeth when she flew off on a five-month world tour.

King George's death came in his sleep at Sandringham a few days later on 6 February 1952. He and the Queen had earned wide popularity, but Almina was never on close terms with Lady Elizabeth Bowes Lyon, albeit she and the 5th Earl had witnessed her early appearances at Court Balls (overlapping with Lady Evelyn's coming out) and had jointly attended fundraising events for the Marie Curie Cancer Fund. Almina confined sending her condolences to the King's mother, Queen Mary, at Marlborough House.

It filled Almina with huge pride that her grandson, Lord Porchester, was one of the soldiers chosen to guard the old monarch's coffin lying in state at Westminster Hall as people filed past to pay their respects. Happy to avoid large Society gatherings herself after the shame of her public bankruptcy proceedings the previous year, Almina paid her respects to the King at her local church in Cleeve on 16 February 1952.

Almina kept a low profile for the rest of the year. She was estranged from her son, so took little interest in the drama at Highclere following a break-in by thieves whilst the 6th Earl was absent in New York.[785] Meanwhile, Almina received news of the death of Sir Milsom Rees (1866–1952), a doctor who had tended the Royal Household in her nursing home days and also Alfred de Rothschild's best friend and a close acquaintance of the 5th Earl. Once the death may have opened the door for more financial manoeuvring – Rees had been Alfred's principal executor following the death of Marshall Hall, but was less agreeable to her adventurous financial schemes and rash disposal of funds than Alfred or Sir Edward – but now, penniless, the death was merely another reminder of Almina's own advancing years.

Refusing help

In 1953 Almina's plight was a talking point at the wedding of 83-year-old peer Walter Patrick Hore-Ruthven (1870–1956), the 10th Lord Ruthven, to his ex-secretary. The best man (Lord Ruthven's brother) was Alexander (Sandy) Gore Arkwright Hore Ruthven (1872–1955), the Earl of Gowrie, a former Governor General of Australia, the current Deputy Constable and Lieutenant Governor of Windsor Castle and, as we shall see, a dear friend to Almina. Among the attendees was Ruthven's son-in-law, Sir Walter Monckton, the legal figure of the abdication crisis of 1936, and his wife, Bridget Helen Hore-Ruthven (1896–1982), Lady Monckton, and a dear friend of Almina who visited her often before and after Walter Monckton's death. Monckton was also Almina's Member of Parliament, representing Bristol West.

Both Gowrie and Monckton considered that the country owed Almina a debt of honour. Her husband, the 5th Earl of Carnarvon, had played a legendary role in British history in unearthing the great Tutankhamun treasures in Egypt. Moreover, Almina had made an important contribution to the war effort in running her wartime hospitals. It shamed these fine gentlemen to know that the aging Countess had been dragged through the bankruptcy courts. Thus they visited Almina several times to persuade her to have the case reheard, Gowrie even arriving with a full military escort from Windsor Castle. Monckton was prepared to fight her corner, at his own expense. Both men expected an appeal could be launched, to have the debts cleared and Almina's good name restored.

But Almina was resolute: she would not accept *any* offer to appeal her case. She was determined, it seems, to stand strong in the face of her son's act against her, to maintain a state of martyrdom over his wrongdoing, in her estimations, to as ever refuse to face up to her offences and the consequences of her own actions. She responded to these two old friends with the remark: "My family wanted me bankrupt, now they have their way."[786]

She was remarkably stoic in the face of her fall from grace. While JTS (and later Tony Leadbetter) took an almost proprietary interest in keeping track of the art treasures Almina had sold over the years to raise cash, especially when pieces reappeared in antiques sales at Sotheby's and Christies auction houses.[787] Almina was disinterested. She viewed such matters as water the bridge, feeling exactly the same about close personal relationships in her life that had crumbled. In her heyday, when she had money, she was generous in the mould of her one time mentor Alfred de Rothschild, shelling out to causes without strings. But now, in poorer circumstances, Almina considered that she had no cause left to fight save her own survival, and she was ever practical and unsentimental.

Further farewells

As the years passed by, it was inevitable that Almina would mourn the deaths of more of her contemporaries and old friends. On 8 March 1953 she was sad to receive news of the passing of Dr Marcus Beauchamp Johnston, (Dr Johnnie), the 5th Earl's committed doctor and Almina's friend, who "passed away peacefully"[788]in a London nursing home.[789] He was cremated at Golders Green. In his last years, including the war years, Almina's dear friend Dr Johnnie had remained a regular face at Highclere for Christmas or New Year, when Almina was in attendance at the same time. They shared unique memories, obligations and secrets.

Later that month, on 24 March, death came for Queen Mary. The austere and uncompromisingly regal Queen was aged 85, and passed away before she could see her granddaughter Princess Elizabeth (her dearest Lilibet, whom she had helped to rear and mentor) crowned sovereign. The coffin, with its scarlet and gold standard, lay on a high catafalque in state at Westminster Hall[790] and her funeral took place a week later at St George's Chapel, Windsor. Almina mourned a grand old lady whom she loved and admired and whose second son, George, and his wife had re-established the integrity of the monarchy. Almina empathised with the Queen over the defiance against the Crown of her playboy son David, albeit he was someone Almina liked and had come to know between 1931 and 1932 as Prince of Wales when his newly acquired lady friend, Mrs Wallis Simpson, was admitted to Alfred House for the removal of her tonsils, and later the treatment of ulcers.[791]

But the mournful season soon passed when the coronation of the 25-year-old Elizabeth II followed on 2 June of 1953, and the whole of Britain lit up from years of post-war gloom with parties, bonfires and fireworks. In Somerset, Anne's cake-making skills were in great demand for competitions, schools, hospitals and street celebrations. The coronation proceedings were also televised and dominated the newsreels; and Almina rejoiced along with everyone else when the young Queen took her solemn oath. It heralded a new age, with the end of wartime rationing, and offered hope for a period of calm and prosperity ahead.

Getting back on the scene

Despite suffering a tarnished reputation due to her bankruptcy, which was creating difficulties such as the loss of tradesmen's accounts and arrangements for household credit, Almina endeavoured to keep up appearances. The reaction of the older toothed in London Society was to shun a bankrupt, and Almina was at first excluded from the Season's invitation lists by some of her fellow peeresses and was given the cold shoulder by some diners in her favourite restaurants. But by 1954 she was once more moving around on the local scene and London circuit, comparatively undiminished by her blackened financial standing, with people treating her more or less as they had done before her fall of 1951.

In London, she called in at all old haunts. She made appearances at the celebrated Grosvenor House antique dealers' fairs, and stayed on good terms with the partners at Duveens, Sparks and Stuart & Turner.[792] She attended Society christenings and weddings, and funerals – usually those of the good and lamented friends, especially from the Great War era, or past staff and patients from Alfred House.

One noticeable absentee from Almina's appearances in public was Lady Evelyn Beauchamp, although Almina made a point of calling on her if the Beauchamps were in residence at The Ritz hotel. To avoid her disapproving son-in-law (who felt Almina had got everything she deserved), she only visited when Sir Brograve was busy attending business meetings on his various boards of directors. Otherwise, mother and daughter kept in touch by telephone throughout Almina's financial ordeal. Evelyn was a sympathetic party but powerless to confront her brother, who was in successful business partnership with her husband.[793]

At the age of 78, the enduring train journey from the West Country to Paddington and the return trip was hard for Almina. She still had the stamina of a woman ten years younger, but felt that going by road was less stressful. Thus, JTS often drove Almina up to London by car. The journey required an early start, which was not inconvenient to Almina, who was always an early riser: up and bathed in a piping hot bath by 6am. Comfort for the journey was provided by a configuration of soft and hard cushions, several travel rugs and a footstool. Tony Leadbetter recalls fondly:

> The cushions, rugs and foot stool were always impossible to position in a comfortable way before departing; they were often thrown out, and then replaced, sat on, and placed in the back and following a lot of agitation all around, finally being accepted.

> ... the fact that Almina was leaving home for the day was a just reward for being very patient and then relief at eventually seeing the car reversing out of the garage fore-court into the road.[794]

In Bristol, Almina also enjoyed days out, often with Anne for company, at a gallery or lunchtime concert, with tea (almost always Earl Grey for Almina[795]) taken at the Grand Hotel. Anne could be relied on to keep track of new art exhibitions, the visiting orchestras and guest conductors appearing in their midst. Sir Malcolm Sargent was one old associate of Almina's who came to Bristol in 1954 and 1955 for live broadcasts with the BBC Philharmonic Orchestra.[796]

Family affairs

Hollywood sources reported that the 6th Earl was stepping out with film stars like the actress Gene Tierney, but she and others quickly rejected his advances. Back in London, Henry was among those who buzzed around the whirl of fashionable meeting places like The Ritz, Savoy Grill or Café Royal. He was often sniffing out sexual conquests around mothering duchesses and their debutante daughters.

Almina didn't mention her son's name for some considerable time after he'd secured her financial ruin, and she refused to talk to him. She did, however, maintain a close relationship with his ex-wife, Catherine, now Mrs Momand after remarriage.[797] Almina was interested in hearing Catherine's news of what her grandson Henry, Lord Porchester, was doing.

The handsome, fair-haired and six-foot-tall Carnarvon heir, Henry Herbert of the Royal Horse Guards, was close to members of the Royal Family, especially, from childhood onwards[798], the Princesses

Elizabeth and Margaret Rose. Indeed, following the famous balcony scene with the King, Queen, Princesses and Winston Churchill at Buckingham Palace on VE Day, 8 May 1945, during the celebrations to recognise the end of the Second World War, it was with Porchester that the Princesses slipped away into the throngs of revellers in St James Street, Parliament Square, up Whitehall and down Piccadilly, for a short taste of anonymity.[799]

Concurrently running the family estate at Highclere (having trained at agricultural college in managing pigs, cows and crops[800]), Porchester was on the army staff of the Royal Household. Having been one of a number of eligible escorts, but discounted as a husband for Princess Elizabeth, he remained a loyal, respected friend and her life-long confidante; one of "Elizabeth's small circle of intimate friends"[801] which "had altered little since her youth".[802]

The 6th Earl's dashing son was a favourite of King George VI; an informant described him as "the son he never had".[803] The King had enjoyed a day's shooting with Porchester as well as conversations about horse racing, and both the King and Queen had encouraged the Carnarvon heir to be on good terms with their daughters. The 6th Earl once claimed that, along with Prince George (Duke of Kent), he'd been requested by courtiers to make a last attempt to persuade the Prince of Wales not to marry Mrs Wallis Simpson.[804]

Catherine and Almina had long nurtured aspirations for Porchester at Court. But Catherine's divorce and Almina's headlines over the bankruptcy did not help; nor did the public loves and losses of his womanising father, who with no wife had no chaperone for the prospective daughters-in-law to visit Highclere. Nevertheless, between 1948 and 1955 Porchester was part of "The Margaret Set"[805], the small collection of men friends who buzzed around Princess Margaret Rose "to fill the emptiness of her life with laughter and noise"[806]. Matchmakers judged him as "a near probable"[807] for Margaret's hand before her ill-fated relationship with Group Captain Peter Townsend, the divorcee with two children, no money and few prospects whom she dumped. Almina thought that "a lot of gush"[808] was written about that romance when the truth was that Margaret, with her flair for the dramatic, never intended to marry to Townsend, 15 years her senior, as she was much too fond of being a Princess.

So instead, it was with Elizabeth, the future Queen, that Porchester remained closest; in large part because they shared a common love of the turf. Porchester, whose family motto is "Only One Will I Serve",[809] was at the centre of a furore in 1954 when it was suggested she placed bets on horses though him.[810] He ultimately became her racing manager, a post especially created for him in 1969. Almina did not live to see this accolade, but she treasured the letters he sent her as he travelled around with the Royal entourage to Windsor, Sandringham and Balmoral, and with the King, Queen and Princesses and later Queen Elizabeth's own horses to the major race meetings over the many years of their association. One of these letters[811] thanks his "Darling granny" for the woollies she presented him that proved a lifesaver on the bitterly cold Scottish moors, with one of the garments (knitted by Anne, of course) being loaned to Commander Colin Buist, an Equerry to King George VI. Almina was forever a writer of notes, on her specially headed stationery; some of these survive. But most of Almina's contact was by telephone.

Move to 19 Hampton Road

The Official Receiver allowed Almina £60 per month to live on. The trustees of the Carnarvon estate agreed to provide the cost of accommodation for the aging Dowager Countess. As the Cowlin sisters were not prepared to sell Park Cottage, Almina was instructed to look for another residence. No one at Highclere knew anything about JTS, despite the fact he had lived with Almina for 12 years. The presumption was that she'd require a rented flat with enough space for herself and housekeeper-companion, Anne Leadbetter, along with Anne's teenage son. But moving to a flat proved impossible: most of those visited had endless steps to the entranceway, which Almina thought "too common for words".[812]

Almina was in despair. In desperation, she went to Lord Porchester in floods of tears, and he agreed to purchase a house for her in Bristol. It was Almina who chose 19 Hampton Road, in the Redland district of the city, an unremarkable three-bedroom house, with a large basement, in row of Victorian terraced houses. [813] Builders made numerous renovations and Almina, JTS, Anne and Tony moved in during the autumn of 1954. But despite the building work there was no hot water system, and Almina considered the toilet and bathroom facilities to be inadequate; thus she made further appeals to her grandson and more building work was undertaken.

During her halcyon days, Almina had always prized her ownership of land and real estate. She deemed the small garden at the back of the house another "cabbage patch", a piece of ground that was only fit for growing a few cabbages. The acid description, first used at Orchard Grove, was intended to highlight to her family her feelings of contempt, especially towards her son Porchey for reducing her to living the life of a landless, rootless pauper.

The house at Hampton Road was a far cry from the beautiful, vast homes Almina had once known, and it must have been depressing to reconcile herself to living out her days in such insalubrious surroundings. One comfort, though, was the unexpected return of her beloved antique furniture. It had been seized as an asset at the time of her bankruptcy examination, to be sold at public auction; but in a surprise move the residue was purchased by Highclere (probably by the 6th Earl)[814] and returned to Almina at Hampton Road. JTS also persuaded her to have additional items retrieved from storage, which were in any case expensive to store. The ownership of these pieces was transferred to JTS to avoid detection with the consequence of Porchey's writ meaning possible seizure by the bailiffs.

The passing of an old lover

On 6 May 1955 Almina attended the funeral of her champion the Earl of Gowrie at Shipton Moyne near Tetbury, Gloucestershire.[815] She also went to his memorial service at the Royal Military Chapel, Wellington Barracks, and London. "Sandy", as he was known to Almina, and the Countess had been devoted friends for many years, and sometime lovers.

Almina had admired Gowrie as a soldier in India and Egypt (with Kitchener) and took an interest in his case when he was severely wounded at Suvla in the Gallipoli Campaign. She knew him when he commanded the Welsh Guards and in the late 1920s, when Gowrie was a Commander at Aldershot, and later, when the Colonel's health brought on a depression, around 1933, Almina fell heavily on Sandy. According to Tony Leadbetter,[816] Almina and Sandy made leisure trips together, under the cover of "Mr and Mrs Smith". Their favourite hideaway was on board the London to Paris luxury train, with a full carriage booked in assumed names. In Paris similar subterfuge took place over hotel rooms. Both were, of course, married to others at the time.

When Gowrie was Deputy Constable and Lieutenant Governor of Windsor Castle, from 1945 to 1953, they resumed close contact. She was appalled at the meagre pension that he been given, and especially that he was denied any adage of the portion for his service in the Sudan which had earned him a Victoria Cross.[817] Tony Leadbetter recalls that it was a feature of any school trip he made to Windsor Castle that Almina would provide him with a letter addressed to Gowrie that had to be delivered by hand.

Almina was shaken by Gowrie's death and often returned to his grave, sharing her grief with their one time go-between Tony Leadbetter by sending him (by then a soldier doing his National Service in Cyprus) a photograph of Gowrie's grave. [818]

Using contacts

For Almina, moving onwards and upwards was all about who you knew, and she was never one to shy from networking. Thus, at sixteen Tony Leadbetter left Hampton Road to work as a footman with the Watney (brewery) family at Cornbury Park, near Oxford. Almina knew the Watneys: there was a marriage link with the Wallops, and Cornbury's owner, Oliver Watney, had once been a patient of Almina's at Alfred House while recovering from TB, at which point in his life he had been seeking a wife but was spurned by one of the Mitford girls.[819]

In 1956, Tony was 18 and he expected to be called up for National Service. Almina arranged an interview for him with an old ally from the Great War, Major General Patrick Henderson, with whom she kept in touch with regularly, by greeting card and by telephone.[820] The General promptly ensured her "dear boy" was recommended for the Royal Army Medical Corps.

Almina also kept in touch with the dwindling band of medical luminaries she had obliged as surgeons and physicians in her nursing homes. Sir William Gilliatt MD, MS, FRCS (1884–1956) was amongst the famous of that elite; a man she had first known as an Officer in the Royal Army Medical Corps during the Great War. When he was killed in a road accident, Almina led a campaign to set up a memorial fund in his name. Despite Almina's poor standing in some walks of Society as a result of her bankruptcy, a number of other titled women, including Lavinia, Duchess of Norfolk, Edwina Mountbatten and Mary, Duchess of Marlborough[821], added their names at Almina's initiative, and without any reluctance. For Almina, such gestures revived hope that she may return to the fold after being branded a social pariah.

For Almina was nothing if not determined and resilient. Perhaps the most striking example of her spirit is from 1956 when the taxi that was taking her shopping from Hampton Road was involved in a collision with a bus at the junction of Temple Way and Victoria Street. One side of the taxi was caved in as a result of the smash, and the accident made headline news in the *Bristol Evening World*. Yet the 80-year-old Countess of Carnarvon remained calm and did not murmur a word after the impact; though Anne Leadbetter told reporters: "I think she is a bit more shaken than she shows. She is not hurt in any way, but it must come as a shock to a lady of her age."[822]

Welcome additions of the family

The year 1956 saw happy news for the Carnarvon family, with the engagement of 31-year-old Lord Porchester to his 20-year-old cousin, Jean Margaret Wallop, eldest daughter of Hon. Oliver Wallop of Big Horn, Wyoming, USA, one of the largest horse and cattle ranches in the country. The couple had found romance the previous summer in England, when Jean(Jeanie) was a guest of the Nevills at Uckfield House, Sussex.[823]

Porchester set sail on the *Queen Mary* for New York, informing reporters, "Only my immediate family will be there, including my mother and father."[824] The marriage took place on 7 January 1956 at the chapel of St James's Episcopal Church, New York. Walking down the aisle on her father's arm, the bride was beautiful in an ivory-tinted satin gown trimmed with family lace and with a full train. Her veil of Brussels lace over tulle belonged to her late mother.

Alice Butler, "The Rat", helped dress Jeanie Wallop for her big day, and for all intents and purposes represented Almina at the ceremony. Alice had known Porchester for several years; she'd made him an elaborate cake for his 21st birthday in 1945, which was transported from Orchard Grove with military style precision, and Porchester's relations, the Wallops, were also friends of Alice's employers, the Trees. Alice also knew Jeanie.

The newlyweds arrived back in England in the spring of 1956 and took up residence at Milford Lake House, Burghclere, within the Highclere Estate, which always remained their main home. Lord Porchester visited his grandmother soon after at 19 Hampton Road, to introduce his wife and attempt to smooth the troubled waters between "Granny" and his father, the 6th Earl. Almina organised a cocktail party to welcome the new Lady Porchester. [825] Subsequently Almina was invited to a subsequent gathering at Highclere by her son for an "At Home" party on 28 March 1956, intended for family and estate workers to meet Jeanie, the new Lady Porchester, and see the wedding presents.

Tony Leadbetter attended the party from Cornbury. Robert, the 6th Earl's butler, introduced Tony to the company in loud ceremonial style, and Lord Carnarvon was heard to say in explanation, "That's Annie's boy."[826] Almina immediately pounced on Tony, whom she had not seen for some while. Lord Carnarvon instructed, "That's right, Mother, take Tony around." But in fact, it was Tony who escorted Almina for the rest of the event, for none of the family seemed interested in her. For Almina was always gregarious, yet her family were not particularly interested in listening to her. This attitude extended to her grandchildren: one of Lady Penelope's letters refers to "Granny" going on and on about something that no one else had the faintest idea or interest; and in a letter to Almina from this era Lord Porchester declares the hope that she is "tranquil".[827] The incumbents at Highclere deemed Almina high maintenance – she was loved but tolerated.[828]

The party at Highclere was a step forwards in the strained relationship between Almina and her son. But meetings of Porchey and his mother were only sustainable on neutral ground, and for the next decade an occasional lunch or tea in a London or Paris hotel was the norm; a balance between no contact and just keeping in touch.

November of that year brought another new member of the Carnarvon clan: a son and heir, George Reginald Oliver Molyneux Herbert, was born to the Porchesters on 10 November 1956. He (Geordie[829]) is the current 8th Earl of Carnarvon.

The Queen was one of the child's godmothers, and the Carnarvons were delighted when she agreed to attend the christening service. The Court Circular of 12 December 12 1956 states: "The Queen was present and stood Sponsor at the Christening of the infant son of Lord and Lady Porchester which took place at St Paul's Church, Knightsbridge", and *The Times* printed a photo of the Queen holding the new Carnarvon heir. Almina attended the ceremony with Anne Leadbetter as chaperone; Anne had made the child's christening shawl and dedicated a poem in the form of a prayer to the newborn Carnarvon.[830] Two other children followed for Lord and Lady Porchester: Hon. Henry Herbert in 1959 and Lady Carolyn Herbert (later Warren), born in 1962. Like their relatives, they've formed close links to the Royal family: their names prominently feature as contemporaries of Diana, Princess of Wales, and there are ongoing links still with Highclere Stud, horse racing and the present Queen.

The Queen and Lord Porchester

Lord Porchester, of course, remained very close to the Queen himself. The Queen
spoke to Porchester about horses every day, and they worked together on horse deals, stud management – which led to some impressive wins[831] – and (albeit Porchester was branded more reprehensible) in the highly controversial sacking of Dick Hern, the monarch's long serving horse trainer.[832] She often stayed at Highclere without any mention of this in the Court Circulars, arriving by helicopter and foregoing her great fear of this form of travel; and Prince Philip and Prince Charles[833] often popped in too. Lady Porchester played the Royal hostess before and after the death of the 6th Earl [834], and the Queen enjoyed roast dinners (or just whatever the family was having). Servants were not always informed a VIP was present, causing more than one of them to drop a tray on discovering to whom they were serving afternoon tea. Such was the closeness between the families that the Queen and Prince Philip even went on to holiday at the Wallop family ranch in Wyoming in 1984.[835] Some commentators infer a good deal more than a business partnership between the Queen and Lord Porchester. In 1991 the late Nigel Dempster insinuated, in a comment as subtle as a Hooray Henry's party joke, that Porchester was Prince Andrew's father. [836] Despite this being deemed "malicious, untrue and denounced",[837] there is no mistaking the depth of affection between the two friends. Somewhere between Dempster's mischief and the judgement of

Robert Lacey in his book Royal (a sequel to Majesty), in which he refutes Dempster's suggestion, even enumerating the calendar days when the Queen and Prince Philip were together to show the rumour was "hugely unlikely to be true",[838] lies unrequited love. Almina was, of course, delighted by her grandson's success in making friends in high places. But she didn't push him to relate every detail of his royal friendship. Tony Leadbetter recalls Almina inviting her grandson and his wife to Hampton Road for lunchtime cocktails and a meal. It was not just a social call (it never was); there were often family documents requiring Almina's signature.[839] Anne Leadbetter cooked the meal and Tony served it up, and atmosphere was informal and relaxed. Tony recalls Lord Porchester was "so relieved we didn't ask him anything about the Queen or Princess Margaret because he got that everywhere he went and was thoroughly sick of it all".[840]

The chosen family

In the final years of the 1950s, Almina found more comfort in spending time with her 'chosen' family of JTS, Anne and Tony than her blood relatives.

During the period from 1954 to 1959 Anne Leadbetter facilitated one young man's ambition for meeting Almina. He was Alfred Lewis Jones, a graduate studying psychology at the University of Bristol. Alfred's father had taken him to Egypt as a boy. As an adult Alfred became interested in Egyptian history and Egyptology. Anne came to know the young man as he was lodging in a house nearby and they often exchanged pleasantries at the local greengrocers. [841] The young man's hope was realised, as he recalls in this memory more than 50 years later:

The servant did, in time tell her ladyship about the psychology student who was very keen and knowlegable about Egypt. The fact that I was doing research as it pertained to the National Health Service was sufficiently acceptable to earn me an invitation to come to tea. At one point the Countess asked me if I knew anything about glass picture slides.[842] I told her that as a matter of fact, I did. My father had a collection from his time in Hawaii and he was called upon to show them to organizations from time to time. She then asked Anne to fetch them for me to see with a view to my helping her find a buyer for them. Things like this fascinated me and I had a few pieces of Egyptian artefacts which I collected on my own and some my father gave me. I said I would buy them if we could settle on a price. This being 1954 or so, they had virtually no value due to the advances in colour photography. I told her that I would be prepared to give her 2/6 each. She seemed pleased feeling that they were items of no real value. I gave her a cheque and took them with me when I left.

Thus I came away with some lanternslides of the historic work her husband and team had done in Egypt. They were of poor quality; some were broken, but very, very, much appreciated. [843]

6th Earl's life saving operation in USA

Almina was no doubt anxious in August 1958 when the 59-year-old 6th Earl was taken seriously ill during a trip to New York,[844] but the mother and son's relationship was still so strained that there was little to do beyond wait for news; and happily he

quickly recovered following a life-saving operation, and returned home on the *Queen Mary*. Almina was similarly distant when Lady Margaret Duckworth, the 5th Earl's last surviving sibling, died on 13 September of that year. She did not attend the funeral; but then neither did any family member from the Carnarvon side.[845]

In 1959 Almina took a holiday to La Bastide du Soleil, paid for by the Carnarvons. It wasn't the first trip away that Almina had managed to wrangle from the Highclere coffers post-bankruptcy: she had been to France for a golfing holiday (for JTS) at Le Touquet, and they'd enjoyed trips to Cornwall. A number of photographs survive of the La Bastide trip, suggesting a close-knit unit of Almina, JTS, Anne and Tony (back home from the army in from Cyprus) relaxing contentedly in the sun-drenched beaches, cafes and bars. Indeed, it seems that Almina had come to regard this group as her family of sorts. She was certainly closer to JTS (his children, especially his daughter, Doreen[846]), and to Anne and Tony than her own children.

Back home, the residents of Hampton Road had settled into a comfortable routine. Almina and JTS each had their own study, bedroom and bathroom, Anne and Tony their space. JTS was contributing financially to the household income by selling AGA cookers, and Anne Leadbetter assisted him at demonstrations. But if they were a family, it was an incestuous one, for by now JTS and Anne were long standing lovers. They engineered an ingenious system to ensure their affair was kept unknown (or at least not obvious) to Almina, with great success: Almina was clueless about the betrayal until years later. As each gave the other the obligatory, chaste good-night kiss before slipping away to their respective bedrooms, their signal was that JTS would place his hand on top of

Anne's. She'd then go to him and stay part of the night, but was always in her own bed by dawn.

Almina was oblivious to the chemistry beneath her roof, and maintained her role as matron of the house, and sometime wife, sometime manager of JTS. She encouraged JTS with the AGA-cookers enterprise by keeping a register of the places he'd visited and different types of cooker and appliances sold. Where he did not win a sale but was asked to return at a later date, she noted this. To bolster his spirits, she would slip a pound note into his top-jacket pocket every day as well as a packet of cigarettes, the latter brought back from their holidays in France, drawn from a formidable cache stored inside her Queen Anne desk. She likewise took an interest in JTS's appearance, ensuring he wore the correct suit, a starched shirt (monogrammed with his initials), a smart tie, (also monogrammed) and smartly polished shoes. [847] On occasion Almina required JTS to display the Carnarvon, Rothschild or Dennistoun colours; the house was full of club ties, handkerchiefs, shirts and cufflinks bearing the insignia of the 5th Earl, Alfred de Rothschild and the Colonel, and Tony Leadbetter was expected to wear these emblems too.

As the swinging 1960s approached, albeit Almina was approaching her mid-eighties, a sense of security and continuity existed among the Hampton Road family, a feeling that nothing would ever change.

Orchard Grove

Orchard Grove: Almina and her new Family 1950s

**JTS in bathing robe and Almina (centre) with friends
A hotel on the French Riviera**

**Almina with her Highclere Family : 1945
The 6ᵗʰ Earl has pride of place in the centre front**

**James Timothy Stocks or Stocking
JTS**

**Almina at 19 Hampton Road Bristol with Alice Butler
on a visit**

Anne Leadbetter with Almina   **Anne Leadbetter**

Almina with Tony Leadbetter

Chapter 13
1960–1969
Almina's Final Years

Reminiscing

The 1960s saw the publication of various materials that related to Almina's life, outlining some events that had shaped her story. Almina was particularly interested in mentions of her first husband. She prized a small enamel miniature portrait of the 5th Earl, which occupied its place with other family photographs on her desk in all her homes,[848] and talked of Carnarvon on days like his birthday and whenever there was a radio programme, book or article published which featured the story of his historic exploits with Carter in the discovery of Tutankhamun's tomb.[849] Almina herself was ignored in such accounts; no historian or commentator ever noted her financial input in Egypt until after her death.[850] Other books in this period of interest to Almina featured retrospectives on the life and court cases of Sir Edward Marshall Hall[851] and Norman Birkett,[852] which rekindled harsh memories of *Dennistoun v. Dennistoun*. Almina was fascinated by the materials; blasé about some, but overtly hostile to others, remarking to Tony Leadbetter that the narratives were often inaccurate: "It was nothing like that, Dear Boy, no nothing like that at all..." [853]

Relaxing on the Riviera

Beginning in the 1950s and extending into the 1960s, Almina made an annual pilgrimage to the South of France. She was adept at wringing money from her family for her holiday. Tony recalls Almina "play-acting on the regular phone-around":[854]

> She warned us that she was going to tackle the family for money and put it on a bit... "Wait until you hear this performance, dear boy, and don't laugh," she quipped. Then she cried huge tears down the phone... to extract the sums needed, usually with appropriate sized portions of £250 or even £500 coming from her son, Lady Evelyn and Lord Porchester. She always successfully pulled off these money coups.[855]

Her preference was to take a villa on the French Riviera near Cannes. JTS would go ahead by motorcar, to keep his presence unknown, often conveying vast amounts of baggage. Almina, Anne and Tony, meanwhile, travelled in style on the Continental train from London Victoria. Almina was a veteran of "Golden Arrow" trips to Paris and the Riviera from her days with Lord Carnarvon, especially the Continental train to Marseilles for the boat to Egypt. At Dover the cross-Channel steamer went to Calais, where the Calais passengers transferred to the Paris Express. These trains were the height of luxury, with the finest of cuisine. Some of the sleeping cars formed the famous French railway's "Blue Train" or "The Millionaire's Train", featuring in the works of such authors Agatha Christie, Evelyn Waugh and P. G. Wodehouse. They boasted armchair accommodation for travellers, and catering, wine and spirits of a high standard. On the "Blue Train" there was even a piano lounge.

For Almina, the train ride was heaven; like stepping back in time to when she had been a grand and wealthy lady. The neatly uniformed staff knew Almina well and greeted her with the respect of serfs. She was one of their life-long celebrities, recognised and given special treatment. On board were old friends, and the whole excursion was spent catching up with news of their families, and discovering who had died recently – for the death of old friends featured in sad numbers, as Almina outlived many of these contemporaries. The Countess was interesting company for a willing listener; after all, she had lived a long life and knew the inside story of countless noble families. At Victoria Railway Station Almina had a habit of casting an eye on her fellow passengers before they boarded. If she saw someone she knew, and could expect to be of reasonable company they were captured prisoner.[856]

Anne was on hand, as always, as her companion, and did all the packing, unpacking and general organising. Almina insisted on French being spoken to waiters and waitresses, and Anne tipped, except when Tony was travelling too, when he was given the task of rewarding service or handling a complaint about Almina's dissatisfaction. [857]

During the train journey Almina needed constant reassurance about her luggage, due to the lingering memories of the theft of her jewels from a train in 1902. Though in truth, Almina had little worth stealing now. The lady who had once worn some of the world's finest jewels for receptions parties and balls, including a wonderful girdle made of diamonds and magnificent tiaras and aigrettes for her hair, was now reduced to wearing paste copies: a sad reflection that this was the woman who previously had such a vast collection of gems but that she had even once threatened to dispose of her best jewels, "out of sheer boredom"[858] as she was always expected (by Lord Carnarvon) to wear them instead of her own choice for Highclere and Court functions.

Once installed at the villa there followed four weeks of complete relaxation in the gardens, in cafes and on the beach or by swimming pools. Almina occasionally saw members of her family nearby if they were also on holiday or passing through. She was open to invitations from friends with their own villas for a reception, lunch or a drinks party. If she did not require a companion, JTS dropped her off and she returned home by taxi. If JTS was playing golf (a frequent getaway for him), Tony increasingly acted as her chaperone, and they travelled together by taxi when she was required to attend functions. Tony sometimes went back to Bristol if he was unable to obtain long leave from his nursing work.

The return journey home involved changing trains in Paris. Almina had a commanding knowledge of the city. She usually found time to go to Sacre Coeur, the Basilica of the Sacred Heart of Jesus, with which her mother's family, the Boyers, had associations.[859] Another obligatory stop was to Debauve & Gallais for chocolate and glazed fruit. This shop had been Alfred de Rothschild's favourite establishment too, and he and Almina had often visited together. In addition, with JTS going home to Bristol by road, the coast was clear in Paris to meet up with Porchey for breakfast at The Ritz hotel, or with Lady Evelyn's in her usual Parisian hotel, adjoining a casino, to indulge her pastime of gambling. Almina was always quick to use the opportunity of meeting her children to extract further sums, whether sterling, dollars or francs, for general living costs and travelling expenses.

Perhaps I should tell you who I am...

Wherever Almina went, she retained the demeanour of a strong, resilient, aristocratic lady, despite her advanced age and her fall from grandeur. Tony Leadbetter recalls arriving at the Cumberland Hotel, London, with Almina late on Year's Eve 1961 after attending the wedding of JTS's daughter, Doreen. The foyer was heaving with drunk and semi-drunken New Year revellers, and it seemed there was no way that they could get through the entangled crowds of people and so reach the lifts or stairs to their rooms. But Almina was every inch the Countess of Carnarvon. "Follow me, dear boy, look to the front and avoid the common herd," she told Tony, and the determined and dogged small woman and her minder made their way effortlessly through a scene comparable with the parting of the Red Sea.

To some, it seemed incredible that this tiny lady, living in a modest terraced house, was indeed a Countess. Both JTS and Tony Leadbetter kept silent to work colleagues about living under the same roof as the Dowager Countess of Carnarvon, and were careful to limit who they brought to Hampton Road to meet Almina. But when on one occasion a friend of Tony's assumed Almina was his grandmother, she soon put an end to that with a line she often used: "Perhaps I should tell you who I am..." Later, Tony's friend was concerned and told him, "Your granny thinks she's the Countess of Carnarvon!" [860]

All the taxi-drivers of Bristol were in no doubt, however, that the great Countess of Carnarvon lived at 19 Hampton Road. After her bankruptcy the car firms Almina had used declined an account, so she had been forced to use local taxicabs. The ordinary cabbies were in an extraordinary way protective of her: she was a Bristol VIP. Tony Leadbetter recalls returning home after a spell away. He got into a cab at Bristol Temple Meads station and announced his destination. Exhausted from travelling all day, he looked a little dishevelled. The cab driver observed him very closely through the mirror. Then, on dropping Tony at 19 Hampton Road, the driver insisted on getting out and going to the door to ensure his passenger was known (and welcomed) by the residents.

Almina was also to keep up entertaining, in keg with her long history of hostessing. She insisted on the Highclere tradition of holding a New Year party with guests coming into the house, and on occasion had invitations specially printed for drinks parties. [861] JTS's grown up children were also most welcome at Hampton Road, for celebrations including their marriages and children's births; and one of JTS's sons lived at Hampton Road for over a year whilst working in Bristol.

Other guests at the house included an American doctor, Gordon Johnstone, whom she'd known from her visits to the American Military Hospital at Musgrove Park, Taunton, during World War Two. Johnstone and his wife stayed for three weeks, and Almina was touched when the doctor later wrote to tell Almina that funds had been provided for a bed to be named after her in his hospital in

245

Maine. Roger Grey, 10th Earl of Stamford (1896–1976), of Dunham Massey Hall, was another guest – although entirely less welcome because he "pestered Almina for years about antiques".[862] Almina found Stamford, a relation of the unfortunate Lady Jane Grey, Queen of England for only nine days, a strain. However, Anne organised several lunch parties for him, and they all enjoyed days out, visiting Lord Methuen, a notable painter at Corsham Court, who was the custodian of some wonderful art treasures and beautiful gardens that Almina greatly admired.[863] Another mutual friend of Almina, Stamford and Methuen who lived nearby was Sir Robert Sinclair (later Lord Sinclair of Cleeve; 1893–1979), a tobacco magnate whose companies supplied most of the cigarettes smoked by Britons, and who also often visited Hampton Road for lunch, and Almina would call on him and his wife Mary at their mansion of Cleeve Court.

Since frequent outings were tiring for the Countess in her later years, she busied herself at home. She was on the telephone near constantly [864], to gossip with old friends, most of whom knew of Porchey's vengeful act and considered the whole affair "shocking and unnecessary",[865] and of course Almina enjoyed the sympathy. She was especially fond of chatting to her daughter, Lady Evelyn, who was active on the London social scene and a frequent visitor to the Riviera.[866]

Almina also enjoyed listening to Tony's collection of gramophone records, and followed the horse racing on the radio and later on the television[867], when it began to be televised. She enjoyed a flutter, and *The Sporting Life* newspaper was delivered every day. She followed the highs and lows of the Highclere Stud, which Porchester was increasingly involved in administering on behalf of his father. She was delighted when a horse named Almina owned by the 6th Earl won a race for two-year-olds at Doncaster on Monday 11 June 1962.

Despite her age, Almina was determined to still be seen on the Society circuit when she was able, and she was delighted to accompany Porchester to the races. Ascot was always a must-go event. Almina was deposited in the Royal Enclosure, with the certain prospect of reunions with old friends. Although Almina held centre stage as usual, she remarked to Tony Leadbetter that on these occasions some heads turned away and the Queen and Queen Mother snubbed her.[868] Although determined to hold her head high, the truth was an undischarged bankrupt would always remain a social outcast to the House of Windsor.

Losing JTS

Almina was approaching 87, and growing old gracefully. Her health was excellent, but as the Carnarvon estate owned the house at Hampton Road, JTS and Anne Leadbetter had to make plans for their future in the event of Almina's death. JTS and Anne pledged themselves to each other. They hoped to perhaps eventually buy Hampton Road or at least set up home together. But it was not to be, as it turned out, because JTS passed on before Almina.

The holiday of 1963 was the group's last one together. Almina, JTS, Anne and Tony took an apartment in Benidorm, Spain – the result of JTS sticking a pin in map of Western Europe, as he favoured a change from France. It was not just the location that broke the mould, but the method of travel also: despite Almina's misgivings, the group travelled by aeroplane. Upon arriving at Heathrow, Almina was appalled to discover that, in this era of the package holiday boom, she would be travelling with legions of what she called "the common herd". She remonstrated with JTS, and refused to get on the plane, but JTS calmed her. He was one of the few people whose reasoning she heeded and he had acquired a talent for managing her moods and foibles. Once in Benidorm, Almina's mood improved. She even agreed to attend the obligatory bullfight. She did not, however, take the time to drive up the coast to visit her great adversary Dorothy Dennistoun (then Madame Woevodsky) at Cap Roig. There is no evidence that the two women ever met again after the upheavals of 1925.[869]

It was 11 days before the Christmas of 1963 that JTS, aged 63, was found dead in his bed. The night before Anne had not gone to him, and now, in the morning, she was greeted by the gruesome sight of her lover sitting up, cold and blue, still with the bedside light on, having died unexpectedly of a heart attack in the night. [870]

JTS's death came as a terrible shock to the 87-year-old Almina; it was the third time she had lost her male companion. A telegram was sent to Tony Leadbetter (who was training in Cardiff), and he took a train to Bristol. When he arrived at Hampton Road he found Almina dressed from top to toe in mourning black, including the veil she'd worn at her bankruptcy hearing. She whisked Tony off to a local jeweller's shop to have "Monsieur's signet ring" sized (and fitted with a guard ring) so that she could wear this, together with as her two wedding rings, for the rest of her life.[871] Tony recalls:

> To ensure privacy the manager of the shop locked the main door (it was lunchtime). In a moment of high drama, with tears being shed on both sides of the counter, she placed Monsieur's ring of platinum and gold with an octagonal seal, onto her finger and secured with the newly purchased guard ring – and there she said it would stay for life. And it did.

Almina took charge of arranging the funeral. It was a difficult occasion, not least because it brought together JTS's work associates, who did not know Almina,[872] and his family with the occupants of Hampton Road. Almina struggled to share the moment with so many others. After a funeral service in a nearby Church she deliberately told everyone that the cremation was scheduled 15 minutes later than the actual time, hoping she would be able to be the only one present. But an alert taxi driver scuttled her plans. [873]

JTS's widow (he had never divorced his wife) dealt with the post-funeral process. A request by her for a copy of his death certificate, in order to claim a widow's pension, aroused Almina's scorn. In the years spent living with Almina a small sum of money (jointly determined by Almina and JTS) was sent in a registered envelope to his wife every week, and she was the chief beneficiary of his estate.

When the contents of JTS's will[874] were revealed, Almina was furious. In the will JTS had included intimate terms of endearment towards Anne, and had left her £500 from the proceeds of a life insurance policy. It was clear now to the Countess that her housekeeper and her companion had been deceiving her, and she felt as betrayed as any wife of a philandering husband might. For Almina had presumed a good deal from JTS in exchange for domestic bliss. He was 20 years younger and undoubtedly sexually active, whereas beyond her middle life Almina was probably not amorously driven and their relationship, whilst affectionate at times, was almost certainly more companionship-based than carnal. Yet she had presumed he would be chaste.

Despite JTS's huge betrayal at seducing *both* the Butler sisters under Almina's roof, she missed him. He was one of the few men she cared about and who had reciprocated her feelings. She had also been fond of her lovers Berkeley Moynihan and Sandy Gowrie. But neither Carnarvon nor Dennistoun had held the same attraction. Other predatory conquests of men or of her by men were long forgotten; she retained male friendships, which upheld her dignity, based on her past decades of endeavour. And the strongest of these friendships had been with JTS: undoubtedly her great true love.

Almina inevitably suffered a period of emotional withdrawal after JTS's death. Each Sunday she would arrange a local taxi driver named Rodney (whom she had adopted, as she had done with others) to take her, alone, to the gardens of the Arnos Grove Cemetery and Crematorium, where JTS's ashes were scattered, to spend time there with her 21 years of memories. His marker was a simple cross engraved his initials, and she told no one of its location. She also worked quietly, yet earnestly to encourage suitable friends she knew to make donations to organisations to better inform the public about the danger signs of oncoming heart disease.[875]

Like Catherine Momand, the 6th Countess who had lost her second husband in World War Two, Almina sought comfort in her grief in the Roman Catholic faith. She told Tony Leadbetter that she'd "always wanted to be a Roman Catholic, as her Mother".[876] She took to reading her Bible every day and had close contact with the Catholic priests and Monsignors of her local Bristol diocese, including attending confession with her Catholic mentor, a Monsignor Hughes.[877] Almina was also a regular attendee, (but more of an observer) in the children's' Sunday schools.[878]

There were occasions at Hampton Road when subjects arose that Almina would not discuss. JTS was one of these. Tony Leadbetter remarks:

When she did not wish to discuss something Almina would look to the heavens rolling her eyes, clutching imaginary pearls around her neck. (She never had any pearls to wear by this time or anytime I remember, they were sold off.) [879]

Because JTS was an unknown figure in her connecting life with family and friends, Almina had to grieve privately.

Almina's absence from the London scene was noted; William Hickey made a short reference in the *Daily Express* under a headline of "Active 87":

It is a long time since I heard news of Almina, Lady Carnarvon, who was 87 last April. Today I am glad to hear that she is well and still active. She lives quietly in a green-painted Victorian terraced house in Bristol with a companion.

A faithful companion

Almina did have one loyal and constant companion to comfort her in her sadness: the devoted Anne, who had been with Almina for almost 28 years now, always in the background, supporting and protecting Almina, striving hard to ensure the household ran smoothly. There was no better cook, no better seamstress, no better organiser, [880] and no one else she would trust to manage her finances (since Almina was an undischarged bankrupt, the Carnarvon Estate allowance was paid into an account in Anne's name and she signed the cheques). In Anne, Almina had an irreplaceable ally and friend, and the pair was able to mutually support each other in their shared grief over losing their loved one, JTS.[881]

But for Anne, there was more than the loss of JTS to contend with. She had kept silent about a lump in her breast, and it was discovered that she was suffering from terminal breast cancer. A mastectomy was arranged, followed by radium treatment, at the Chesterfields Nursing home, paid for by medical insurance. Coincidentally, Anne's surgeon, Gordon Paul, had trained in London and was known to Almina through her past nursing home links with Lord Moynihan.
[882]

Tony, her son, was now in his late twenties, and was living in his own flat and working as a nurse in a Bristol hospital. Despite his efforts to build his own life, he was an only son and Almina's ever-faithful "Dear Boy", and was therefore persuaded in March 1965 to abandon plans to go to the USA, where he had a job lined up, and return to Hampton Road to help his mother upon her return to the house. The basement area was cleared to allow him a more assured degree of privacy.

Letters from Almina's family in this period are moving. Anne was genuinely loved by Almina's daughter, Lady Evelyn, by Jeanie Porchester and by Catherine, the 6th Countess, who all sent thoughtful personal gifts and offered spirited support. Once home, Anne could tolerate small amounts of alcohol, and she enjoyed small bottles of champagne sent by Lady Evelyn.

Stepping out in London

For the elderly Almina, journeying to London was by now exhausting, but nevertheless she was determined to enjoy a social life and made several visits to the capital in 1966.

The Porchesters had bought a house in Belgravia, converted stables in Cadogan Place, a regular meeting place for Porchester and the Queen to discuss racing business matters. Almina, Anne and Tony were invited to stay at the house while attending the wedding of Ronald Warwick, who was later a Commodore with Cunard. Almina knew his father, William (Bill) Eldon Warwick (1912–1999), also with Cunard, and Ronald was an occasional visitor at Hampton Road.[883]

In April 1966, Almina celebrated her nintieth birthday at a Bristol restaurant. The 6th Earl must have been feeling generous, for he arranged a second birthday party in London, at The Ritz. Catherine Momond arranged hotel rooms for Almina and Anne at Claridges. Over dinner Almina headed one of the tables; for the last time in her life she held court over the three generations of her family. She was triumphant, restored that evening as the incomparable head of the Carnarvon dynasty.

Finally, on 21 June 1966, Almina occupied centre stage at a special service of dedication at Highclere (arranged by the 6th Earl) for the life of the 5th Earl on what would have been his 100th birthday. His grave, on Beacon Hill, overlooking the Highclere Estate, was also renovated and a name plaque unveiled. [884]

Battling illness

By September 1966, Anne's health had stabilised, and for the first time since JTS's death three years before, Almina, Anne and Tony took a holiday, to Cannes in the South of France. The restorative properties of the break were marred, however, when Almina developed a severe chest infection upon her return, which landed her in bed for three weeks.

Almina's illness was a source of concern for her family; at the age of 90, any illness could spell the end. Her bedridden state compelled her daughter, Lady Evelyn Beauchamp, who was living in a sixteenth-century converted farmhouse in Sussex with 50 acres, large garages, stabling outbuildings and gardens[885], to pay her mother a visit at Hampton Road, which had never happened before, and Almina was delighted to have her daughter close.

Tony Leadbetter nursed Almina[886], and the Countess made a full recovery. With Anne now in remission from her cancer, a short period of peaceful normality resumed.

Out in the cold

Tony had persuaded his mother that the Carnarvons should be approached over payment of some kind of salary or pension. The solicitors Scott Son & Chitty devised a scheme whereby Anne would receive "a series of gifts". They wrote to Anne on 4 December 1967:

> It has been decided to simply matters that instead of being paid a wage, the Trust will pay you a series of gifts in recompense for your faithful service to Lady Carnarvon, and in fact, you will be receiving £34.13s 4d a month which you should not return to tax as these are capital payments."[887]

Almina was livid. Anne was delighted. Tony was relieved. For the first in over 25 years Anne had an income independent of Almina. However, Anne did not enjoy this newfound wealth for very long. In the following year or so that culminated in Anne Leadbetter's death, a good deal of mixed feelings existed between Tony and Almina. She was still his "My Lady"; he was still her "Dear Boy". Almina could be kind and helpful: she got an old colleague, the eminent eye surgeon Sir Benjamin Rycroft, to write a reference for Tony, securing him a senior nursing post at the Bristol Eye Hospital. But she could also be exhausting in her demands, expecting Tony to be at her beck and call, which was not made easy by his nursing job, where he had in any case sought to alter his working hours to ensure he could see as much of his mother as he could. He was living in his own flat now, but visited 19 Hampton Road almost every day. He continued to clean the silver and do the French polishing (a constant routine)[888] and perform the other domestic chores he had done for 20 years. [889]

Amongst the people that Almina came to depend on was one of Tony's nursing colleagues, Josephine (Jo) Giles [890], who had worked with him as a staff nurse at the Bristol Eye Hospital. Jo organised

Almina's New Year party in January 1969. She first supported Anne and Almina together, but after Anne was admitted to a nursing home, her cancer having returned, Jo became Almina's new support and full time carer. The two women travelled to London together for Almina to make her usual round robin contacts and to the surrounds of Bristol for shopping, tea and cultural pursuits. During this time with Jo Almina had her picture painted, in which she appeared to be enjoying life to the full.

Anne Leadbetter died in a nursing home on 28 March 1969, aged only 55. There was a funeral service and cremation, and the turnout by JTS's family was a demonstration of how much Anne was loved and respected by them. Tony and Almina where both present, but they did not speak. He recalls: "Since I had not done exactly what she wanted me to do [which included leaving from Hampton Road for the funeral], I was blanked, they [Almina with Jo] both blanked me at my own Mother's funeral." [891] Tony's refusal to go to Hampton Road was a practical one, since his own flat was very close to Arnos Grove Cemetery.

Tony picked up his mother's belongings: just two suitcases represented 28 years of her life serving Almina. Jo Giles continued to support Almina day by day, and Tony was left out in the cold. Almina's 93rd birthday, on 14 April 1969, was celebrated, but Tony was not invited to visit and a neighbour told him that there had been a considerable amount of noise that evening coming from his old basement at 19 Hampton Road, suggesting that the event was duly marked.

A grim and lonely death

Life ended for Almina in a sudden drama. The Countess had long had a deep dread of fish and chicken bones: everyone who served her food over the years, from chefs across establishments in her favourite haunts in London, Paris and Monte Carlo, to catering staff on board trains and ships, and her personal domestic staff, the Butler sisters included, knew that great care must be taken to refine Almina's food. Thus it was a cruel irony that after so many years of careful consideration, it was choking on a piece of gristle in a home-made chicken stew that brought Almina's long and colourful life to a close.

It was the unfolding of the worst nightmare scenario. Only Almina and Jo Giles were in the house. Despite desperate attempts, neither

Almina nor Jo was able to shift the obstruction in her esophagus.[892] An ambulance was summoned and Almina was taken to the Frenchay Hospital, Bristol, and since forceps could not remove the blockage she was rushed into surgery. To extract the residue of food causing the problem, an emergency *esophagogastrectomy* (the removal of the lower esophagus and the upper part of the stomach that connects to the esophagus) was performed, which almost certainly severed her food tube, which could not be repaired. Almina was, after all, aged 93, and her body worn down by the usual ravages of old age.

After lingering pitifully in a state of semi-delirium for three weeks, during which time Jo Giles and members of the family from Highclere kept watch over the situation until finally Almina, Countess of Carnarvon, passed away. In death Almina was liberated. It had been a full life, and the mutilations to her body from surgery could not have allowed any remaining quality of life.

The end game

Since Almina had been at death's door for three dark weeks, the Highclere family were prepared for Almina's end game. It was a blessing that the dead 5th Countess's grandson, Lord Porchester, who cared very much about her, attended to the registration of the death and oversaw the funeral arrangements. *The Bristol Evening Post* carried the family's brief announcement:

> DEATHS: Carnarvon: Lady Almina, beloved mother of Lord Carnarvon and Lady Evelyn died peacefully May 8. Funeral service, 2.30 pm next Monday at the Pro-Cathedral, followed by private cremation.

It was generous of the 6th Earl to include the words "beloved mother"; after all, no doubt aware that with each year that advanced she moved closer to death's shadow, Almina had neglected to make peace with her angry son. She had died isolated and lonely, without even her "Dear Boy" Tony Leadbetter at her side. It is unclear whether Almina asked for Tony; the Carnarvons did not think of the man who had been, to all intents and purposes, a surrogate son, and did not bother to inform him of her death until it was too late to pay his respects.

The funeral was functional, not emotive, although met Almina's wish for a Catholic Mass. But there was no family memorial service held for her at which a eulogy could be given and comfort offered to those who mourned her and deserved a final farewell. After the funeral Mass Almina's remains were probably taken to Highclere. It is unclear what became of her remains; no grave is known of and the author has found no local reports in Berkshire/Hampshire newspapers concerning Almina's final resting place. She is, in death, lost.

Almina's estate

The Times published a short obituary on Almina[893] and other newspapers reported on fragments of her life and death. Her old friend Lord Sinclair of Cleeve sent a follow-on tribute to *The Times*, highlighting her successful war-hospitals.[894] The local Bristol newspaper obituaries contained some errors[895] but her interest in nursing received praise, and deservedly so, for it was in tending the sick that Almina had her finest hour. A curious, accurate and moving obituary appears in the *Newbury Weekly News and General Advertiser* of 15 May 1969:

Almina, Countess of Carnarvon

Almina, Countess of Carnarvon died peacefully in hospital at Bristol on Thursday, in her 94th year [sic].

She was a most remarkable person. Her father was an Englishman, and her mother being half French and half Spanish, contributed to making her a vivid character, beloved by many – beautiful in her youth, looking somewhat like a tiny Dresden figure, with exquisite colouring.

Her greatest joy in life was everything that contributed to the nursing of the sick. At the outbreak of World War One she immediately established a hospital at Highclere for the wounded on their return from France and, to this day, there are many who remember her kindness in helping them back to health.

She continued her activities in this field, first at 48 Bryanston Square, and then at Alfred House, Portland Place, London right up to the beginning of World War Two, when she moved her nursing home to the country. While some of her patients were rich people, many who could not afford the fees were treated free, and given the best of everything her money could provide.

When her husband was ill in Cairo in 1923 she chartered a Puss Moth and flew to his bedside – a truly courageous act when one remembers how fragile these machines appeared to be at the time. Courage and kindness were her greatest virtues and I think in that context she would wish to be remembered by her many devoted friends and patients.

C

The identity of the author "C" is not known. It may have been written for/by the 6th Earl of Carnarvon.

Although Almina had informed Anne that she'd changed her will a few months before her death, no will was ever probated.[896] Hichclere therefore took charge of her estate, which, as an undischarged bankrupt, was effectively worthless. In a dressing table drawer was the last of her pasted jewellery, and all her private papers were removed to Highclere Castle, though such records, photographs and memorabilia were not expected to be of significance beyond the ephemeral.

With Almina gone, the family were at liberty to empty the house at Hampton Road to make it ready for sale, but this did not happen quickly (it was, however, eventually sold to the BBC). All the furniture was given away, the major recipient being Almina's last housekeeper, Jo Giles. Tony Leadbetter advised the Highclere solicitors that there were a number of important Carnarvon relics still in the house and that these should removed and passed on to the family. An example of this was one of the 5th Earl's "passports that opened up, like a map".[897]

Tony's tribute

It was a sad day for Tony when he handed over his front door key to 19 Hampton Road to the Carnarvon solicitors, Fyzers. Almina had presented the key to Tony at the age of 21 in a grand "coming of age ceremony", which involved her imperiously demanding that he at once leave the house and come in again of his own accord using his own front door key. For Tony, the handover represented the end of an era. He was grieving and in shock, since he had lost both his mother and Almina in the space of only a few weeks. This barren feeling was worsened a few weeks later when he saw Jo Giles, Almina's last charge, and beneficiary, wearing one of "My Lady's" best fur coats.

Despite their differences in the last months of Almina's life, it is not surprising that her passing is deeply mourned, even to this day, by

Tony Leadbetter. Her influence on his life from a young child of four (in 1942) to a man of 31 (in 1969) was profound. Latterly, Tony received a cheque from Lady Evelyn Beauchamp as a contribution to his mother's final nursing care and funeral costs, which he had needed a bank loan to cover. This seemed to signal the Carnarvons' desire for their own final closure.

The tribute that follows was written by Tony Leadbetter in the spring of 1979 and stands as a most moving epitaph to the woman he called "My Lady":

> These words are compiled as a tribute to a great lady, who throughout her life did so much for others. She was often misunderstood and finally accused and taken to court for bankruptcy, as a result of her generosity and extravagance. She worked and cared for the sick between 1914 and 1945. She enabled me to be part of, and learn to understand her side of life, in a way but for fate, that would have not otherwise been possible. She gave my Mother hope and help in her hour of need and I am grateful to her for this, and for her service to others.[898]

Almina, the last Countess

Almina's life was tumultuous. She certainly gave those who led duller lives, and there were many, something to talk about. She spent her life forever striving for more – more money, more status, more happiness – often courting controversy yet insisting that she never wanted to blow her own trumpet. Hers was a fulfilling life when things went her way, especially when she was nursing. But often life didn't go according to plan, when she plunged herself into doomed situations and relationships, motivated by a need to control and dominate and to buy, rather than earn, the love she craved. She made mistakes, many; but was also unfortunate – used by people who exploited her generosity, and let down by weak men.

She was uncompromising, and manipulative, but also thoughtful when it suited her and generous to a fault. Money had a way of slipping through her fingers as she single-mindedly pursued her ambitions to live a lavish lifestyle and to run her nursing homes, in the case of the latter with a degree of folly reserved only for the eccentric or seriously rich. She was strong-willed, resilient and lived on her nerve, delighting in surrounding herself with notable figures of the 19th and 20th centuries – mostly men, for she loved men. She had genuine feelings for some members of her family, but was unable to commit to them beneath the surface; her relationship with her children, especially the love–hate nature with her son, was a sad reflection of this character flaw. She was, despite her faults, a very great lady, a strong-willed old world aristocrat, a Countess through and through.

Almina's story epitomises the fall of her class in the post-war period. She stands out as one of the last surviving Countesses of the Victorian era. She deserves this retrospect to place in context and in history her whole remarkable life, the good deeds done by her incomparable generosity to those she chose to treat, as well as her more unscrupulous side evident in her indulgences, mistakes and often disgraceful acts. Negatives aside, Almina was Almina, a lady of her own making. There will never be another to match Almina, Countess of Carnarvon.

Epilogue
Almina's secrets

The biography that never was: A missing link

In death, Almina, Countess of Carnarvon, casts a shadow over the incumbents of Highclere Castle. She has left behind the greatest of dilemmas for her descendants, who have opted thus far, it seems, to conceal the *full* facts of their relative's life.

One Almina secret may have come to light by chance. In the mid-1990s, Henry, the 7th Earl of Carnarvon, instructed a guide at Highclere – to compile a biography of his wayward grandmother. This public announcement appeared in *The Times* of 22 January 1996:

> THE EARL of Carnarvon, the Queen's racing manager, is helping one of his guides at the family seat, Highclere, in the writing of a biography of an extraordinary woman. The Rev David Sox is writing the life of the Earl's grandmother, Almina, Countess of Carnarvon, who was a spirited and spendthrift nurse. The illegitimate daughter of the bachelor bon viveur Alfred de Rothschild, she ploughed through the family fortune, funded the 1922 Tutankhamun discovery and set up a nursing home in Portland Place where Noel Coward was treated for piles. "It's a wonderful story. She was really rather remarkable dreamt up the National Health Service years before it existed," enthuses Carnarvon.

Yet despite the family's apparent enthusiasm for this project, no biography was ever published. So what happened to scuttle things? Could it be that in researching the Countess, certain facts deemed too controversial to reveal were unearthed, and that it was resolved to conceal, and suppress Almina's true legacy?

Tony Leadbetter was one of a number of contributors to significantly add to the work undertaken by David Sox, the Highclere guide. Tony has spoken frankly and at length to the present author about his involvement in this previously proposed book on Almina. He met with that first biographer several times, at Highclere, in a Berkshire pub and during an overnight stay in a country cottage, in order that the biographer could fully discuss the 7th Earl's project and extract the fullest information about Almina's remarkable life story.

Tony made his unique collection of material on Almina's life and times available for the 7th Earl's tribute to his grandmother (as he has equally done for this book). In addition, at the steer of the 7th Earl and Sox, the resourceful guide, many folk were canvassed (some of whom are inaccessible to the present author: several are dead, and others have chosen silence and have ignored requests for information).

Sox's work appears to have been exhaustive and commendable, including visits and correspondence with the Herbert linked families, the late Miriam Rothschild, the Wombwell family and people who knew Almina on the Highclere estate. Lord Porchester (the 7th Earl's favourite title) also mentioned the nature and pace of the project to H. M. Queen.[899]

Eventually, Tony Leadbetter was permitted to review a draft manuscript, of just over 120 pages in length, and this was, or later a modified version of it was subsequently punted around commissioning editors in London and County publishing firms. Tony expected there would be grand celebrations at Highclere Castle upon the book being launched. But it was the epic that never was.

The entire project was dumped, and no explanation was ever given of the reason(s). When Tony Leadbetter visited Highclere again during August 2001, in the company of two other writers also searching out details of Almina's story,[900] Almina's great-grandson, Geordie, was faultlessly charming. [901] But there was no mention of what had become of the planned biography. In fairness to the 8th Earl, his father was the spark in the original plans for the book on Almina and he was to die shortly afterwards in September 2001.

But what happened to the book the 7th Earl's commissioned? And why was it abandoned? A two page letter in Leadbetter's possession has been unearthed – dating from 1996 - on *Highclere headed notepaper*[902] – which suggests that the most likely reason for non-publication was the discovery that the true father of Almina's son, later the 6th Earl of Carnarvon, was *not* the 5th Earl. It was a bombshell. The implications arising from it were judged (it seems) an admission too far for the 7th Earl.

Of course, various other uncomfortable secrets of Almina's chequered past existed. Highclere could not admit to Almina's 20-year cohabitation with JTS, nor of her carnal affairs with other men. They would be similarly unwilling to publicise her defrauding of the Inland Revenue, and her own children of their inheritance from

Maria Wombwell (of course, *if* these irregularities were discovered by Sox's investigations?) Then there was Almina's less-than-exemplary record of questionable financial affairs generally and money laundering with the Colonel, not to mention the ignoble spectacle of *Dennistoun v. Dennistoun* possibly being replayed again. Almina's conversion to the Roman Catholic faith was another sore point for the Carnarvons, since those in the mainstream of the Herbert family have prided themselves (as has the monarchy and state) on adhering to the Church of England's supremacy.[903] There were also savage truths about Almina's topsy-turvy relationship with the 6th Earl and the insight she had of Porchey's first marriage to Catherine Wendell, and their joint and several marital skeletons, including its mix of serial adultery and alcoholism, which would equally make unappetising headlines.

This is awkward for the family. To revisit matters breaks an edict of the 7th Earl who had (as this book reflects in several part) compelling reasons to block the publication of *any* book or article revealing Almina's skeletons. However, when the clean-up operation was put into effect to sweep the unsavoury details of the Countess's adultery under the Highclere red carpet it may have amounted to an act of patricide upon the 6th Earl and a snub upon his true ancestral legacy.

A recent approach to the former Highclere guide, David Sox, met with the following response to the present author:

"I can't help you. I agreed with the late Lord Carnarvon not to do any more about Almina. I don't know why they [Highclere] are the way they are about her – but that's that."[904]

The 7th Earl of Carnarvon also spread the net to ensure others who had known Almina would not disclose sensitive private information. It was feared that Almina's maid, Alice Butler, who had died in 1988, might have left behind potentially incriminating material in her recollections about her time with Almina and the Colonel on the Isle of Wight and at Orchard Grove, especially about JTS or any other of Almina's misdeeds. The Tree family were contacted about this, and the 7th Earl personally intended to collect material from America.[905]

Since the 7th Earl's move to conceal Almina's biography, especially whatever was judged to be repugnant, no researcher has been given access to Almina's surviving papers; indeed, these papers may have been sanitised or destroyed. The 8th Earl refused the present author access, and that embargo has also been applied to other writers.[906] The cause for the embargo now seems crystal clear and undoubtedly the reason why the custodians of Almina's history are only willing to offer a scanty, contrived, incomplete picture of her life.

The author of this book has reviewed a recent publication (from 2011) derived from Highclere sources, which he describes as " Almina's Half Life, Only Half Told" [907]

For a family who constantly seek media publicity and who pride themselves on their place in history and their record of public acts, an act of suppression as this is at the very least painfully rude to Almina's memory.

The name disclosed in the document issued from Highclere Castle in 1996 (if it is true) offers a most remarkable link for the family back in the history of Britain's past. Therefore, as well as Highclere displaying the 5th Earl *and Almina's* respectable (and well earned) links with Egypt's past, should not those whose blood is Almina's blood acknowledge and also be proud of this ancestry?

The laws of privacy (rightly) must be respected here. Any disclosure of that name encroaches directly upon the present family, and although not on those for whom the law holds no brief, disclosure must be withheld. [908] It is for Highclere to answer, if they wish, only they can provide transparency and clarity as to what the overwhelming reason was that the Sox biography of Almina was stopped dead in its tracks.

If there is any truth to reveal about Almina's only son's paternity this moment is a chance to reveal that untold story. This moment marks a golden opportunity for Almina, Countess of Carnarvon, to be remembered as more than the wife of Lord Carnarvon, discoverer of the legendary tomb of Tutankhamun. More than the daughter of a Rothschild. It would be a wrong righted if her *full story* was now finally aired, the story of this tiny lady with the great spirit; the pioneering war-time nurse; the colourful bon viveur; the aristocrat who fell from grace but remained ever a Countess and always a lady?

Appendix 1
Later events of interest

Tutankhamun exhibition at the British Museum

In 1972, three years after Almina's death, her daughter, Lady Evelyn Beauchamp, was in the limelight. She was the last survivor of those who'd entered King Tut's tomb in 1922. Evelyn was present at the official opening by the Queen of the Tutankhamun exhibition, which brought the great treasures discovered by her friend Carter and her father to London. Over a million people visited the exhibition at the British Museum. Most people in the long line-up (including the author, when he was a 19-year-old student) talked about wanting to see the golden mask. The beaten gold burial mask of the boy king, just over 21 inches top to bottom and weighing just over 22 and a half pounds, was considered the most amazing item on display. But nothing could prepare one for the sight of the boy king's sarcophagus. It was breathtaking.

The British Museum, *The Times* and the *Sunday Times* sponsored the 1972 exhibition. The 7th Earl and Countess, Lady Evelyn and Sir Brograve Beauchamp attended at a dinner at the British Museum on 29 November 1972, marking 50 years after the opening of the tomb of Tutankhamun. The 5th Earl would have been delighted by the events, and the buzz they created. After all, he had courted publicity in 1922-3 for his find. It was a shame for him, given his debts, that he had never benefited financially from the discovery as his relatives later did.

The 6th Earl's memoirs

In his last decade the 6th Earl of Carnarvon enjoyed the limelight. He walked tall with dukes and with Prime Ministers, and his succession of mostly younger girlfriends made him a soft target for the gossip columnists who enjoyed speculating on who would be his next Countess.

In 1976 he published his memoir *No Regrets*, followed in 1980 by *Ermine Tales*.[909] The books painted a vivid, albeit complimentary, picture of the Earl, saying he was: "never close to his parents and was raised by governesses... had a career in the British Army, with service in the two World Wars, actor, jockey, horse breeder and winner of the Derby, spy, polo player, twice a husband divorced by his wives, and an adoring grandfather..." [910] Both books were bestsellers; readers enjoying the tales of the Earl's adventures in the saddle and in the bedroom. The indiscretions unveiled caused libel bells to ring at Highclere. The Earl's ghost writer, Barry Wynne, was paid £10,000 to forget about doing a series of taped interviews that revealed much more than was in print, with names of those bedded and discarded.[911] His mother, Almina, no doubt, also suffered a savage indictment which never made it into print.

The Earl enjoyed the rounds of publicity and TV appearances to promote the two volumes. He appeared on the British circuit of chat shows, including *The Michael Parkinson Show* [912], and was observed taking the Concorde to America with his valet Robert Taylor, with the poor employee struggling to haul 500 copies of *No Regrets* intended for the American market.

A snob and a cad to the last, the 6th Earl was in and out of nursing homes in his final years suffering from Parkinson's disease. The *Daily Telegraph* obituary delivered the essence of Almina's son following his death, aged 88, in 1987: "A relentless raconteur and most uncompromisingly direct ladies' man whose chief concern when staying at The Ritz hotel in London was to find a suite not so much over looking the Park as overlooking the rent."[913]

Other deaths

On 25 August 1976 came the death of Almina's son-in-law, Sir Brograve Beauchamp, from pneumonia at the age of 79. He'd been married to Lady Evelyn for 53 years. His estate was valued at £24,909.

Lady Evelyn Beauchamp died on 31 January 1980. She suffered a series of strokes over the years going back to her car accident in 1935. The family announcement of her death read: "On Jan 31 1980 Lady Evelyn Beauchamp after a long illness with great courage. Funeral service at Putney Vale Cemetery, Kingston Road, SW15 on Tues 5 Feb at 10.45." Lady Evelyn was laid to rest in the same cemetery where Howard Carter was buried. On 28 May 1980 *The Times* stated that Lady Evelyn's estate was valued at only £2,825.

Almina's housekeeper Alice Butler was uprooted in the USA following the death of Ronald Tree in 1976, whose widow Marietta survived until 1991. Alice returned to Britain, and lived for a short time with Collins, Ronald Tree's ever faithful butler, until he died. [914]She latterly lived at Eton Square, London, on the staff of Mary, Dowager 10th Duchess of Devonshire, and died in 1988 of lung cancer. [915]

Almina's grandson, Henry, Lord Porchester, the 7th Earl, died on 11 September 2001, that notable day in history when the twin towers of New York fell. He suffered a heart attack, aged 77. *The Guardian* said he was "one of the most influential figures in the world of horseracing. A man of immense energy and diverse talents".[916] In his will he left £21 million, most of the lands and property being left to his widow, Jeanie, and their two sons and daughter. The Royal Family was represented in force for his memorial service in January 2002.[917]

Others who have featured in this book and who survive to this day include Tony Leadbetter and Jeanie, the Dowager Countess of Carnarvon, widow of the 7th Earl and mother of George, the present 8th Earl of Carnarvon.

Highclere

In 1988, some 300 objects relating to King Tut were "rediscovered" at Hichclere. That year, the 7th Earl opened Highclere Castle to the public at large, charging an entrance fee for tourists to come and see what a dazzling headline on the front page of *The Times* labelled "lost treasure".[918] In fact, for most objects there was a tentative link only to the boy king; the items were those which Almina had not been able to sell off to America in 1927, or which Howard Carter had deemed "unimportant items"[919] and failed to catalogue.

Since Almina was left the rights to all of the 5th Earl's Egyptian artefacts in her husband's will, these were her property; but there was never any acknowledgement of this. That said, it is doubtful that the hoard, if remembered in 1951, could have saved her from bankruptcy. Their value is nowhere near that of the relics from Tutankhamun's tomb.

Charles Wilson of *The Times* set part of the record straight in 1988: "All the objects found were recovered from archaeological digs in the Valley of the Kings before the discovery of Tutankhamun's tomb.[920] Further information came from an Egyptian expert, no less a figure than Harry James, the British Museum's Chief Egyptian Collection Curator, who declared: "They're not immensely valuable. They're not treasures in the sense that those from Tutankhamun are treasures. This is a less important part of the Carnarvon– Carter Collection."[921]

Regardless of the historical significance of the objects, tourists were happy to visit Highclere and see such marvellous artefacts as a "wooden mask of Tutankhamun's grandfather dating back 3,200 years".[922]

Today, Highclere remains the family seat of the Carnarvons, the home of the 8th Earl, his second wife Fiona, and their family. Times are hard for those running the stately homes of England; thus in recent years the Carnarvons have developed a successful business side to Highclere, which has been featured as a backdrop for weddings, pop concerts, TV antique shows, movies and TV series, notably, in 2010/2011, the period drama series *Downton Abbey*.

In referring to Almina in a recent interview promoting the house and its family, Fiona, the 8th Countess, is reported as saying that "it's quite possible she [Almina] may have strayed".[923] Indeed.

Almina's story

The reasons for writing this book were simple: to tell the true story of a remarkable woman, and to correct the errors of fact and substance in guidebooks and histories relating to Almina and Lord Carnarvon's lives.

In the last ten years two other books have thrown some light on Almina Carnarvon. In 2002, joint authors Andrew Collins and Chris Ogilvie-Herald published *Tutankhamun: The Exodus Conspiracy*, which charted some aspects of Almina's life and times; and in 2006 the late H. V. F. Winstone gave some biographical details on her life in the reprint of his biography of Howard Carter. The author acknowledges the personal help and advice given to him by Chris Ogilvie-Herald and the late Victor Winstone, and hopes that this book can fill many of the remaining gaps in the public knowledge of Almina, Countess of Carnarvon.

Appendix 2

The Research, Acknowledgements and Author's Thanks

The author has reviewed practically everything in paper format or traceable electronically that features reference to Almina Carnarvon and the 5th Earl of Carnarvon, and the other people caught up in their lives through diaries, timelines, histories, biographies, narratives, references and comments in publications and on the Internet. He graciously acknowledges the various authors of material quoted in the text and their respective publishers and copyright holders. The quotations have been acknowledged in the footnotes. Such quotes have been kept modest and incidental. Care has been taken *not* to exceed the spirit of the copyright principles laid down in the respective *" Permissions and Fair Dealing"* guidelines in terms of the limits under the criteria for *" the purposes of criticism or review".* Otherwise individual rights/ ownership permission of copyright holders has been sought and given.

The author first became aware of Almina, Countess of Carnarvon during 2008 whilst he was researching the story (for a book called *A Beautiful Nuisance*) about a Welsh heiress, the Hon. Gwyneth Ericka Morgan. Gwyneth's rotting corpse was fished from out of the River Thames on 20 May 1925. The timing of Gwnyeth's sad discovery came at the very height of the court case of *Dennistoun v Dennistoun.* When reading and extracting the details about Gwyneth's end it was impossible to ignore the lurid newspapers headlines about the scandalous case that gripped the English speaking world, when Almina's second husband Lt Colonel Ian Dennistoun was sued by his former wife, Dorothy. Later the author became more and more curious about Almina, the merry widow of the 5th Earl of Carnarvon, of Tutankhamun fame. More interest followed and he soon became hooked on Almina's story. He began by looking at the history of her various nursing homes and this widened into a full-blown biography. It has been an interesting labour the past three years. The author owes a lot of people for their help, good faith and kind support.

This book could not have carried such an incisive portrayal of Almina had the author not been assisted throughout the research and in the writing process by Anthony (Tony) Leadbetter, who has been his principal source of information about the Countess, especially in her latter years. Tony knew Almina at very close quarters for almost 30 years, between 1942 and 1969. The author acknowledges Tony's superb and sincere contribution to his much better understanding of Almina and records his great thanks to him with much affection and regard.

Public and private archives have been plundered almost to saturation. Among the public records to acknowledge is the material in Crown Copyright extracted from National Archives, Kew. In the private arena particular thanks is due to the staff of The Royal Archives, Windsor Castle and Rothschild Archive, London. The author acknowledges the kind permission of Her Majesty Queen Elizabeth II and the Directors of Rothschild, London to quote from their repositories and collections.

The author has received generous advice also from authors Chris Ogilvie Herald and the late H.V.F. Winstone, both of whom have written and previously published material on Almina's life. He also acknowledges the advice given by authors Derek Wilson, an authority of the Rothschild family and Peter Bance, an authority on the Duleep Singh family. Another writer who has provided input is Henry Keown –Boyd. In the editing process of the manuscript the author wishes to record his profound thanks and gratitude to Charlie Wilson, for her input, knowledge, spark and wisdom.

The outcome of all this research would also not have been possible – or been as successful - but for the tireless support received by the author from Monty Dart and her husband Tom. Monty spent endless hours at National Archives, Kew and elsewhere copying images and transcribing letters and newspaper articles. Her comments have also been constructive throughout. Tom Dart has copied material in the Leadbetter Collection and tens of hours of interviews with Tony Leadbetter.

The author's enrolment at The University of Newport at Caerleon has enabled him to access online The *London Times* and the British Library's database of 19th Century newspapers. He would like to thank Viv Davies, Jan Pinder, Oliver Hewer, Jill Morgan, Jayne Hunt and Peter Brown of the Life Long Learning department.

The photographs used in the book are taken from Tony Leadbetter's unique Collection, that he largely inherited from his mother's albums. Both Tony and the author ultimately intend to offer *all* their research papers and memorabilia to a suitable Archives for full, unrestricted public access to be given to the book's sources once the material is catalogued and indexed.

The author is indebted to many titled individuals and where appropriate their respective Archivists for replying to enquiries including (in alphabetical order) Lord Carrington, Lady Elizabeth Cavendish, Deborah, Duchess of Devonshire, The Earl of Dudley, the late 5th Earl of Gainsborough, the late Earl of Harewood, The Duke of Marlborough, Lord Montagu of Beaulieu, the late 4th Lord Mottistone, The Countess of Mountbatten, Lord Palmer, and Elizabeth, Countess of Sutherland.

Sadly, the Carnarvon family did not co-operate in granting access to Almina's papers at Highclere Castle Archives. As a result the missing aspects of Almina's story remain a question mark. Besides this enforced dead-end some other enquiries went unanswered but these obstacles did not halt the author's investigations nor diminish a search for truth. The author is very thankful to those individuals who did answer queries and who showed him great kindness and an interest in the researches including the Williamson family of Alvie, Ken Grist, Christine and David Jones, Ian Pickard and Roger Smith, Isle of Wight. He also wishes to thank Bill Buchanan for checking Census returns. Special thanks to Beryl Attaway, John Briggs, Alex Cameron, Sylvia Darley MBE, Brian Hughes, Alfred Jones PhD, Pearl Kilpatrick, Martin's Gallery, Abergavenny, Kathy Perkins, Sophie Pigott, Nash Rambler, Margaret Sharp, Tithe Barn, Abergavenny, Annabel Venning, Christopher Wilson, Philip Wray and Ching-Yi Huang. Any other help given him is also acknowledged.

Any errors in the text etc are the author's and his alone. He welcomes corrections, with sources and any additional data to include in any future reprints of the book. Thanks are also due to Newspaper Archive.com, Abe Books, Amazon Books, Google Books, Scotsman Digital Archives, Shropshire Archives, Somerset Archives, The City of Bristol Library, The British Library, including the Newspaper Library, National Library of Scotland, Manuscript Division. Finally, he records considerable thanks to his wife Perry and to Newport colleagues at NYO, for their enduring patience, constant love and insufferable encouragement.

END NOTES

[1] This is the spelling used throughout the book. Representation of the name of boy King varies across publications, with *Tutankhamun* being largely used, followed by *Tutankhamen*. The latter spelling is often seen in American publications.

[2] Princess Elizabeth, later H.M. Queen Elizabeth II, was born on April 21 1926 at 17 Bruton Street, London.

[3] Advertisements for 18 Bayswater Terrace in *The Times* from 1878 and 1884 add " Owned by a Jewish property magnate named Reuben Levy " The rooms were spacious, with drawing, sitting and bedrooms provided and a full table d'hote. " "

[4] Leadbetter, interviews 2009 and 2010. Tony Leadbetter adds " ..*when Almina spoke French heads turned, because the tone was the oldie world style of French associated with aristocrats... and it sounded very beautiful...* "

[5] Maria Victoria de Los Dolorés Gogorza was born at Maracaibo, Venezuela on 28 July 1819. The source for this is the *"Acte de Mariage"* of 1876, relating to her second marriage.... See footnote 7 below.

[6] According to Dennis Cunniff " the informant (who seems to have been the concierge) did not know the names of Alexandre's (deceased) parents. The only additional information is that he died at age 78, which would make his birth year about (1875-78=) 1797, and that he was born in Marseille, Bouches-du-Rhone, France, and that he died in his home on the rue de Lisbonne, 18th arrondissement, Paris, France..."

[7] This extract from a translation from the *"Acte de Mariage"* (kindly supplied by Dennis Cunniff) provides an insight into Almina's maternal links. " On 14 September 1876, at 9:30 in the morning, Marriage certificate of: Alexander Mellinet, Minister Plenipotentiary of France to Tehran in Persia, born 13 September 1808, Rome (Italy), currently residing in Paris, 74 rue de Lisbonne; adult son of Anne Francis Mellinet and Aglaia Eulalie Dosne, his wife, both deceased and Maria de los Dolores Victoria Gogorza, of independent means (gentlewoman), born 28 July 1819 in Maracaibo in the Republic of Venezuela (America), living in Paris, 74 rue de Lisbonne, widow of Alexander Antoine Boyer, who died 11 November 1875 in Paris, eldest daughter of Bernardo Gogorza and Josefa Salmas, his wife, both deceased......."

NB Dennis Cunniff adds "Josefa Salmas in the printed announcement in the *Annuaire Noblesse de France, 1877*, does not look like "Salmas" in the [hand written] Acte... more like Salsisras or Salsisias or Sasisuras or Salsirras."

[8] 1871, UK Census, 3 Bryanston Street, Marylebone, London Ref: RG10/165/21.

[9] Marie's parents were married before 1838 – as Marie had a brother Alexandre born in that year. He was a witness to his mother remarriage in 1876. NB *Historical Archive of Zulia* 1852, vol. 8, bundle 21, *folio* 40 to 40v also records the following on the establishment of a settlement in Venezuela : " The Frenchman Alexandre Boyer was the major factor in its final momentum *and* force... in the decades of 1840 to 1860.... undoubtedly of great significance in the process production of mid-century, had arrived to Maracaibo to 1827 *and* from those years was devoted to trade *and* other businesses in the region." His

projects had a major injection of capital from its partners in Europe. In 1847 he had established in Paris "French Society in Maracaibo".

[10] The French had longstanding financial interests in the whole of the continent and between the three American continents, North, South and Central America, and one adventurous project (possibly involved a member of Almina's grandmother's de Gogorza family in the building of the Panama Canal. [An Anthoine de Gogorza , born USA of French parents was a pioneer in the Canal's early development.]) The Rothschilds, with other European bankers, were also big time investors in these continents and greedy to be leading on such projects as the Panama Canal.

[11] *Pall Mall Gazette* of 16 September 1898 records " After the restoration, Charles II avenged his father by "causing the body of Oliver Cromwell to be exhumed from Westminster Abbey and sending it to Tyburn, to be first hanged and then decapitated and quartered at the foot of the gallows. Cromwell's daughter, Lady Fauconberg, whose husband at that time owned Newburgh Priory, is asserted, by means of bribing the guards, to have succeeded in substituting another corpse for that of her father, and to have obtained possession of his remains, which she conveyed to the priory."

[12] See Carnarvon, Fiona [Eighth] Countess *Carnarvon and Carter*, Highclere Enterprises LLP, (2007).

[13] Thornbury Walter and Walford Edward *Old and New London: Westminster and the western suburbs* Cassell, Petter & Galpin (1891) records "At the corner of Conduit Street and George Street is Limmer's Hotel, once an evening resort for the sporting world; in fact, it was a midnight "Tattersalls'," where nothing was heard but the language of the turf, and where men with not very clean hands used to make up their books. "Limmer's," says a popular writer, "was the most dirty hotel in London; but in the gloomy, comfortless coffee-room might be seen many members of the rich squirearchy, who visited London during the sporting season. This hotel was frequently so crowded that a bed could not be had for any amount of money; but you could always get a good plain English dinner, an excellent bottle of port, and some famous gin-punch. See also *The New Sporting Magazine*, December, 1844, p352.

[14] According to her brief obituary notices, Lady Georgina Wombwell died at 9B John Street, Berkeley Square, on 10 May 1875, in her 68th year.

[15] Henry Chaplin (1840-1923), 1st Viscount Chaplin, politician, landowner and racehorse owner.

[16] Hastings lost everything in a single bet on the 1867 Derby. The story of this famous Derby, which cost the luckless Marquis of Hastings his fortune and won for his arch rival in love Henry Chaplin the colossal sum of £100,000, is revealed in Blyth, Henry : *The Pocket Venus*, Walker and Co. (1967). The night before the race it was reported that Hermit, the horse that won it, had gone lame. Hastings considered the event a certainty, put his whole fortune to the hazard at 100 to 1, and was completely ruined. This Derby was run in a snowstorm. Hastings in grave health, through alcoholism, died the following year, a broken man. Fred Wombwell lost a friend and a patron.

[17] *Reuters Telegrams* : 7 June 1871 Paris and Interim.

[18] A Boyer family appear on the 1871 Census English returns for 19, Marine Parade, Dover. Dover would have been a ferry crossing point to / from France. The data records :

Madame Alexander Boyer Wife Aged 53 Born France
Alexander G Boyer   Son Aged 33 Unmarried Born France
Jules Boyer   Son Aged 31 Unmarried Born France

The only inconsistency is over the birthplace for "Madame" (if this is Maria Victoria) being recorded as France as opposed to Maracaibo. "Madame Boyer" described, as a "Wife" is credible since her husband Alexandre was still alive in 1871, and died on 11 November 1875.

[19] Married 19 December 1864. This was far from being a *"good"* marriage. It was not a happy union, but produced one child, a son, Walter Alexander Charles Lethbridge (who died Paris, 1931, aged 65). See also *Freeman's Journal and Daily Commercial Advertiser*, 2 December 1884 regarding the subsequent divorce case *Lethbridge v Lethbridge*.

[20] Married 31 October 1865. See *The Era,* 5 November 1865. Henry became 3rd Earl of Effingham in 1889. The marriage produced one son, another Henry, who later inherited the Earldom as the 4th Earl, but who died in 1927, childless. The Earldom then passed to a cousin.

[21] *Leeds Mercury*, 14 January 1868.

[22] Among these cronies were a few notable gentleman (who, sadly, like Fred died relatively young) The Marquess of Blandford, (George Charles Spencer-Churchill, the eldest son of the Duke of Marlborough, later the 8th Duke, who died aged 48 in 1892) Hon. Oliver Montague (a son of the Earl of Sandwich who died aged 48 in 1893) and Hon. C Carrington (later Marquess of Lincolnshire and sometime an Equerry to Queen Victoria).

[23] *The Times*, 18 October 1913. George's caricature appears in *Vanity Fair* of 24 January 1874 by *APE* described as Soldier and Farmer.

[24] Lady Julia Sarah Alice Child-Villiers (d.1921) daughter of George Augustus Frederick, 6th Earl of Jersey and Julia Peel , the latter was a daughter of Sir Robert Peel.

[25] *The Morning Post* of 8 June 1868 refers to an event at the *Bois de Boulogne* (a large public park in Paris) where (on 5 June 1868) the visitors *" Amongst the fair sex present in the pavilion … [were] the Duchess of Manchester, Madame Alphonse Rothschild, Marquise de Gallifet, Madame de Pourtales, Duchess of Castries, Mrs Philip and Miss Miles, Lady Mary Craven, Mrs Reginald Herbert, Madame Bowyer and Mrs Frederick Wombwell…"*

[26] *The Plantagenet Roll of the Blood Royal* gives the date of Frederick's birth as 8 April 1869.

[27] See Gower, Lord Ronald FSA *My Reminiscences* (1883-4) p.383; and Ryan, Charles E *With an Ambulance During the Franco- German War 1870-71* (1896) pp.116, 287.

[28] According to the Census of 1871, Frederick and Marie's son Frederick, age 2, was staying with his grandmother Georgina, Lady Wombwell in Brighton.

[29] The legal age was 21, below that lay the defence of claiming " infancy".

[30] Ryder v Wombwell LR, 3 Ex. 90 (described in Finch, Gerard Brown, *A Selection of Cases on The English Law of Contract* (1886). Exchequer, 1868. L.R, 4;32.)

[31] *The Times,* 29 January and 7 February 1872.

[32] *The London Gazette* of 13 February 1872 records a bankruptcy petition against Frederick Wombwell of 3 Bryanston Street, Bryanston Square dated 10 February 1872.

[33] *Ashworth Trustee & Company v Wombwell* Case No A4 : Kings Bench Division pleadings. A single document relating to this case (naming Frederick Wombwell) can be found in National Archives, Kew, ref J55/3/174. The writ is dated 4 January 1876 and the proceedings (in the Queen's Bench Division) is dated 30 May 1876). At the time of receiving this writ (January 1876 : just a few months before Almina's birth) Fred Wombwell may have fled the country again (for France), it is possible Marie actually joined Fred in Paris, following Almina's birth.

[34] Marie moved sometime to live at 20 Bruton Street, Mayfair whose lease was in the name of Boyer. See *Boyer v Bancroft. The Law Journal* Vol 18 (1883). This records a case of a tenants dispute over these premises which backed onto 18 Berkeley Square. The case was heard in the Chancery Division of the High Court on 21 March 1883.

[35] Hetherington John Aikman : *Nellie Melba : A Biography,* Faber and Faber. (1968).

[36] See Morton, Frederic *Rothschilds A Family Portrait,* Secker & Warburg. (1962).

[37] Hetherington, John Aikman : *Nellie Melba : A Biography,* Faber and Faber. (1968).

[38] See Lindsay, David, Crawford Papers: *The Journal of David Lindsay*, Twenty-seventh Earl of Crawford and Tenth Earl of Balcarres, 1871-1940 During the Years 1892 to 1940, Manchester University Press (1984) pp 599-600.

[39] Algernon West, (1832-1921) , Gladstone's private secretary, records in his Diary for 1895 "We very often walked over in the Sunday afternoons to Halton, Alfred Rothschild's, who was ever willing to show us his beautiful pictures and gorgeous surroundings. His kindness was not limited to personal friends, for I was told that in the cold bitterness of winter mornings he sent a cart round every morning with hot coffee and bread and butter to every labourer on his estate."

[40] In an obituary on Alfred in *The Capital Times*, 9 February 1918, it remarks: " He was a little autocratic in his ways, and often evinced his disapproval of anything that offended his artistic eye, having several times created a sensation by suddenly demanding the removal of a gaudy bunch of flowers from the buttonhole of some astounded railway porter or minor official..."

[41] See also Battersea, Lady Constance, *and Reminiscences.* London (1922).

[42] Tony Leadbetter, who lived in Almina Carnarvon's households from 1945-1969 recalls that Almina spoke sparingly of Alfred's parties. When she did comment reference was made to Alfred's assembly of men, who stayed at weekends, many of them "bohemians from the world of art and the theatre". A transcript of the Guest Book for Halton is available at the Rothschild Archives.

[43] See *Country Life* Vol. 154 (1973). A much-quoted review of what constituted Rothschild hospitality. It's originator may have been the Jewish historian Cecil Roth (1899-1970) author of *The Magnificent Rothschilds.* R Hale (1939).

[44] No exact date is known for when Alfred and Marie first met and/or when the relationship advanced to a personal level. In the early years of their marriage, Fred and Marie Wombwell and Alfred de Rothschild are listed as present together in Court circles as early as 1871. There may also have been a tie-in to

Marie's father, Alexandre Boyer, or stemming from Alfred first knowing Fred Wombwell. The Rothschild clan in Britain and France were involved in Paris over many decades of the 19th Century, including supporting English expats in distress at the time of the Paris Siege. The paths between the parties may have crossed then. The British Rothschilds as among the " *Jewish leaders*" also named as wheeling and dealing with the Shah of Persia, Nasser al-Din Shah Qajar (1831-1896) who visited Britain in 1873, 1878 and 1889. During the 1878 visit the Shah presented Alfred with the " Order of the Lion and Sun", " possibly in token of appreciation of certain financial affairs" (See *The Globe* 3 August 1878).   Marie's stepfather, Alexandre Mellinet, was French Minister to Iran from 1872 until 1879. [He died in 1884.] He would have known Alfred and was often present to represent French interests when the Shah visited key countries and people in Europe. These dates for Marie's stepfather being in Rothschild company straddle Marie's pregnancy with Almina but must fall short of being regarded as evidence of how Marie and Alfred came to be on closer terms with each other.   Three events in the early 1880s provide a better public linkage. On 19 January 1881, Alfred acted as best man at the wedding of his brother Leopold to Marie Perugia. Marie (as Mrs Wombwell) is listed as giving a wedding gift. Marie is also listed (as is Alfred) as attending the wedding of Nellie Baldock to the Earl of Kilmorey on 23 June 1881.   On 21 June 1883 Marie is listed (as is Alfred) at an afternoon party held at Hertford House. [See *Morning Post* of 20 January and 24 June 1881 and 22 June 1883.]

[45] Rose, Kenneth : *Elusive Rothschild : The Life of Victor, Third Baron.* (2003) Weidenfeld & Nicholson p.12 " *For many years Alfred lived contentedly with a mistress, Mrs Wombwell….*" But no primary source is given for this statement. Scrutiny of the dates when Alfred took possession of the two principal homes he is best associated with, show that he bought his London address at 1 Seamore Place, Mayfair (from Christopher Sykes MP) in 1879 and only used Halton House (his place in Buckinghamshire) after it was completed in July 1883. These dates are several years after Almina's birth, in 1876.   It seems *very* unlikely that Alfred and Marie ever cohabitated. Benjamin Disraeli (when Lord Beaconfield) was also a long term guest of Alfred's at 1 Seamore Place from 1880-1. [For further details of the Rothschild homes from 1825 see Arthur Irwin Dascent's " *Piccadilly In Three Centuries : With Some Account of Berkeley Square and the Haymarket* " Macmillan and Co London (1920).]

[46] In " *Lady Almina And The Real Downton Abbey*" (2011) p.32 Fred is merely branded *"a drunkard and a thief"*.

[47] Henry, Carnarvon, the 6th Earl of (1898-1987) produced two volumes of autobiography *No Regrets*" (1976) and *Ermine Tales* (1980) published by Weidenfeld and Nicolson, London.

[48] The Inland Revenue documentation in National Archives, Kew files IR 59/519-521 describes Almina (coldly) as a " *Stranger in Blood*".

[49] A recent study that reflects on this is Poole Andrea Geddes: *Stewards of the nation's art: contested cultural authority 1890-1939.* University of Toronto Press (2011) who comments that this " *was received with real distress and resentment*" among Alfred's Rothschild relations. Poole's authority is   Kenneth Rose's *Elusive Rothschild*, his biography of Victor, 3rd Baron Rothschild where the corresponding reference (p.196) is " *Alfred alienated much of his estate…by leaving it to his mistress's child, Almina…*"

[50] File IR 59/521 in National Archives, Kew uses values from Christies of the contents of 1 Seamore Place, including wine and articles in store at 10 Bruton Street at £495,258. Silver and plate is valued additionally at £4,186.

[51] *Liverpool Mercury*, 28 December 1875 and *Freeman's Journal*, 30 December 1875 quoting from *Figaro*.

[52] Ibid.

[53] Wilson, Derek : *Rothschild : A Story of Wealth and Power*, Andre Deutsch. (1988) and revised edition Mandarin Paperbacks (1994).

[54] IR 59/519–521 National Archives, Kew. An Indenture of Settlement was made on 25 June 1895.

[55] Emails between Author and Derek Wilson 20 February to 7 March 2010.

[56] See Davis, Richard : *The English Rothschilds* (1983) p225. University of North Carolina Press (Chapel Hill).

[57] It is a curiosity too that at the Spanish Court in Madrid in the 1870s was one Countess de Almina who was an attendant to the Queen of Spain and the Duchess de Prio. Given Marie's mother's Spanish ancestry this offers another possible source for the name chosen for her daughter. See *The Daily News* of 1 February 1873

[58] Almina's Birth Certificate is registered as entry No 246 of Kensington Registration District, Sub District of St John Paddington on 24 November 1880, issued "on authority of the Registrar General". She was born 24 April 1876 at 18 Bayswater Terrace.

[59] Almina's Death Certificate is registered as entry No 114 of Sodbury Registration District on 8 May 1969 giving her date and place of birth as " About 1878, France".

[60] Wilson, Derek : *Rochschild: A Story of Wealth and Power* Revised edition Mandarin Paperbacks (1994) p.262. Part of the accusation by Wilson against Almina (to merit such a harsh description) revolves around the identity of a peeress who was blackmailing the unmarried Lionel Walter de Rothschild (1868-1937, the 2nd Baron) who had fathered an illegitimate daughter. No evidence naming Almina has emerged in the author's researches. Tony Leadbetter says he was informed (by a 3rd party – contact author for the source) that Almina was **NOT** the "blackmailing peeress".

[61] Email to author from Derek Wilson, 7 March 2010.

[62] See Rothschild, Miriam : *Dear Lord Rothschild*", Hutchinson (1983) p.12 " " Porchy" [sic] Carnarvon (who claimed to be Alfred's grandson) "

[63] Private source - please refer to author.

[64] A corresponding negative element to highlight (noted by a Rothschild insider (now deceased) – contact Author for source) is the observation that Almina did NOT look like any of the other Rothschild women, albeit there was recognition for Almina's daughter Lady Evelyn Herbert's " looks" being similar to other Rothschild women. Evelyn does have a strong edged look – some see Jewish- some see oriental – some see a Wombwell. To ensure that the fuller residue of genetic material is included this comparison should embrace the French, North African and Spanish American characteristics on her maternal side.

[65] The Author has seen letters in The Royal Archives, Windsor Castle (Royal Archives, RA AEC/GG/01/1-131.) which may originated from Alfred's Scrapbook, which he mentions in his Will of 1917 as an heirloom left to Almina.

The letters at Windsor include a touching letter from Alfred to King George V expressing his sorrow on the death of King Edward VII, in 1910.

[66] Tony Leadbetter recalls seeing the Alfred de Rothschild scrapbook when he visited Highclere Castle in 2000, but he had no time to digest its contents. The opportunity to reveal serious proof of Alfred's paternity from Herbert sourced material within Highclere Archives came with the publication of *" Lady Almina And The Real Downton Abbey"* (2011) from Hodder and Stoughton on 29 September 2011. However, this book can only very feebly declare that *" the question of Almina's paternity can't be conclusively determined with any certainty...."*

[67] Allrey, Anthony *Edward VII and his Jewish Court,* Weidenfeld & Nicolson. (1991) p.198.

[68] Cited by Rose, Kenneth *Elusive Rothschild: The Life of Victor, Third Baron.* London, Weidenfeld & Nicolson. (2003).

[69] Leadbetter Collection.

[70] Ibid.

[71] According to Brighton and Hove Directories a highly fashionable address.

[72] Almina (almost certainly) didn't see Frederick's sentimental offering or the tender, loving message he imparted with it in his Will.

[73] Probate Registry, London. Indexes to Wills and Admons, 1889.

[74] Survey for National Burial Project by Cleveland Family History Society.

[75] *Aberdeen Weekly Journal,* 10 May 1893.

[76] On 5 July 1893 one of the great event of the summer season was a garden party given by the Prince and Princess of Wales at Marlborough House (See *The Morning Post* of 6 July, 1893, which includes Prince Victor Duleep Singh, The Earl of Carnarvon and Alfred de Rothschild as attendees.)

[77] For the succession of Lord Porchesters, "Porchey" or "Porchy" was the shortened form used. Lady Burghclere uses "Porchy" in her biographical sketch of the 5th Earl in 1923. "Porchey" is the spelling mostly used by the 6th Earl in his memoirs, although this lapses sometimes in *The Carnarvon Letters*, Privately printed (1994) (by 7th Earl as compiler) and becomes " Porch" and again " Porchy" .

[78] For the background to the Earldom of Carnarvon, see National Archives, Kew, file HO 42/25/237, folios 612-3, being *" a letter of thanks [dated 25 June 1793] from Lord Porchester for the news of the King's intention to create him an earl, asking that he should be styled Earl of Carnarvon".*

[79] Nevill, Ralph (Ed) : *Reminiscences of Lady Dorothy Nevill* (1906) pp.139-141

[80] The relationship between Disraeli and Anne, Countess of Chesterfield (1802-1885), and her sister, Selina Bridgeman, Lady Bradford, (1819-1894), is the subject of over 500 letters (the originals are in Staffordshire Record Office); many were published in *Letters of Disraeli to Lady Chesterfield and Lady Bradford* edited by the Marquis of Zetland. (1929). According to the Oxford Dictionary of National Biography " Though Disraeli proposed marriage to Anne, he was really in love with Selina, and Anne lapsed gracefully into the role of confidante". Benjamin Disraeli (1804-1881) was "a frequent guest at Bretby." Disraeli's own house in Curzon Street was abandoned whilst being renovated. He lived with Alfred de Rothschild at 1 Seamore Place, Park Lane, Mayfair. The often quoted remark on the Rothschilds by Disraeli was " I have always been of

opinion that there cannot be too many Rothschilds". This is also referred to by Lady Battersea (herself a Rothschild) in her *Reminiscences"* (1922).

[81] Vandenberg, Philip *The Golden Pharaoh,* MacMillan Publishing Company (1980) p.82.

[82] According to Patricia Jalland in *Death in the Victorian Family,* Oxford University Press. (1999) "puerperal fever caused 33-38% of maternal deaths in England and Wales from 1847-1874". As she lay dying, Lady Carnarvon suffered the great personal loss of two members of the Highclere staff , including the housekeeper, Mrs Laverick, who was killed in the Shipton-on-Cherwell railway disaster of 24 December 1874, and whose funeral took place a few hours after the Countess.

[83] *Hampshire Advertiser*, 3 February 1875.

[84] The Oxford Dictionary of National Biography entry for Lady Evelyn's mother, Anne Elizabeth Stanhope [née Forester], Countess of Chesterfield (1802-1885), records of her husband " He lies in bed half the day, " reported Greville in 1846, and he confessed himself saddened by Bretby: "a princely fortune dilapidated by sheer indolence, because the obstinate spoilt owner will neither look into his affairs nor let anybody else look into them' (GEC, Peerage).

[85] Probate Registry, London. Indexes Wills & Admons, 1875.

[86] Lady Burghclere: *Biographical Sketch of the Late Lord Carnarvon* (1923). British Library Catalogue D -7705.r.1 . The " slight sketch" is included in some editions of the Carter- Mace book *Tomb of Tutankhamun*. It is used as a source for Lord Carnarvon's entry in the Oxford Dictionary of National Biography. Lady Winifred Burghclere writes cautiously about her brother, stopping the leak of any embarrassing fall out. Almina is demolished by Winifred's trumpet in a single dull sentence.

Such contrived, diminished text represents a pattern among chroniclers of Herbert history placed in the public domain. There is a heavy handed gloss on the truth by Elizabeth (Elsie) Howard (the (second) 4th Countess), who rigorously controlled and censored the posthumous biography of her husband, Henry, 4th Earl of Carnarvon. Lately *" Lady Almina And The Real Downton Abbey"* (2011) is a hackneyed account of Almina's life, which ends abruptly in 1920s.

[87] *Hampshire Telegraph and Sussex Chronicle*, 17 April 1880, describes Porchey as " delicate".

[88] Lady Burghclere Biographical *Sketch of the Late Lord Carnarvon* (1923). Also seen in a tribute to Lady Gwendolen Herbert in *The Newbury Weekly News*, on 11 November 1915, following her death on 26 October 1915 aged 73.

[89] Ibid.

[90] Vandenberg, Philip *The Golden Pharaoh,* MacMillan Publishing Company. (1980) p.82. Gwendolen (or Gwendoline) was the younger daughter of the 3rd Earl of Carnarvon born 1842; lived at Putney, Surrey and at Highclere, she died unmarried in 1915; The Earls of Portsmouth were leading lights in the fox-hunting fraternity of Devonshire. Their seat was Eggesford House, North Devon. Isaac Newton Wallop, (1825-1891), the 5th Earl, married Lady Eveline Alicia Juliana Herbert (1834-1906). The family of Wallop have a remote link back to Sir Isaac Newton, one of the Wallops married a daughter of the philosopher's niece.

[91] Elisabeth Catherine Howard and the 4th Earl of Carnarvon were cousins. Elisabeth's father Henry Howard (1802-1875) was a brother of Henrietta Anna Howard (1804-1876) the 3rd Countess of Carnarvon, Porchey's paternal grandmother.

[92] Hon. Aubrey Nigel Henry Molyneux Herbert (1880-1923) and Hon. Mervyn Robert Howard Molyneux (1882-1929).

[93] James' first wife Florence was the only daughter of Isambard Kingdom Brunel. He died at Bay Mount, Paignton in 1921 in his 81st year. See *The Times*, 9 August 1921.

[94] NB "Duleep" is sometimes recorded in texts as "Dhuleep" or as " Dilip". At Eton Victor's nickname was "Tulip", a sloppy derivation of "Duleep/ Dilip".

[95] See Bance, Peter, *Sovereign, Squire and Rebel : Maharajah Duleep Singh and the Heirs of a Lost Kingdom*, Coronet House Publishing Ltd. (2009); *The Times*, 4 October 1880; Francis Denzil Edward Baring, later 5th Baron Ashburton (1866-1938); John Walter Edward Douglas-Scott-Montagu; after 1905 the second Lord Montagu of Beaulieu, famed motor car pioneer (1866-1929); Ralph Nevill (1866-1927), writer and traveller - son of writer and hostess Lady Dorothy Nevill, a regular at Highclere. Prince Victor Duleep Singh (1866-1918), life long friend of Porchey; Another fellow pupil was , George William Coventry, (1865-1927). Viscount Deerhurst, heir to the Coventry title. His sister Lady Anne married Prince Victor Duleep Singh in 1898.

[96] The gambling habit for Porchey started at Eton Collge under Duleep Singh's steerage. A contemporary, Ralph Nevill, refers in *Florest Etona : Anecdotes and memories of Eton College*, Macmillan and Co, London, (1911) to the high stakes involved (p.323) *"a new boy (the son of the Maharajah Duleep Singh, whose arrival at Eton created some sensation) ...offered to bet him a fiver against a certain horse, which wager had been accepted. This was the largest wager we ever heard of as being made at Eton, and it was looked upon as extraordinary.. "*

[97] The *Otago Witness* of 23 August 1900 says of the 5th Earl " In the Newbury District he was nicknamed Motor- Carnarvon, in Berkshire Auto-Carnarvon."

[98] *The Times*, 25 July 1945 ; *Notes and Records of the Royal Society* Vol. 4, No. 1 Apr 1946 pp113-120.

[99] *Freeman's Journal*, 31 July 1885 and *Leeds Mercury*, 1 August 1885. The 4th Earl and Porchey travelled from Ireland to the funeral of Anne Chesterfield. Afterwards they returned to Ireland. The ceremony was private and she was buried in the family vault at Bretby.

[100] Jeune, Mary: Lady St Helier *Memories of Fifty Years*, E. Arnold. London (1909).

[101] To his family, Porchey was awkward, shy and clumsy, especially with women. "Tulip"(Prince Victor Duleep Singh) delighted in leading his weaker, inexperienced friend. Whilst at Cambridge both men formed all male social associations – their contemporaries there included the notorious " Prince Eddy", Duke of Clarence (son of Bertie, Prince of Wales) and Lord Francis Hope – of the Hope diamond fame- but evidence is slight that Porchey and Victor were deflected into seeking pleasures in the company of these fellows.

[102] *Hampshire Telegraph and Sussex Chronicle*, 19 July 1890.

[103] *Morning Post*, 25 February 1889. NB The maternal family of Prince Victor Duleep Singh also resided in Egypt.

[104] *Observer*, 11 May 1889.

[105] The Nile Campaign 1884-1985, Diary of Colonel Sir Percival Marling in Journal of Royal African Studies Vol 35, 139, Apr 1936.)

[106] A famous affair from 1890 (and later Court proceedings) of cheating at cards by Lt Colonel Sir William Gordon-Cumming of the Scots Guards. Bertie, Prince of Wales was present at the event held at a country house at Tranby Croft, near Doncaster, Yorkshire. See The Times, 2 June 1891 for details of the Court proceedings that followed. The case is also dealt with by H Montgomery Hyde in Bridgeman and Drury *Society Scandals*, David & Charles (1977). pp. 100-119.

[107] Julian Osgood- Field, (1852 –1925), in his scandalous reminiscences *Uncensored Recollections* (1924) p247 says " When I first knew Lord Porchester as he was then, he was a fine handsome youth, but Victor Duleep Singh led him into wild ways." The preferred course was of visiting common prostitutes, who were available (and tolerated) on the Continent and in Egypt – thus keeping any scandal at arm's length from their families in Britain.

[108] *Observer*, 11 May 1889. . The 4th Earl's diaries in the British Library Manuscripts Division record his concerns over "property and family matters including Porchester's serious financial problems".(BL Add.60929).

[109] *Washington Post*, 25 November 1911.

[110] Victor was at Sandhurst Royal Military College between 1887-8. See Campbell, Christy, *The Maharajah's Box*, Harper Collins, London (2000) Chapter 37. In 1887, Victor's mother, the Maharani Bamba, died in London.

[111] *Omaha daily bee*, 28 April 1890.

[112] *Guardian*, 2 July 1890 (quoting from *The Times*).

[113] Robin Harcourt Williams, Archivist of Hatfield House advises in an email to the author dated 17 December 2009 "We have two letters from the Fifth Earl to the Third Marquess of Salisbury, dated 1890, but they are simply concerned with the funeral of the Fourth Earl of Carnarvon."

[114] *The Times*, 2 October 1925.

[115] *Hampshire Telegraph and Sussex Chronicle*, 2 August 1890.

[116] Hardinge, Sir Henry Arthur, *The Life of Henry Howard Molyneux Herbert* (1925)

[117] See Woolf Virginia, *Moments of Being* (edited by Jeanne Schulkind) Grafton Books (1989) p.185. [This included at Court presentations. An example of this can be found in The London Daily Mail of 19 May 1896 which describes her dress at the Fourth Drawing Room of that year " *Elsie, Countess of Carnarvon, wore a train of black peau do soie, lined with glace silk and ornamented with black tulle, caught up with plumes of black feathers and moiré ribbon. The gown was black velvet trimmed with fine cut jet and Brussels lace.*"]

[118] See also National Archives, Kew file CO 323/916/4 f61-65 regarding a comment on Lady Elisabeth Carnarvon being rude to two civil servants whilst attempting to obtain access to her husband's old departmental papers. In defence another civil servant records " Oh, no, she was pressing but not provocative.."

[119] This is highlighted in Christopher Wilson's article in the Daily Mail of 21 October 2011 " *Downton's greatest secret: A lonely countess and her illicit love affair with an Indian Prince…..*". Tony Leadbetter adds further from what Almina told him about the Earl's " *malady*". " Lord Carnarvon contracted the

pox in Egypt, after visiting whorehouses with Duleep Singh. Not long after he became the Earl he lapsed into a serious state of health, and was not expected to live... Victor Duleep Singh, who at the time was on leave from the Army stayed at his bedside...Carnarvon continued to suffer long terms side effects. " It is inferred that the side affects caused the cessation of Carnarvon's sexual activity.

[120] *The Belfast Newsletter*, 14 May 1892.

[121] *The Hampshire Advertiser*, 25 June 1892.

[122] On 8 February 1893 *The World* reported that John Gretton, a partner in the Bass Brewery Company, tenant of Drakelow Hall was to acquire Bretby. A further announcement in the Derby Mercury of 22 February 1893 gives the terms of purchase as £400,000. This highlighted the extent of Carnarvon's growing debts and financial difficulties.

[123] See Julian Osgood- Field's *Uncensored Recollections* (1924) p247 " *When I first knew Lord Porchester as he was then, he was a fine handsome youth, but Victor Duleep Singh led him into wild ways.* "

[124] Leadbetter, interviews 2009 and 2010. Photographs of the 5[th Earl] give credibility to such abrasions. In her posthumous tribute in 1923, Winifred Burghclere also refers to him having " serious injury to his mouth and jaw" sustained in the motorcar accident in Germany in 1909. These scars were from the related surgery.

[125] In the early 1890s Alfred was a regular visitor to Nice and Monte Carlo and successfully played the tables. One report from the *Bristol Mercury and Daily Post* of 16 December 1891, refers to him making a substantial win of " *three maximums of 12,000 f (francs)...*" and, displaying the banker's sense he " *went away immediately with his winnings*". It is highly likely that Alfred would have seen Carnarvon (and Duleep Singh) lose at the tables, making the Earl game for Alfred's scheme to find Almina's a titled husband, who would jump at the offer to clear their debts.

[126] At another level the whole covenant entered into by Alfred in favour of the Carnarvons was the hiring price for to secure the title of Countess for Almina. The money was to be paid at a rate of £12,000 per year and would continue to be paid to the surviving partner in the event of death of either Almina or Carnarvon.

[127] In 1823, the 3rd Earl, John had been declared "of unsound mind and condition, and incapable of managing himself and his affairs"

[128] *The Penny Illustrated Times*, 1890 "How The World Wags" . Carnarvon and Victor were in Berlin together in October 1893, when news came through of the death of Victor's father, the Maharajah Duleep Singh, in Paris, on 22 October 1893.

[129] After Lord Carnarvon first met Almina he disappeared with Prince Victor Duleep Singh on a yachting trip to South America, which is described in some detail in Lady Winifred's biographical sketch of Carnarvon, from 1923. She dates this trip as " In 1894" . This was in effect the last time that the two friends were able to spend time with each other, on his return to England, Carnarvon married Almina.

[130] *The Morning Post*, 30 October 1894.

[131] *Birmingham Daily Post*, 30 October 1894.

[132] Ibid.

[133] Hoving, Thomas : *Tutankhamun : The Untold Story,* Simon and Schuster. (1978).

[134] See Adonis, A : *The Survival of the Great Estates .* Historical Research Vol 64, Issue 153 pp.54-62. (1991).

[135] Hampshire Archives : REF: 75M91/S3 *1895:* Letters concerning wedding of 5th Earl (stepson) and Almina Wombwell including request to 6th Earl Stanhope to advise on the propriety of allowing Mrs Wombwell to host the wedding breakfast, with his reply. Also includes letter from Eveline, Countess of Portsmouth, and copy letters to the 5th Earl.

[136] Situated on the south west of Berkeley Square. Previous owners / occupants included past Prime Ministers John Stuart, 3rd Earl of Bute; William Petty (Marquess of Lansdowne); William Pitt and Lord Rosebery. William Waldolf Astor (1848-1919): American born hotelier, benefactor and financier. 1st Viscount Astor. Lansdowne House (Now the Lansdowne Club) was much altered by reconstruction in the 1930s.

[137] Millicent Wilson (1872-1952) (daughter of an MP) married Sir Charles Edward Cradock Hartopp (1858-1929) at St Mark's Church, North Audley Street. Almina was *" gowned in a white muslin cape and wore a panama hat".* The marriage was not a success and the Hartopps divorced after sensational court cases, in 1902 and 1904. Millicent later became the wife of the 3rd Earl of Cowley, but she divorced him in 1913.

[138] *" Pocket Venus"* is a term used to depict very petite, but lovely and voluptuous women.

[139] *The Times* of 27 June 1895 lists Frederick Wombwell, Almina's brother, as among the guests.

[140] Madame Patti (1843- 1919) had been a favourite guest of Alfred's, especially giving concerts at his house at 1 Seamore Place from the early 1880s onwards. An intriguing newspaper item appears in *The Western Mail* of 30 May 1893, about the time that Almina was beginning her round of debutante appearances. Among the guests staying with Patti at her home at Craig-Y-Nos (near Swansea) was the *" Hon Mrs Wombwell and Miss Rothschild".* This may well refer to Marie and Almina. Was this Marie's doing in giving the press such names, or a slip up by one of Patti's staff ?

[141] *Pall Mall Gazette,* 27 June 1895.

[142] For a wedding breakfast c 1895 dishes were generally served in course, with bouillon in cups, oysters in different way, game, cold meats, salads, ices sweets with sherry, Burgundy and champagne.(Source Illustrated London News)

[143] Marie Wombwell also made wedding gifts to Almina on her marriage to the 5th Earl comprising " emerald and diamond ear-rings, a pearl and diamond brooch, a turquoise and diamond tiara, a ruby and diamond necklace, and a ruby and diamond pendant " (Source: Newbury Weekly News and General Advertiser, 27 June 1895).

[144] *Newbury Weekly News and General Advertiser,* 27 June 1895.

[145] *Derby Mercury,* 3 July 1895.

[146] Leadbetter, interviews 2009 and 2010.

[147] Jameson, Mrs Anna *The beauties of the court of Charles the Second: A Series of Portraits* (1833). Writing in 1912 in *The Life of James, First Duke of Ormonde, 1610-1688* Lady Winifred Burghclere describes the evidence of murder as *" slender".*

[148] Delnadamph Lodge was built in 1860, at Torran Deallaig, on the south bank of the River Don. In 1895 it was on lease to Sir Charles Forbes. This 12-bedroom lodge now lies on the Balmoral estate, and is the highest shooting-lodge in Scotland. It was gifted by The Queen to Charles and Diana on their marriage, but Diana found it uninviting and was not interested in repairing it. The lodge was gutted in 1987, but 20 years later is being rebuilt as a retreat for Prince Charles and Camilla.

[149] *Derby Mercury*, 18 September 1895.

[150] Later the Marquess of Ripon (1852-1923) shared with the Singhs and Lord Ashburton a passion for shooting game. He and Lord Carnarvon were a comfort to each other during the Great War. The Marquess lost his wife, Constance Gwladys Herbert, (one of the Herberts of Lea) in 1917. She was one of the patrons of Covent Garden Opera, her photograph albums in their special collection. Lord Carnarvon exhibited a " striking portrait of Lord Ripon, with an ancient vase in his hands" entitled *"The Connoisseur"* at the Camera Club, Adelphi in 1916.

[151] *The Scotsman*, 14 December 1895.

[152] Leadbetter Collection.

[153] Ibid.

[154] *Hampshire Telegraph and Sussex Chronicle*, 14 December, *Pall Mall Gazette*, 16 December and *Morning Post*, 18 December 1895.

[155] *The Times*, 18 December 1895.

[156] Leadbetter Collection.

[157] *Vogue Magazine*, 1895.

[158] In the 1901 Census Marie is described as a widow living on private means. Her place of birth is given as Paris, to which is added " British subject". There were five members of staff in the household, a lady's maid (Sylvia Purchase) two housemaids, two footmen and a kitchen maid.

[159] *Pall Mall Gazette*, 7, 8 and 15 February 1896. Later reports suggest that Alfred had been ill, and the cruise and stay-over at Monte Carlo was to aid his recovery.

[160] *Pall Mall Gazette*, 7 March 1896.

[161] Louisa, 8th Duchess of Devonshire, famed hostess and bridge-player, nicknamed the " Double Duchess". German born Louisa Von Alten (1832-1911). She was the widowed 7th Duchess of Manchester until 1892 when she married the 60 year old 8th Duke of Devonshire. See Vane, Henry, *Affair of State*, Peter Owen (2004).

[162] Prince Dimitri Soltykoff, of Russian extraction, a Mayfair resident and racehorse owner, died 1903.

[163] *Hampshire Telegraph and Sussex Chronicle* 6 June 1896. The Alliance Electrical Company Ltd featured a photograph of Highclere Castle in its advertisements in the late 1890s " Fitted throughout with Electric Light for the Earl of Carnarvon."

[164] *London Daily Mail*, 20 June 1896.

[165] Sir Alfred Cooper, FRCS, died 1908, aged 70. He was a London surgeon to members of the Royal Family, the Inns of Court and several army regiments. Obituary : The Times 5 March 1908. Cooper's eldest son was Alfred Duff Cooper, Viscount Norwich, (1890-1954), who married Lady Diana Manners in 1919.

[166] One newspaper report dated 12 September 1896 spells out the seriousness of this health attack, since Carnarvon's London physician had to be summoned by telegraph. Victor's arrival (he too was summoned by Almina) soon bucked Carnarvon's spirits up, such was Victor's strength in personally handling the situation of the Earl's recurring deep seated malady, first contracted in the Egyptian whorehouses with its debility, high fever and distress.

[167] *The Bristol Mercury* and *Daily Post*, 23 October 1896.

[168] *The London Daily Mail* of 29 March 1897 records the Carnarvons were present at the Restaurant de Paris, Monte Carlo (during the previous week) at the same time as Bertie, Prince of Wales was present.

[169] *The Bristol Times and Mirror*, 15 June 1897.

[170] Mrs Hwfa (pronounced Hoofa) Williams (a member of the Farquharson family of Invercauld) a notable Edwardian hostess, and known as the best-dressed woman in England records in her memoirs, *It Was Such Fun*, Hutchinson & Co, London (1935) " It was the greatest fancy-dress ball that I had ever seen…. there was a spirit of festivity in the air…old books and pictures were consulted to make sure that the historical figures were accurate in every detail, and in many cases those taking part assumed the characters of famous ancestors. "

[171] *The Times*, 29 June 1897 and 3 July 1897.

[172] Akbar was a Muslim, and he made India tolerant to all religions.

[173] See Murphy Sophia, *The Duchess of Devonshire's Ball*, Sidgwick & Jackson Ltd, (1984).

[174] The daily routine at this one of the most popular of the German spas comprised rising at 6.30am (Almina was always up at 6am and in the bath throughout her life) and drinking a glass of water from the springs. This is followed by a half hour walk among the trees followed by another glass of water from the springs. Breakfast was at 8am followed by a mud bath at 10am. It was expected that you would sit in the mud for 20 minutes then take a clean bath and lie still for an hour, This was repeated over two days, on the third day a steel bath was substituted. The fourth day was a holiday, no bath was taken. On the fifth day the process began again from the start. In the afternoon everyone rested till 4pm when two more glasses were drunk from the springs, with an interval of half an hour between glasses. At 5 pm a band played and visitors promenaded up and own and took walks. See *Pall Mall Gazette*, 13 August 1892.

[175] Johnson, DE, *Victorian shooting days: East Anglia 1810-1910*. Boydell Press (1981).

[176] National Archives, Kew Ref : J77/586/17907.

[177] Writing to Victor's father from Windsor Castle on 6 July 1886 (reported in *The North- Eastern Daily Gazette* of 3 August 1895) Queen Victoria records " think of me as your best friend and the godmother of your dear son who bears my name."

[178] *Lowell Sun*, 21 March 1905.

[179] Such comments stem from one story that Victor's grandmother Maharani Jindan Kaur (1817-1863) was a dancing girl and the daughter of a trooper in the bodyguard of Ranjit Singh, Victor's grandfather. Other histories say that the Maharani was the daughter of an " overseer of the Royal kennels".

[180] Bance, Peter, *Sovereign, Squire and Rebel: Maharajah Duleep Singh and the Heirs of a Lost Kingdom*. Coronet House Publishing Ltd. (2009).

[181] Ibid. According to Peter Bance Victor and Anne were dubbed " the odd couple". Bance says that on the return of the Duleep Singhs from their honeymoon " they attended a ball thrown by Queen Victoria at Buckingham Palace July 8, 1898...the ball was soon followed by a request from Queen Victoria for a private audience with Princess Victor where she received the most distressing and chilling of orders....She was told by the Queen that she must not have any children with the Prince and that she must live abroad with her husband. " Bance, a Sikh, says he obtained this information from a close "Coventry family source" a relative of Lady Anne. He adds "This person, who told me not to mention his name, asked Lady Anne once, 'why didn't you have any children?' and that was when Lady Anne spoke about Queen Victoria's instructions...... She went by those instructions."

The present author believes, however, from a report in an American newspaper c1918, reflecting from the time of Anne's engagement to Victor (a year before- in July 1897) that Queen Victoria wrote to Lady Anne saying she should be ashamed of herself. Coupled with this, extracting a promise from Anne at the time of the engagement (described as a " nine day wonder" by the *Hampshire Telegraph and Sussex Chronicle* of 24 July 1897) (rather than waiting until after the marriage) points to the more likely timing of the Queen's command of chasteness.

[182] *The World,* of 26 January 1898 comments that Viscount and Lady Deerhurst (who was the American, Virginia Bonynge) "did everything possible to prevent" the marriage, declaring it was " a frightful disgrace for a member of the family to marry a man of colour". Deerhurst himself was no angel, having gone through the bankruptcy courts (in 1890) and sought a rich wife in America to bail him out of financial disgrace.

[183] *The Bury and Norwich Post*, and *Suffolk Standard* 4 January 1898.

[184] See *The World,* 26 January 1898.

[185] E-mail exchange between the author and Peter Bance dated 18 February 2011. *The Graphic* (January 1898) has photographs of Lady Anne and Prince Victor, by Russell & Sons Studios, Baker Street. Victor is in morning dress.

[186] See Ruffer, J G, *The Big Shots: Edwardian Shooting Parties*. Debretts. (1977) p.55. " After this incident, the Maharajah, who regarded the diamond as rightfully his, referred to Her Majesty[Queen Victoria] as "Mrs Fagin".

[187] See Fowler, Marian, *Hope Adventures of a Diamond*, Pocket Books. (2004) pp29, 202. In 1948 when India was made independent of Britain the return of the Koh-I-Noor to " its proper repository " in the Golden Temple at Amritsar (the most sacred place of the Sikh religion) was claimed but resisted. A request was also unsuccessfully made by Zulifikar Ali Bhutto, Prime Minister of Pakistan in 1976. See FCO 37/1799 and PREM 16/1037 in National Archives, Kew. Sikh historian, Peter Bance, told the author (at a meeting in London on 17 February 2011) that " there will always be claims on the Koh-I-Noor" adding " the difficulty is what Sikh group it should be given to in the India of today?"

[188] See *Pall Mall Gazette* 4 February 1898.

[189] Leadbetter, interviews 2009 and 2010. Whilst there are no gardens up to the windows at Highclere (the ground is now covered in chippings), Almina's solitary appearance at the window was the signal, which the man could see from where he was working.

[190] Ibid.

[191] An informant (please contact the Author for source) claims that following the death of the 5th Earl, in 1923, the Herbert family hierarchy (this would have included the Pembrokes of Wilton House, Wiltshire) demanded that Almina swear an affidavit to the effect that Porchester was the 5th Earl's son.

[192] Letter to Highclere Castle by author, e-mails between author and Hampshire Archives, 2009.

[193] Leadbetter recalls an endless stream of visits from the Carnarvon Estate solicitors (when Almina was living in her various West Country homes) usually to have her sign something. Her signature was required throughout her life. Among Almina's own papers was Alfred de Rothschild's Scrapbook (left to her in Alfred's will). According to Tony Leadbetter this was left by Almina to her grandson, Lord Porchester, who may have presented it to the Royal Archives, Windsor Castle. The author has seen letters there from Alfred to King George V following the death of Alfred's great friend, King Edward VII.

[194] *The Times*, 22 January 1996 contains this item. " THE EARL of Carnarvon, the Queen's racing manager, is helping one of his guides at the family seat, Highclere, in the writing of a biography of an extraordinary woman. The Rev David Sox is writing the life of the earl's grandmother, Almina, Countess of Carnarvon, who was a spirited and spendthrift nurse. The illegitimate daughter of the bachelor bon viveur Alfred de Rothschild, she ploughed through the family fortune, funded the 1922 Tutankhamun discovery and set up a nursing home in Portland Place where Noel Coward was treated for piles. ``It's a wonderful story. She was really rather remarkable dreamt up the National Health Service years before it existed,'' enthuses Carnarvon. "

[195] A letter seen by the Author in the Leadbetter Collection fully supports the basis of this claim. This matter is highlighted in Christopher Wilson's article in the Daily Mail of 21 October 2011 " *Downton's greatest secret: A lonely countess and her illicit love affair with an Indian Prince…..*".

[196] Leadbetter Collection.

[197] Heresay evidence does not rule out a seedier scenario. Almina was not seduced but was the seducer. They were all together in Egypt. Almina was frustrated at being unloved – albeit her mother, Marie, (an accomplished woman with men), had provided her daughter with guidance and instruction. Victor was vulnerable. His future marriage with Anne was dismal and sexless (although Victor's own sexual appetite is unclear, and he may have accepted the celibate marriage). An opportunity presented itself to Almina to which Victor (ever willing to help the Carnarvons) agreed.

[198] Victor and his wife Anne were virtually inseparable in the years that followed, with most of their public appearances taking place together. Curiously (given Anne's undertaking to remain chaste), Victor was *not* implicated with any other woman. Whether this was on account of his declining health (he suffered badly with rheumatism), his sexual preference or his own decision to stay celibate (or a combination of these factors) the reality is unsubstantiated. Victor continued to gamble and play bridge and he and Anne often went cruising, one example being a cruise to the Far East, reported in the *Straits Times* of 20 April 1909, with the American publisher and yachtsman, J Gordon Bennett. According to *The News – Newport* of 18 July 1913 he always had one close companion for affection, a red

toy Pekinese dog that "he was passionately fond of which he took everywhere and slept on his pillow."

[199] Bance, Peter, *Sovereign, Squire and Rebel: Maharajah Duleep Singh and the Heirs of a Lost Kingdom*, Coronet House Publishing Ltd. (2009).

[200] Dr. Marcus Beauchamp Johnson (1867-1953)

[201] *Pall Mall Gazette*, 2 September 1898.

[202] *The London Daily Mail*, 9 November 1898. Charlotte Carleton, Lady Dorchester, (1831-1914), had a house at 42, Berkeley Square, a few doors away from the Carnarvon residence at 13.

[203] See *The Bury and Norwich Post* of 22 November 1898 under "The Society Papers" (quoting from *The World*) " There are, of course, great rejoicings over Lord Carnarvon's son and heir, and Lady Carnarvon is doing capitally."

[204] *The Times*, 13 December 1898. Henry George Alfred Marius Victor Francis born 7 November 1898 died 22 September 1987.He was the 6th Earl of Carnarvon from 1923-1987.

[205] Lady Agnes Cooper (born Agnes Cecil Emmeline Duff, formerly Viscountess Dupplin, and Mrs Herbert Flower) (1852-1925).

[206] Victor was an accomplished musician and writer of songs.

[207] Unknown source in British Library's 19th Century newspapers database.

[208] *London Daily Mail*, 5 June 1899. Almina sold *objects de art* from France.

[209] *London Daily Mail*, 13 July 1899.

[210] *London Daily Mail*, 8 June 1899.

[211] *London Daily Mail*, 15 June 1899.

[212] Ibid.

[213] Jottings from the *Northern Echo*, 17 March 1899.

[214] *The Gleaner*, 8 August 1899.

[215] *London Daily Mail*, 5 October 1899.

[216] *London Daily Mail*, 23 February 1900.

[217] *London Daily Mail*, 28 March 1900.

[218] The cruise took the Carnarvons to Ostend where they attended the Battle of Flowers in the presence of the Shah of Persia, a friend of Alfred de Rothschild. See Black and White 1 September 1900.

[219] Lady Evenly Leonora Lamina Herbert, later Beauchamp, (1901-1980). Her paternity is also borne out by correspondence seen in the Leadbetter Collection. Contact author for further details.

[220] *London Daily Mail*, 12 February 1901

[221] Almina presented a " Mrs Ernest Pearse" at the May Court of 1902.

[222] *The London Reader* of 19 July, 1902 records " *Lady Carnarvon is pretty, piquante, and petite. She is, of course, a smart Society lady, but is intensely resourceful; and, if denied the companionship of her fellows, can interest herself with books, pictures and furniture. Outdoor exercises and sports do not greatly interest her ladyship, though naturally she is very proud of the fact that her husband is one of the best shots in England.*"

[223] *Country Life* Vol XII No 303, 8 November 1902.

[224] *Daily Express*, 24 December 1902.

[225] Ibid.

[226] *The Times*, 23 December 1902.

[227] *The Scotsman*, 27 December 1902.

[228] The police periodically made arrests of jewel thieves. The thieves were male and female; indeed, temporary ladies' maids were often suspected of being involved. One other story is notable from the time. According to *The Times* of 21 March 1912, Herbert Grimshaw, a 38-year-old jockey, was found guilty of being involved "for the past four or five years... connected with the most notorious gang of Continental jewel thieves in existence". Grimshaw's gang, which was responsible for stealing £40,000 worth of pearls from the Café Monaco (a fashionable continental-style den in Shaftsbury Avenue), dwarfed Almina's theft of £5,000 worth of property.

[229] Dr. Marcus Beauchamp Johnson (1867-1953) son of Walter and Mrs Johnson of Farnham, Surrey, born in Melbourne, Australia, but attended Malvern public school in England (See The Malvern Register 1865-1904) and studied medicine at Trinity College, Cambridge University. He qualified in 1896 and was a member of the Royal College of Surgeons and the Royal College of Physicians. His first practice was at 9 Henrietta Street only a short distance from the Carnarvon's London home at Berkeley Square. Joseph Lindeon Smith in *Tombs, temples and Ancient Art* comments that the 5th Earl's reliance on Marcus " a continued semi active life was in large part due to a Dr Johnson, familiarly known as " Johnny" who was a permanent member of the Carnarvon household. " Johnson may have first met Carnarvon at Cambridge University.

[230] Jacob Pleydell-Bouverie, the 6th Earl of Radnor (1868-1930)and Julian, Countess of Radnor (1891-1946).

[231] *The World*, 6 February 1903 : Rosalind, Lady Chetwynd : born Rosalind Secor of New York; she married Sir Guy Chetwynd in 1902 (later divorced). Appeared as Rosa Lynd on the music hall stage. She died in 1922.

[232] *New York Times*, 1 February 1903.

[233] Mamie Stuyversant Fish : (1853-1915) : American eccentric and hostess.

[234] Harry Lehr (1869 - 1929) : leading New York socialite and Court Jester.

[235] James, ET, James JW and Boyer P S : *Notable American women 1607-1950: a biographical dictionary* Vol 2 (1971).

[236] Leadbetter Collection.

[237] Ibid.

[238] Countess Marguerite Cassini, mother of dress designer Oleg Cassini and New York Society Columnist Igor ("Chol-ly Knickerbocker") Cassini, a spirited Russian matriarch, died 1961.

[239] Rt. Hon. Sir Michael H.Herbert: (1857-1903) (died Switzerland): fourth son of Sidney, 1st Baron Herbert of Lea. Ambassador to US 1902-3.

[240] William Alvord : (1833-1904) San Francisco merchant, banker and political leader. Letters from the 5th Earl and Almina in William Alvord Papers at Bancroft Library, University of California, Berkeley. Dated 24 March 1903.

[241] Jeremiah Lynch : (1849-1917) of Irish-American parentage. Traveller and adventurer in Egypt (1889). San Francisco stockbroker (Callaghan and Lynch) and later New York business man. Author of *Egyptian Sketches* (1890) and *The Lady Isis in Bohemia* (1914). In 1907 (only four years after meeting Lynch) Lord Carnarvon sponsored the excavation of the tombs in Deir el-Bahari (Thebes).

[242] *The San Francisco Call* of 31 March 1903 lists the attendees as Miss Charlotte Russell, Miss Alice Hager, Miss Ethel Hager, Miss Linda Cadwalader, Miss King, Miss Helen Wagner, James D Phelan, Enrique Grau, Clement Tobin, Donald de V Graham, Dr Johnston and Richard McCreary.

[243] The San Francisco Call, 31 March 1903.

[244] Lynch, Jeremiah *Egyptian Sketches* London: Edward Arnord, (1890).

[245] Great San Francisco Earthquake and subsequent fires took place on 18 April 1906.

[246] Lord Kitchener was Consul General in Egypt, 1911-1914.

[247] *Oakland Tribune*, 12 September 1903.

[248] As described in " The Carnarvon Letters 1943-1944" 7th Earl of Carnarvon (1994).

[249] According to Tony Leadbetter this was Almina's favourite tipple.

[250] *New York Times*, 25 September 1904.

[251] Leadbetter Collection.

[252] *Guardian*, 17 April 1903.

[253] *London Daily Mail*, 23 July 1903.

[254] Leadbetter Collection.

[255] *Washington Post*, 27 November 1904.

[256] *The Mercury* of 28 September 1901 records " Lord Carnarvon travels all over England on his machine, and frequently makes the journey from Highclere to London."

[257] *Daily Mail*, 11 August 1903.

[258] Ibid.

[259] Jules is described in the English probate records as Jules Joly Boyer died 10 July 1903 at 6 rue-de-Pharlsbourg, Paris. Almina's mother Marie was granted administration of his estate in London on 16 May 1907. His estate was modest valued at £314.

[260] Prince Frederick Duleep Singh 1868-1926. Soldier and patron of the Arts.

[261] In Paris in 1906, Ashburton married Frances Donnelly, of New York, an actress known on stage as Frances Belmont, who appeared in " Floradora sexette", " My Lady" and was Charles Hawtrey's leading lady in " A Message From Mars." Ashburton died of a heart attack on the return trip of the Queen Mary to Britain in 1938, aged 71. Frances survived him until 1959.

[262] *The Sketch*, Vol 48, Issue 619.

[263] The exception being a photograph of them, together, on their way to the Ascot races in 1920.

[264] See Rose, Phyllis : *Woman of Letters : A Life of Virginia Woolf*, Routledge & Kegan Paul Ltd (1978). The charge against Duckworth of molesting Woolf is described as " unfounded" in " Mr Charles Booth's inquiry : O'Day, Rosemary and Englander, David : *Life and labour of the people in London reconsidered* (1993).

[265] *The Intelligencer / Record*, 21 May 1969.

[266] Flora, Luisa and Zamith, Maria Candida, *Virginia Woolf : Three Centenary* (2007).
" Woolf recalls in a memoir " Old Bloomsbury" the hypocrisy and repression of a Kensington evening with George Duckworth and Countess Carnarvon [Else, 4th Countess] around 1900 – in the course of which George kissed Lady Carnarvon behind a pillar."

[267] Carter was born in London in 1874, the son of an animal painter. He grew up in Norfolk. He first went to Egypt in 1890 and was soon assistant to the archaeologists Percy Newberry and Professor Flinders Petrie. He was sometime Chief Inspector of Antiquities in Upper Egypt. He was associated with the

discovery of three royal tombs besides that of Tutankhamun and died in London on 2 March 1939.

[268] Leadbetter, interviews 2009 and 2010.

[269] *The Times*, 1 July 1905.

[270] Richard Luttrell Pilkington Bethell (1852-1930) 3rd Lord Westbury. Famously died by suicide and was reported as a victim of the King Tut curse. Westbury's son Richard, an assistant to Howard Carter, also died suddenly in 1929. Westbury's suicide note said " I cannot really stand any more horrors."

[271] Lord Charles William Augustus Montagu, (1860-1939), 2nd son of the 7th Duke of Manchester.

[272] Lady Grace Fane (1860-1933), wife of the 2nd Earl, daughter of 12th Earl of Westmoreland. Socialite. Her daughter Lady Irene Denison married the Marquess of Carisbrooke.

[273] *The Straits Times*, 6 January 1906, 8 February 1905, 26 February 1906.

[274] *Eastern Daily Mail and Straits Morning Advertiser*, 3 February 1906.

[275] *Eastern Daily Mail and Straits Morning Advertiser*, 2 March 1906.

[276] Salaman v Secretary of State for India in Council – reported in *The Times*, 5 April 1906.

[277] An annual summary of winners and losers and prize money appeared in The Times for many years.

[278] *The Bystander* Volume IX, page 38.

[279] The Washington Post of 10 March 1907 records the Carnarvons had arrived at the Savoy Hotel, Cairo.

[280] Libel action (dubbed " The Cult of the Clitoris") by actress Maud Allan against Noel Pemberton Billing MP. An article in the newspaper *The Vigilante* in January 1918 written by right wing MP Noel Pemberton Billing alleged a pro-German conspiracy involving British homosexuals and perverts. Billing proclaimed the existence of a secret German Dossier or Black List containing the names of 47,000 men and women in Britain who practised vices *"all decent men thought had this had perished in Sodom and Lesbos…"*

It was claimed that those listed included Cabinet Ministers and Privy Councillors all subject to potential blackmail by Germany into disclosing war secrets. In February 1918, *The Vigilante* went further. Under a headline *"The Cult of the Clitoris"*, they condemned a private London production of Oscar Wilde's *Salome* –by a Canadian dancer, named Maud Allan (a particular favourite of Lord Carnarvon's to watch on stage). The paper said that the audience would consist of many of those on the *"47,000* deviants list". Maud Allan sued Pemberton Billing for libel, but lost the case. The names of many notable people echoed in the Court proceedings including Lord Carnarvon, Colonel Aubrey Herbert . Marshall Hall made an impassioned speech to Mr Justice Darling that he was ready to act for the Carnarvon brothers. The Carnarvons are mentioned in The Times 31 May and 1 June 1918 but only in connection with questions about the war effort. Several titled women received unwelcome exposure including several of the Rothschilds, whose names were apparently on the list. Billing received acquittal amid popular rejoicing.

[281] See James, T.G.H:. *Howard Carter: The Path to Tutankhamun;* Kegan Paul International (1992). Quoting diaries of A.C. Mace (1923) " Carter talks to him like a naughty child".

[282] Leadbetter , interviews 2009 and 2010.

[283] See A C Mace, Diary from 1923 quoted in James, T.G.H. *Howard Carter: The Path to Tutankhamun;* Kegan Paul International. (1992) p245.

[284] J P Morgan (1837-1913) See Jackson, Stanley, *J.P.Morgan, a biography,* Stein and Day (1983). Morgan was also interested in Egyptology. Alfred introduced him to Lord Kitchener and to the 5th Earl of Carnarvon.

[285] *The Times*, 20 June 1908.

[286] See the 6th Earl's memoirs *No Regrets,* Weidenfeld & Nicolson, (1976) pp13-15. See also Horn, Pamela: *High Society : the English social elite*, 1880-1914, Sutton Pub Ltd, (1992) p54.

[287] The 5th Earl of Carnarvon visited Germany several times, including one long period at the turn of the century when he was receiving medical treatment there for a serious condition/illness. However, the tie in between a motor car accident in 1901 or 1902, and this prompting him to go to Egypt (which he had been known to visit from 1889 onwards) is at best a mistake of the 6th Earl of Carnarvon, who was a very small boy at the time, so was drawing on second hand testimony. The 5th Earl's doctors, knowing of the past improvements to his health brought on by previous visits to Egypt (the climate eased his diseased lungs/ breathing) would have recommended that the patient return there, to further recuperate.

[288] *The Times*, 15 September 1909.

[289] Ibid.

[290] *The Observer* of 7 November 1909 records that Almina gave a dance for a hundred guests in the large Gothic hall. The dancing began at 10 o'clock and went on till 2 o'clock in the morning. A buffet supper was served at midnight in the dining room and bridge tables were set up in the various reception rooms. Almina wore a gown of apricot coloured soft satin, embroidered in silver with a tiara and necklace of emeralds and diamonds. Guests included Marie Wombwell.

[291] Leadbetter, interviews 2009 and 2010.

[292] *London Daily Mail*, 23 November 1911.

[293] Leadbetter, interviews 2009 and 2010.

[294] *London Daily Mail*, 9 December 1911.

[295] Leadbetter, interviews 2009 and 2010. This comment is also reflected in a snippet from the Daily Mirror of 6 April 1923. " He[Lord Carnarvon] cynically said (once) that his choice of the turf in preference to politics, which his forebears had adorned, was due to a desire to attach himself to something in which there was a semblance of honesty!"

[296] Sir Ernest Wallis Budge takes the credit for once saying to Lord Carnarvon " Go to Egypt, excavating dead cities is the most fascinating pursuit in the world. "

[297] Tony Leadbetter advises that Almina did not mention her brother/ half-brother Frederick Wombwell in any recollections and memories he could recall. But he knew of Frederick, so thinks Almina must have told him just that she had a brother. Evidence emerged during the research from Beryl Attaway that a nursemaid named Clare Simms was employed by Almina at Highclere. Clare was well liked by the Carnarvon family and on leaving Almina gave her a large framed, signed photograph. Later Almina recommended Clare to her brother and his wife. Clare was with the Wombwells when Frederick's only son Philip was born in July 1910. She had charge of the child during Frederick's

subsequent illness and took the child to stay with her sister Mara at Stancil Farm, Tickhill, seven and a half miles from Doncaster.

[298] *Observer*, 17 March 1912.

[299] The trio of Arthur Portman, Charles Seymour Pearce-Serocold and Marie Wombwell were very close friends and often appear together for weekends and holidays at Highclere.

[300] *The Newbury Weekly News*, 9 January 1913.

[301] *Daily Express*, 18 March 1913.

[302] Arthur Edward Pearse Brome Weigall was Inspector General of Antiquities under the Egyptian government. He retired in 1914. In his journal Mervyn Herbert (Carnarvon's half brother) describes Weigall as " The prince of swine".

[303] Hankey , Julie: *A passion for Egypt : Arthur Weigall : Tutankhamun and the Curse of the Pharaohs*, Tauris Parke Paperbacks, (2007) p.190.

[304] *The Newbury Weekly News* of 19 June 1913 lists the house guests including Sir John and Lady Milbanke, The Earl and Countess of Drogheda, Lord Westbury, Lady Leucha Warner, Sir John Maxwell, Arthur Portman and his regular racing chum Mr Serocold.

[305] *The Newbury Weekly News*, 31 July 1913.

[306] Ibid.

[307] Ibid.

[308] Ibid. The window was executed by Messrs C E Kempe and Co, London and depicts " two warrior saints (St Martin and St George) who while typifying military prowess also typify bravery in its highest form – Christian heroism.." . The Author has created a website on this.
http://ladyalminacarnarvonstributetoherbrother.yolasite.com/

[309] Her death Certificate indicates that Marie died on 30 September 1913 principally from pneumonia and heart failure. The doctor who certified the death was Marcus B Johnson, MRCS. The 5th Earl was the informant, and the death was registered the same day.

[310] Although exiled in Paris, Victor Duleep Singh acted with the same speed, as he had done for Carnarvon (and Almina) four years earlier, in going to help after the motor car accident in Germany . Upon hearing of Marie Wombwell's passing, Victor travelled to England to offer Almina his considerable-sized shoulder to cry on. Alfred de Rothschild could see that Almina was suffering under the strain, and whilst Marie lay dying he took a let of Castle Ashby, Northampton as an ample house with beautiful gardens, where Almina could retreat.

[311] Probate Registry Family Division of High Court, Wills and Admons 1913; The Times 6 November 1913.

[312] Rothschild Archives, London Ref 000/174A (1918) and 000/174B (1918).

[313] Ibid.

[314] Leadbetter, interviews 2009 and 2010.

[315] Carter had newly discovered the entrance to the lost tomb of Amen-hotep I and planned to excavate this with Carnarvon in the following season (says The Times of 9 June 1914). Carnarvon had also secured a concession to dig (in succession to the American, Theodore M. Davies) in the Valley of the Kings from June 1914. Carter convinced Carnarvon that despite Davies years of

activity in the Valley, and a view that the site was exhausted there were still untapped areas to explore.

[316] *The Times*, 18 July 1914.

[317] See *Observer*, 16 March 1919. Sir George White, remarked that Cowans was in the same league as Moses in providing for his people. Sir John's greater reputation was founded on a more down to earth remark namely that " whatever went wrong the soldiers *always* got their grub". See *Guardian*, 12 September 1928.

[318] Oxford Dictionary of National Biography Kitchener, Horatio Herbert. Earl Kitchener of Khartoum (1850-1916) army officer by Keith Neilson.

[319] The text of Alfred de Rothschild's telegram sent to the German Emperor at 3.45 pm on 1 August 1914 was published by *The Times* on 24 December 1919.

"Sirs – I am fully aware that your Majesty is straining every nerve in favour of peace, and it is because I am aware of this, and because I have always been such a warm and devoted admirer of your Majesty's policy, that I venture to address your Majesty at such a very critical moment, when the blessings of peace or the horrors of war are evenly balanced. Will your Majesty therefore send me a proposal which I could at once lay before my friends, and which would be of such a nature as would find favour both at St Petersburg and at Vienna, and which could be warmly supported by my friends? I venture most earnestly to hope that your Majesty will most graciously reply (? to one) who begs to subscribe himself your Majesty's most faithful and obedient servant. ALFRED DE ROTHSCHILD, 1, Seamore Place."

The telegram was received in Berlin at 7.30pm that same day. The Kaiser endorsed it with these words " An old and very respected acquaintance of mine! About 75-80 years of age ! [Alfred was 72.]

[320] Leadbetter, interviews 2009 and 2010.

[321] 6th Earl's memoirs *No Regrets*, Weidenfeld & Nicolson. (1976) p. 20.

[322] Latest cable Pictures from Europe Introductions : Lady Carnarvon reading to wounded soldier. *Oakland Tribune*, 27 December, p3.

[323] A lengthy tribute to Elizabeth(Elsie) Howard can be found on pages 36-46 of *Lady Carnarvon's Nursing Homes : Nursing the Privileged in Wartime and P*eace : compiled by William Cross, published 15 October 2011. ISBN 1905914032.

[324] Ronald D Knight's website on Purse Caundle has a comprehensive tribute to Lady Victoria Herbert.
http://pursecaundlehistoryappendices.blogspot.com/search/label/Lord%20Carna
rvon

[325] Obituary for Lady Burghclere, *The Times*, 29 September 1933.

[326] See Sandhurst, Viscount, *From Day to Day*. (1928) p.81 " Oct 24, 1914 Carnarvon tells me he has eighteen wounded at Highclere, 1st and 2nd floor turned in Hospital and Lady C very busy."

[327] *The Illustrated London News* Vol. 162, Part1 (1923) remarks " Lady Carnarvon was celebrated for inventing and wearing the very prettiest and most graceful nursing uniform seen at any private hospital during the war......."

[328] Ogilvie Herald, Chris, *Riches to Rags*, Unpublished biography of Almina, Countess of Carnarvon (2009).

[329] Major General Patrick Hagart Henderson (1876-1968) CB, DSO, MB, CH.B DPH, AMS (Ret.). Obituary in British Medical Journal, 10 August 1968.

[330] Campbell Captain David, M.C., *Forward The Rifles*, The History Press, Ireland (2009).

[331] See also page 30 of *Lady Carnarvon's Nursing Homes : Nursing the Privileged in Wartime and P*eace : compiled by William Cross, published 15 October 2011. ISBN 1905914032.

[332] The 6th Earl names the officer as George Paynter (1880-1950), But see pages 28-30 of *Lady Carnarvon's Nursing Homes : Nursing the Privileged in Wartime and P*eace : compiled by William Cross, published 15 October 2011. ISBN 1905914032.

[333] 6th Earl's memoirs *No Regrets*, Weidenfeld & Nicolson. (1976) p.24.

[334] Ibid.

[335] Buchan, John, *Greenmantle*, Hodder & Stoughton, London. (1916).

[336] *The Newbury Weekly News*, 29 April 1915.

[337] According to Sandhurst, Viscount in his war diary *From Day to Day*, (1928) p.105 " 13 November 1914. Ripon (Marquess of) told me he had seen Carnarvon's hospital at Highclere, it was so good in every particular. C never says anything." After the move of Almina's hospital to London, on one occasion Carnarvon insisted on showing Ripon round the wards, which was met with Almina's wrath and she soon sent the two peers packing.

[338] Highclere Castle, *The Windsor Magazine*, vol. 41, 1915, p580.

[339] Vandenberg, P, *The Golden Pharaoh*, MacMillan Publishing Company. *(1980)*. p119.

[340] More details about the workings of Highclere Military Hospital, based on the testimony of Tony Leadbetter, Almina's godson, are in *Lady Carnarvon's Nursing Homes : Nursing the Privileged in Wartime and P*eace : compiled by William Cross, published 15 October 2011. ISBN 1905914032.

[341] Simon Joseph Fraser Lovat (1871-1933) ADC to King George V and Hon. Laura Lister, Lady Lovat, (d.1965) niece of Margot Asquith, wife of H.H.Asquith, (British Prime Minister 1908-1916). The Lovats put 48, Bryanston Square up for auction in 1930. It was later occupied by the League of Remembrance (1930-1949) and for many years by the Industrial Welfare Society. It is now Wetherby Preparatory School for Boys.

[342] *The Newbury Weekly News*, 6 January 1915.

[343] *Newbury Weekly News* of 11 January, 1918 records : "Illness of Lord Carnarvon: We regret to announce that the Earl of Canarvon has had to undergo serious operations for appendicitis and other internal trouble. His Lordship was shooting at Highclere last week apparently in his usual health but was taken ill immediately after lunch. He proceeded to London and in a short tome after arrival at his town house in Bryanston-square, was operated upon. For a day or two his Lordship remained in a critical condition, but yesterday's report was that he was progressing satisfactorily, and there is hope of recovery. He is being nursed by the Countess and their daughter Lady Evelyn Herbert."

[344] Lady Burghclere: *Biographical sketch of the late Lord Carnarvon* (1923).

[345] Ibid.

[346] Ibid.

[347] The 5th Earl's will was made on 29 October 1919.

[348] Leadbetter, interviews 2009 and 2010.

[349] *The Times*, 9 April 1915.

[350] Billington, Mary Francis: *The Roll-call of serving women: a record of Woman's work for combatants in the Great War.* London The Religious Tract Society. (1915), p.187.

[351] Frank William Walter Fane (1864-1931). Born in Kent, England. Joined the Canadian Mounties, married Margaret Duff of Lethbridge in 1890. They had four daughters. Fane was invalided home to Canada in 1916. He died in 1931, his wife died in 1942. See Lethbridge Herald 1 April, 1931 and 7 February 1942.

[352] Fane is mentioned on a web site for *Alberta Pioneers*. This states he was a Major, Commanding "C" squadron, 19th Alberta Dragoons, during the Great War.

[353] Winnipeg Free Press, 26 February 1916, p.23.

[354] Tennyson, L H, [3rd] Baron, *From Verse to Worse,* London. Cassell.(1933)

[355] Roberts, SC, *Adventures With Authors*, Cambridge University Press.(1966)

[356] Nickalls' army file (National Archives Kew, WO 339/39101) *specifically* refers to the fact that *"he requires treatment in hospital (Lady Carnarvon's). "* A letter on specially printed lilac notepaper headed " *Lady Carnarvon's Hospital for Officers, 48 Bryanston Square..."* survives.

[357] Nickalls, V, *Oars, Wars and Horses*, Hurst & Blackett. (1932)

[358] Anthony Battersby informs the Author " *My father Reginald St John Beardsworth Battersby spent a part of 1917 and 1918 convalescing at Lady Carnarvon's Hospital after he had his leg blown off. He was then 17 yrs and 1 month old. He was probably the youngest commissioned officer in WW1. He was commissioned when he was 15 years and 68 days old."* See also National Archives, Kew WO339/34889.

[359] Fallon, David, MC, *The Big Fight* (Gallipoli to the Somme). W J Watt & Company.(1918). Fallon's file in National Archives, Kew, Ref WO374/ 23524 has correspondence which questions whether he actually took part in the Gallipoli campaign.

[360] Furse, (Sir) R F, *Aucuparius*, London, Oxford University Press. (1962)

[361] Ibid.

[362] Ibid.

[363] Tony Leadbetter advises that Almina had heart felt memories of dealing with the additional medical burden brought about with the epidemic of Spanish flu that raged through Europe at the close of the Great War Years. Tracy Whinnett has informed the Author of the sad story of her Great Uncle, Arthur Frederick Britton, a Lieutenant and an observer in the Royal Flying Corps. He spent part of 1917 convalescing at 48 Bryanston Square (after a leg amputation), however, less than two years later he died in the flu epidemic, aged 31.

[364] Furse, (Sir) R F, *Aucuparius*, London, Oxford University Press. (1962)

[365] Royal Archives Ref RA/ MRH/MRH/SOV/MIXED/131/67, 99

[366] War Secretary's List, War Office 3 March, 1917.

[367] Leadbetter, interviews 2009 and 2010.

[368] Almina never grudged *any* expense to make life more bearable for her charges. No attention was too much trouble, large London stores often providing exceptional foodstuffs. Alfred paid for hampers from Harrods for Ambulance Stations and refreshments in BEF. See Rothschild Archives Ref : 000/115/116.

[369] Tony Leadbetter recalls that after the First World War the members of the Royal Flying Corps presented Almina was a golden teapot as a token of their appreciation, together with a book signed by members of the Corps' survivors.

[370] Lady Burghclere says in her tribute to her brother in 1923 that he was consulted by military intelligence during the course of the war about interpreting aerial photographs of sites on the war-stricken Continent of Europe.

[371] Obituary for Lady Margaret Duckworth, *The Times*, 19 September 1958

[372] According to his obituary in *The Times* of 17 September, 1955, R C Dawson (1865-1955) was *" a great trainer of racehorses"*. His early success was with Lord Carnarvon, out of the Whatcome Stables, near Newbury, running Carnarvon's horses including *The Solicitor* when it won the Hunt Cup at Ascot in 1902, and the same year with *Mauvezin* which took the Steward's Cup at Goodwood. Later Dawson and Lord Carnarvon had much success with the horse *Robert de Diable*.

[373] *The Time,* 17 September, 1955.

[374] Examples of Lord Carnarvon's intimate studies of young women were published from time to time in contemporary newspapers and Journals. *The Daily Mirror* of 8 November 1917 has an example, which is a glamorous photograph of the actress Lilian Davies, star of Ivor Novello's musical comedy *Theodore and Co,* which ran for several hundred performances at London's Gaiety Theatre. There is nothing on record of how Almina viewed her husband's hobby. Alfred de Rothschild held a financial stake in the Empire and Gaiety Theatres, but remained in the background as an anonymous theatrical "angel". The extent of Alfred's commitment, and exactly what his return was on such investments was not common knowledge, but he with Carnarvon and camera were allowed to roam freely behind the scenes. Perhaps this was reward enough to satisfy their voyeuristic proclivities towards certain women. Moreover, Alfred provided regular patronage to theatre managers across London with a view to raising funds for good causes and the war effort during the Great War. Actresses were willing to act as programme sellers at such gatherings, and Alfred's influence almost certainly facilitated Carnarvon and camera being given unfettered access.

[375] *The Times*, 1 July 1916.

[376] According to Thuillier, R and Litchfield P, in *Marcus Adams, photographer royal*, Salem House, (1986) Carnarvon's " great friend " the painter/photographer Bertram Park did a series of nude photographs for the Earl. Carnarvon had put up £3000 to enable Bertram to open a studio in London at 43 Dover Street. This is further elaborated by Beaton, C and Buckland G, in *The magic image*, Weidenfeld and Nicolson (1975) who state that Carnarvon " built a large studio where he developed and enlarged his picturesque studies of nude female models posing among the water-lilies of the lake at Highclere-Castle.."

[377] *The Scotsman*, 15 September 1916.

[378] The guides tell present day visitors to Highclere Castle of this.

[379] National Archives File WO 138/7 Lt Col C a Court Repington was cited in a divorce case from 1901. He was retired from the army as he " broke his word of honour as an officer and gentleman" that he would not again see Lady Garstin, wife of Sir William Garstin wife of PUS Public Works, Egypt.

[380]Repington, Charles a Court : *After the War: London, Paris, Rome, Athens, Prague, Vienna, Budapest, Bucharest, Berlin, Sofia, Coblenz, New York, Washington: A Diary* , Houghton Miffin Company (1922)

[381] At the outbreak of war in 1914, Victor and Anne were among a group of Britons stranded in an hotel at Carlsbad, Bohemia, but who made their escape to Paris, via Vienna. See *The Scotsman,* 19 September 1914. Victor died on 8 June 1918 only in his 52nd year. He had been ill for some time and had long retreated from London to live in Paris and the south of France. An obituary in the *Washington Post of* 2 July 1918 records " His London clubs, in particular the Carlton, saw him but little, and he became to a great extent forgotten.save by a handful of college chums and boyhood friends, who never failed to look him up when they were on the continent, among them being Lord Carnarvon.." Victor was buried in Cimetiere du Monaco, which lies high on the hills above Monte Carlo. His wife, Lady Anne Coventry, died on 2 July 1956 and her cremated remains also lie there. Victor and Anne were to be seen very occasionally in England at the races. Several women of the aristocracy looked down on Anne for marrying Victor, another reason for them staying away from England. Their home in Paris was on the Avenue de Trocadero (later named the Avenue du President Wilson), but season upon season they were in residence at the Hotel de Paris, Monte Carlo, with a sighting of them at Nice in 1914 (see reports *London Daily Mail* of 2 February 1914. Also a note in the Guardian of 12 June 1918 which says that " Victor harboured a grievance, which seemed always to separate him from other people.")

[382] Alfred died on 31 January 1918. Escott records in The *Story of Halton House* " *his death in January 1918, after a short illness ending in pneumonia, came as little surprise to those who knew him...He was 75*". Alfred was buried at Willesden (Jewish) Cemetery on 4 February 1918. His funeral costs were a mere £161 pounds nine shillings and sixpence.

[383] Sum disclosed by Almina in the witness box during Dennistoun v Dennistoun (1925).

[384] Rothschild Archives, London Ref : 000174A.

[385] 6th Earl's memoirs *No Regrets*, Weidenfeld & Nicolson. (1976) p.21.

[386] Ibid.

[387] Nichols, Beverley: *All I could never be : some recollections*. Jonathan Cape. (1949).

[388] Allrey, Anthony: *Edward VII and his Jewish Court,* Weidenfeld & Nicolson. (1991) p.285

[389] Ibid.

[390] Alfred de Rothschild made his last will on 17 September 1917. A copy of the will can be found in *The Story of Halton House* (Original Text by Squadron Leader Beryl E Escott). When Alfred's share of the Rothschild partnership assets is included, his available resources were close on £2.5 million. He made 72 specific legacies and over 50 pecuniary payments including payments to Almina, (£50k) Lord Carnarvon (£25k), Lord Porchester (£25k) and Lady Evelyn (£25k), with the payments (excluding the Carnarvons) totalling in excess of £175k.

[391] The freehold of 1, Seamore Place, Mayfair, was valued by Christies at only £27,500, the contents were valued at close on £500,000.
See also *London As An Art City* by Mrs Steuart Erskine, A Siegle, London (1904) p71-2 " Passing up Park Lane we can scarcely refrain from pausing to consider the beautiful pictures and objects d'art owned by the Rothschild family, especially the exquisite collection of Mr. Alfred de Rothschild in Seamore Place. Three great Gainsboroughs are let into the white panelling of his dining-room –

Mrs Mears, Mrs Beaufoy and Mrs Lowndes Stone; while a fourth, the portrait of Mrs Villebois hangs in the drawing-room above. Romney's Mrs Tickell and the Lady Hamilton by the same painter are also in this cabinet, which contains also a particularly fine collection of Dutch pictures, including Ter-Borch's " Music Lesson" and some exquisite specimens of the voluptuous art of Greuze. The French furniture, much of it of the Louis Seize period, the clocks, the snuff-boxes, the Limoges enamel, the miniatures, the goldsmiths' work, the sevres china, the three specimens of the rare and valuable Henri II. ware.."

[392] Details of the original settlement (later known as " the half million fund ", which Almina sold to her family in 1939) are contained file IR 59/159 in the National Archives, Kew. The income from the 1895 marriage Settlement was worth £12,000 a year. Alfred paid the latter sum annually to Almina and Lord Carnarvon. Therefore, deducting what had been paid between 1895 and 1918 the final balance payable out of Alfred's estate to the Carnarvons was £212,000.

[393] Lionel's share of Alfred's will was worth around £483,000. Alfred's country home and contents at Halton, Buckinghamshire was valued by Christies in this sum. But Lionel detested Halton. It was sold to the RAF after 1918 for £115,000, in whose ownership it remains. Much of Alfred's furniture, Continental porcelain and other objets d' art left to Lionel de Rothschild were sold at Christies on 4 July 1946, making £41,000.

[394] Probate records for Alfred de Rothschild indicate that 1, Seamore Place comprised 11 bedrooms, 7 reception rooms, 3 bathrooms, a vestibule, hall, passenger lift and basement offices.

[395] Writing in 1920, Arthur Irwin Dascent, records in " Piccadilly In Three Centuries With Some Account of Berkeley Square and the Haymarket" p 227 "The small house next door (No 13) [Berkeley Square], recently vacated by Lord Carnarvon, has been superstitiously rechristened No 12A. Presumably its new owner regards thirteen as an unlucky number. "

[396] This is included " an unusually long series of portraits of race horses by J F Herring" many wearing the Chesterfield colours. See The Times, 4 June 1918.

[397] Bretby Park was sold to J.D. Wragg in 1915, and was bought in 1925 by Derbyshire County Council as an orthopaedic hospital.

[398] The Times,26 November 1955, 10 January 1956, 17 June 1966 and 27 July 1966.

[399] The Times, 19 February 1919.

[400] Carter worked for the war effort in Cairo. Between lulls he played a major role in the campaign against tomb-robbing which was rife during the Great War. This is well described by Arnold C Brackman in : The Search for the Gold of Tutankhamen, Hale , London. (1978).

[401] There are additional details relating to Almina's life in the Great War years at Highclere and 48 Bryanston Square, London in Lady Almina And the Real Downton Abbey : The Lost Legacy of Highclere Castle : Hodder & Stoughton (2011), See especially Chapters 9-17 of that publication.

[402] Maxwell had made a harsh reputation for himself during the Easter Rising in Ireland (1916), and had attracted the nickname "Bloody Maxwell" over his ordering of executions in Ireland.   He was also President of the Egyptian Exploration Society and sometime commander of British forces in Egypt.

[403] See James, T.G.H.: Carter The Path to Tutankhamun. Kegan Paul International. (1992). pp 212-3. The American archaeologist James Henry

Breasted (1865-1935) refers to dining with the Carnarvons in a letter dated 5 February 1920. Sir John Maxwell (a member of the Milner Commission, which was gathering evidence on British –Egyptian relations) also dined with them.

[404] Hoving, Thomas : *Tutankhamun: The Untold Story,* Simon and Schuster. (1978) p. 60. See also Winstone, H.V.F. *Howard Carter and the discovery of the tomb of Tutankhamun.* Barzan. (2006) p.128. According to Tony Leadbetter Almina was goaded, but in a light hearted way into raking out these jars.

[405] One Carter biographer, Victor Winstone, believed (as does Tony Leadbetter) that Lady Evelyn and Carter were on the threshold of becoming more intimate (at least at one stage) and Carnarvon/ Almina broke the whole thing up, as they wanted a different course, notably for their daughter to marry a title.   In the end Evelyn's choice of husband was a dull baronet, and sadly this stopped her continuing to take part at ever being involved with the follow up on her late father's work. According to Winstone, Evelyn's daughter (who survives) scoffed at there ever being any kind of romance between Carter and her mother. But see also Hawass, Zahi A, *The golden age of Tutankhamun: divine might and splendour in the New Kingdom,* (2005) which makes lurid and specific aspersions about Lady Evelyn and Carter, which led to a bust-up between Carter and the 5th Earl. But several dates given in this book are inaccurate.

[406] *London Daily Mail*, 14 May 1920.

[407] Ibid.

[408] Aleksander Stamboliyski (1879-1923). Bulgarian Prime Minister, 1919-1923, then ousted in a coup. He attempted to raise a rebellion against the new Bulgarian government, but was captured by the military, tortured and killed. A hated figure, his head was sent to Sofia in a box of biscuits.

[409] *Reynold's Newspaper*, 15 February 1891 *Birmingham Daily Post,* 13 February 1891. Francis Henry Paget died at Link End, Malvern on 17 January 1921 aged 80.

[410] In the late 1890s, Ian Dennistoun was a regular participant at the Northern Meeting (a Society gathering in the Highlands of Scotland) held at Inverness, in the company of his relations the Macpherson-Grants of Ballindalloch Castle. Prince Victor Duleep Singh knew the Macpherson –Grants (and the 5th Earl is also bound to have known them) from shooting holidays taken in Scotland.

[411] Dorothy's own story was syndicated after the trial by numerous newspapers in the USA e.g. *Syracuse Herald* 19 April 1925.

[412] Ibid.

[413] Ibid.

[414] Ibid.

[415] Almina gave evidence in Court in Dennistoun v Dennistoun on 19 March 1925.

[416] Ibid..

[417] Evidence in court in Dennistoun v Dennistoun from 3 March to 26 March 1925 reported in all the major London and international newspapers.

[418] *The Times*, 2 April 1921.

[419] *The Times*, 20 March 1925.

[420] Lady Cowans was born Eva May Coulson, she died in 1934. She had no children.

[421] Tony Leadbetter advises that Almina told him that she had occasionally asked Sir Edward Marshall Hall to act for one or other of her friends. A case was cited

of a former nurse of Almina's from the Great War era who was arrested and charged with giving her terminally ill mother a lethal dose of morphine. Almina organised for Marshall Hall to take the case.

[422] *The Times*, 20 March 1925.

[423] Colonel Dennistoun gave evidence in court on 19 March 1925.

[424] Ibid.

[425] On 1 June 1921, in Madrid, (where Mervyn was serving as Secretary at the British Embassy) he married Mary Elizabeth Williard, daughter of Joseph E Williard, the US Ambassador to Spain.

[426] *The Times*, 20 March 1925.

[427] Ibid.

[428] Leadbetter, interviews 2009 and 2010. In her later years recalling this incident, Almina referred to Dorothy as " a vile, disgusting, wicked bitch. ". Leadbetter adds " At the same time that we were having this conversation Almina went on to say " especially as I had recently given her [Dorothy] my engagement ring as a present."

[429] *The Times*, 20 March 1925.

[430] Evidence read in court in Dennistoun v Dennistoun.

[431] *The Times*, 20 March 1925.

[432] Ibid.

[433] See file in National Archives, Kew on Alfred de Rothschild Probate: IR59/519. Portrait of Mrs Lowndes Stone Norton in pink dress with a dog by her side. Full length. Christies valuation £30,000; Portrait of Mrs Mears in mauve and white dress resting her arm on a pedestal. Full length. Christies valuation £35,000; Portrait of Mrs Beaufoy in pink dress with her right hand to her breast. Full length. Christies valuation £40,000. The schedule in IR 59/519 records " Sold 9 October 1923 All Three 120,000" . Almina sold another Gainsborough in Alfred's collection at Christies for £35,000 on 13 November 1919 entitled Portrait of Mrs Villebois in blue and white dress her hair done high.

[434] *The Times*, 20 March 1925.

[435] See *The Times*, 16 February 1921and 17 March 1921.

[436] *The Times*, 31 January 1922.

[437] Wild, Auguste, *Mixed Grill in Cairo*, Sydenham & Co. (1954).

[438] *NZ Truth*, 23 September 1922.

[439] Leadbetter, interviews 2009 and 2010. This story was told by Catherine herself to Tony Leadbetter during one of her many visits to see Almina in her later years.

[440] *Daily Express*, 4 November 1997.

[441] Williams, Valentine, *World of action*, Houghton Mifflin Company. (1938).

[442] Carnarvon's own description in The Times article of 11 December 1922 is at variance with Carter's famous remark of seeing " wonderful things" inside the hole made for the original party of Lord Carnarvon, Carter, Lady Evelyn and Carter's assistant Arthur J Callender.
" We again reached a sealed door or wall bearing the same seals as in the case of the former one. We wondered if we should find another staircase, probably blocked behind this wall, or whether we should get into a chamber. I asked Mr Carter to take out a few stones and have a look in. After a few minutes this was done. He pushed his head partly into the aperture. With the help of a candle, he could dimly discern what was inside. A long silence followed, until I said, I fear

in somewhat trembling tones, " Well, what is it?" " There are some marvellous objects here," was the welcome reply. Having given up my place to my daughter, I myself went to the hole, and I could with difficulty restrain my excitement."

In The Times of 29 March 1972 (during the exhibition of Tutankhamun at the British Museum), Lady Evelyn describes " The Day We Found The Treasures"; the article repeats Carter's phrase of seeing " wonderful things".

[443] George Valentine Williams (1883-1946). Reuters reporter. See Williams, Valentine, *World of action*, Houghton Mifflin Company. (1938).

[444] Ibid.

[445] McKenzie, Vernon, *Behind the Headlines : Journalistic Adventures of Today* (1931) Article by Valentine Williams "Uncovering Tutankhamen".

[446] George Valentine Williams (1883-1946). Reuters reporter. See Williams, Valentine, *World of action*, Houghton Mifflin Company. (1938).

[447] James, T.G.H. : *Howard Carter: The Path to Tutankhamun* Kegan Paul International. (1992).

[448] Williams, Valentine, *World of action*, Houghton Mifflin Company. (1938).

[449] National Archives file FO141/483/1 contains the minutes of a meeting with Egyptian officials on 7 February 1923 in which Carnarvon called for the dismissal of Rex Engelbart, Inspector of Antiquites in Upper Egypt. Engelbert's constant watch on the tomb was resented. The heated debate that ensued is a clear cut example of Carnarvon's arrogance, short fuse and of a man determined to get his own way.

[450] Brackman, Arnold C, The Search for the Gold of TUTANKHAMEN, London, Hale (1978) says Carnarvon's " relationship with Almina was strained" p.17 .

[451] Private source – please refer to the Author.

[452] James, T.G.H.: *Howard Carter : The Path to Tutankhamun*, Kegan Paul International (1992)

[453] The 6th Earl describes in No Regrets the hue and cry that went up when it was clear that Lord Cararvon's illness was serious. Porchester cites a telegram about his father's illness as follows:

FROM SIR JOHN MAXWELL COMMANDER-IN-CHIEF EGYPT TO SIR CHARLES MONROE C-IN-C INDIA URGENT PLEASE EXPEDIATE AN IMMEDIATE PASSAGE FOR LORD PORCHESTER TO CAIRO WHERE HIS FATHER IS VERY DANGEROUSLY ILL

However, the two military leaders mentioned had both retired from the army some years before these events. The 6th Earl either deliberately made an error, or he got it wrong, which can be excused over 50 years afterwards. He could not have been drawing on any document. In 1923 General Lord Rawlinson was the Commander in Chief, India (appointed 20 November 1920), General Sir Charles Monroe (Monro in Oxford Dictionary of National Biography) had retired during that year. (See : Rawlinson Obituary The Times 28 March 1925; Oxford Dictionary of National Biography: Monro). Maxwell retired in 1922. In crisis before and after independence Lord Allenby was in overall charge of the military in Egypt until he retired in 1925. (See also Oxford Dictionary of National Biography: Allenby).

[454] Tuesday 20 March "Left for Cairo owing to Lord C's illness." Wednesday 21 March " Arrived Cairo. Found Ld. C. very ill with an acute attack of erysipelas and blood poisoning.."

[455] Whilst there is information about Almina being with the Colonel in Paris (from Alice Butler, Almina and the Colonel's maid on the Isle of Wight in the 1930s) confusion arises as this seems to relates to when Carter made the first discovery of the tomb, on 22 November 1922, not when the news broke of the 5th Earl's illness on 19/20 March 1923.

[456] There was widespread coverage of Almina's fleeing to be at Carnarvon's side by all the London and international newspapers on 20 March 1923.

[457] Captain Barnard, one of Imperial Airways most experienced pilots was killed in 1927 at Filton Aerodrome, Bristol while testing a racing aeroplane. He was aged 32.

[458] Sir Ernest Alfred Thompson Wallis Budge: (1857-1934) was a regular visitor to Highclere Castle and was interviewed after Carnarvon's death. This quote is reported in several newspapers.

[459] Newspaper Archives Online http://www.newspaperarchive.com

[460] Ibid.

[461] In Brackman, A C, *The Search for the Gold of Tutankhamen*, Robert Hale, London (1978) an "Author's Note" at page 177 records " As for Carnarvon the only material extant in his own hand is in a series of articles in *The Times* of London. These appeared between December 1922 and April 1923. Carnarvon's private papers were largely destroyed in the Blitz in 1940.." In Heald, T, *Honourable Estates*, Pavilion Books (1992), which is based on an interview with the 7th Earl it records at page 97 " Immediately after the 5th Earl's death the family had tried to destroy all memory of the Egyptian links. Papers and books were destroyed.."

[462] *Steubenville Herald Star*, 7 April 1923.

[463] Ibid.

[464] Armitage, Albert Borlase, *Cadet to commodore*, Cassell and company. (1925) .

[465] Ibid.

[466] 1 May 1923.

[467] Probate granted to General the Right Hon. Sir John Grenfell Maxwell, GCB, KCMG of 103, Lancaster Gate, W, and Major General Sir Robert Hutchison, KCMG, of 57 Catherine Street, Buckingham Gate , SW, and Mr Arthur Fitzhardinge Berkeley Portman, of 29 Montagu Square, W. See *The Times*, 18 May 1923.

[468] *The Times*, 30 July 1923.

[469] Ibid.

[470] Adverts from 1919-1922 in *The Scotsman*.

[471] Leadbetter, interviews 2009 and 2010.

[472] Some reports suggest Aubrey's death was self-induced, since resorting to this mouth surgery was misguided; another fatal cause, deemed by Almina (says Tony Leadbetter) was the rupture of a stomach ulcer. This is confirmed in the biography of Aubrey by his granddaughter, *The Man Who Was Greenmantle*, Oxford University Press. .(1985).

[473] The Lima News of 27 September 1923 remarks " His [Aubrey's] friends recall he objected to the Earl Carnarvon's activities at Luxor.."

[474] *Time*, 8 October 1923.

[475] Evidence from Alfred Jones, PhD, of Texas, suggests that the lantern slides used by Carter
(from images on glass, made by the 5th Earl) belonged to Almina. She sold the slides to Alfred Jones in the 1950s. See Chapter 12.

[476] The Bowery Boys New York History Blog 26 April 2010. Online at http://theboweryboys.blogspot.com/2010/04/bringing-news-of-king-tut-and-his-curse.html

[477] *The Ogden Standard-Examiner*, 9 September 1923.

[478] The Near East, Vol. 24 (1923) p375 refers to Almina spending the early autumn in Glenborrodale.

[479] Evidence given by Almina in Dennistoun v Dennistoun, 19 March 1925.

[480] Ibid.

[481] Ibid.

[482] Read in court in Dennistoun v Dennistoun March 1925.

[483] Ibid.

[484] Ibid.

[485] *The Scotsman*, 20 December 1923.

[486] Evidence heard in Dennistoun v Dennistoun and widely reported in the press March 1925.

[487] Leadbetter, interviews 2009 and 2010.

[488] According to files IR59/519-521 relating to Alfred's estate, Almina paid over £100,000 legacy duty to Inland Revenue, but only in 1925.

[489] See Hewins, R, *Mr Five Percent, the story of Calouste Gulbenkian.* (1957) "Joe" Duveen (later Sir Joseph), later still Lord Duveen" (1869-1939).

[490] *The Times*, 19 March 1924.

[491] Portrait of Emma Hart afterwards Lady Hamilton in white muslin dress and black hat her hand to her throat. Engraved under the title of " Emma". In Alfred de Rothschild Probate file at National Archives IR 59/519 the picture is estimated to be worth £ 6,000. It was sold at Christies on 29 February 1924 for £17,000.

[492] *The Scotsman*, 14 August 1924.

[493] Correspondence between the author and Jamie Williamson, current owner of Alvie Estate, Kingussie, 2009.

[494] Among the best overall summaries of the Dennistoun case are Bardens, Dennis, *Lord Justice Birkett,* Robert Hale Ltd (1962) Chapter VIII, pp. 71-83; and Hooke, Nina Warner & Thomas Gil, *Marshall Hall :* Arthur Barker Ltd (1966) pp. 239-248

[495] In mid February 1924, Howard Carter closed the King Tut Tomb after a dispute with the Egyptians, (notably with Pierre Lacau, Director General of Antiquities, Cairo). This centred on wives of Carter's collaborators being forbidden admission to the site. The dispute ran for 11 months, during which the Egyptian Government sought to have Carter , Almina and the Carnarvon executors renounce *all* claims on the contents of the tomb. See *The Times,* 13,14 and 15 February 1924.

[496] When the tomb was first opened by Carter he found many duplicates (i.e. exact copies) of artefacts. The new agreement was a complicated compromise (later withdrawn) in which the Egyptian government " reserved absolute discretion" to give to Carter " for scientific purposes such duplicates as it may

select where their separation from the rest will not affect the scientific value of the collection" See *The Times*, 13, 14 and 26 January 1925.

[497] The Cunliffe-Owens often attended (as did Marshall Hall and Carter occasionally) the séances arranged by the 5th Earl at Highclere Castle. There is reference to Carnarnon's superstitions by the 6th Earl in his memoirs and by Barry Wynne in *Behind the Mask of Tutankhamun*, Souvenir Press Ltd. (1972). Almina did not share the 5th Earl's interest with any commitment.

[498] Newspaper coverage of Dennistoun v Dennistoun in various publications.

[499] Norman Birkett, Marshall Hall's junior, reflecting on the Dennistoun case in *The Gleaner* of 3 September 1961 wrote, " Marshall Hall always enjoyed a fashionable audience but, this time, he was to appear at his worst. Only a sick man could have behaved as he did when cross-examining Mrs Dennistoun.."

[500] Newspaper coverage of Dennistoun v Dennistoun in various publications.

[501] Ibid.

[502] Ibid.

[503] Ibid.

[504] Ibid.

[505] Ibid.

[506] Oscar William Pocklington-Senhouse (1891-1915) was a young man whom Dorothy had known in her early years, a relative of Ian's aunt Lady Mary Macpherson-Grant and Dorothy's friends, the Millers of Manderston and of the Curzons. He was a soldier but was killed in the Great War, at Loos. It was alleged in Dorothy's cross-examination that she committed adultery with Senhouse *before* he left for the Front. Ian alleged she had been seeing him from 1912 onwards.

[507] LCO 2/775 National Archives Kew.

[508] Newspaper coverage of Dennistoun v Dennistoun in various publications.

[509] Ibid.

[510] Ibid.

[511] Ibid.

[512] Ibid.

[513] Ibid.

[514] Ibid.

[515] The close friendship that had once existed between Dorothy and Almina was put under the microscope in Marshall Hall's grilling of Dorothy. She agreed that Almina had been " *marvellously kind"* during the two years when she was on the *"greatest of terms"* with the Carnarvon family.

[516] On 15 October 1923, two months *before* marriage to the Colonel Almina paid £15,000 into the Colonel's bank account, on 17 December 1923 £2,500 was paid in and on 2 January, 1924, the sum of £50,000 was deposited. Hume-Williams reminded the jury in his closing remarks that Ian was " *a man who was once down and out"*….. but who in part of 1923 had these and the sum of £7000 paid into his account and in the second half of the same year the sum of £48,650.

[517] Newspaper coverage of Dennistoun v Dennistoun in various publications.

[518] Ibid.

[519] Ibid.

[520] Ibid.

[521] Ibid.

[522] Ibid.

[523] This quote is from Dorothy 's letter, written two days after Almina's marriage to the Colonel. The inference is that Dorothy lost Almina's friendship when the Colonel became her lover and this is suggesting the Colonel and Almina were lovers *before* Lord Carnarvon died. The evidence from Alice Butler (Almina's maid, whom she spoke to about the affair with the Colonel) is that Carnarvon knew and tolerated Almina's relationship with the Colonel. However Dorothy's letter was a " thunderbolt" (the description of it by Hume-Williams) and was to embarrass Almina and prompt her to settle out of court.

[524] Newspaper coverage of Dennistoun v Dennistoun.

[525] Ibid.

[526] Ibid.

[527] Ibid.

[528] Hume-Williams, Sir Ellis, *The World, the House and the Bar*" John Murray. (1930)

[529] Lady Helen Cunliffe-Owen had entered Almina's nursing home, Alfred House at Portland Place at the end of 1933; she returned on 3 January 1934 and was operated on the same night. On release she had a relapse and died on 14 January 1934, leaving four young children. She was a great furniture collector and (like her husband) a horse owner and racing personality.

[530] LCO 2/775 in National Archives, Kew.

[531] WO 374/ 19236 in National Archives, Kew.

[532] Ibid.

[533] Ibid.

[534] Ibid.

[535] Ibid.

[536] In 1934, a Mr C Benjamin Riley wrote to the War Office from 88, Church Street, Kingston, Jamaica, asking for the address of " ex-Major I O Dennistoun, MVO who was once attached to the Grenadier Guards and was Private Secretary to the late Sir W H Manning former Governor of Jamaica." Protecting confidentiality, the army said it was only willing to send on a letter to Mr I O Dennistoun MVO. but it seems that the communication was later returned " Gone Away" from the home of Almina and Ian at Temple Dinsley. By 1935-1936 the Colonel had already been removed to the Isle of Wight. Whatever the skeleton is in the closet around this matter it remains unknown.

[537] Lois Meredith (born 1897) had a few screen and stage credits from 1914 onwards including films called " The Legacy of Folly" and " Over the Top". The Paris film scene was fuelled with alcohol, sex, drugs and death. Lois was a close friend of Olive Thomas also an actress, and ex -Ziegfeld girl married Jack, Mary Pickford's brother; Olive committed suicide in 1920. (Olive Thomas: the life and death of a silent film beauty " Michelle Vogel. p77) . On Olive's death (after swallowing an alcoholic poison) Meredith rose to being " the most popular American movie actress before the French public." Ian Dennistoun met her at the Auteull Race Track, Paris.

[538] The Meredith case featured in American and French newspapers between 31 March and 17 April 1925.

[539] *The Bee* (copied from the Chicago Tribune), 17 April 1925.

[540] Ibid.

[541] Catherine gave birth to her daughter at Hill Street, Berkley Square, London on 3 March 1925. When the child was christened at Highclere Church on 12

April 1925 the godparents included Catherine's sister, Philippa Fendall Wendell, Countess of Galloway; the socialite Poppy Baring (whose wedding to William Piers (Peter) Thursby in 1928 saw both of Catherine's children appear in the limelight as "attendants") ; the child's uncle, Sir Brograve Beauchamp and Highclere regular, Arthur Portman. See *The Times* 13 April 1925 and 18 December 1928.

[542] Five family portraits in all, originally from Bretby Hall including two Gainsboroughs of Anne, Countess of Chesterfield and her husband.

[543] Royal Archives : Queen Mary's Diary 15 May 1925 : "Fine nice day. I went at 2.15 with Mary Trefusis to Hampton Court and walked for an hour in the lovely garden. Back for tea. At 6 to Christies to see the lovely furniture, china etc from the Alfred Rothschild collection, which Lady Carnarvon is selling."

[544] *The Argus*, Melbourne, Victoria 25 May 1925

[545] An amusing fact is that Utica, the estranged wife of Almina's conductor friend Sir Thomas Beecham, bought up a good deal of Almina's furniture in the Christies sale. Beecham was furious about it all as Utica tried to get him to pay up , after he'd taken out an advert in the newspapers saying he would not be liable for his wife's debts. The matter went to court. See The Times, 4 July 1925. The Beechams were later divorced in the 1940s, in the USA.

[546] See De Hamel, Christopher, *The Rothschilds and Their Collections of Illuminated Manuscripts*: The British Library (2005). Also see *The Times*, 21 May 1925.

[547] Auction houses were still using this antiquated currency.

[548] Referred to in these terms by Alfred in his Will of 1917.

[549] A note in National Archives, Kew, file IR 59/521 gives the proceeds as furniture (19 May) £79,973, 15s 6d (net of duty £73,973. 12s.10d); pictures (22 May) £ 49,275.9s (net of duty £45, 579.15s.10d) and engravings (1 July) £ 703.10s (net of duty £615.11s3d.).

[550] IR59/521 National Archives, Kew. A further cheque for £10,000 was paid over to Inland Revenue in October 1925.

[551] A press report from August 1925 (in an American newspaper) suggested a rift between Almina and the Colonel. She was *"contemplating a trip to California to seek rest and quite after her trying experiences"*. It was added that *" Colonel Dennistoun probably won't accompany her , as it is whispered that he may be involved in another action."*

[552] One of Almina's correspondents was Alice, 4th Marchioness of Salisbury (1867-1955) who had been an extra Lady of the Bedchamber to Queen Alexandra. One fragment from a letter survives in the Leadbetter Collection, which may have been an acknowledgment of Almina's condolences sent on the death of the Queen. Alice Salisbury (Lady Cicely Alice Gore) was, in common with Almina, a close friend of Lord Kitchener.

[553] The 6th Earl was an accomplished amateur rider.

[554] See *The Gleaner*, 30 November 1926 .

[555] Lady Anne Penelope Herbert, daughter of the 6th Earl, wife of Gerrit van der Woude, died in 1990. Gerrit remarried Hon. Esmé Mary Gabrielle Harmsworth (b.1922) daughter of Esmond Cecil Harmsworth, 2nd Viscount Rothermere & Margaret Hunam Redhead.

[556] Leadbetter, interviews 2009 and 2010.

[557] Whilst Moynihan's patient casebook is available at the Royal College of Surgeons, London, the year in question remains closed. Catherine may have been carrying an unwanted third child, and not the 6th Earl's. Catherine had a close relationship with Prince George, (later Duke of Kent) during this time. Alternatively, Catherine's abdominal operation may have been the consequence of her increasing alcohol dependency.

[558] *The Observer*, 13 February 1927.

[559] Parts of this cache were displayed at an exhibition of Egyptian works of art at the Burlington Fine Arts Club in 1922. See The Times 22 February 1927.

[560] *Daily Express*, 23 February 1927.

[561] Ibid.

[562] Ibid.

[563] A surprising twist in the drama came in 1988 when, after the 6th Earl's death, it emerged that there was still a cache of Egyptian artefacts hidden away at Highclere Castle. Cupboards were sealed up between the rooms where the items were stored. The inference is Almina (under the 5th Earl's will the owner of *all* the Egyptian artefacts) did *not* sell everything from the collection to the Americans. Either some pieces were returned to Highclere or Carter – who had catalogued the collection there – deliberately missed some items from the inventory; or the 6th Earl had managed to hold back some pieces. See also the Epilogue to this book.

[564] *The Times*, 7 April 1927.

[565] An informant remarked concerning Almina's surname that she snubbed ever using her husband's name of Dennistoun.

[566] A veiled reference to Berkeley Moynihan.

[567] Essex Record Office has a sales catalogue for 7-9 Portland Place for 1920 ref Sale /A2973. The property was put up for sale by Alfred Savill & Sons for Hon. Lady Peek on 1 July 1920. See The Times, 7 May 1920.

[568] *Daily Express*, 4 July 1927.

[569] *Daily Express*, 12 July 1927.

[570] *Daily Express*, 19 September 1929.

[571] Ibid.

[572] Burra, Edward John, Well Dearie! The Letters of Edward Burra, William Chappell.(1985)

[573] *London Daily Mail*, January 30, 2010.

[574] Mary was the daughter of Mrs R E Gentles of Coleyville, Manchester, Jamaica. She was a pupil at St Hilda's School, Brown's Town and left Jamaica around 1933 to train as a nurse at Dr Steven's Hospital, Dublin. Later Mary completed her midwifery at Hollies Street Hospital, Dublin.

[575] The Gleaner, August 1939.

[576] *Guardian*, 13 August 1927.

[577] The Barracks was originally built for troops stationed there after the Jacobite rebellion of 1745 See *The Scottish Clans and Their Tartans* : Anonymous author.

[578] Henry Keown-Boyd (born 1932) provided this feedback after reading the 1st version of the book. He writes on 14 May 2011 " *I must have passed the Barracks on Loch Rannoch on several occasions as my wife and I used to spend a week or two every summer in that area...I don't think the London train still stops at Rannoch station but the line to Mallaig is still open and is reputed to be the most spectacular train journey in Britain.. "*

[579] Henry Keown-Boyd, (born 1932,) author and retired businessman. Spent his childhood in Egypt.

[580] It is interesting to note that Carnarvon is described by on newspaper reporter in the *Daily Express* of 15 October 1928 as "small, thick set and cheerful". This could easily be a description of his alleged father Prince Victor Duleep Singh. There is no doubt that as he got older the 6th Earl's physical resemblance to Victor was more pronounced. In Evelyn's case, as she got older she best resembled her mother.

[581] Murley and Hosford, *Memories of Lord Moynihan*: British Medical Journal, Vol 297, Dec 1988, pp 24-31.

[582] Trotter was the author of *Instincts of the Herd in Peace* (1916).

[583] Leadbetter Collection.

[584] *Daily Express*, 19 September 1929.

[585] *Daily Mirror*, 2 March 1929.

[586] Fielding, Daphne, *The Duchess of Jermyn Street*, Futura, (1976).

[587] Holland,Vyvyan: Time Remembered After Père Lachaise, Gollancz,(1966).

[588] *Daily Mirror*, 10 January 1929.

[589] Tennyson, L H, [3rd] Baron, *From Verse to Worse*, London. Cassell.(1933).

[590] Louise Selina Bonynge, Lady Maxwell, was the half-sister of Virginia Bonynge, (1866-1948) Viscountess Deerhurst. NB The extensive personal papers of Sir John and Lady Maxwell are held by Princeton University Library, New Jersey, USA.

[591] *The Times*, 4 February 1929.

[592] In *The Man Who Was Greenmantle*, the biography of Aubrey Herbert by his granddaughter, Margaret Fitzherbert, (Oxford University Press) (1985), she makes clear that the 5th Earl spurned his stepmother as a child. Their relationship was only ever formal. Elsie's life's work in Egypt during the Great War where she was a famed nurse and for Albanian causes meant Almina and Elsie saw little of each other, and by choice.

[593] *The Times*, 9 February 1929.

[594] Interestingly, this wasn't the first time Almina had been misrepresented as dead. On one occasion during the lifetime of the 5th Earl, Almina's death was also reported in Paris, when the venue for the function she was due to attend was burnt to the ground. She was on the invitation list but failed to be accounted for in the aftermath of the fire. In fact she had been indisposed with a migraine (something that was infrequent) and had simply not gone to the event. According to an intimate, the 5th Earl had been preparing to be a widower – we can only guess how he may have felt about this.

[595] Mervyn Herbert was in Egypt in 1923. According to his diaries Lady Evelyn confided to him that her father and Carter had secretly entered and removed (allegedly unrecorded) items from King Tut's tomb *before* the Egyptian government had approved clearance.

[596] *The Times*, 3 June 1929. Lady Winifred Burghclere sent her apologies as she was abroad

[597] Described in Cooper, Diana : *Autobiography* (3 vols in one book); *The Rainbow Comes and Goes; The Lights of Common Day; and Trumpets from the Steep".

[598] When the author contacted the late Lady Diana Duff Cooper's son, the travel writer, (Viscount)John Julius Norwich and asked him of his own knowledge of Almina 80 years later he could only reply :- " So sorry - never met her in my life!"

[599] A lengthy tribute to Evie James can be found on pages 50-58 of *Lady Carnarvon's Nursing Homes : Nursing the Privileged in Wartime and P*eace : compiled by William Cross, published 15 October 2011. ISBN 1905914032.

[600] Patricia Leigh Brown in *Architectural Digest* " At Home in the Surreal World : Expanding on Edward James's Vision in Xilitla". August 2005.

[601] Source: 1st Baron's son, the 4th Lord Mottistone, Captain David Peter Seely CBE, born 1920, died 2011. Correspondence with the author 2010.

[602] A Queen Anne country house, redesigned by Lutyens at the same time as the gardens were designed by his great friend, Gertrude Jekyll. In his book *King's Walden (1925-29)* Ronald Hartless observes " When I started secondary school at Hitchin, I used to travel on the bus with the son of Mr Wright, the head gardener at Temple Dinsley, Preston. I often used to visit him there and walk round the grounds which belonged to Lady Carnarvon, widow of Lord Carnarvon, who with Howard Carter discovered the tomb of Tutankhamun in February 1923. Later this property became the Princes Helena College. See also *The Observer*, 19 February 1928, for details of the link of the house to Sir Ralph Sadleir " *trusted counsellor of Henry VIII and Elizabeth*" . Temple Dinsley was sold to Almina by Douglas Vickers. It was described by the selling agents, Messrs John D Wood and Co, as " *a fine sporting estate, abounding in pheasants, partridges, and hares. There are 1550 acres.* "

[603] The Times, 8 April 1929 : "Cairo Notes 31 March Colonel Dennistoun and Almina Countess of Carnarvon have arrived at the Semiramis Hotel."

[604] Carter was never rich enough to conduct his own excavations; otherwise he would have not required a patron. There was a rumour that he was only ever paid expenses, never a regular allowance or salary, by the Carnarvons. This allegation runs contrary to the 6th Earl's memoirs in which he claims that following his father's death he paid Carter a wage, which is likely to be inaccurate since it was Almina who managed such transactions.

[605] File FO141/481 /1 (National Archives, Kew) has this report from a member of the British Residency in Cairo dated 3 January 1930:- " A very unhappy Mr Howard Carter came to see me the day before yesterday. He said that the Egyptian Government had accepted his offer to finish the work in the Tomb for nothing but Monsieur Lacau had added the verbal condition that Carter must surrender the keys to the local Inspector of Antiquities, and not enter the Tomb without the latter's permission."

[606] FO 141/483/1 National Archives Kew.

[607] Ibid.

[608] Almina promised Howard Carter a quarter of the compensation from the Egyptian government. This sum was reduced as Almina instructed that he should only receive 25 per cent of the sum involved" *after payment of duties, and expenses.* "Subsequently A W Fryzer sent him a cheque for the sum of £ 8012. A further £546.2s 9d was sent to him as a portion of the *"legacy duty refund"* received by the 5th Earl's trustees.

[609] Ronald Balfour married Deirdre Hart-Davies ,(1909-1998), sister of publisher Rupert Hart-Davies (father of Adam, famed TV historian) Balfour was employed at the Admiralty. After his flat in London was bombed he lived in the country; he was killed on the way there when, after working all night, he fell asleep at the wheel.

[610] She knew her through Maria Wombwell's great friend Nellie, the 3rd Countess of Kilmorey. who was Ellen Constance Baldock, second daughter of Edward Holmes Baldock, MP. Nellie married the third Earl of Kilmorey in 1881, who died in 1915. The Countess died in 1920. [Some controversy surrounds Constance's relationship with Prince Francis of Teck, the younger brother of Queen Mary. In effect she was the Prince's mistress, who died in 1910, aged 39. He left Nellie some fabulous emeralds in his Will. Queen Mary stopped publication of the Will, which created the precedent for non publication of all Royal Wills. See also David Leigh in *The Guardian* 27 March 2007 " *Secret wills of the royals- a tale of mistresses, jewels and cover ups.* "]

[611] See Hale, G and Roberts N, *A doctor in practice,* Routledge and Kegan Paul (1974) p71.

[612] *The Times*, 9 July 1930.

[613] The 5th Earl of Carnarvon was a member of the Royal Yacht Squadron with links there in the 1880s onwards.

[614] *The Times*, 6 August 1930.

[615] Lethbridge died on 3 January 1931, aged 65. He is described in the family intimation of his death in *The Times* as a " late Captain in the Northamptonshire Yeomanry". He was the only son of Marie Wombwell's sister Eleanor Boyer, later Lethbridge. He had two sons who went to live in Canada. The only other cousin Almina had from off her mother's two sisters, was Henry Alexander Gordon Howard (only son of Victoria Boyer), 4th Earl of Effingham, (1866-1927), who died childless.

[616] *Daily Express*, 2 January 1931.

[617] *The Times*, 1 and 4 July 1931.

[618]On 4 April 1930 a millionaire heir was added to the list of the notables born at Alfred House when Muriel Dodge, wife of Horace Elgin Dodge, son of a rich American automobile manufacturer (later Chrysler) gave birth to a son, David Elgin Dodge.

[619] An article in the *Daily Express* children's column indicates that Almina's charges at Alfred House also included children. An appeal is mentioned on behalf of "a little member of the Rupert League who is in a nursing home after being very ill and undergoing an operation". The patient was 14-year-old Bettina Marks.

[620] A lengthy tribute to Nurse Jean Robertson can be found on pages 71-76 of *Lady Carnarvon's Nursing Homes : Nursing the Privileged in Wartime and P*eace : compiled by William Cross, published 15 October 2011. ISBN 1905914032.

[621] *Daily Express*, 25 August 1931. See also Frankland, Noble *Prince Henry, Duke of Gloucester*, Weidenfeld and Nicolson, London (1980) p112. For further details on the Duke of Gloucester, see also pages 60-64 of *Lady Carnarvon's Nursing Homes : Nursing the Privileged in Wartime and P*eace : compiled by William Cross, published 15 October 2011. ISBN 1905914032.

[622] The unmarried third son of King George V and Queen Mary had spent his life in the army. He was a dull, be-speckled and shy man, unlike his dashing,

glamorous older brother, the Prince of Wales. One commentator in the *Syracuse Herald* of 6 May 1928 remarks of Henry " He is a great lover of dogs and often travels alone, accompanied by no equerries, but only by two of his pet dogs. " Henry later married in 1935, Lady Alice Christabel Montagu -Douglas - Scott.

[623] Leadbetter, interviews 2009 and 2010. See also Thornton, Michael , *Royal feud*, M Joseph , London (1985).

[624] Leadbetter, interviews 2009 and 2010. It was Winston's wife Lady Clementine Churchill who required an operation at Alfred House.

[625] See Frankland, Noble *Prince Henry, Duke of Gloucester*, Weidenfeld and Nicolson, London (1980).

[626] Besides the Colonel several invalids were on board, including George Ulick Browne, 6th Marquess of Sligo, (died 1935), Harry Lawson Webster Levy Lawson Viscount Burnham – whose father had been involved in running the Daily Telegraph (died 1933). Among the more charismatic of their fellow passengers was Sir Claude Champion de Crespigny, 1847-1935, a great adventurer, fighting soldier and man of the turf, and Lady Ursula Stewart, who was born Ursula Chetwynd –Talbot and published under the name of Laura Talbot. As " La" she famously had a long affair (and later married) writer/ playwright Patrick Hamilton, 1904-1963. Ursula was killed in a plane crash with her fourth husband in 1966. Also on board the same cruise were Viscount and Viscountess Coke, from 1941 the 4th Earl and Countess of Leicester, of Holkham Hall. See *The Gleaner* 13 February 1932. Viscountess Coke, Marion Gertrude Trefusis (1882-1955) was a correspondent of Almina, a fragment of a letter to Almina from " Marion Leicester " is in the Leadbetter Collection.

[627] The Gleaner, 11 February 1932 Readers were told that Almina was " well known for her social work and is head of a big nursing home in London. "

[628] *The Daily Express*, 16 July 1932.

[629] Lancaster, Osbert : *With An Eye to the Future,* John Murray. (1967).

[630] Evelyn Waugh was Almina's nephew twice over through his two marriages: first to Evelyn Gardner (1903–1994) the famed 'She Evelyn', daughter of Lady Winifred Burghclere, whom he divorced in 1931; and later to Laura (1916–1973), a daughter of Aubrey Herbert.

[631] Amory, Mark (Ed) *Letters of Evelyn Waugh*, Weidenfeld & Nicolson. (1980) and (1995)

[632] *Lethbridge Herald*, 14 October 1933.

[633] Ibid.

[634] Cronin, A J, *The Citadel*, London, Victor Gollancz Ltd. (1937). Almina's hospitals are also given a passing reference in later fiction including Alfred Shaughnessy's novel *Hugo,* (1996), and Charlotte Bingham's *The kissing garden* (1999).

[635] Coward, Noel : *Future Indefinite*, Heinemann, London. (1954).

[636] See Lesley, Cole: *Remembered Laughter vol 2 of Life of Noel Coward*, Cape. (1976)

[637] *Daily Express*, 20 December 1933.

[638] Brooklands Society; *The Scotsman*, 27 June 1933 (Funeral).

[639] Culled from obituary tributes. Lady Winifred took after her father the 4th Earl. She was most literary and scholarly of his six children, with a flair for editing the letters of notable figures including the Duke of Wellington . She wrote several exacting biographies of 17th century noblemen and penned a slanted, over

sentimental tribute to her brother, George, 5th Earl of Carnarvon, after he was dead in 1923.

[640] Leadbetter, interviews, 2009 and 2010

[641] *The Times*, 3 October 1933.

[642] Examples include Young, JHB, *Francis Brett Young: a biography*, Heinemann (1962); and Hart-Davis *Hugh Walpole: a biography* Hamish Hamilton (1985).

[643] Leadbetter adds that Almina was always seeking out (to buy) the latest hospital / surgical equipment, a matter that had always interested her from the time of the Great War. She sent a team of her theatre sisters from Alfred House, on a tour of America to research the latest gadgets.

[644] Firstly the wealthy Consuelo Vanderbilt, (1877-1964) who left him in 1908 and whom he divorced in 1921 followed by his long standing mistress Gladys Deacon, (1881-1977) who was effectively deposed and removed herself from Blenheim just before the 9th Duke's painful death from cancer in 1934.

[645] Leadbetter Collection.

[646] *The Times*, 24 November 1933.

[647] The present Duke of Marlborough (11th) has confirmed there are no papers at Blenheim on this matter. [Letter from Blenheim Palace to author 20 October 2009.]

[648] Dr Moore was with the Royal Army Medical Corps in Gallipoli and France and in 1917 commanded the Military Hospital, Gibraltar. He was Physician in Ordinary to Princess Beatrice from 1928 to 1944. See *The Times* 14 November 1957. Almina also attended the following year's luncheon given by Mrs Moore, at Claridge's on 11 July 1935.

[649] On 18 August 1934, Almina attended the Requiem Mass at St James, Spanish Place, London, for the Infante Don Gonzalo, the 19 year-old son of Queen Ena (and King Alfonso) of Spain. The boy had died in a car accident.

[650] This was probably lifted from the Preston Women's Institute *History of Preston* (1953) which recounts the same story but adds that Almina's "interests lay chiefly elsewhere but her husband did much for Preston" – Ian Dennistoun was elected a school manager.

[651] Source Philip Wray, a local historian.

[652] *The Times*, 2 July 1935 and 9 July 1935.

[653] This is now a substantial property called The Plantation House. On a site visit in November 2010 the currents owners, Christine and David Jones made available to the author an aerial view (c1935) showing Eastmore and surrounds.

[654] The Red House, Hove is cited as the home of Major Seymour Caldwell (died 1938 at 7, Brunswick Place, Hove) and his wife Marjorie. Their daughter, Diana Caldwell, (1913-1987) married Jock Broughton (of Nairobi's Happy Valley Sect, featured in the book/ film *"White Mischief"*). she was later Lady Delamere.

[655] Leadbetter, interviews 2009 and 2010. Tiddles was forced to run down her home at Amport House, Hampshire, where Alice was a maid.

[656] The Colonel was a well-known name in model yachting, whilst at Temple Dinsley he was a member of a club in Bedford. His model yachts competed in international competitions in the years 1934-5.

[657] *Syracuse Herald*, 20 June 1935.

[658] Ibid.

[659] *Daily Express*, 4 July 1935.

[660] Royal Archives, RA AEC/GG/01/70.

[661] Royal Archives, RA AEC/GG/01/1-131.

[662] Royal Archives, RA AEC/GG/01/18 and RA AEC/GG/01/39.

[663] Royal Archives, RA AEC/GG/01/29.

[664] *The Daily Mirror* of 2 July 1935 says that Lady Carrisbrooke went back to Alfred House. It became necessary as a direct result of making too speedy progress after her previous operation. She was convalescent in Spain and had reached the stage where she was allowed to walk a few steps. Then the Spanish revolution broke out and she had to hurry across the frontiers from Madrid with the Spanish Royal Family.

[665] Royal Archives, RA AEC/ GG/01/55.

[666] Royal Archives, RA AEC/GG/01/76.

[667] *The Times*, 6 April 1936.

[668] Michael Lewis of Newbury recalls in the 1930s, taking part as a boy soprano in a concert on the Highclere Estate, in which he sang " a small solo part". He remembers " a little old lady" came up to him afterwards and said she had very much enjoyed his performance and handed him a £5 note. Lewis was puzzled and asked who she was. Almina replied " Never you mind who I am, your parents know perfectly well who I am." Lewis recounts that Almina's generosity of spirit (of which this was typical) was much appreciated by those working and living near Highclere.

[669] *The Times*, 28 May 1936

[670] Almina and Jean Jacomb were professional rivals. On Jean's retirement in 1949, Almina sent her a warm letter, a copy of which was given to the author by Kathy Perkins, the Archivist of the London Clinic, who is compiling Jean's biography. Almina ends the letter with this flurry "Such a life of Christian sacrifice can only be understood, truly appreciated, by one who had lived and worked under similar conditions and I am proud to sign myself - Yours affectionately, in principle and in understanding. Almina Carnarvon."

[671] *The Times*, 15 January 1937.

[672] Private source, please refer to author. This informant adds " Catherine was still having an affair with the Duke of Kent at the same time as Princess Marina of Greece (Duchess of Kent), was involved in an on/off affair with the conductor Sir Malcolm Sargent" [See also Watson, Sophia, Marina: *the story of a Princess*, Weidenfeld and Nicolson, London (1994). p.192] suggesting Catherine's close relationship with "Georgie" continued *after* the Prince married in 1934. Rumours surround the background to George being instructed to marry, and later attempts to "banish" him to a colonial post. As Prince George, " PG" or " Babe" to his intimates he was implicated in homosexual affairs, including a fling with a young Frenchman, and discovery of a spate of compromising letters that were retrieved (at cost) by the Royal guardians (described in the Diaries of Sir Robert Bruce Lockhart and Sheridan Morley's biography of Noel Coward (2005)). Philip Hoare provides further details of George's romantic escapades in Noel *Coward: A Biography (1998)*. George was also briefly linked as a very young man with the black American singer Florence Mills. A torrid love affair with Helen Azalea (Poppy) Baring, and a fling with Napier (Naps) Alington's sister the actress Hon. Lois Sturt (later Viscountess Tredegar d.1937). The Prince shared Poppy and Lois with one or more of his brothers. Post marriage

George adored another American Paula Gellibrand, (1898-1986), a Cecil Beaton fashion model, and sometime wife of fascist supporter William Allen, MP. (See *The Evening Independent* (Ohio) 8 and 11 January 1937.) Almina told Tony Leadbetter that after the Prince married " Marina was a bitch to him". Earning her the title of being a "fag hag" and to rub salt into George's sexual frustrations Marina surrounded herself with several feminine men (some of whom he'd bedded). Marina, Duchess of Kent died in 1968.

[673] Catherine married Porchey Carnarvon (later 6th Earl) on 17 July 1922, and her son Henry (later 7th Earl) was born on 19 January 1924. Yet, the question of Henry's paternity remains a curiosity. The physical resemblance of the 7th Earl as a young man to Prince George is striking and remarkable. . Prince George, Duke of Kent, died in a mysterious plane crash during the Second World War in 1942, giving rise to conspiracy theories to the present day. If Prince George fathered the 7th Earl of Carnarvon, that would make Henry a cousin to Princess Elizabeth, later H.M.Queen. This might explain why Porchester was so much favoured at Court. For Almina, the consequence of such a truth would be that she was not Porchester's blood relation. To Almina that would have been unthinkable, but it is significant mystery on other counts. See also the Epilogue to this book.

[674] *The Times*, 21 April 1924. Includes a photograph of the 6th Earl & Countess with the child

[675] 21 September 1938 to Geoffrey Grenfell, who was killed in the Second World War. Another of Catherine's lovers was a cousin of the Grenfell family, the conductor Sir Malcolm Sargent.Catherine attended a function at Claridges Hotel, London on 5 March 1935 when Sir Malcolm " arranged a programme of Gluck, Handel and Debussy" for the Olympian Party. Almina's daughter Lady Evelyn Beauchamp was also present. The other event attended by Catherine was a " Fashion Plate Ball" at Grosvenor House on 2 December 1935.Sargent was branded a conqueror of umpteen women ("even the ugly ones") and was also on intimate terms with Almina. Sargent's secretary Sylvia Darley, MBE, confirms in an email to the author "Sir Malcolm was a friend of the Carnarvon family." He was almost certainly treated at Alfred House for tuberculosis (in the 1930s), although he recuperated mostly in Switzerland.

[676] Reports vary about whether Wigram died of natural causes or by suicide. A moving tribute to him is in Lawford, Valentine: *Bound for Diplomacy*, John Murray. (1963)

[677] Ava Bodley, later Wigram, 1896-1974, subsequently Viscountess Waverley.

[678] Correspondence by e-mail with Pearl Kilpatrick, a daughter of Margaret Lawson of Dunfermline, Fife, March 2011.

[679] A lengthy tribute to Margaret Lawson (nee Sharp) can be found on pages 77-88 of *Lady Carnarvon's Nursing Homes : Nursing the Privileged in Wartime and Peace* : compiled by William Cross, published 15 October 2011. ISBN 1905914032.

[680] Henry Keown-Boyd (born 1932) , who was born in Alfred House Nursing Home, advised after reading this passage in the book that he believes that his brother David was given the Colonel's collection of model soldiers, something that he also remembers playing with as a young boy. Keown-Boyd writes on 14 May 2011 " Apart from my brief acquaintance with her [Almina]

(perhaps the first occasion was the day of my birth!) there are several other points of personal interest .. for example, you mention Tiger's collection of toy soldiers, some of which I believe my late brother David " inherited". He told me that as a boy he had been given some of these either by Tiger himself or by Almina after his death….."

[681] Cribbed from the song in Iolanthe by Gilbert & Sullivan " None shall part us from each other"

[682] Royal Archives, RA AEC/GG/01/104.

[683] Royal Archives, RA AEC /GG/01/100.

[684] Royal Archives, RA AEC /GG/01 103.

[685] Tony Leadbetter recalls his Aunt Alice saying that Almina had her make up numerous food hampers for the undertaker, who was also installed in a London apartment at Almina's expense. Almina was " besotted by him".

[686] On a site visit to Eastmore by the author in November 2010 he met Roger Smith, whose grandfather was a Yarmouth resident at the time of the Colonel's death and one time chauffeur and valet to William Smith Nicholson, the owner of Eastmore until 1913. He corroborated Alice Butler's story of the embalmed figure kept at the house. David Jones, joint-owner of The Plantation House showed the author the heart shaped stone on this same visit. NB Part of the site is now called Eastmore Court (utilising buildings erected after Almina's time) and the main house is now called Carnarvon House. After the Second World War the "Brothers of Christian Schools" also known by the name of the La Salle Brothers ran Eastmore as an Approved School until it was taken over by the Isle of Wight County Council in the 1960's and closed in the 1990s, when it was converted back into residential use.

[687] An Inventory of Eastmore, by Stuart & Turner Ltd, of 13 Soho Square London W1, a month after the Colonel's death valued the contents for insurance or replacement at £14,783- 2s.

[688] Dr Alfred Jones, PhD, an American psychologist who worked as a volunteer in the Egyptian department of the British Museum in the mid 1950s adds the following: " Let me share some thoughts regarding Carter, from a psychological vantage point. My knowledge comes from the British Museum chaps who knew him personally and my reading between the lines in the historical literature. He was a strange fellow all of his life. Very self-serving at all times. He was very much of a treasure hunter as opposed to being a true archaeologist. He had a wonderful system of recording everything from the tomb, but the way he treated the actual body looking for amulets was shocking. I am sure Thomas Hoving was correct in his book "Untold Story" about the entry into the tomb and they [Carter and Carnarvon] doubtless pocketed small pieces for themselves. Carter sought out Carnarvon looking for backing. At that time Carnarvon was well off and could afford it. He too was a treasure hunter. I have to give Carter credit for being skilled, knowlegable and determined. In all fairness, many of the diggers in Egypt were out to make a fortune as opposed to adding to the body of knowledge. This continues to this day.

[689] Royal Archives RA AEC/GG/01/108 Princess Beatrice adds in the same letter of being " touched with a gift of Worcester china in remembrance of your charming home in the Isle of Wight.."

[690] Stated in Almina's bankruptcy proceedings in 1951.

[691] Ottilie Ethel Losch (1904-1975), of Austrian origin, she was a child star of the Corps de Ballet of the Vienna Staatsoper, later of CB Cochran's This *Year of Grace* (Noel Coward) in London and as a nun in Max Reinhardt's film *The Miracle* and appeared with Fred and Adele Astaire in *The Band Box*. Tilly first married Edward William Frank James (1907-1984) and was at the centre of a spectacular divorce case in London in 1934. In her later years she became a popular celebrity painter.

[692] Leadbetter, interviews 2009 and 2010. The description of someone being "a bitch" was an often-used Society phrase in the era for maligning women, made by both men and other women; the remark was usually a spiteful one made behind the subject's back.

[693] Almina gave a grand house warming party in the grounds of Avenue Road, during July 1939. Guests were introduced to Queen Ena of Spain and her daughter the Infanta Maria Christina. A dinner and dance was held in a marquee set up on the lawn. Porchey, Almina's son, acted as joint host. See The Observer, 16 July 1939 for guests including former Alfred House patient, Dona Gina Regis de Oliveira, (wife of the Brazilian Ambassador), fellow Society belles Helen Percy, the Duchess of Northumberland, and Edith, Marchioness of Londonderry, (daughter of Henry Chaplin), Royal physician, Sir Lois Knuthsen, and Hansel, the Prince of Pless (son of Daisy Cornwallis- West).

[694] A summary of Alfred House patients (in the Leadbetter Collection) shows that between 11 July 1927 and 1 September 1939, 4025 were treated there in the period.

[695] Royal Archives, RA AEC/GG/01/116.

[696] Ibid.

[697] See Bloch, Michael *Wallis & Edward Letters 1931-1937 The Intimate Correspondence of the Duke and Duchess of Windsor*. pgs 59-60, Penguin Books (1986).

[698] Royal Archives, RA AEC/GG/01/117.

[699] Almina continued living in London till the end of December 1939. She is listed as attending a dinner party on 14 December 1939, given by the Chilean Ambassador and his wife for the Brazilian Ambassador and his wife (all long standing friends of Almina). Additionally at this small dinner, were the Ambassadors of Egypt, Japan, Argentine, Spain and Italy. It was almost certainly concerned with the " What ifs? surrounding the early course of the war. The dinner companions also included Ronald (later, Sir Ronald) Cross, Minister of Economic Warfare (1939-40, later the Minister of Shipping); Lady Austin Chamberlain, a friend of Mussolini; Sir John Monck, an influential figure in diplomatic and Court circles and Lord Greville, an experienced hospital administrator. See *The Times* 15 December 1939.

[700] Arthur Fitzhardinge Berkeley (" Audax") Portman was a regular house party guest at Highclere for many years. He was the proprietor and editor of the *Horse and Hound*, and wrote under the name " Audex". A notable shot, Lord Carnarvon often invited him for pheasant shooting. Writing in "Horses Guns and Dogs" p171 (Pub 1903) he records the places where he had demonstrated his skills at pheasant shooting " and Highclere Castle, where the present Lord Carnarvon has some immense bags, and where in 1902 a party of five guns of which I was one, got 1302 pheasants in a day. "

Portman was also one of Carnarvon's Executors. His wife Mary (whom he married in 1915) was the widow of Fitzpatrick W B Praed.

[701] See *Resident alien : an Englishwoman in New York and Washington 1939-43,* Robert Hale. (1990) p.153.

[702] Seen in correspondence in Royal Archives Collection.

[703] Royal Archives, RA AEC/ GG/ 01/119.

[704] In later years Prince William of Gloucester died aged only 30 when his plane crashed near Wolverhampton on 28 August 1972. A study of porphyria (the malady suffered by William's ancestor George III) revealed that Prince William was treated for the same disease. William's parents outlived him and his brother Richard became Duke of Gloucester.

[705] Alice, Duchess of Gloucester had suffered previous miscarriages. See *The Memoirs of Princess Alice, Duchess of Gloucester.* Collins (1983) p.116. Almina spoke in later years referring to that fact that the Duchess's stay at The Glebe was inordinately long and cost [Almina] a fortune.

[706] Royal Archives, RA AEC/ GG/01/121.

[707] Deborah Vivien Cavendish, Dowager Duchess of Devonshire DCVO (born 31 March 1920), *née* the Hon. Deborah Freeman-Mitford.

[708] Correspondence between the author and Deborah, Duchess of Devonshire 2010. See also *Wait for Me* the Duchess's memoirs, published in 2010.

[709] A private source (please refer to author) indicates that at the height of the wartime air attacks on London, when the sirens rang out, Almina and her entourage encamped at the local shelter until the raid was over. Recalled later it was said that Almina " was always interested to know what was going on above ground" and coaxed someone to go and find out whether an explosion nearby was a bomb from the air or a gun fired from the ground.

[710] JTS's will records his name as James Thomas Stocks or Stocking.

[711] Leadbetter, interviews 2009 and 2010.

[712] Both JTS and Jack Humphries served in the Kings Royal Rifles in the First World War. Both men were excellent shots. JTS suffered burns and Jack was badly gassed in the trenches.

[713] Tony Leadbetter believes that his aunt Alice Butler was sent by Almina to train as a nurse at Salisbury General Hospital. This was after Eastmore closed, and it may have been after the Second World War had started. The venture was short lived, Alice was not cut out for nursing. One abiding memory (told to Tony by his aunt) is that Almina had sent Alice a set of silvered hair brushes, whilst at Salisbury.

[714] Alice Butler followed her mistress to London after the closure and sale of Eastmore on the Isle of Wight. Alice's elder sister Beatrice Anne Laura Butler (later Leadbetter), was always known as Anne. The girls' father Stanley Butler was a native of the Isle of Wight. On marriage Stanley moved to Amport in Hampshire, where the girls were born. His wife died of breast cancer and he later remarried, and had a further daughter, Audrey, a half-sister to Alice and Anne. Alice and Anne were *" put out to service"*. Anne ended up working in London for the Cory-Wright family as a nanny; the lady of the house she worked at being Felicity Tree, daughter of the actor/ manager Sir Herbert. Beerbohm Tree.

[715] Like JTS Peter Leadbetter served in the Kings Royal Rifles, he also served in the Black and Tans in Ireland and drove ambulances in the London Blitz.

[716] 32 Avenue Road was offered for sale by Maple & Co with a 21-year lease. It was described as a "delightful Regency Period Residence modernized at considerable cost, and having a fine underground ARP shelter." See *The Times* 30 September 1941.

[717] Ibid.

[718] E-mail correspondence between the author and Henry Keown-Boyd 2009.

[719] Almina wrote personally to all her staff at The Glebe to inform them of the reasons for the closure and sale. The letters were on black edged In Memoriam paper with the "AC" Coronet on the top, a style of writing paper she copied from Queen Alexandra.

[720] Souhami, Diana, *The Trials of Radclyffe Hall*, Weidenfeld & Nicolson. (1998).

[721] Ibid, but see an earlier biography of Radclyffe Hall by Lady Una Vincenzo Troubridge

[722] Ibid.

[723] In *Laughter From a cloud* Weidenfeld and Nicolson London (1980) Laura, Duchess of Marlborough, refers to the recruitment as matron for her Red Cross Hospital at Himley as " a most charming woman called Lewis. She had been at Lady Carnarvon's luxurious and well known nursing home in London"

[724] Leadbetter Collection.

[725] Ibid.

[726] Ibid.

[727] Ibid.

[728] Ibid.

[729] The name Bicknoller is supposed to be derived from the ancient British words Bychan, meaning small and Alwar, meaning a treasury.

[730] Jack Humphries stayed with a Mr and Mrs Thomas. He died in the 1940s from a chest infection. Tony Leadbetter recalls him with affection as he taught him a good deal, including how to tell the time and tie his shoelaces.

[731] Leadbetter, interviews 2009 and 2010. JTS's children Doreen, John (Jack) and Jim were allowed to call Almina " Auntie".

[732] Tony Leadbetter adds that the same photograph (that he describes as Almina in her VAD / Red Cross uniform) was placed beside JTS's bed wherever they lived.

[733] Leadbetter Collection.

[734] Ibid.

[735] Ibid.

[736] Among Tilly's personal papers in the Max Reinhardt Archives at the State University of New York at Binghamton.

[737] A petition through the London courts by the 6th Earl was dismissed in November 1945 on the grounds that the court was not satisfied that Tilly had deserted him. In July 1947 a decree nisi was granted and the marriage finally ended. See also the late Michael Davie's article in *The Observer* of 18 January 1976 reflecting (in the week of her memorial service in London) on Tilly's life and her contemporaries from the days of CB Cochran. Porchey attended her memorial service.

[738] Born Ivy Sweet (1908-2003), her stage name was "Jeanne Stuart", married and divorced Sir Bernard Docker, Jeanne also used the title " Lady Docker". She later married Baron Eugene de Rothschild.

[739] The Leadbetter Collection. See The Carnarvon Letters (1984).

[740] Almina was worried about this further instance of cousins marrying each other, especially with the past occurances of premature deaths in the Wendell and Herbert /Howard family and (in her medical experience) there was a high risk of congenital deformity.

[741] Leadbetter, interviews 2009 and 2010.

[742] *The Times*, 26 July 1978.

[743] A private source (refer to author for details) describes how Alice had fallen in love with a farmer (although unnamed this is unmistakably JTS) who turned out to have more interest in Almina.

[744] Ronald Tree had two sons to his first wife, Nancy Perkins Field (later Lancaster), and a daughter with Marietta, Penelope Tree (born 1950) – well-known model companion of society photographer David Bailey. Marietta had a daughter Francis (Frankie (born 1940) Fitzgerald from her marriage to Desmond Fitzgerald. See Seebohm, Caroline: *No Regrets: The Life of Marietta Tree,* Simon & Schuster. (1997).

[745] Leadbetter Collection.

[746] Tony Leadbetter says the letters were read and written by his mother with the help of an English-French dictionary.

[747] Perhaps a memory of observing the Red Indians of North America during Almina's visit there in 1903.

[748] Ibid.

[749] One of the Highclere gun dogs. There were other dogs kept as pets in the 1940s onwards. A cocker spaniel named Betsy and Rover, an Old English sheepdog that Almina insisted on calling "Tiger" (Colonel Dennistoun's pet name).

[750] Tony Leadbetter recalls that at Orchard Grove Almina had a good deal of Rothschild Sevres white and gold dessert and tableware and " masses of Carnarvon glasses, for every type of drink.."

[751] JTS discouraged Almina from talking at any length or detail about her past life. It was only after JTS's death 1963 that she rejoiced in remembering things and shared these memories with Anne and Tony Leadbetter.

[752] Jim Criddle who was a butcher slaughtered all the animals for the table at Orchard Grove by trade. Criddle also salted and cured the carcases.

[753] Almina had a habit of sprinkling lavish quantities of white pepper on her food.

[754] Popular from the First World War onwards, a combination of bourbon, cognac, conintreau, lemon juice and crushed ice. The trick was to get the right mix of sweet and sour

[755] Later vicar of Withycombe, Minehead died 1964. See The Times, 4 February 1964.

[756] Ibid.

[757] Tony Leadbetter cites an instance – many years after Almina's death when he was reunited with a schoolboy contemporary from the 1940s. Almina had arranged and paid for the boy to go to London to have a squint corrected in his eye.

[758] In later years Tony Leadbetter discovered a series of nude photographs of JTS and Anne that each had taken of the other's private parts.

[759] Leadbetter, interviews 2009 and 2010.

[760] Cyril Bowdler Henry FDS, LRCP, MRCS, a legendry Society dentist based in Harley Street. Following his death at a great age on 26 March 1981 his memorial service at Marylebone Parish Church was filled to capacity by a who's who of the rich, famous of the previous generation of Society folk.

[761] Wenets Denture Fixative Powder.

[762] Almina's favourite meal in these establishments was Vienna "Wiener" Schnitzel

[763] Royal Archives, RA AEC /GG/01/122.

[764] Among the Carnarvon jewels presented by the 5th Earl to his bride included a " diamond coronet, an emerald and diamond tiara, a pearl and diamond necklace, two rows of pearls with diamond cluster, one long row of pearls, a diamond aigrette, a diamond and sapphire bracelet, a ruby and diamond bangle, an emerald and diamond devant corsage, Louis XVI bows and a pearl and diamond ring..." (Source : Lord Carnarvon's wedding day coverage in Newbury Advertiser, 1895)

[765] Winstone, H.V.F., *Howard Carter and the discovery of the tomb of Tutankhamun,* Appendix 1 Barzan Publishing. (2006). Tony Leadbetter expands on the use of "green ink", which was commonly used by the British Secret Service. The 6th Earl was a great horse racing pal of Major The Hon. Lionel Samuel Montagu, DSO (1883-1948), who often visited Highclere, and told tales of his service with the Special Operations Executive in WW2. Porchey lapped all this up and envied his friend doing such work, since he was stuck in a dreadfully dull admin job at Salisbury. [Montagu's file is in National Archives, ref HS9/1052/4.]

[766] Leadbetter, interviews 2009 and 2010.

[767] Jim Criddle, his wife Sally and their daughter Mary moved into Higher Hopcott with Almina. They had their own living room and kitchen and two bedrooms.

[768] Leadbetter, interviews 2009 and 2010.

[769] Ibid.

[770] The 6th himself had wounds from his past encounters with the Inland Revenue. In 1935 he lost an appeal over income of the Carnarvon Estates Company (amount to £23,591) which the Courts ruled was *his* income and subject to super tax. See *The Guardian* of 9 April 1935.

[771] Ibid. See also Appendix to Winstone, HVF (2006), *Howard Carter and the Discovery of the Tomb of Tutankhamun.* Barzan Publishing (2006).

[772] *Tilloy,* a filly that Lord Carnarvon bought in France for £10,000, won at Newbury and Birmingham, but failed to win the St Ledger (although it was well tipped)

[773] Leadbetter Collection. The room was one of the drawing rooms that Almina had redecorated c1900 with Alfred de Rothschild funding. The curtains were of green silk, a wedding present from Alfred.

[774] Culled from Bristol newspapers of 1951. See also *The Times* and *Guardian* of 22 September 1951.

[775] Ibid.

[776] Ibid.

[777] Ibid.

[778] Ibid.

[779] Ibid.

[780] See National Archives, Kew file IR59/520–2.

[781] *The Times*, 18 July 1945.

[782] Leadbetter Collection.

[783] Ibid.

[784] Barow, A. *Gossip: A History of High Society from 1920 to 1970*. Pan Books. (1978).

[785] *Daily Mirror*, 23 February 1952, describes how raiders stole five miniature paintings and a fur cape owned by the 6th Earl's daughter, Lady Penelope.

[786] Leadbetter, interviews 2009 and 2010.

[787] In July 1958, *L'Amour Oiseleur*, an early painting by Boucher of four amoretti playing with doves, which had made 600 guineas in the Sale of the Century in 1925, fell under the hammer for 1,250 guineas.

[788] A short family intimation of his death is in the *British Medical Journal*, 4 April 1953, p. 792.

[789] Probate Registry, London records: "1953: Johnson, Marcus Beauchamp of Camberwell House, Peckham, London died 8 March 1953. Administration London 31 July to Stella Mary Kennington (wife of William Kennington) Effect £3,555.1s 3d."

[790] See also Brown, Ivor , *The Bedside Guardian 2. 1952–3*. London: Collins (1953).

[791] In *The Heart Has Its Reasons Michael* Joseph (1956), the Duchess's memoirs, she refers to going into Alfred House in November 1931. See also Bloch, M, *Wallis and Edward Letters 1931-1937 The Intimate Correspondence*, Weidenfeld & Nicolson (1986). For more details of the Duchess of Windsor's illnesses see Higham, Charles, *Mrs Simpson: Secret Lives of the Duchess of Windsor*. Sidgwick & Jackson. (1988).

[792] Almina conducted private sales with a number of London dealers including Duveens and Peter Sparks of John Sparks and Co, which specialised in Chinese artefacts. A schedule from PhD student Ching-Yi Huang from the Sparks Archives shows scores of transactions between 1916 and 1940. Almina also received the occasional gift from Sparks. Messrs Stuart and Turner, with a London shop at 13 Soho Square and at Newberry, valued the contents of Eastmore in 1938. Almina was on friendly terms with Cecil Turner of that firm.

[793] Sir Brograve had been an MP from 1931 –1945 and a company chairman with Pyrotenax Ltd (dealing in copper cabling) from its founding in 1936 until he retired on health grounds in 1962, albeit remaining a director. During part of that time the 6th Earl extensively invested in this company and describes the rewarding success of this in his memoirs *No Regrets*.

[794] Leadbetter Collection.

[795] Almina adored lapsang souchong tea. This was served at the launch of *The Life and Secrets of Almina Carnarnon* in Newport, in 2011.

[796] *The Times*, 10 April 1954 and 15 October 1955. Dr Nicolas Bell, Music Archivist at the British Library, advises "From Sir Malcolm's 1954 diary I can tell you that he went to Bristol on 9 April for a rehearsal in the evening, stayed at the Grand Hotel, rehearsed 2.30–3 on the 10th before the concert at 7.30 (broadcast live), and on the 11th (Palm Sunday) he has written '10–1 BBC Bristol 2.45'; he then caught the 7.25 train arriving in Paddington at 10.25. But alas there is no sign of Almina, and the 1955 diary is one of the few that is missing."

[797] *The Times*, 23 September 1950, reported Catherine Grenfell married Don Stuart Momand in London on 22 September 1950. Almina and Catherine kept in touch and met together in the South of France and London – for one of Almina's birthdays Catherine organised a joint weekend at Claridge's hotel. Sometimes Catherine would make the journey to see Almina at her home, and then the visits were quite an occasion, the Momands arriving in their huge American car, often a Cadillac, "and always bearing great gifts" of hampers and clothes. Tony Leadbetter recounts a gift of a sports jacket from Catherine. The 6th Countess, who had also suffered at the end of the 6th Earl's wrath, was overwrought on hearing of her ex-mother-in-law's fate and that the head of the Carnarvon family had stooped to such lengths to hurt his mother. The Times, 12 April 1977, reported that Catherine died at Lausanne on Saturday 8 April 1977 "beloved wife of Don and adored mother of Porchey and Penelope". Her funeral was held at Highclere on Wednesday 13 April 1977. Don, who had a daughter, Virginia, died in 1983.

[798] However, according to Amanda Murray in " All the King's Horses's : A Celebration of Royal Horses from 1066 to the Present Day"(2006)... Princess Elizabeth first met Porchester in the autumn of 1943.

[799] See Shawcross, William, *Queen and Country*. BBC. (2002). The tale is related with quotes from Lord Porchester.

[800] *Waterloo Sunday Courier*, Iowa, 30 September 1951.

[801] Flamini, Ronald, *Sovereign: Elizabeth II and the Windsor Dynasty*. Bantam Press. (1991)

[802] Ibid.

[803] Private source, please refer to author for further details.

[804] *The Avalanche Journal*, 14 November 1976.

[805] In addition to Porchester, regular members included the Earl of Dalkeith (1923–2007), the Marquis of Blandford (b.1926), Billy Wallace (b.1927), Mark Bonham Carter (1922–1994), Colin Tennant (1926–2010) and Tom Egerton (1918–1999).

[806] *Wisconsin Rapids Daily Tribune*, 28 April 1960.

[807] *Ogden Standard Examiner*, 10 August 1952.

[808] Leadbetter, interviews 2009 and 2010.

[809] At Highclere the Herbert (the Carnarvon family name) coat of arms is on display. Beneath that is the family motto in old French, *Ung Je Serviray* (One Only Will I Serve).

[810] *The Brownsville Herald* published a report dated 13 April 1954 saying that the Queen used Lord Porchester to place bets on horses. The next day the offending columnist published an abject apology making clear the Queen, whilst a horse owner and racing fan, did not bet.

[811] Leadbetter Collection.

[812] To Almina such stairs represented a working class household, and she spoke of seeing women on their knees endlessly cleaning and scrubbing and whitening them.

[813] Tom Page, who was born in Bristol and lived in Cotham Vale between 1961 and 1963 remembers Almina living in the end house on the corner of Hampton Road and Aberdeen Road, Bristol. " I remember an elderly lady dressed in old fashioned clothes with a chauffeur driven Black Morris Oxford car.."

[814] Leadbetter, interviews 2009and 2010

[815] *The Times*, 7 May 1955.

[816] Leadbetter, interviews 2009 and 2010.

[817] See personal file of Earl of Gowrie VC, GCMG, CB, and DSO in National Archives, Kew Ref: WO 138/56.

[818] One of Almina's last Society appearances, on 30 July 1965, was to attend a memorial service for Lady Gowrie (Sandy's widow) at St George's Chapel, Windsor Castle, at which Joan Sutherland sang *Ave Maria* as a tribute to the Gowries' strong links with Australians, as much loved colonial dignitaries. Despite conducting an on/off affair with Sandy Gowrie, neither Gowrie nor Almina broke their secret pact of time spent together. Almina also admired her lover's wife, Zara, Lady Gowrie and especially her supreme courage over the loss of her eldest son in action in North Africa in the Second World War.

[819] See Mosley, Charlotte, *The Mitfords: Letters between Six Sisters*. Harper. (2007)

[820] A card in the Leadbetter Collection from Henderson dated 9 December 1957 says: "I hear very regularly from Lady Carnarvon."

[821] Among the co-signatories was Lavina, Duchess of Norfolk (1916–1995), Edwina Mountbatten (1901–1960) and Mary, Duchess of Marlborough (1900–1961).

[822] *Bristol Evening World*, 1956.

[823] Home of Lord and Lady Rupert Nevill. It was at Uckfield House that Princess Margaret and Peter Townsend spent a dramatic last weekend together before Margaret announced that their romance was over.

[824] *Billings Gazette*, 29 December 1955.

[825] Tony Leadbetter recalls that when asked what she wanted to drink Jeanie requested a glass of milk, to which Almina responded with " Nonsense, you will have a gin and tonic."

[826] Tony Leadbetter recalls that the 6th Earl always called his mother "Annie".

[827] Leadbetter Collection.

[828] Almina was often driven to Highclere by another of her regular taxi drivers named Stanley Morse. In the late 1950s and early 1960s this was to deliver food hampers – made up by Anne Leadbetter for Lady Porchester's guests. One of Anne's specialities was a chocolate cake made from French chocolate.

[829] This is sometimes recorded on the Internet as "Jordy".

[830] The Leadbetter Collection retains a copy. "A Christening Prayer. Into Thy hands dear Lord we place our little son, he is very holy for his life has just begun. May he be with happy spirit blessed and hate and greed and selfishness never steep into his breast. May he serve his God and fellow man, and dear Lord please give him full span to justify the beating of his little heart, in this troubled world to take his humble part. Guard and protect him not to be bitter in strife. Teach him the greatest power on earth, is the power from above, which gave him birth. George Reginald Oliver Herbert Nov 10, 1956."

[831] Including the French Oaks and the St Ledger, notably in the Queen's Jubilee year of 1977.

[832] See Willett, Peter, *Dick Hern*. Hodder & Stoughton, 2000. In December 1984 Hern was seriously disabled in a hunting accident, after which time he used a wheelchair. In 1988 he was controversially sacked from his position as trainer for Queen Elizabeth II at West Ilsley by her racing manager, the 7th Earl of Carnarvon – Hern was recovering from heart surgery at the time. Later a

compromise was reached whereby Hern shared the stable with the new incumbent – William Hastings-Bass (later Earl of Huntingdon) for a year before moving to Hamdan Al Maktoum's Kingwood House Stables in Lambourn. Dick Hern died in 2002 in Oxford, England at the age of 81.

[833] When Prince Charles was at Cheam School, Headley, Berkshire in the late 1950s, his parents often stayed at Highclere with the Porchesters.

[834] Anne Leadbetter provided catering hampers for Jeanie Porchester's Royal visitors, notably supplying such treats as cucumber sandwiches, chocolate cake, éclairs and coconut macaroons. Tony Leadbetter remarks " All Jeanie Porchester had to do was to get her staff to boil the kettle."

[835] The Queen went to the Wallop ranch in order to see the horse stocks after a Canadian tour with Prince Philip, who'd visited the ranch in 1969. Philip returned to the UK and the Queen, with her entourage of detectives, enjoyed three days of Wallop hospitality, an event overshadowed by the IRA attack on the Grand Hotel, Brighton, and its attempt to kill Margaret Thatcher. See Shawcross, William, Queen and Country. BBC (2002). pp. 128–9.

[836] In 1993, the New York Times Magazine repeated the conundrum 'Get hold of a picture of Prince Andrew and then one of Lord Porchester at the same age. You'll see that Prince Philip could never have been Andy's father.' See also Kelley, Kitty " The Royals" Warner Books. (1997).

[837] Interview with Jeanie, Lady Carnarvon, in The Times, 12 February 1996.

[838] Lacey, Robert, Royal: Her Majesty Queen Elizabeth II. Little, Brown, (2002).

[839] Almina was still a key part of matters relating to the actions and decisions of the remnants of the 5th Earl's legacies, administered by Carnarvon estate trustees. It's Tony Leadbetter view that in order to obtain Almina's co-operation, the 6th Earl used Lord Porchester as a " go-between" with Almina as her grandson was " the apple of her eye". In exchange for her signature, Almina did not miss the opportunity to extract funds from the 6th Earl for general living costs. In one instance a solicitor arrived acting for Highclere arrived to see Almina. She sent him away with a flea in his ear, suggesting she was no pushover, bargaining on getting things on her terms.

[840] Leadbetter, interviews 2009 and 2010.

[841] Tony Leadbetter advises that the greengrocers shop was A J Todd's (known as Toddie) "on the corner, the other end of Aberdeen Road, now an Oxfam charity shop." Alfred Jones, PhD writes : "Anne Leadbetter was what I would call a typical "in service" person. I was honest with her wanting her to know that I was not trying to be friendly with her for any other reason than to seek her help in meeting the Countess I told her about my father taking me to Egypt as a child before the war, of my work in cataloguing scarabs at the British Museum and my great interest in Egyptology in general. At the same time, I think she liked the attention paid to her by a young university student, I found her to be likable. intelligent and suspected that she perhaps did not have much of a social life. At that time, one did not talk very much about personal things. Had it not been for her help, I would never have been able to meet the Countess."

[842] Tony Leadbetter comments " The coloured slides must have been in Almina's Queen Anne walnut desk.."

[843] E-mails between Dr Alfred Jones and the author 25-27 February 2011.

[844] The Daily Express, 30 August 1958. Tony Leadbetter recalls this was for a prostate operation. Almina's reaction at the time was " Why on earth does he

have to go to New York, for such an operation, when there are surgeons who can do it in London?"

[845] Lady Margaret's funeral attendees are reported in *The Times*, 17 September 1958. Her husband, Sir George Duckworth, Secretary of the Royal Commission on Historical Monuments from 1908-1933, died in 1934. [For a moving tribute on Lady Margaret see Vanessa Bell's *" Sketches in Pen and Ink"* pages 83-93 *" My Sister-In-Law"* (1998) Pimlico.]

[846] JTS's daughter Doreen Stocking (now Mrs Watkins) declined to contribute her memories of Almina to the author adding in an email (2010) "Without seeming discourteous, I have no wish to give any personal details of my relationship with Lady Carnarvon."

[847] JTS was a Freemason and an active member in a Masonic Lodge at Exeter. There was often great anxiety felt (by Almina and the household) when JTS went off alone to evening meetings of his Lodge and considerable worry expressed about him driving back in the dark in all weathers over the old A38.

[848] According to Leadbetter this picture features on the cover of the 8th Countess's book on Carnarvon and Carter. See Carnarvon, Fiona [8th] Countess Carnarvon & *Carter*, Highclere Enterprises LLP, (2007).

[849] *Tutankhamen: Life and Death of a Pharoah* by Christiane Desroches-Noblecourt, New York Graphic Society, (1963) was one book purchased by Almina in this period, the author being a French Egyptologist. Almina was irked by the dedication in the Acknowledgements to the 6th Earl. He had been consulted, and was praised for his "forthright information" and his " an element of first-hand experience".

[850] One single cutting in the Leadbetter Collection (marked up in manuscript *"The Times*, 20 October 1940" but believed to be quite a bit later than this date) is notable for being retained by Almina (or perhaps Anne). "Tut-ankh-Amen: Thousands of former patients, of Almina Countess of Carnarvon, whose nursing home was for many years one of the best known in London, must have thought of her when they tuned into the BBC broadcast about Tut-ankh-Amen's tomb, which was discovered by the fifth Earl of Carnarvon in association with Howard Carter. The broadcast dealt somewhat luridly with Lord Carnarvon's untimely death, supposed by superstitious people to have been one of a chain of misfortunes befalling those who unearthed the royal mummies and treasure. But if the many friends of Lady Carnarvon (who later married Lieut. -Col. Dennistoun), remembered her, the BBC did not. It would have been courteous, not to say prudent in the interest of accuracy, to have consulted her about a broadcast concerning her husband's death and an enterprise whose completion she herself afterwards financed."

[851] Hooke, Nina Warner and Thomas, Gil, *Marshall Hall*. Arthur Barker Ltd. (1966)

[852] Birkett died in 1962. See Bardens, D, *Lord Justice Birkett*. Robert Hales Ltd and Hyde (1962) Montgomery, H, *Norman Birkett: The Life of Lord Birkett of Ulverston*. Hamish Hamilton (1964).

[853] Leadbetter interviews 2009 and 2010. Tony Leadbetter adds: "Almina discussed the Colonel openly when the Norman Birkett book was published in 1964 - a year after JTS's death. (JTS discouraged Almina from talking about past deeds and misdeeds, because some matters were painful; recalling some people (like Dorothy Dennistoun) upset her, brought on tears and had a

tendency of leading to her to partaking of too many whiskies and soda.   ). The Birkett book was on display in most of the bookshop windows in Bristol. Everyone who came to 19 Hampton Road made some reference (tactfully) about it and Almina seemed happy to discuss it and put her case forward." Curious, given the cost to her of still defending the Colonel.

854 Ibid.

855 Ibid.

856 One instance recalled by Tony Leadbetter was of Almina seeing Hon. (William) Neville Berry (1914-1998) at Victoria Station wearing brown shoes. He was a newspaper magnate (of Allied Newspapers(Kemsley House) whose brother had married a Rothschild. Neville was carrying a vast collection of newspapers with him to review. The poor man was given no chance to go through these on the journey. Almina grabbed him, demanding he keep her company all the way down to Cannes.

857 Tony Leadbetter recalls that Almina had a short fuse when it came to being dipleased about poor service in hotels or on board trains. When any part of a meal was not much liked Almina made no bones of crying out loudly and harshly. A typical remark being " Take *that* away from me, at once!"

858 *Daily Mirror*, 22 May 1920.

859 Leadbetter, interviews 2009 and 2010.

860 Almina became agitated on the telephone when giving her surname, and then being asked to repeat it. She spelt out the letters C-A-R-N-A-R-V-O-N, adding she was *not* a Welsh town.

861 Almina received complimentary supplies of wine from a London wine merchant she knew from her nursing home days. Some of this wine was brought into use for parties, but much of it was bartered with a Bristol wine merchant in exchange for whisky.

862 Leadbetter, interviews 2009 and 2010. See also Lomax, James and Rothwell, James, *Country House Silver: From Dunham Massey*. The National Trust, (2007) p. 102.

863 Leadbetter, interviews 2009 and 2010

864 Almina always had a telephone beside her bed. It was her favourite means of keeping in touch. She pounced on any telephone calls coming into the house. Tony Leadbetter remembers that their telephone number was identical to a local hospital, but for one single digit.   Many stray calls were received as a result. Almina took charge of the situation with gusto. She delighted in redirecting such callers.

865 Leadbetter, interviews 2009 and 2010.

866 A telegram [in the Leadbetter Collection] from Lady Evelyn in Marseilles to Almina in Bristol dated 7 April 1963 reads "looking forward to a gossip with you".

867 There was a television at Hampton Road from around 1958. Almina enjoyed Armchair Theatre but usually fell into a very deep sleep during the programme, sometimes scaring Anne enough into checking her breathing with a mirror. JTS enjoyed Grandstand and the Boxing.

868 Almina had come to expect being kept at a distance from any Royal embarrassment, based on an earlier event at Highclere. Tony Leadbetter writes: "One of the visits by Almina to Highclere coincided with the Queen calling in to

see her new godson [Geordie, the present 8th Earl]. She [Almina] was bustled away to ensure neither woman met each other."

[869] During research the author gleaned a little about Dorothy Dennistoun's later life from Adrian, Lord Palmer of Manderston, whose mother befriended Dorothy while on a trip to Spain in the 1970s. In the summer of 1928 Dorothy remarried Colonel Nicholas Woevodsky, who had been cited in her close company during trips abroad during the court proceedings if 1925. The Colonel was the son of Admiral Woevodsky, an ADC to the last Russian Czar. He had been an Air Attache in the Russian Embassy during the Great War. Dorothy enjoyed life as the proprietor of an antique furniture business, under the name of "Rufus" in Brook Street in the West End of London, which Woevodsky helped her to run as manager. They left England and both became domiciled in Spain, where they created the most beautiful gardens at Cap Roig. Dorothy died in 1980. The author also exchanged emails with Amanda Bradley, a lecturer at a Japanese University, who owns a wristwatch allegedly owned by Almina, but possibly given to Dorothy as a present. Amanda writes: "Many years ago in Barcelona, we were talking about the supposed owner of the watch in a class of wealthy and gossipy housewives and one told me that she [probably meaning Dorothy] had run off with a Russian diplomat and that they had both lived in the villa next to hers, indeed on the Costa Brava."

[870] Tony Leadbetter is not sure whether it was his mother, Anne, or Almina who first found JTS dead. The morning house routine was for Almina to rise first and bathe, followed by Anne, who would see to the breakfast. Almina retreated to her bedroom, for up wards of an hour to massage her face with Ponds cold cream. Alarm bells would have rung as JTS was expected to rise and run his own bath. There is evidence to indicate that JTS suffered an earlier heart attack. This was when he was admitted to hospital a year or so before his death after damaging an Achilles tendon in an accident whilst pushing his car (which had stalled). He had an operation and may have suffered a post-operative heart attack.

[871] Tony Leadbetter recalls: "I was once allowed to examine the signet ring [which must have been a gift from Almina to JTS]. There was an inscription and the word 'Marie' [inside], which I feel was the one name that JTS used for her during their relationship."

[872] An exception was the owner of the company that JTS worked for. JTS's boss and his wife were also regular visitors to Hampton Road at social evenings. Almina found a medical interest too as the man was an amputee.

[873] Tony Leadbetter recalls the scene as being one from a black, almost comic farce. It seems that the taxi driver knew the men at the Crematorium well enough to be allowed inside the area where the coffins were placed for the incinerators. He spotted that JTS's coffin was about to be placed inside, (since Almina had already had a funeral service for him, with only her being present). The taxi driver alerted the staff to the fact that the mourners were only just arriving, outside the Crematorium. The funeral service had to be repeated.

[874] Probate Registry, London: "Stocks, James Thomas of 19 Hampton Road, Bristol 6 died 12 December 1963. Probate London 4 March 1964 to Norman Eric King, heating engineer and Audrey King (wife of the said Norman Eric King, Effects £2,711." Almina may have told JTS that she would ensure he took possession of 19 Hampton Road following her death. The will dated 18 February

1962 includes this part "if the house 19 Hampton Road, Bristol 6 be standing in my name at the time of my decease that the deeds and ownership be passed to the said Anne Leadbetter, I do this in appreciation of the love and devotion she has shown me over the many years of association of the same love she has shown to my children."

[875] Leadbetter, interviews 2009 and 2010. Tony Leadbetter saw at first hand the rapid rise in cases of heart disease in Britain in the 1960s. He remarked that very often when he cleared out a deceased patients' locker, proprietory brands of indigestion tablets (e.g. Setlers or Rennies) were found. Many people misdiagnosed themselves as suffering from indigestion when they were really suffering angina attacks and each time this was wrongly treated it increased damage to their heart muscles.

[876] Leadbetter, interviews 2009 and 2010.

[877] Ibid.

[878] Ibid.

[879] Leadbetter Collection.

[880] The morning ritual at Hampton Road was for Anne to prepare breakfast. Almina always made some polite complimentary remark such as. " Oh, I see we have some glorious buttered toast this morning." Anne came to know (by name) Almina's Society friends and associates. She always scrutinised The Times obituaries before Almina read the morning paper and so prepared her for any "shocks".

[881] Tony Leadbetter remarks that he was also affected by JTS's death in a way he didn't expect, because of the strain he saw that it had on his mother and Almina.

[882] Tony Leadbetter recalls " *Gordon Paul was the surgeon who operated on my mother, twice. He was a Bristol consultant, and a Fellow of the Royal College of Surgeons. He was one of the few men still around c1966 who had worked and had been partly trained by Lord Moynihan, and had attended operating sessions at Alfred House. He referred to Almina as " the old girl" and always asked how she was keeping. Paul used to be invited to most of Almina's important lunch-time meetings at Hampton Road. He was among the last links whose company she enjoyed who could share memories of the close friendship with Berkeley Moynihan and the heyday of nursing activities at Alfred House.*"

[883] Captain Bill Warwick commanded the Queen Mary and *Queen Elizabeth* and QE2 liners. His son Ronald's bride was Karen Chassiron. Ronald retired from Cunard in 2006.

[884] According to Leadbetter the 6th Earl told his mother about this time that he had been approached by a Holywood film company who wanted to make a film about the discovery of Tutankhamun. Almina remarked. " Well, who's going to play my part, Elizabeth Taylor?"

[885] Little Streele, Framfield, bought 1936. Classified from 1953 as a Grade II building. See *The Times*, 11 March 1936.

[886] Tony always delighted Almina with breakfasts of Melba toast and scrambled eggs (sometimes with smoked salmon added). She also relished Tony's mash potato with cream, butter, egg yolk and white (added separately) with plenty of salt and pepper. During the scare over Almina's health he was dispatched by Almina to see Anne (whilst she was receiving in care at a nursing home) to obtain the exact recipe for hollandaise sauce.

[887] Leadbetter Collection.

[888] Tony adds " I polished the dining room table until it shone like glass. "

[889] Tony was accomplished at folding table napkins, a skill learned as a footman at Cornbury.

[890] Tony Leadbetter advises that in the early days of visiting Almina, Jo Giles came to the house in her nurses uniform. It gave the impression to neighbours that Almina was being attended upon because of ill-health. But these early visits by Jo were purely social.

[891] Leadbetter, interviews 2009 and 2010.

[892] Tony Leadbetter believes that Almina's GP Dr Hugh Pyke may have been consulted (by telephone) or could have been called out to first examine Almina. Efforts by the author to trace Almina's last companion, Jo Giles, have not been successful.

[893] The Times, 9 May 1969.

[894] The Times, 12 May 1969.

[895] The Bristol Evening Post, 9 May 1969, contains errors relating to her birth, her age at marriage, the reasons for not attending the opening of King Tut's tomb, and the period of her life when she was involved in nursing.

[896] Almina had further antagonised Tony Leadbetter as she had asked Highclere's solicitors to enquire about whether Anne Leadbetter had made a will.

[897] Leadbetter, interviews 2009 and 2010.

[898] Leadbetter Collection. Tony Leadbetter (born 1938) spent his career as a nurse, in Cyprus during National Service with the RAMC, he later did his SRN training in Cardiff, Almina attended his graduation, with Tony's mother, Anne. In the Leadbetter Collection is a telegram from Almina's daughter, Lady Evelyn Beauchamp, to Anne, sending her congratulations on Tony gaining his SRN status. Tony worked at various hospitals including St Cadocs, Caerleon, Newport, South Wales and throughout the Bristol area, in particular at the Bristol Eye Hospital, and Chesterfield and Homeopathic Hospitals, Bristol. One of Tony's proudest possession, (a gift from Almina), is the gold pin she wore to keep her nurses's hat, made of organza silk, in position on her head when touring the hospital wards.

[899] Leadbetter, interviews 2009 and 2010.

[900] Andrew Collins and Chris Ogilvie Herald who were researching for their book Tutankhamun: The Exodus Conspiracy: The Truth Behind Archaeology's Greatest Mystery. Virgin. (2002).

[901] Geordie, Lord Porchester (the 8th Earl from September 2001 to date) was fully aware of who Tony Leadbetter was in the context on his great grandmother's life. Tony's mother Anne made Geordie's christening shawl. But he had met Tony only as a child. In 1968, two of the 7th Earl's children (including Geordie, then Lord Porchester) were taken by their nanny, Angela, to see Almina at 19 Hampton Road. They stayed a few days.

[902] Letter dated 1 June 1996 held by Tony Leadbetter.

[903] From the time that Elisabeth, Countess of Carnarvon (second wife of the 4th Earl, who was very much High Church of England), demanded French Protestant tutors for her two sons Aubrey and Mervyn, but some acknowledgement of the Church of Rome was later tolerated.

[904] Letter to the author received 20 November 2010.

[905] Private source, contact the author for details. Attempts by the author to verify this further has met with silence.

[906] Email exchange and personal meeting with Peter Bance, author of *Sovereign, Squire and Rebel: Maharajah Duleep Singh and the Heirs of a Lost Kingdom*, Coronet House Publishing Ltd. (2009). Given the regularity of visits to Highclere Castle by Princes Victor and Frederick Duleep Singh (which is invariably reflected in the Highclere visitors book) such information, as this would have been very useful to Bance.

[907] See Review of *Lady Almina And the Real Downton Abbey : The Lost Legacy of Highclere Castle* : Hodder & Stoughton (2011) by the Author on Amazon web site and Google Books.

[908] See however, Christopher Wilson's article in the Daily Mail of 21 October 2011 " Downton's greatest secret: A lonely countess and her illicit love affair with an Indian Prince…..".

[909] The dedication in the 6th Earl's first book was not to a parent or ex-wife or child; it was to the Earl's faithful secretary Crystal Stubbins. Miss Stubbins, " *My Dear Friend Crystal"* . served the 6th Earl for more than 40 years.

[910] From newspaper reports syndicated throughout the USA in November 1976 when the 6th Earl was in America to promote his book *No Regrets*.

[911] William Hickey, *Daily Express*, 5 November 1976.

[912] A transcript of the interview is reproduced in Michael Parkinson's *Parky's People* published by Hodder & Stoughton (2010) . See pgs 319-323 *Lord Carnarvon – a portrait of an English aristocrat.*

[913] *The Salina Journal* of 20 March 2000 cites this from *The Daily Telegraph Book of Obituaries: A Celebration of Eccentric Lives* (produced in several volumes).

[914] Collins died from cancer. He is buried next to Ronald Tree in Spelsbury churchyard near Charlbury.

[915] In her last hours Alice Butler was comforted at Westminster Hospital by (the late) Lady Anne Tree and Lady Elizabeth Cavendish, the two daughters of Mary Devonshire (1895-1988). Source: correspondence between the author and Lady Elizabeth Cavendish and also Deborah, Duchess of Devonshire, 2009.

[916] *The Guardian*, 14 September 2001.

[917] At St Nicholas' Church, Newbury on 17 January 2002. See *The Times*, 18 January 2002 and *Daily Express*, 16 October 2002

[918] *The Times*, 8 March 1988.

[919] Ibid.

[920] Ibid.

[921] Ibid.

[922] See Reeves, Nicholas, *The Search for Tutankhamen. The Final Chapter*, Aramco World, Vol 39, no 6 (November–December 1899), pp. 6–13.

[923] *Mail on Sunday*, 3 October 2010.

Contact William Cross at williecross@aol.com

About the Author

William Cross (Will) spent 28 years as a Civil Servant in London. He took early retirement in July 2005 to concentrate on writing and research. His roots are Scottish, although he now lives in Wales. He is the author of many articles and booklets on Scottish history and genealogy topics.

He is a regular Lecturer at the Society of Genealogists, London, on Scottish subjects. He was Editor of Renfrewshire Family History Society's Journal from 1999-2011. A Fellow of the Society of Antiquaries of Scotland since 1984, he is also a founder member of Newport's *Screwpacket* Playwrights and an authority on the Morgan women of Tredegar House, the one time seat of the Lords Tredegar. Will is also a member of the Society of Authors.

Along with a writing partner Monty Dart, he completed in 2010, a biography (as yet unpublished) of Hon. Gwyneth Ericka Morgan entitled *A Beautiful Nuisance*. Since then they have taken up their own individual writing projects and worked jointly on others, their latest joint work is on Ronald Firbank, whose grave in Rome's *Campo Verano* Cemetery Monty and Will have been restoring over the last few years.

Will Cross is married to Perry and they have two grown-up sons and two grandchildren.

In 2011, Will published a follow up book on Almina, Countess of Carnarvon, *Lady Carnarvon's Nursing Homes : Nursing the Privileged in Wartime and Peace.*

Two new books are planned for 2012. *The Dustbin Case* (due out in the Spring) will reproduce the 17 days of proceedings in the High Court in London involving the scandal ridden case of *Dennistoun v Dennistoun*, in which Almina became embroiled in 1925. *Lordy! All About Tutankhamun's Patron George Carnarvon* is a retrospection on the 5th Earl of Carnarvon, This will be produced to mark the 90th anniversary of the discovery of the Tomb of Tutankhamun, which falls in November 2012.